The Trouble I've Seen

The Trouble I've Seen
The Big Book of Negro Spirituals

Bruno Chenu

Translated from the
French by Eugene V. LaPlante, A.A.

Judson Press
Valley Forge

Library of Congress Cataloging-in-Publication Data

Chenu, Bruno, 1942–
    [Grand livre des Negro Spirituals. English]
    The trouble I've seen : the big book of Negro spirituals / Bruno Chenu : translated
    from the French by Eugene V. LaPlante.
       p. cm.
    Includes song texts.
    Includes bibliographical references, discography (p.), and index.
    ISBN 0-8170-1448-9 (pbk. : alk. paper)
    1. Spiritual (Songs)—History and criticism. 2. African-Americans—Music—History
    and criticism. I. Title.

ML3556.C513 2003
782.25'3—dc21

                                                                    2002040573

Printed in the U.S.A.
10 09 08 07 06 05 04 03
5 4 3 2 1

In remembrance of Louis T. Achille (1909–1994),
tireless missionary of Negro spirituals in Lyons and beyond

*"They say us can carry de song better than white folks.
Well, maybe, us does love de Lord just a little better,
and what's in our mouth is in our hearts."*
—Dinah Cunningham,
former slave

"When we sing, we announce our existence."
—Bernice Johnson Reagon,
singer of spirituals

Contents

Foreword

SINCE THE FREEDOM SONGS that guided much of the Civil Rights Movement in the United States of the 1960s, one can discern the slow but steady emergence of a new idiom of popular music in African American church circles. The beat and rhythms of this new sound increasingly have an accelerated tempo, joyful cadences of praise, and emotive lyrics of thanks.

This new sound in the black church is simply, but curiously, called "contemporary gospel music," as contrasted with that earthy, Southern, rural harmonization in "traditional Gospel" of the Mighty Clouds of Joy, Shirley Caesar, or the Dixie Hummingbirds. Usually contemporary gospel music of the Kirk Franklin, Yolonda Adams, or Donnie McClurkin variety has lyrics laced with personal testimonies, interspersed at times with RAP, on spiritual coping and the importance of faith in Jesus as a deliverer and a God-send for every season of life's challenges.

Whether in black churches or in campus ministries or prison chaplaincies, contemporary gospel music has become ubiquitous. It has virtually eclipsed the long reign and apparent, almost universal appeal of the remarkable "Negro Spirituals" that emanated from the African American slave experience.

It is the height of irony perhaps, as the classic Negro Spirituals have receded in most of the black churches in America—they are non-existent in charismatic churches—that out of France comes this delightful and most informative new book on the Negro Spirituals. Readers are in for much more than a rehash of familiar themes and lyrics from the lamentations from the legacy of African American slaves. Bruno Chenu instead welcomes the reader into a rich exploration of those uniquely African American "popular religious hymns" that emphasize equally the important motifs of a desperate yearning for freedom and a quest for human dignity—subjects seldom mentioned, as sad as it is to acknowledge, in either traditional or contemporary gospel music!

Chenu selects 210 spirituals out of the known corpus of some 6,000 for detailed study. (He actually quotes from nearly 400.) One should be grateful, as I am, for Chenu's decision to open this book with a useful synopsis that reviews the historical context out of which these popular hymns of the enslaved Negro emerged. Today it is simply tragic that so many African Americans, not to mention other American Christians, have scant appreciation of the historical background that gave rise to these deeply moving African American laments and paradoxical odes of joy.

The Trouble I've Seen will familiarize readers with the names of slaves whose own voices are here given new life—Harriet Jacobs, Olaudah Equiano, and Solomon Northrop. These are but a few of those whom the author allows to speak from the past about their challenging experience with an America that is so often hidden and gilded in retrospect by the majority culture in the United States.

Above all, *The Trouble I've Seen* is a careful, systematic, and comprehensive examination of the themes of the Negro Spirituals. For his study, Chenu draws on important sources such as William B. McClain's *Songs of Zion* and *Lead Me Guide Me: The African American Catholic Hymnal,* published by GIA in 1987. One only wishes that Chenu had available the more recent *African American Heritage Hymnal* for which my colleague, Dr. Delores C. Carpenter, served as General Editor. Her volume was also published in Chicago by GIA, but in 2001.

Moreover, while Chenu has an extensive bibliography which he draws upon nicely throughout the book, his efforts would have been even more fruitful if he had access to Hansonia L. Caldwell's *African American Music: A Chronology 1619–1995* or the valuable insights on African American sacred music by Dr. Jon Michael Spencer. Still, *The Trouble I've Seen* is a most pleasant reminder that the Negro Spirituals have an enduring legacy that continues to strike resonant chords around the globe.

As Chenu himself recognizes, *The Trouble I've Seen* is quite timely. This is so not only because of the rise of "enculturation," wherein diverse people are adapting the Christian faith to the natural rhythms and textures of their own racial and cultural self-understandings, but also because of another factor. The advent of this new millennium is bringing about a long-overdue rediscovery of the profundity of the classic Negro Spirituals. The stone that the builders once threw away is now becoming the cornerstone in several regions of the country—and not just in black churches!

One might even say that the rediscovery of the value and depth of many Negro Spirituals by African Americans themselves is an odd kind of *re-enculturation* that is sure to have a salutary effect on the health of the black church in America.

—*Cain Hope Felder*
Howard University, School of Divinity
Washington, D.C.

Introduction

THIS BOOK is the fruit of a long-standing desire. As soon as I immersed myself in the religious universe of the African Americans, when I first visited the United States in 1970 and 1971, I knew that someday I would write a book about the Negro spirituals. I alluded to that in my book *Dieu est noir* [*God Is Black*], in 1977, when I wrote: "The theology of the spirituals, the Bible in sound-images, would in itself deserve a whole book."[1] Since then, that thought has always been on my mind and has led me to write several other works.[2] It took a sabbatical year in the United States for my dream to take form and then to emerge, on my return to France, as a reference book on the subject.

Today's musical and ecclesiastical context seems favorable to the subject. Indeed, the success of gospel music in regions far from the American ghettos is evident. In France, numerous groups that recruit their members in the Caribbean, Africa, and Madagascar dedicate themselves to this type of music for performances connected with evangelical churches. In my view, the only problem lies in the fact that the term *gospel* tends to include all religious music that has issued from the American black milieu. Yet it is important to distinguish between these two types of hymns—spirituals and gospels—since they reflect two different situations and two theologies. The *Negro spiritual* is a popular religious hymn, originating in rural areas of America during the era of slavery, between 1760 and 1875. An anonymous collective work, it is at the crossroads of an African vision of the world and a spirituality borrowed from the white Methodist or Baptist "awakenings" and from the tragic experience of slavery. It manifests a predilection for the Old Testament as a witness to a collective liberation in history. On the other hand, the gospel is a religious hymn of the urban ghetto. It is related to the white gospel hymns (which began at the turn of the twentieth century) and the blues (the expression of personal distress on the periphery of a racist society). The authors of gospel songs are well known and use the New Testament as witness to an individual hope beyond history. The all-powerful God who frees God's people gives way to the intimate Jesus who frees my soul. The world to change becomes the world to endure.

Another element makes the present environment favorable for a study of the spirituals. In the Catholic and Protestant churches there is an increased interest in new expressions of Christian faith. At the dawn of the third Christian millennium, there is much talk about "enculturation," that is, the need for new incarnations of the faith in the cultures of different peoples. We yearn for an African Christianity, an Indian Christianity, an Asian Christianity, and so on. Yet this long-term desire has already had interesting and even surprising realizations. Black American Christianity is one of the most beautiful examples of enculturation that we can find in twenty centuries of Christian history. And the crown jewel of this original Christianity is found in the Negro spirituals—hymns that are perfectly local, since they sprang from the hearts of black Americans and from nowhere else, and that at the same time are completely universal, since they are sung and appreciated to the far ends of the earth. Thus we will try to enter into the world of the spirituals.

There has, to date, been no systematic study of the themes of the spirituals. That is my task, which I will carry out while keeping in mind three objectives. First (and I believe this is not superfluous), I will examine the odyssey of Africans on the soil of the United States from the seventeenth through the nineteenth centuries, including their discovery of the Christian faith and their way of adapting this creed. This primarily historical objective will be taken up in the first three chapters. Second, I will study the spirituals themselves. However, since their number is estimated to be at around six thousand, I thought it proper to select 210 (without neglecting the others) and give their texts in Appendix 1. Why 210? That number provides a broad enough spectrum of the various musical genres and texts. With this representative selection of the spirituals that are most original and most often sung today, the reader will have in hand a really good sample.[3] However, my study of the themes will draw from all possible sources. In total, I will quote from nearly four hundred spirituals.[4] Third, it will be my objective to give priority to the words of the slaves or former slaves. True, their words have often been lost in the night of history and have left no visible traces. Yet, as soon as slavery ended, researchers took care to record the testimony of the "damned of the earth" and had them tell about their descent into hell, so that we have excellent collections of stories and interviews. Even before the suppression of slavery, the abolitionist campaign was supported by the accounts of various freed slaves who still bore in their flesh the painful stigmata of servitude. We think especially of Olaudah Equiano, Frederick Douglass, Harriet Jacobs, and Solomon Northup. Through the hymns, as through the testimony and the prayers, it is the word of the slave that will resonate in this book.

It just so happened that the first phase of this work took place in a residence under the patronage of Saint Peter Claver, in Berkeley, California. I saw that as more than a mere coincidence. Indeed, this Spanish Jesuit, who lived from 1585 to 1654, had been sent to Cartagena, in New Grenada (now Colombia), in 1610. Ordained a priest in 1616, he took as his motto "Peter Claver, forever the slave of the Ethiopians."[5] At the time, Cartagena was the great port of entry for slaves destined for Spanish America. At the beginning of the seventeenth century, this port received at least three thousand slaves per year, unloaded from some twenty slave ships, for the mines and the plantations. At each arrival Peter Claver would sneak through the crowds of colonists and succeed in boarding the ship to bring the captives the comfort of his presence and give them first aid. He would even carry them on his own shoulders. He baptized those who had not been baptized before boarding and instructed them in the faith with pictures and sketches. It is said that he helped and evangelized some one hundred thousand slaves. Peter Claver wanted to be a slave to the slaves, to be enslaved in order to serve better. The Catholic Church honors him as the Francis Xavier of the black people, the patron saint of the mission to African Americans.

If this book helps the reader to hear directly the words of the African American slaves and discover one of the most extraordinary expressions of thirst for freedom and desire for dignity that have ever inhabited the human heart, then it will not have been written in vain. Those who had been considered as the least among humans give us a splendid lesson in humanity and faith. This music will never disappear.

Notes

1. Bruno Chenu, *Dieu est noir: histoire, religion et théologie des Noirs américains* (Paris: Centurion, 1977), 165.

2. Examples: Bruno Chenu, "Le Spiritual, un people en mouvement vers son Dieu," *Lumière et Vie* 140 (1978): 65–71; Bruno Chenu, *Le Christ est noir* (Paris: Desclée, 1984), 53–79.

3. My selection is based on two recent collections of hymns: *Songs of Zion* (Nashville: Abingdon, 1981); *Lead Me, Guide Me: The African American Catholic Hymnal* (Chicago: GIA, 1987). I have also found to be useful a recent anthology of two hundred spirituals: Richard Newman, *Go Down, Moses: A Celebration of the African American Spiritual* (New York: Potter, 1998).

4. The entire list is given in Appendix 2. There is no published list of all the "historical" spirituals. The most complete work is the following: Erskine Peters, ed., *Lyrics of the Afro-American Spiritual: A Documentary Collection* (Westport, Conn.: Greenwood, 1993).

5. At that time, the term "Ethiopian" designated all Africans.

Bibliography

Chenu, Bruno. *Le Christ noir américain.* Paris: Desclée, 1984, 53–79.

————. *Dieu est noir: histoire, religion et théologie des Noirs américains.* Paris: Centurion, 1977, 158–78.

————. "Jésus dans la diversité des cultures." In *Jésus. Des Évangiles aux multimédia.* Nîmes: Université d'été assomptionniste, 1996, 44–52.

————. *Théologies chrétiennes des tiers mondes.* Paris: Centurion, 1987, 82–88.

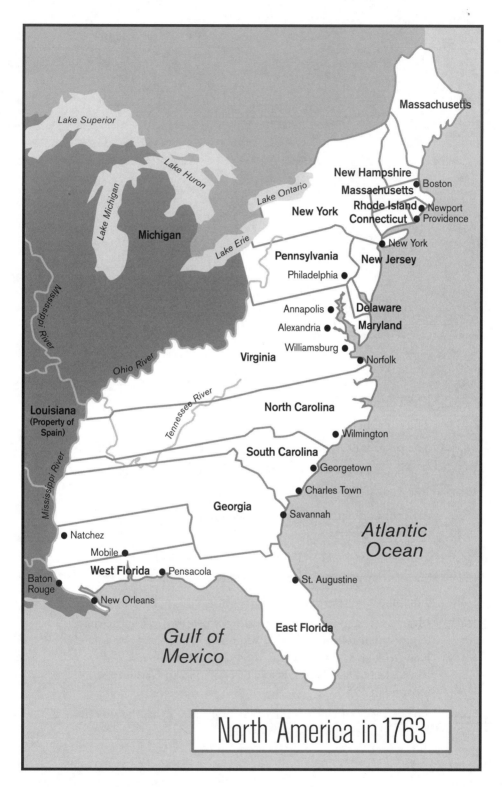

Lake Superior

Lake Huron

Lake Michigan

Lake Ontario

Lake Erie

Michigan

Mississippi River

Ohio River

Tennessee River

Mississippi River

Louisiana
(Property of
Spain)

Massachusetts

New Hampshire
Massachusetts ● Boston
Rhode Island ● Newport
Connecticut ● Providence

New York

New York ● New York

Pennsylvania
New Jersey

Philadelphia ●

Annapolis ● Delaware
Alexandria ● Maryland
Williamsburg ●
Virginia ● Norfolk

North Carolina

● Wilmington

South Carolina

● Georgetown

● Charles Town

Georgia

● Savannah

● Natchez

Mobile ●

West Florida ● Pensacola

Baton
Rouge

● New Orleans

● St. Augustine

East Florida

Atlantic
Ocean

Gulf of
Mexico

North America in 1763

Chronology of Slavery

1444	The Portuguese begin the African slave trade.
1452	The papal bull *Dum Diversas* of Nicholas V is promulgated.
1455	The papal bull *Romanus Pontifex* of Nicholas V is promulgated.
1456	The papal bull *Inter Coetera* of Calistus III is promulgated.
1502	The first African slaves are put ashore in Cuba.
1520–1530	Africans participate in Spanish expeditions in the New World.
1607	The English colony of Jamestown (Virginia) is founded.
1619	Some twenty Negroes are disembarked at Jamestown.
1620	The Pilgrims arrive on the *Mayflower.*
1641	Massachusetts becomes the first English colony to legalize slavery. Connecticut follows in 1650; Virginia in 1661; Maryland in 1663; New York and New Jersey in 1664; South Carolina in 1682; Rhode Island and Pennsylvania in 1700; North Carolina in 1715; Georgia in 1750.
1688	The Quakers of Germantown (Pennsylvania) make the first protest against slavery in the Western world.

1701   The Society for the Propagation of the Gospel in Foreign Lands is founded by Thomas Bray.

1712   Slaves revolt in New York.

1740   The Great Awakening begins.

1770   The Boston Massacre occurs, in which Crispus Attucks, a free mulatto, becomes the first martyr of the American Revolution.

1774   The first independent black church is founded at Silver Bluff, South Carolina.

1776   The Declaration of Independence is ratified.

1777   Vermont becomes the first state to abolish slavery. It is followed by Massachusetts in 1780, by New Hampshire in 1783, and by Connecticut and Rhode Island in 1784.

1787   Richard Allen and Absalom Jones found the Free African Society of Philadelphia.

1793   Eli Whitney invents the cotton gin.

1794   Absalom Jones founds the African Church of St. Thomas in Philadelphia. In the same city, Richard Allen inaugurates the African Methodist Episcopal Church of Bethel.

1800   The Gabriel Prosser conspiracy occurs in Virginia. The Second Great Awakening begins.

1808   The importation of African slaves is officially banned.

1822   The Denmark Vesey conspiracy occurs in South Carolina.

1829   The abolitionist pamphlet *The Call,* by David Walker, is published.

1831   Nat Turner's rebellion occurs in Virginia.

1852   *Uncle Tom's Cabin,* by Harriet Beecher Stowe, is published.

1853   James Augustine Healy, the first African American Catholic priest, is ordained in Paris.

1857   The Dred Scott decision is handed down, declaring that no black person, free or slave, has rights that a white must respect.

1860   Abraham Lincoln is elected president of the United States.

1861   The Civil War begins.

1863   The Emancipation Proclamation is issued on January 1.

1865   The Civil War ends. Abraham Lincoln is assassinated. The Thirteenth Amendment abolishes slavery. The Ku Klux Klan is born.

1

"Nobody knows the trouble I've seen."

The Terrible Ordeal of Slavery

*"I was in the kitchen of suffering and I cleaned all its
pots and pans with my tongue."*
—a slave

ON AUGUST 8, 1444, "very early in the morning because of the heat," Portuguese sailors unloaded an African cargo near Lagos in Portugal. It consisted of 235 slaves, "some white enough, fair enough and well proportioned"; "others were less white, like mulattoes"; "others again were as black as Ethiops and so ugly both in features and in body . . . as almost to appear . . . the images of a lower hemisphere." Reported with a certain emotion by the chronicler Gomes Eannes de Zurara, this event inaugurated the systematic exploitation of Africa by Europe. The merchants of Lisbon had expected gold. They did get a little, but slaves were easier to find. The Portuguese, needing workers (to the tune of a thousand slaves per year), would be the first to open the African trail for all the European nations that would rush in ardently without a trace of human scruples.

One man would have been able to stop the trade in the children of Africa immediately: the pope. Yet neither Nicholas V nor Calistus III opposed Portuguese expansionism. They were only too happy to see Christian armies mobilized against Islam. Nicholas, in his bull *Dum Diversas* of June 18, 1452, gave King Alphonse V of Portugal "full and free permission to invade, seek out, capture and enslave all Saracens, pagans, infidels and other enemies of Christ . . . and to condemn them to perpetual slavery." Shortly after the fall of Constantinople (1453), on January 8,

1455, Nicholas issued another bull, *Romanus Pontifex,* in which he encouraged the conversion to Christianity of the African populations, who had been deprived of all rights by the Muslims, and sanctioned the monopoly of Portuguese commerce in black Africa. His successor, Calistus III, confirmed these privileges in his bull *Inter Coetera* of March 1456. We cannot, then, be surprised to see Pope Innocent VIII, in 1488, offer African slaves to his cardinals and to the Roman nobility when the king of Spain put a hundred of them at his disposal.

In reality, of course, the year 1444 did not mark the beginning of European traffic in slaves, and still less, the history of the enslavement of human beings. Slavery has existed in all times, only with varying degrees of humiliation for the enslaved person. It was practiced in Assyria, in Babylon, in China, in Egypt, in India, in Persia, in classical Greece, in Rome. If it declined in Western Europe after the fall of the Roman Empire, it persisted in the Mediterranean basin with the wars between Christians and Muslims. The Italian sugar plantations of the fourteenth century used black and Russian slaves. Even before the "discovery" of America by Christopher Columbus, Africans were exploited in the Madeira Islands and São Tomé off the West African coast.

After the colonization of the New World, the Atlantic slave trade would rival in size the Muslim slave trade that coursed through Africa from the eighth and ninth centuries on, whether through the Sahara or on the east coast. It must be underscored that the ancient practice of slavery did not have a racist tone, since whites as well as blacks were enslaved, and slavery was not an irreversible status or even the lowest status. It was, primarily, a domestic institution of prestige rather than a source of revenue. In America, though, the slaves would be the victims of implacable racism and constitute the workforce of a rural society based upon agriculture.

Why the English?

That slavery could have become the foundation of the English colonies in America is astounding. Indeed, the first English settlers did not even think of it: they defined themselves as English or Christians, never as slave or free. How did it come about that the status of slaves, which did not exist in English law and had disappeared from the English purview, was recognized in Massachusetts in 1641 for the people of West Africa? How is it that those who presented themselves as the pioneers of freedom and of the kingdom of God on earth became the diabolical organizers of a slave empire?

Historians are divided into two camps: the ideological and the economic. For some, racist ideology was present in England well before colonization of the New World. The English believed themselves to be the epitome of civilization, the center of the world. They wanted to be the missionaries of this refined cultural ideal to those furthest from it, namely, the Indians and the Africans. Three stereotypical qualities were attributed to the Africans: they were "black," "savage," and "pagan." Beginning in 1530, travelers' tales invited people to compare "the beasts that resemble men" (orangutans) and "the men who resemble beasts" (the black Africans). Physical color is not neutral. In sixteenth-century English, *black* was synonymous with baseness and filth, not to say evil and sin. "Blackness" could only be a divine malediction, since there was only one couple at the origin of humanity—and that couple was white! The black Africans were the descendants of Ham. This discrimination points the way to open racism. From the religious point of view, the explorers found only magic and superstition. This paganism later would be used to justify slavery. The organization of the African family would horrify the Europeans and confirm in their opinion that this was a savage people, sensual and close to animals. From 1555 on, the English would be able to judge directly, since Africans would be on English soil, voluntarily at first and later by coercion. At the end of the sixteenth century, there was a quite significant black presence in England. Even if Africans had inferior jobs, they did not face social discrimination.

For other analysts, racism came later. The economics and demographics of the North American colonies caused the substitution of black slaves for European indentured laborers. At first, and for decades, the status of the Africans was not automatically one of slavery. In the historical record we can find free blacks, blacks hired for a specific time period, and black slaves. And a person's status was not first ·of all a question of color. Blacks were few in number and often shared the same conditions as white servants. The only difference lay in the fact that they had not come to America voluntarily!

It would seem that we should not give precedence to either racial prejudice or economic necessity; history seems to underscore the interaction of both factors. The contemptuous view of the Africans promoted their enslavement. But the desire for economic development and success also induced racist attitudes with a rigid classification of human groups.

Why, then, slavery for Africans and not for the American Indians? An attempt *was* made to enslave the first inhabitants of the country, but they were averse to the process. The settlers had to be cautious if they did not want bloody reprisals. And the Indians knew the territory too well and would disappear into the forest. Besides, illnesses brought from Europe decimated them. Finally, their numbers were limited. It was different with the Africans: they could take the climate of the South; they cost less than the white workers; they already had a certain experience with tropical farming; they were easily located because of the color of their skin; no exterior power would protect them; and the African lode seemed inexhaustible. The slavery of some would guarantee the freedom of the others!

In short, conditions in the second half of the seventeenth century were favorable for the transition from white labor to black labor. In England, the economic situation was improving, and it was no longer necessary to try one's luck in the New World. The birth rate fell so steeply in the 1640s that the number of

indentured English individuals declined rapidly. At the same time, African resources were more than ever available with the creation of the first English slave
trade company, the Royal African Company, in 1672.

The Infamous Traffic in "Ebony"

As the English turned to the New World, the Atlantic slave trade was already in
full swing. The Portuguese were the first to open the way in the sixteenth century
and held a sort of monopoly in South America for nearly a century. But the other
maritime powers would rush in: the Spaniards, the Italians, the Dutch, the English,
the French, the Swedes, the Danes, the Brandenburgers, and the Americans. "Only
far away Russia and the Balkan countries are missing, who however receive their
small contingents of slaves through the Ottoman Empire."[1] North America was
never an important market, and the colonists would invest in slave commerce only
from 1730 on. The period from 1720 to 1780 would be the high-water mark of
the world traffic in African slaves.

The figures we are able to find prove that the English colonies in North
America were a truly marginal region for the importation of slaves. Today, it is
estimated that they received only 6 percent of the slaves transported across the
Atlantic, that is, 600,000 Africans out of a total of about 10 million. Of these
Africans, men were much more numerous than women: 63 percent to 37 percent,
or two men for every woman. Although the first slaves brought to what was to
become the United States were from the Caribbean region, the majority (at least
70 percent) were imported directly from Africa.

These Africans came from a coastline more than three thousand miles long,
from Mauritania to Mozambique, and represented a variety of ethnic groups, all
designated by one name: Guinea. The countries most visited were the Ivory Coast,
the Gold Coast, the delta of the Niger (called the Slave Coast), and the coast of
Angola. The English colonists had their preferences: the South Carolina planters
preferred the Africans from Senegambia; the Virginians liked the Africans from
the Gold Coast. In the end, however, the Congolese-Angolans would be the most
numerous in North America, along with the Nigerians.

Most of the time, these slaves were sold by African merchants or tribal chiefs
to white buyers. Petty kings and African traffickers easily sold their prisoners of
war, their undesirables, and their own subjects. They began to make war on their
neighbors for that sole purpose. "During the entire period of the slave trade,
violence was the hallmark of African history" (G. Mbaye). In this somber story,
the Africans served as intermediaries, and the European raids were only comple-
mentary. In 1550 the price of a slave was ten English pounds, rising to fifty pounds
at the high point of the slave trade in 1760. Usually, however, the African merchant
was paid in European merchandise (cloth, firearms, hardware, alcohol, tobacco).

Throughout the colonial period, North America depended on England for
its "ebony," since the British traffic represented 41 percent of the European total.

The three ports of Liverpool, Bristol, and London specialized in this commerce. When it entered into the trade, it was Rhode Island that distinguished itself among the North American colonies for slave trading by organizing a thousand trips to bring in one hundred thousand Africans.

In this "triangular traffic"—generally leaving Europe, going to Africa, crossing to America, and then heading back to Europe—the most delicate stage was crossing the Atlantic with a cargo of human beings torn from their continent. Hubert Deschamps called "the black passage" a terrible descent into hell. The logbooks of the slave ships give us an idea of what it must have been like for the captives, but nothing equals the words of the Africans themselves on this horrible experience. We are lucky to have the 1789 account of Olaudah Equiano, the first slave to have told his adventure without white abolitionists as intermediaries.

> The first object that saluted my eyes when I arrived on the coast was the sea, and a slave ship, which was then riding at anchor, and waiting for its cargo. These filled me with astonishment, that was soon converted into terror, which I am yet at a loss to describe, and much more the then feelings of my mind when I was carried on board. I was immediately handled and tossed up to see if I was sound, by some of the crew; and I was now persuaded that I had got into a world of bad spirits, and that they were going to kill me. Their complexion too, differing so much from ours, their long hair, and the language they spoke, which was so different from any I had ever heard, united to confirm me in this belief. Indeed such were the horrors of my views and fears at the moment, that if ten thousand worlds had been my own, I would have freely parted with them all to have exchanged my condition with the meanest slave in my own country. When I looked round the ship too, and saw a large furnace or copper boiling and a multitude of black people, of every description, chained together, every one of their countenances expressing dejection and sorrow, I no longer doubted of my fate; and quite overpowered with horror and anguish, I fell motionless on the deck, and fainted. . . . At last, when the ship in which we were, had got in all her cargo, they made ready with many fearful noises, and we were all put under deck, so we could not see how they managed the vessel.
>
> But this disappointment was the least of my grief. The stench of the hold, while we were on the coast, was so intolerably loathsome, that it was dangerous to remain there for any time, and some of us had been permitted to stay on the deck for the fresh air, but now the whole ship's cargo were confined together, it became absolutely pestilential. The closeness of the place, and the heat of the climate, added to the number

in the ship, being so crowded that each had scarcely room to turn himself, almost suffocated us. This produced copious perspiration, so that the air became unfit for respiration, from a variety of loathsome smells, and brought on sickness among the slaves, of which many died, thus falling victim to the improvident avarice, as I may call it, of their purchasers. This deplorable situation was again aggravated by the galling of the chains, now become unsupportable; and the filth of necessary tubs, into which the children often fell, and were almost suffocated. The shrieks of the women, and the groans of the dying rendered it a scene of horror almost inconceivable.[2]

These Africans were not going to accept their deportation without making a move. Believing, as did Equiano, that the whites were going to eat them, many in despair threw themselves into the sea. Some refused to eat during the crossing or refused medicine when they fell ill. Because of the iron discipline (in both the literal and symbolic senses!) on the slave ships in which Africans were "packed like sardines," according to the expression of D. P. Mannix, mutinies were relatively rare. On average, a mutiny occurred once every two years on crossings that could last from three weeks to three months, depending on favorable or unfavorable winds. Because of scurvy, smallpox, and dysentery, there was a 10 percent mortality rate among the human cargo, though the rate would decline in the eighteenth century. On the other hand, the white crew was not spared by the tropical illnesses and shipwrecks! In wartime, the principal risk was capture by the enemy. Pirates scoured all the seas, so much so that certain ships practiced both trade and piracy.

Was it a lucrative trade? This commerce could not have lasted so long if the slave traders had not made a profit. The beautiful residences of Nantes and Bordeaux are witnesses to that on French territory. A quite precise English estimate on the trade between 1761 and 1810 indicates a profit of below 10 percent on the capital investment.

What was the demographic impact on Africa? That is extremely difficult to calculate, because we do not know the population of Africa before 1850. Patrick Manning, an American specialist, holds a prudent position: "For the entire coastal region of West Africa—which extends from Senegal to Angola to a depth of 600 kilometers inland—there was a population decline from 1730 to 1850."[3] Others estimate that the draining of ten million slaves caused a net loss of one hundred million people. The scarcity of adult males caused a change in family structures and farm production.

In any case, this odious commerce left an indelible imprint on the African American conscience. "The descendants of the slaves still feel the hot iron that marked their ancestors" (H. Deschamps). The collective memory of a people never forgets an excess of humiliation.

A Progressive Institutionalization

Traditionally, the history of the African Americans began on August 20, 1619, when a Dutch frigate anchored at Point Comfort, a few miles from Jamestown in Virginia. The crew then exchanged its cargo of "twenty strange Negroes" for urgently needed provisions. In reality, Africans had already trod on North American soil, either as explorers or as slaves. In 1492 Pedro Alonzo Nino, identified as a black African, was the pilot on the *Santa Maria,* Christopher Columbus's ship. During the sixteenth century, a few Spanish attempts to settle in South Carolina or in Florida included groups of African slaves. Their first revolt took place in 1526. In April 1619 the new governor of Virginia counted twenty-two Africans in his territory. Yet 1619 remains the symbolic date that inaugurates the African presence in the English colonies. A year before the Pilgrims of the *Mayflower,* the Africans were there. They would always be able to claim that they were present on U.S. soil right from the beginning. The first arrivals, however, had the status of indentured servants and not of slaves.

Indeed, perpetual slavery was not part of the initial plan to populate the English colonies. The 120 adventurers who landed in a place they called Jamestown (Virginia), in April 1607, had received as their mission "firstly to preach and to baptize in the Christian religion . . . and to take back from the arms of Satan a certain number of poor and miserable souls." A truly religious enterprise! Slavery, however, was gradually established.

The story of a certain Anthony Johnson shows how ambiguous the situation was all through the seventeenth century. Arriving in Virginia in 1621, he was put to work on a plantation along the James River. He married an African woman, Marie, and raised four children. In the 1630s Johnson and his family bought their freedom. Soon they owned 250 acres, which they farmed with the help of indentured European servants and an African slave, called John Casar. In 1654 Johnson sued for the return of this slave, who (he claimed) was stolen by two neighboring white planters. He did obtain the return of John Casar, lived until 1670, and knew his grandchildren—a rare privilege in those days. The lesson here is this: there were then free Africans, indentured Africans, and African slaves. The latter were few in number. Those who were able to prove that they were baptized were granted freedom. In an eastern Virginia county, in 1669, 29 percent of the African Americans were free.

In fact, the English history of African slavery does not begin in Virginia but in the Caribbean Islands. In the 1630s the English on Barbados had already decreed a status of slavery for the Africans present on the island. What happened in the Antilles would have repercussions on the mainland. The English would copy the model set up by the Portuguese in Brazil, establishing a connection between the production of sugar and the practice of slavery. In 1660, because of its sugar exports, Barbados became for the English "the crown jewel" of the New World. Blessed profits! But the "sugar revolution" required an adapted population that the Old World could not and did not want to give. In 1638, the six thousand inhabitants of Barbados included only two hundred Africans; in 1660, twenty-seven thousand Africans lived alongside twenty-six thousand Europeans in Barbados. The economic forces had done the work: the Africans were perfectly adapted to this type of work. And the Dutch fleet would undertake to bring the workers to their destination, then transport the sugar to Europe.

The Barbados experience inspired the colonization of South Carolina in the region called the Lowcountry. Indeed, some of the new colonists came from Barbados, and in their view, slavery was a *sine qua non* of economic success. Thus slaves would be found there in great numbers even before the cultivation of rice in the eighteenth century. Carolina would be the only colony to have an African majority in 1708.

Let us get back to Virginia, the first colony to receive the uprooted Africans. Having landed in 1607, the first colonists hoped for quick success, but they would have to lower their expectations because of the climate. Land was given over to private ownership, and a representative assembly was elected. This type of organization allowed them to concentrate on a product much in demand in Europe: tobacco. Beginning in 1617, Jamestown would throw itself frantically into the production of tobacco. The first inhabitants of the land, the Indians, were rapidly dispossessed or exterminated. The workforce was at first furnished by indentured European servants. Africans were few, comprising 3.5 percent of the population in 1660. They seemingly were not counted on for economic reasons. Fewer than twenty were imported each year. White indentured servants and Africans suffered the same domination, even if the former came voluntarily and the latter involuntarily.

The situation changed in 1660 with the arrival of English slave ships. In 1680 there were scarcely four thousand Africans in Virginia and Maryland; thirty years later there would be more than thirty thousand. A system of slavery was firmly rooted in both colonies. The African became the "possession" of the master, a form of property. It was not a crime to kill a slave in an attempt to punish him or her. The social division was no longer between Christians and pagans, as in the first part of the colonial times, but now between whites and blacks. Racial discrimination was visible for all to see.

Although documents prove that in the 1620s the African Americans received just about the same treatment as the whites (they could testify in court, be property owners, and if they were indentured servants, be free at the end of their contract), the situation deteriorated progressively between 1630 and 1660. Proof of this is the story of John Punch, an African servant in Virginia, who fled his master's house with two white servants. When caught, the whites were whipped and four years were added to their contract, but John Punch had to serve his master for the rest of his life!

The year 1660 marked the turning point in Virginia. New laws encouraged the slave trade and the development of slavery. In 1662 it was decreed that all children born in Virginia inherited their mother's status. This was contrary to English law, which before had always referred to the father's status. It would soon be forbidden, almost everywhere, for a black to have white servants. It was also decreed that baptism did not affect the slave status. Interracial marriages were banned. The population of African origin was progressively locked into hereditary slavery. At the end of the seventeenth century, free Africans would be the exception. In Boston, in 1690, one family in nine had a slave; in New York, in 1703, two families in five had slaves!

The Eighteenth Century

If the seventeenth century was that of the institutionalization of slavery in the New World, the eighteenth was that of its consolidation and rapid expansion. From a society "with slaves," it became a "slavery society," according to the distinction of Ira Berlin.[4] The high point of the slave trade was from 1763 to 1775. Prior to the American Revolution, three times as many Africans as Europeans crossed the Atlantic.

It would be wrong, however, to imagine a uniform system of slavery spreading over all the English colonies. The historical studies of the past thirty years, to the contrary, show the diversity in time and space of this "peculiar institution" that long defined American society. We must not forget, of course, that the majority of the white population did not possess slaves.

We must distinguish at least four distinct situations: (1) the colonies of the North, where the basic institution was not the plantation but the home and where African presence remained marginal; (2) the Chesapeake region (Virginia and Maryland); (3) the Lowcountry (the Carolinas, Georgia, East Florida); and (4) the lower Mississippi valley, where slavery was organized around a predominant agricultural product. Of course, in all four cases, the African origin was common and the oppression was the same. But the relationship between whites and blacks, the nature of the terrain, and the nature of production colored the varying configurations of servitude, which would evolve according to historical forces.

Following the lead of the historian Philip D. Morgan, we will take two examples, those of Virginia and South Carolina.[5] These two societies "welcomed" three-fourths of African Americans in the eighteenth century. In 1700 "Virginia had a plantation economy in search of a labor force, whereas South Carolina had a labor force in search of a plantation economy."[6] Founded about seventy-five years before South Carolina, Virginia grew tobacco and began to import slaves on a large scale only when the source of indentured servants dried up. At the beginning of the century, the Africans represented only a sixth of the population. On the other hand, South Carolina was born with slavery. Right from the start, it was a slave society. Its problem was to find a profitable product. On both sides, the first African immigrants came from the Caribbean and not directly from Africa. That would evolve quickly. And the relations between the whites and blacks (which had been relatively flexible at the beginning, with a kind of complicity between white indentured servants and black slaves, even though the Africans were always considered inferior beings) became progressively rigid. They needed to differentiate themselves more clearly from the new arrivals. The masters would see to that.

In reality, the type of agriculture—tobacco on the one hand and rice on the other—gave rise to the differences of the colonies. To get into the cultivation of rice, one had to have at least "thirty Negroes," admitted a planter in 1769. On the other hand, with just a few workers, you could envisage cultivating tobacco by adding a few other resources. Rice plantations would always be larger than tobacco plantations; that type of cultivation had to be on a large scale with an abundant workforce in order to be profitable. In 1720, in South Carolina, more than half of the slaves would be on plantations that had at least twenty slaves. That was the case for only 10 percent of the slaves in Virginia. The farms would always be bigger and more stable in South Carolina. The big property owners of Virginia divided their slaves among different properties. South Carolina was the area of specialized monoculture; Virginia, that of diversification.

These two types of plantations produced different populations. The basic production modulated the forced migration of Africans. South Carolina imported twice as many Africans as Virginia, which nevertheless had begun earlier. And the slaves were not from the same areas: the Ibos dominated the Virginia market; the Angolans, that of South Carolina. But with the increased demand, the African population would become more heterogeneous.

For our purposes, it is interesting to note that already in the second decade of the eighteenth century the slave population of Virginia began to grow by natural reproduction, which was unique in the New World. In a more severe atmosphere, South Carolina would follow the same road fifty years later. At the time of the American Revolution, only one-fifth of the Virginia slaves had been born in Africa. Slave women, on average, could give birth to six or seven children. Also, the North American slaves were generally bigger than those of the Caribbean. That leads one to think that their nutrition in North America was not terribly bad. The growth of the indigenous African American population, with a balanced distribution between children and adults, men and women, would not be without consequence for the ties to Africa.

One significant fact of the eighteenth century was the simultaneous emergence of a class of masters and a class of slaves, both born in North America. These two developments would give American slavery its particular coloration. Indeed, the masters would not direct their plantations from afar, from a big city or from the home country; most of the time they would be present on the plantation and be involved in its life. That was not the case in Jamaica, Cuba, or Brazil. The American planters considered themselves permanent colonists. They did not look to England but instead took interest in their government, their community, and their property. They wanted a society in the image of their plantation.

The ties with Africa having been broken, the black slaves would turn inward to their own group, create a new culture, truly African American. They remained African in their hearts and desired to return to their country at death. They refused to comply with the illegitimate situation they were placed in and resisted in a thousand ways. Since they came from different ethnic groups, their presence on American soil united them, grouped them, and integrated them insofar as the basic division was between whites and blacks. The slaves would hold to their traditional religious vision of a world without a clear distinction between the sacred and the profane, impregnated with a spiritual presence. We will be able to verify that in the music as well as in the magic. At the same time, the broken ties with Africa cannot be underestimated. Their American situation was, in many ways, another world.

With the cultural adaptation of the African population, the slaves would no longer refer to their ethnic origins. They had daily interaction with the whites, which meant a mutual influence. Progressively, they would no longer give African names to their children but would prefer biblical names. And they would use names to strengthen the family ties so severely tested by their servitude.

We must not forget that slavery was first of all a physical violence, a status of subordination, a reduction of the human person to his or her work, with the whip as the barometer. The newly arrived Africans did not easily accept the plantation discipline. However, the gamut of punishments and tortures was extremely refined, from branding with a hot iron, to the amputation of fingers or toes, to castration. All resistance had to be "broken," and fear instilled to the point of blind obedience. As the century wore on, however, physical force tended to lessen, if only to prove the legitimacy of slavery to those who had begun to raise their voices against it, such as the Quakers. A certain number of owners had more humane feelings for the slaves they had seen born and grow up—they were "our people," the owners declared with a condescending and paternalistic attitude that would triumph in the next century. They were part of the family, albeit inferior members, liable to extreme forced labor.

The American Revolution

For the thirteen states of the Union, the American Revolution was a long process of decolonialization in which pride, wounded by vexatious measures by England, progressively created a unique national identity. The process that took more than twenty-five years (1763–1788) placed on the pedestal of the young republic the great names of Liberty, Happiness, and Property, which remain the mobilizing myths of American life. But did the African Americans profit from this struggle for freedom? The coexistence of the rhetoric of liberty with the exploitation of slaves, at the time of the revolution, is a contradiction that deserves some attention because it concerns the entire future of the new United States.

Right from the beginning, African Americans were present at the fronts of the War of Independence. One of the events that began the revolutionary process was the Boston Massacre on March 5, 1770. Among the leaders and victims of this event was a mulatto with African and Indian blood, Crispus Attucks, a very strong man. A seaman, he had fled slavery. On the occasion of a brawl between English soldiers and citizens of Boston, blows were exchanged. Feeling threatened by the crowd that had quickly gathered, the English soldiers thought they had no other recourse than to open fire. Crispus Attucks was in the first row, "the first to defy, the first to die," as we can read on his monument. This mulatto is considered the first martyr of the struggle for independence.

When George Washington took command of the army in 1775, he insisted that the slaves not be authorized to serve. He feared conspiracies and insurrections. In a clever maneuver, the British governor of Virginia, Lord Dunmore, offered freedom to all the slaves who would join the English troops. Their response was so enthusiastic that Washington was forced to retreat and willy-nilly accept the enlistment of slaves. He did not have occasion to complain, since the African soldiers showed themselves to be particularly adept at espionage, guerrilla warfare, and piloting ships. They participated in all the big battles, including Lexington, Concord, and Bunker Hill. It is believed that five thousand African Americans served in the American army and navy.

For their good and loyal services, a certain number of slaves were emancipated after the war. But the official status of the slaves did not change. Freedom was given to a few individuals, but not to the ethnic group as such. In serving the cause of the American citizen, the slaves had only prolonged their obedience to their white masters. That was quite logical. And at the end of the revolution, there would be more slaves than before! The peculiar institution had spread to the western territories.

Yet the people of the United States had just given themselves constitutional texts that spoke an entirely different language. Having crossed the Red Sea of the Atlantic, the colonists really had the impression that they were creating a new world founded on universal values, as Thomas Paine had stated at the beginning of 1776: "It is in our power to recreate the world. Such a situation has not presented itself since the time of Noah. The birth of a new world is within our reach and a race of men, perhaps as numerous as all of Europe, is destined to receive its portion of freedom from the events of a few months."[7]

A rich thirty-three-year-old Virginian, Thomas Jefferson, a poor orator but excellent writer, wrote the Declaration of Independence, which even today cannot be read without admiration:

> When in the Course of human events, it becomes necessary for one people
> to dissolve the political bands which have connected them with another,

and to assume among the powers of the earth, the separate and equal
station to which the Laws of Nature and of nature's God entitle them, a
decent respect to the opinions of mankind requires that they should
declare the causes which impel them to the separation.

We hold these truths to be self-evident, that all men are created equal,
that they are endowed by their Creator with certain unalienable Rights,
that among these are Life, Liberty, and the pursuit of Happiness. That to
secure these rights, Governments are instituted among Men, deriving
their just powers from the consent of the governed. That whenever a Form
of Government becomes destructive of these ends, it is the Right of the
People to alter or to abolish it, and to institute New Government, laying
its foundation on such principles and organizing its powers in such form,
as to them shall seem most likely to effect their Safety and Happiness.

For the first time in human history a colony emancipated itself from the power of
a monarchy by appealing to the universal rights of humanity.

Yet in the entire text of this declaration, adopted by Congress on July 4,
1776, there is not the least allusion to slavery. It was as if the institution did
not exist. A tormentor of slaves could sign the text without the least scruple,
since the right to property, and not the principle of equality, was evoked under
the vague expression of "pursuit of Happiness." It is worth noting, however, in
the minutiae that lie under the great events of history, that Jefferson had wanted
to expressly mention slavery. In the first draft, he had put in a whole paragraph
on the subject:

[The king of England, George III] has declared a cruel war against human
nature itself, violating the most sacred rights of life and liberty in the
person of a distant people that had never offended him, imprisoning it
and reducing it to servitude in another hemisphere, when he did not cause
it to perish in a miserable death in the vessels that were transporting it
there. This war of pirates, which would be the shame of pagan powers, is
waged by the Christian King of Great-Britain. Decided to maintain open
a commerce in which can sell and buy MEN, he has dishonored his right
of veto by blocking all legislative initiatives tending to ban it or reduce it;
and so that nothing of note be lacking in this list of horrors, he has now
urged this same people to take up arms against us and thus buy this
freedom of which he himself deprived them; thus repairing former crimes
committed against a people by crimes that he encourages them to commit
against another people.[8]

Jefferson's cunning lay in his placing the entire responsibility for slavery on
England. Yet this cunning was not enough to convince the representatives of

Georgia and South Carolina, who did not see such an abomination in the slave trade, and they obtained the suppression of the paragraph.

The discussion should have begun anew with the elaboration of the Constitution that marked the birth of the nation. In reality, the question of slavery was never taken up directly during the Constitutional Convention. All believed that it was better to remain silent on the issue if the Union was to be preserved. Even as divergent interests manifested themselves between the northern and the southern states, the final compromise mentions slaves three times (not directly but in circumlocutions):

Article 1, section 2: The slaves are counted as "three fifths of all other persons" as regarding representation in Congress and for direct taxation.

Article 1, section 9: "The Migration or Importation of such Persons as any of the States now existing shall think proper to admit, shall not be prohibited by Congress prior to the Year one thousand eight hundred and eight." The slave trade was to be permitted for another twenty years. But there would be an end to it.

Article 4, section 2: "No person held to Service or to Labour in one State, under the Laws thereof, escaping into another, shall in Consequence of any Law or Regulation therein, be discharged from such Service or Labour, but shall be delivered up on Claim of the Party to whom such Service or Labour may be due."[9] Thus, fugitive slaves could be returned without delay.

The text that caused the biggest problem was that regarding representation for the slaves calculated at three-fifths of other persons. It was not anger at giving the African Americans three-fifths of human identity; it was an underlying question of a totally different order: the division of power between the North and the South. Who would control the nation? If the slave had counted for a whole person, the South would have been in a position of strength. The North was adamantly opposed to that, and against its own convictions reasoned like this: "You consider your slaves as goods. Goods do not have a right to vote. So be logical!" The final decision was seen as a victory for the South. But we have to remark that the slave was partway between the status of owned property and the status of a human person. It was not by chance.

Indeed, one must not think that at the time of the Revolution the pro-slavery position was weakening. Slavery was in full expansion. It was the system that determined the social structure in the South and was on the verge of expanding to the West. There were plenty of arguments to prove that slavery was a fact of nature and an extension of the right to property, if not even the will of God. People did not hesitate to say and to write that slavery was a blessing for the slave, the fruit of wisdom and divine Providence, and that the owner of Christian slaves was the true friend of the Africans, having saved them from extermination.

Now, however, the opponents of slavery began to stand up. For the first time, people dared to denounce the baseness of the slavery system. Abolitionist societies were born almost everywhere, in the South as in the North. What were the arguments of these humanists? It will suffice to present the position of a key person of the times: Thomas Jefferson. He reflects the idealism and the contradictions of the first opponents of slavery.

Personally implicated in the slave trade, and owner of more than two hundred slaves, Jefferson made strong statements against slavery, especially at the beginning of his political career when he tried to pass legislation condemning slavery in Virginia and on all the territory of the United States. He felt a certain guilt regarding a situation that deprived other human beings of their fundamental human rights. But the damage was less for the black than for the white, for the morality and the security of the white masters was put in danger by this relation of domination. In his *Notes on the State of Virginia* Jefferson said, "Every relation between master and slave is a continual exercise of the most violent passions, unchecked despotism on the one hand, degrading submission on the other. Our children see that and learn to do the same."[10]

At the same time as he spoke clearly against the institution of slavery in his writings, Jefferson harbored doubts as to the aptitude of blacks for full freedom and full humanity. He depicted the Africans as beings "as incapable as children to take care of themselves," mentally "inferior" and sexually "ardent." He expressed a strong aversion for any mixing of races.[11] In the end, if equality was impossible, it was because it would involve a mixing of blood. And the white Americans did not want to "soil their blood."

Caught between a will to humanize the fate of the Africans and a refusal of any racial mixing, the sage of Monticello would preach, as would George Washington, a gradual emancipation. Let's not go too fast! There cannot be a complete citizenship for blacks. In the future, the ideal would be to gather them in some place where they could live in freedom under the compassionate supervision of whites. That could be in the West or in Africa. But as such a displacement was impossible, Jefferson would tend more and more to accept slavery tacitly as inevitable. He had perfectly internalized the position of the ruling class. Besides, eight of the first twelve presidents of the United States would be slave owners.

We can understand now, through its most eminent representative, the hidden content of the revolutionary ideology. Behind the acceptance of human universality lurked a very precise ethnic identity. The norm was white, British, and Protestant (even if a Catholic signature appears at the bottom of the Declaration of Independence, that of a representative of Maryland). Beneath the praise of liberty lay the servitude of a people, the African Americans. The Revolution did not speak for the African American. The Revolution lied to itself. But the call of conscience could not be indefinitely choked off: "Yes, Sirs, having ceased being Englishmen, I hope that it will please you to become men, and, as such, admit the entire human species to your inalienable rights" (Thomas Day).

At the first official census in 1790, 657,527 slaves were counted in the South in a total population of less than 4 million. That figure almost doubled by 1810, with 1,163,854 slaves, since knowledge that the slave trade was ending galvanized the slave merchants. Yet we can consider a more positive effect of the American Revolution: the progressive abolition of slavery in the North (in the thirty years following the Revolution, all the states of the North pledged a complete abolition of slavery), the limitation of the expansion of slavery in the Northwest Territories, and the multiplication of free African Americans in the South (they had profited from the general confusion to flee or were generously freed by their owners). Yet the number of free blacks would decline from 1810 to 1860 because legislation would once more seal the access to freedom. The "politically correct" status of a black in a white society could only be slavery. "Because race was the most easily identifiable difference, it became an increasingly important justification for slavery; the assumption that Blacks were not fit for freedom was crucial to the defense of slavery in an era of liberty and equality."[12] The freedom of the slave owner was that of possessing slaves. And it was the servitude of the slave that made possible, economically and socially, the freedom of the others.

The Triumph of King Cotton

At the end of the eighteenth century, the future of slavery seemed dim. It appeared to be barely profitable, and revolutionary ideas had sapped its legitimacy in the minds of many. The prohibition of the slave trade was a first step that would bring others. Yet between 1790 and 1860, the number of slaves would grow from 697,897 to 3,953,760—a nearly sixfold increase. And institutional slavery had conquered nine new states. But it became the distinctive trait of the Deep South. And on the eve of the Civil War, one would have thought slavery even more solidly in place and for a long time to come.

What caused this considerable expansion? It was the explosion in cotton farming. This agricultural product, which is not native to America, had made a discreet entry a long time before. But two unforeseen circumstances gave a considerable impetus to cotton farming: (1) the Industrial Revolution in England offered new capacities for the treatment of cotton to which the Indian fiber was not well suited, and thus created new demands; and (2) the invention of the cotton gin by Eli Whitney, in 1793, made it far easier to separate the fiber from the seed than it had ever been. The figures speak for themselves: in 1792, a year before Whitney's invention, the United States exported 138,328 pounds of cotton; in 1794, a year after the invention, 1,601,000; in 1800, 17,790,000; in 1820, 35 million pounds. The United States became the premier supplier of cotton for Europe. And that considerably reinforced slavery—the machine needed matter. From then on, in the Deep South, the world of the slave would be the cotton field. Cotton production began in Georgia and North and South Carolina, then spread into Arkansas, Florida, Texas, and elsewhere. But the production would be concentrated especially in three states: Alabama, Mississippi, and Louisiana. These three states accounted for over half of the national cotton production. That brought the displacement of a million slaves to these western states, without consideration for family ties.

Solomon Northup, who spent twelve years of slavery in Louisiana, told of the daily life of slaves working for King Cotton:

The cotton harvest begins in the second half of August. Each slave is given a sack to which is attached a strap around the neck, so that the opening is at the height of his chest, with the bottom practically at his feet. Each one also received a large basket that contains about two barrels, to store the cotton when the bag has been filled. These baskets are brought to the field and placed at the head of the rows.

When a slave is sent to pick cotton for the first time, he is soundly whipped so that he will work as fast as possible. When night comes, his bag is weighed to see how much he can produce. This determines the amount of cotton he must bring in every night. If the amount diminishes, he will be considered lazy and will be given a more or less great number of lashes. . . .

The hands are required to be in the cotton field as soon as it is light in the morning, and, with the exception of ten or fifteen minutes which is given them at noon to swallow their allowance of cold bacon, they are not allowed to be a moment idle until it is too dark to see, and when the moon is full, they often labor till the middle of the night. They do not dare to stop even at dinnertime, nor return to the quarters, however late it be, until the order to halt is given by the driver.

The day's work over in the field, the baskets are "toted," or in other words, carried to the gin-house, where the cotton is weighed. No matter how fatigued and weary he may be—no matter how much he longs for sleep and rest—a slave never approaches the gin house with his basket of cotton but with fear. If he falls short in weight—if he has not performed the full task appointed him, he knows that he must suffer. And if he has exceeded it by ten or twenty pounds, in all probability his master will measure the next day's task accordingly. So whether he has too little or too much, his approach to the gin-house is always with fear and trembling. Most frequently they have too little, and therefore it is they who are not anxious to leave the field. After weighing, follow the whippings; and then the baskets are carried to the cotton house, and their contents stored away like hay, all hands being sent in to tramp it down. If the cotton is not dry, instead of taking it to the gin-house at once, it is laid on platforms, two feet high, and some three times as wide, covered with boards or plank, with narrow walks running between them.

This done, the labor of the day is not yet ended by any means. Each one of them must then attend to his respective chores. One feeds the mules, another the swine—another cuts the wood, and so forth; besides, the packing is all done by candle light. Finally, at a late hour, they reach their quarters, sleepy and overcome with the long day's toil. Then a fire must be kindled in the cabin, the corn ground in the small hand-mill, and supper, and dinner for the next day in the field, prepared. All that is allowed them is corn and bacon, which is given out at the corncrib and smoke-house every Sunday morning. Each one receives, as his weekly allowance, three and a half pounds of bacon, and corn enough to make a peck of meal.[13]

Nineteenth-century slavery presented a variety of situations according to the size of the plantation, the crops produced, the presence of a resident owner or not, and/or the strictness of the discipline. In the Deep South, slaves were more than half of the population; they were the heart of the working class. Cotton, however, did not require large plantations like those in the Caribbean Islands. In 1860 only 2.7 percent of owners had fifty slaves or more, and only a quarter of the slaves lived on such large plantations. Because of the modest size of these plantations (fewer than thirty slaves on average), most of the slaves had a resident owner who personally supervised the work. Often, however, the owner employed a white overseer and black team leaders. Two work systems were possible: (1) piecework in which each slave had to attain a fixed quota, and (2) teamwork in which each slave had a specific task.

The distinction between the slaves in the master's house and the field slaves lasted a long time. It corresponded to a distribution of roles, but not necessarily a social scale, because the size of the plantation did not permit work specialization and the domestic slaves were accused of collaborating with the master. Rosa Starke insisted on a rather complex social scale:

Dere was just two classes to de white folks—buckra slave owners and poor white folks dat didn't own no slaves. Dere was more classes 'mongst de slaves. De fust class was de house servants. Dese was de butler, de maids, de nurses, chambermaids and de cooks. De nex' class was de carriage drivers and de gardeners, de carpenters, de barber, and de stable men. Then come de nex' class: de wheelwright, wagoners, blacksmiths, and slave foremen. De nex' class I 'members was de cowmen and de niggers dat have care of de dogs. All dese have good houses and never have to work hard or git a beatin'. Then come de cradlers of de wheat, de threshers, and de millers of de corn and de wheat, and de feeders of de cotton gin.

De lowest class was de common field niggers. A house nigger man might swoop down and mate wid a field hand's good-lookin' daughter, now and then, for pure love of her, but you never see a house gal lower herself by marryin' and matin' wid a common field hand nigger.[14]

In any case, three-quarters of adult slaves worked in the fields, and they considered as part of the elite the slaves who served the black community rather than the masters: the preachers, the traditional medicine men, the midwives, the musicians, the rebels. The differences in status among the slaves were greater between plantations than within a plantation itself.

A most delicate question, and at the same time one of the most interesting questions to study, is that of the relationship between the master and the slave in the nineteenth century. "Slaves were, at the same time, both objects and subjects, human property held for the purpose of enriching their masters, and individuals who had lives of their own."[15] In order to characterize the contradictory attitude of the slave owners, one word has been much used: *paternalism.* The term does not designate an inoffensive slavery but a situation in which the master imposed himself in the slaves' life by claiming the right to set the terms of that life. He knew them by name; he cared for their well-being; and he wanted to direct their lives. He did not hesitate to talk of his "love" for these human beings, of his "family, white and black." It was Providence that had placed him in that position, and he had to fulfill it with a sense of his responsibilities. And he did so to such a degree that the material conditions, the food, and the health of the slaves tended to improve during this century. In fact, the mortality rate became comparable to that of many European nations. In 1825 the Southern states had the largest slave population of the whole New World. The smallest importer had become the great exploiter. The masters' desire to convert their slaves to Christianity had its roots in this paternalistic atmosphere. They gathered them for religious instruction, prayer, and the reading of the Scriptures.

This attitude of the whites, mixing coercion and persuasion, did not suppress the slaves' autonomy but tremendously reduced it. The lives of the oppressed were boxed in by the rules of the game, from morning till night and from childhood to old age. Practically nothing escaped the purview of the master. He knew what was good for the slaves. He placed them in a situation of utter dependency. It was another version of "Without me, you can do nothing." These Africans, believed the owners, were children who had to be controlled by inspiring in them a gut-level fear. And the possible types of punishment were nearly infinite. Rare were those slaves who were able to avoid whippings, despite all the denials of their masters. The testimony of Solomon Bradley, a twenty-seven-year-old cook and blacksmith, is particularly striking:

The most shocking thing that I have ever seen was on the plantation of Mr. Farraby, on the line of the railroad. I went up to his house one morning from my work for drinking water, and I heard a woman screaming awfully in the door-yard. On going up to the fence and looking over I saw a woman stretched out, face downwards, on the ground her hands and feet being fastened to stakes. Mr. Farraby was standing over and striking her with a leather trace belonging to his carriage-harness. As he struck her the flesh of her back and legs was raised in welts and ridges by the force of the blows. Sometimes when the poor thing cried too loud from the pain Farraby would kick her in the mouth. After he had exhausted himself from whipping her he sent to his house for sealing wax and a lighted candle and, melting the wax, dropped it on the woman's lacerated back. He then got a riding whip and standing over the woman, picked off the hardened wax by switching at it. Mr. Farraby's grown daughters were looking at all this through the blinds. The punishment was so terrible that I was induced to ask what offence the woman had committed and was told by her fellow servants that her only crime was in burning the edges of the waffles that she had cooked for breakfast.[16]

Another clear indication of the state of dependency of the slaves was the interference of the master in their family life. Marriages of slaves were not recognized in any Southern state, and yet, despite all difficulties, the monogamous African American family developed. The importance of a stable family is nowhere witnessed to so well as in the autobiographies of slaves. The numerous escapes of slaves to find their companion also attest to it. Often they had to look for their partner at another plantation, which did not please the master. But the family constituted a fragile refuge against the worst rigors of slavery. It was also the place of human development.

African American women had to bear the sexual assaults of their owners. The rape of a woman slave was unknown as a crime in the law of the South. However, liaisons between white women and black men were not rare either. Mulattos began to proliferate (estimated at more than 10 percent of the slaves in 1860). They would always be assimilated to the black community and be subjected to slavery.

The forced separation of families, according to the fluctuations of the market and the interests of the owners, was the most terrible of trials. A historian has estimated that one-third of marriages were broken by the sale of slaves and that half the children were separated from at least one of their parents. Frederick Douglass spoke of the rare moments he spent with his mother when he was a very young slave:

I never saw my mother, to know her as such, more than four or five times in my life; and each of these times was very short in duration, and at night. She was hired by a Mr. Stewart, who lived about twelve miles from my home. She made her journeys to see me in the night, traveling the whole distance on foot, after the performance of her day's work. She was a field hand, and a whipping is the penalty of not being in the field at sunrise, unless a slave has special permission from his or her master to the contrary—a permission which they seldom get, and one that gives to him that gives it the proud name of being a kind master. I do not recollect of ever seeing my mother by the light of day. She was with me in the night. She would lie down with me, and get me to sleep, but long before I waked she was gone. Very little communication ever took place between us. Death soon ended what little we could have while she lived, and with it her hardships and suffering.[17]

The slave was a possession, a source of labor, before being a person. And the arsenal of laws of the nineteenth century sought to reinforce slavery rather than alleviate it. These laws placed restrictions on travel, forbade the slaves to learn to read and write, and multiplied obstacles to obtaining freedom. The efforts of some to humanize the system were another way of making it last.

The slaves were far from sharing the positive view of the situation that their masters sought to inculcate in them. They combined deference and defiance. At work, certainly, they obeyed. But they sought to profit from the least bit of leeway they could find in the unequal and unjust system, to live by their own system of values and display their personality. To a great extent, outside of the fields, the world of the slaves was free of servitude's constraints. They enjoyed a partial autonomy in their quarters, where they could express they importance they placed on the family, the group, and religion. The distance between the slaves' quarters and the home of the master (a distance desired by the latter) allowed the slaves a certain privacy; they could grow a garden, eat, sing, play, discuss, tell stories, pray, love, raise children, and rest. The African influence was stronger for the slave of the first generation; the Christian influence was stronger after that. But the number of whites and the size of the plantations prevented the black community from being a world apart. They had daily interactions. A collective consciousness among the African Americans could be forged only gradually, with suspicions easily undermining their relations. They were more like individuals seeking to find a place in the system. Popular African American tales do not present us with heroic figures, but sly animals who can profit from the most disadvantageous situations. Just the same, an ethnic consciousness was promoted by the masters who spoke of their "Negroes" and by the slaves who called themselves "brother" and "sister."

In order to survive as human beings, the slaves combined an adjustment to and a resistance to servitude. The resistance took various forms, from the simplest to the subtlest means. A recently arrived slave would feign inability to use a work instrument. Another would beat records of passivity. It was a marvel to see them unanimously stop work as soon as the overseer turned his back. Feigned illnesses were contagious. Even subtler was the children's apprenticeship in learning to hold their tongues when the whites were around. The deepest feelings of the slave community had to remain completely invisible.

During the entire era of slavery there were innumerable thefts (taking what belonged to the master was not stealing) and fires (harvests, barns, and houses).

The dominating class always had to be on guard. They even had to watch their food, for the slaves knew how to use arsenic. As soon as one could find a weapon, it was one more chance for rebellion. And the slaves used all means possible to get rid of those who crushed them. When they could not, they mutilated themselves so as to be unable to work, or in desperation they decided on suicide. The number of infanticides was always high on the plantations.

Incapable of obtaining their freedom through legal means, that is, by buying their freedom, many slaves were tempted to escape individually or in small groups. The North Star was their guide through forest and swamp. In fact, many succeeded, if we are to believe the newspapers of the slave states, filled with appeals from owners describing their fugitive slaves. Between forty thousand and one hundred thousand escapes were organized during the nineteenth century alone. Yet the chances of success were no greater than 10 percent! Most of the fugitives (80 percent) were young men between the ages of sixteen and thirty-five. Most of the time they were trying to find a family member. It was one way of voting with their feet!

As the years passed, the escape toward the North (considered, perhaps too quickly, a place of freedom) was better and better organized. Thus the Underground Railroad was established, which drained thousands of slaves from the South. It consisted of a well-organized network of guides, relays, and hiding places. Everything was done at night, for it was the safest time. Two enemies of the fugitives were to be avoided: the white man (with his dogs) and hunger. Among the most famous "passers" was a woman: Harriet Tubman. She made no fewer than nineteen trips to the South to free three hundred slaves, among whom were her parents.

Of course, there were several violent rebellions. Nineteenth-century history records three of them: that of Gabriel Prosser in Virginia in 1800, that of Denmark Vesey in South Carolina in 1822, and that of Nat Turner in Virginia in 1831. They were quickly smothered, none lasting more than two days. The clearest result was a savage repression.

Rather than a frontal attack on the system, most slaves chose a constant, day-to-day pressure, a silent sabotage. They wanted to survive with as much decency as possible. If they could not wrest their freedom from the owners, as did Toussaint-Louverture in Haiti, they tried to limit white control so that the spark of freedom could one day nourish the flame of liberty. As Peter Kolchin concludes: "If the slaves helped make their own world, they nevertheless remained slaves, and the 'internal' lives they forged in the quarters operated within the confines of the political, economic, and social hegemony of white slave owners who interfered in the daily lives of their 'people' far more intrusively than most masters did elsewhere."[18]

While considering life on slave plantations, we must not forget the presence of two other categories of African Americans: the free blacks and the free blacks who owned slaves. Often they were mulattos who had bought their freedom.

According to the 1790 census, there were 59,466 free blacks (27,109 in the North; 32,357 in the South). Their ranks would grow at the turn of the century, but the growth pattern would not last. In 1860 they would constitute only 9 percent of the black population, living mostly in the more anonymous big cities. State laws sought to keep them in a subordinate position. In all but six states they could not vote. They could not testify against whites. In the South their professions were varied: carpenters, masons, merchants, mechanics, tailors. Some earned a good living.

Among these wealthier free blacks, a certain number were slave owners. In 1830 there were 3,775 blacks who owned a total of 12,760 slaves. That means that one free black family in ten owned at least one slave. The biggest owners lived in Louisiana and in South Carolina. And in truth, their daily behavior was not fundamentally different from that of their white counterparts.

In order to complete our review of American society before the Civil War (1861–1865), let us mention once more the importance of the whites who did not own slaves. They were the most numerous, for at the beginning of the century only one-third of white families owned slaves, and in 1860 no more than a quarter did so. Yet the slave owners were in power, defined the social order, and dominated the government. The nonowners represented the lower classes of the white populations who worked on small farms or as craftsmen in the cities. It was primarily an economic trench that separated them from the Southern aristocracy; in 1860 slave owners earned fourteen times more than the nonowners, and 93 percent of the riches of cotton plantations belonged to them. The borders between the two groups remained porous, however, because the nonowners wanted to be owners as soon as possible and many profited from slavery anyway. Most have identified the interest of the South with the perpetuation of the slave system. The racial division united the whites through common interests.

Let us now take a snapshot of the situation in 1860. The total population of the United States was about thirty-one million inhabitants. The fifteen Southern states had a population of some twelve million inhabitants, including four million slaves with a good male-female population balance. In South Carolina and Mississippi slaves represented more than half the population; in Louisiana, Alabama, Florida, and Georgia they were more than 40 percent. The youthfulness of the slave population was remarkable: 55.8 percent of the men were under twenty years old, as were 57 percent of the women. There were 385,000 slave owners, of whom 50 percent had fewer than five slaves and only 12 percent had twenty or more slaves. This means, however, that more than half the slaves lived on plantations with more than twenty slaves. The biggest plantations did not grow cotton, but rather sugar in Louisiana or rice in South Carolina and in Georgia. Just one planter, Joshua Ward, owned more than a thousand slaves.

Despite its great profitability and adaptability, slavery's days were numbered. The Civil War between an industrial and financial North and a rural and aristocratic South, declared on April 12, 1861, would spell its unexpected end.

The Emancipation Proclamation of January 1, 1863, and the Thirteenth Amendment of the Constitution (enacted December 18, 1865) would effectively kill slavery. The amendment stipulates: "Neither slavery nor involuntary servitude, except as punishment for crime whereof the party shall have been duly convicted, shall exist within the United States, or any place subject to their jurisdiction." A little later (April 9, 1866), a law on civil rights gave to the former slaves American citizenship with all its accompanying rights and obligations. But the African Americans quickly saw that the abolition of slavery did not set racial equality in place. Besides, only ten days after the passage of the Thirteenth Amendment, the Ku Klux Klan was founded in Tennessee.

Notes

1. Elikia M'Bokolo, "La dimension africaine de la traite des Noirs," *Le Monde diplomatique,* April 1998, 16.

2. Quoted in Henry Louis Gates, Jr., ed., *The Classic Slave Narratives* (New York: Mentor, 1987), 34–35.

3. Patrick Manning, "La traite négrière et l'évolution démographique de l'Afrique," in *La chaîne et le lien. Une vision de la traite négrière* (Paris: Unesco, 1998), 162.

4. Ira Berlin, *Many Thousands Gone: The First Two Centuries of Slavery in North America* (Cambridge, Mass.: Belknap, 1998).

5. Philip D. Morgan, *Slave Counterpoint: Black Culture in the Eighteenth-Century Chesapeake and Lowcountry* (Chapel Hill and London: University of North Carolina Press, 1998).

6. Ibid., 1.

7. Text taken from *Common Sense,* published anonymously on January 9, 1776.

8. Quoted in Joanne Grant, *Black Protest: History, Documents and Analyses* (New York: Ballantine, 1991), 17–18.

9. The French text of the U.S. Constitution is found, for example, in Gordon S. Wood, *La création de la République américaine* (Paris: Belin, 1991), 737–49.

10. Thomas Jefferson, *Notes on the State of Virginia* (Chapel Hill: University of North Carolina Press, 1955), 162–63.

11. The writing of these words for the original publication of this book in French pre-dates the finding, based on genetic research, that Jefferson fathered offspring with one of his slaves.

12. Peter Kolchin, *American Slavery, 1619–1877* (New York: Hill & Wang, 1993), 90–91.

13. Quoted in John B. Boles, *Black Southerners, 1619–1869* (Lexington: University Press of Kentucky, 1983), 71–72.

14. Quoted in James Mellon, ed., *Bullwhip Days: The Slaves Remember* (New York: Weidenfeld & Nicolson, 1988), 136.

15. Kolchin, *American Slavery,* 111.

16. Quoted in John W. Blassingame, ed., *Slave Testimony* (Baton Rouge and London: Louisiana State University Press, 1977), 372.

17. Frederick Douglass, *Narrative of the Life of Frederick Douglass, an American Slave* (New York: Signet, 1968), 22.

18. Kolchin, *American Slavery,* 166–67.

Bibliography

Berlin, Ira. *Many Thousands Gone: The First Two Centuries of Slavery in North America.* Cambridge, Mass.: Belknap, 1990.

————. *Slaves without Masters: The Free Negro in the Antebellum South.* New York: Vintage, 1974.

Berlin, Ira, Marc Favreau, and Steven F. Miller, eds. *Remembering Slavery: African Americans Talk about Their Personal Experiences of Slavery and Emancipation.* New York: New Press, 1998.

Blassingame, John W., ed. *Slave Testimony: Two Centuries of Letters, Speeches, Interviews, and Autobiographies.* Baton Rouge and London: Louisiana State University Press, 1977.

Boles, John B. *Black Southerners, 1619–1869.* Lexington: University Press of Kentucky, 1983.

Campbell, Edward D., Jr., ed. *Before Freedom Came: African American Life in the Antebellum South.* Richmond: Museum of the Confederacy; Charlottesville: University Press of Virginia, 1991.

Countryman, Edward, ed. *How Did American Slavery Begin?* Boston: Bedford; New York: St. Martin's, 1999.

Curtin, Philip D. *The Atlantic Slave Trade: A Census.* Madison: University of Wisconsin Press, 1969.

Douglass, Frederick. *Narrative of the Life of Frederick Douglass, an American Slave.* New York: Signet, 1968.

Finkelman, Paul. *Slavery and the Founders: Race and Liberty in the Age of Jefferson.* Armonk, N.Y.: Sharpe, 1996.

Fohlen, Claude. *Histoire de l'esclavage aux États-Unis.* Paris: Perrin, 1998.

Frey, Sylvia R. *Water from the Rock: Black Resistance in a Revolutionary Age.* Princeton, N.J.: Princeton University Press, 1991.

Gates, Henry Louis, Jr., ed. *The Classic Slave Narratives.* New York: Mentor, 1987.

Genovese, Eugene D. *Roll, Jordan, Roll: The World the Slaves Made.* New York: Pantheon, 1974.

Huggins, Nathan Irvin. *Black Odyssey: The Afro-American Ordeal in Slavery.* New York: Pantheon, 1977.

Jacobs, Harriet A. *Incidents dans la vie d'une jeune esclave.* Paris: Viviane Hamy, 1992.

Jordan, Winthrop D. *White over Black: American Attitudes toward the Negro, 1550–1812.* Chapel Hill: University of North Carolina Press, 1968.

Joyner, Charles W. *Down by the Riverside: A South Carolina Slave Community.* Urbana: University of Illinois Press, 1984.

Kolchin, Peter. *American Slavery, 1619–1877.* New York: Hill & Wang, 1993.

Lerner, Gerna. *De l'esclavage à la ségrégation. Les femmes noires dans l'Amérique des Blancs.* Paris: Denoël/Gonthier, 1975.

Mellon, James, ed. *Bullwhip Days: The Slaves Remember.* New York: Weidenfeld & Nicolson, 1988.

Miller, Randall M., and John David Smith, eds. *Dictionary of Afro-American Slavery.* Westport, Conn., and London: Praeger, 1997.

Morgan, Philip D. *Slave Counterpoint: Black Culture in the Eighteenth-Century Chesapeake and Lowcountry.* Chapel Hill and London: University of North Carolina Press, 1998.

Northup, Solomon. *Twelve Years a Slave: Narrative of Solomon Northup.* Auburn, N.Y.: Derby and Miller, 1853.

Parish, Peter J. *Slavery: History and Historians.* New York: Harper & Row, 1989.

Petre-Grenouilleau, Olivier. *La traite des Noirs.* Paris: QSJ, 1997.

Rawick, George P., ed. *The American Slave: A Composite Biography.* 19 vols. Westport, Conn.: Greenwood, 1972–1979.

Scott, William R., and William G. Shade. *Upon These Shores: Themes in the African American Experience, 1600 to the Present.* New York and London: Routledge, 2000.

Wood, Betty. *The Origins of American Slavery: Freedom and Bondage in the English Colonies.* New York: Hill & Wang, 1997.

Wood, Peter H. *Black Majority: Negroes in Colonial South Carolina from 1670 through the Stono Rebellion.* New York: Knopf, 1974.

2

"Have you got good religion?"

The Conversion of the Slaves to Christianity

"My religion is my life."
—Mary

TODAY, NO ONE CAN DOUBT IT—the secular history of America is based on a religious vision. It is the myth of the Promised Land, of the Chosen People, that urged on the first colonists. Dissenting from the Anglican Church, the *Mayflower* Pilgrims were highly conscious of their divine mission. They fled the European Babylon, for they were called by God to be the genesis of a new humanity in this unknown land. "God has sifted through a whole nation so as to send his best seed to this wild country."[1] As John Winthrop stated in 1630, while they were still aboard ship, they (the Pilgrims) were "like a city on a hilltop," offering a new model of Christianity, completely conformed to the gospel ideal.

These seventeenth-century Calvinists, called Puritans, were imbued with a democratic mentality. But their Christian egalitarianism was undermined by their theology of divine election. Indeed, God had secretly chosen certain individuals, and this choice translated into worldly success. "God helps those who help themselves"—such was the great principle of God's action. According to that vision, material success was a sign of salvation. The invisible election was revealed by the amount of money amassed. Those who could not demonstrate such success could have no part in God's salvation. There were the saved and the damned, the pure and the impure. Certain of their salvation, as was proved by their good works, the Puritans could not allow themselves be contaminated by people of color. They kept themselves pure by ferreting out evil where it was—in other peoples, contaminated by all kinds of human turpitude, incapable of being other than slaves. The inferiority of the Africans was God's will for them.

We must admit that, with such a theology, the atmosphere was not propitious for the slaves' encounter with Christianity. The whites, moreover, did not show any great desire to evangelize the Africans. The latter were quite content in their "paganism." Much time would pass before one could detect a significant Christian presence in the slave quarters in the nineteenth century. But the Christian God eventually replaced the African god.

The African Religion of the Slaves

The American blacks come from Africa, humanly, socially, and religiously. Their world found its cohesion in a religious representation, and their African identity necessarily expressed itself on the religious level. That context was perturbed by the Atlantic slave trade and the imposition of slavery, yet that trauma did not completely erase the basic religiosity that defined the black person's existence.

Certainly, the severing of the umbilical link with the motherland was extremely violent. Young men in chains were completely disoriented, lost among other Africans whose language they did not always understand and whose customs or beliefs they did not completely share. It is interesting to note that no African ritual objects have ever been found in archaeological digs in North America. And an oral tradition, by definition, does not leave traces.

Also, certainly, the merchants and the missionaries did not show the least respect for the African religious experience—it was only a gross fetishism, tribal customs, diabolical superstitions, savage paganism, they believed. Human sacrifices cohabited with abominable witchcraft. Could anything come from an inferior people except an inferior religion?

Even today we can hesitate between using the singular or the plural when speaking about African religion. As soon as we do not content ourselves with quick generalities, we discover many variations in beliefs and rites along with the ethnic origins and the tribes. God, or the Supreme Being, was not evident in all the societies, and God's distance from humankind was calculated differently among the African peoples. The hierarchy of beings was more or less complex.

Nevertheless, the black American was structured by an African identity that had a religious dimension, or rather was closely tied to religion. The question is less about easily seen concrete elements than about a kind of grammar of principles of action and reflection. It is a way of being in life and of seeing reality. It is a question of a system of values, criteria for judgment, models of behavior that permit one to distinguish between good and evil. "Like involuntary muscles that keep the heart beating without one consciously thinking about it, this generalized African heritage helped shape the slaves' response to their American situation."[2]

All other religious expressions that we meet both in Africa and in the New World will have to take into account this age-old substratum.

In order to avoid superimposing our present-day categories, and especially a static Christian view of African religion, we will allow Olaudah Equiano to describe how his people, the Ibos, were imbued with their religion. Though he had been kidnapped at the age of eleven in what would become Nigeria, he had an excellent memory. In any case, as he wrote at the end of the eighteenth century after having become Christian, he was not influenced by the violent criticism of traditional religion that would characterize the Christian mission in the following century.

> As to religion, the natives believe that there is one Creator of all things, and that he lives in the sun, and is girded round with a belt that he may never eat or drink; but according to some, he smokes a pipe, which is our own favorite luxury. They believe he governs events, especially our deaths or captivity, but as for the doctrine of eternity, I do not remember to have ever heard of it; some, however, believe in the transmigration of souls, in a certain degree.—Those spirits, which are not transmigrated, such as their dear friends or relations, they believe always attend them, and guard them from the bad spirits, or their foes. For this reason they always before eating, as I have observed, put some small portion of the meat, and pour some of the drink, on the ground for them; and they often make oblations of the blood of beasts, or of fowls at their graves. I was very fond of my mother, and was almost constantly with her. When she went to make these oblations at her mother's tomb, which was a kind of small solitary thatched house, I sometimes attended her. There she made her libations, and spent most of the night in cries and lamentations. I have been extremely terrified on these occasions. The loneliness of the place, the darkness of the night, and the ceremony of libation, naturally awful and gloomy, were heightened by my mother's lamentations, and these concurring with the doleful cries of birds, by which these places were frequented, gave an inexpressible terror to the scene.
>
> We compute the year from the day on which the sun crosses the line, and, on its setting that evening, there is a general shout throughout the land; at least I can speak from my own knowledge, throughout our vicinity. The people, at the same time, make a great noise with rattles, not unlike the basket rattles used by children here, though much larger, and hold up their hands to heaven for a blessing. It is then the greatest offerings are made. . . .They have many offerings, particularly at full moon; generally two at harvest, before the fruits are taken out of the ground; and when any young animals are killed, they sometimes offer up a part of

them as a sacrifice. These offerings, when made by one of the heads of a family, serve for the whole. . . .

We practiced circumcision like the Jews, and made offerings and feasts on that occasion in the same manner as they did. Like them also, our children were named from some event, some circumstance, or fancied foreboding at the time of their birth. I was named Olaudah, which, in our language, signifies "vicissitude or fortunate," also, "one favoured, and having a loud voice, and well spoken." I remember we never polluted the name of the object of our adoration; on the contrary, it was always mentioned with the greatest reverence; and we are totally unacquainted with swearing, and all those terms of abuse and reproach which find their way so readily and copiously into the language of more civilized people. . . .

I have before remarked that the natives of this part of Africa are extremely clean. This necessary habit of decency was with us a part of religion, and therefore we had many purifications and washings; indeed almost as many, and used on the same occasions, if my recollection does not fail me, as the Jews. Those that touched the dead, at any time, were obliged to wash and purify themselves before they could enter a dwelling-house, or touch any person or any thing we eat. I was so fond of my mother I could not keep from her, or avoid touching her at some of those periods, in consequence of which I was obliged to be kept out with her, in a little house made for that purpose, till offering was made, and then we were purified.

Though we had not places of public worship, we had priests and magicians, or wise men. I do not remember if they had different offices, or they were united in the same persons, but they were held in great reverence by the people. They calculated our time, and foretold events. . . . They wore their beards; and when they died, they were succeeded by their sons. Most of their implements and things of value were interred with them. Pipes and tobacco were also put into the graves with the corpse, which was always perfumed and ornamented, and animals were offered in sacrifice to them. None accompanied their funerals but those of the same profession or tribe. These buried them after sunset, and always returned from the grave by a different way by which they went.[3]

In this testimony, we find the belief in a Creator God, the veneration of ancestors, the multiplication of offerings and sacrifices, the respect for the sacred, the rules of purity and impurity, the existence of priests and sorcerers, and a feeling of proximity to Jewish practices. There is nothing really surprising in light of what we now know of the African world.

If we tried to synthesize the major lines of West African religion, we might come up with the following creed: "I believe in a supreme being who creates everything and in divinities, spirits, and inferior powers that keep and control the universe. I believe in the ancestors who keep and protect their descendants. I believe in the efficiency of sacrifices and the power of magic, good or bad; I believe in the fullness of life here and now."[4]

We can never insist enough on the wholistic perspective of African religion. It imbues all the dimensions of life without marking divisions between the sacred and the profane so familiar to the West and of which the West is a victim. For Africans, religion is the source of all meaning and the accomplishment of all existence.

Since religious thought gives the meaning, we find a system of relationships and connections that make the universe coherent. Life is a whole, but it is organized with a graduated and specialized power structure. The participation of all things in the vital energy of the world creates a universal harmony. That energy, that power that comes from God, is distributed in a descending order, first to lesser divinities, then to the ancestors, and finally to the heads of families and to all the members of the family. According to Rene Jaouen, "The concept of vital force seems to be the most apt to account for all the manifestations of African belief, whether they be philosophical, properly religious or even magic."[5]

We must underline the fact that this African religion is not centered at first on God or the cosmos or the forces of evil, but on living men and women and on the ancestors on the side of the dead. The gods exist for the humans, and the humans are in communion with life. According to the well-known phrase of John Mbiti: "I am because we are; and because we are, I am." The human task is to dam up evil, illness, or failure as much as possible. All must collaborate in the celebration and explosion of life. Hence, the cult of fertility. Newel Booth, a specialist, has set out five key terms for a study of African religions: (1) the power of life, (2) humanity, (3) the search for wholeness, (4) the continuity of time, and (5) health. Without a doubt, these themes remained in the consciousness of the slaves being carried to the inhospitable shores of America.

Can we find, however, continuity between African religious behavior and the behavior of the slaves in America? We will be content with three examples—dance, baptism by immersion, and witchcraft—and keep for later on the subject of music, which is at the center of our purpose.

"In the beginning there was dance." Alfred Métraux defines African religion as "a danced religion." It is through dance that people express their deep emotions, are in communion with the universal energy, and vibrate in rhythm with the spiritual world. In Africa, dance accompanies each phase of community life and each moment of human existence, from birth to death, with a special place reserved for the rites of passage. In North America, dance allowed slaves to form ties between people of different tribes, to live moments of great exultation, to take revenge on the white world by showing greater virtuosity. It strengthened the cohesion of the community of the oppressed. It was entertainment and an outlet capable of expressing the gamut of emotions by including the body and constituted the favorite pastime of the slaves. The tradition was perhaps best kept in Louisiana, for in 1817 the city council of New Orleans gave the African Americans a special place to dance, Congo Place. On February 21, 1819, the architect Benjamin Latrobe observed nearly five hundred slaves dancing in groups around musicians playing drums, a stringed instrument, and a gourd.

If baptism by immersion was so successful among the slaves, it was because it was done in a context to which Africans were particularly sensitive, namely, one that involved singing and dancing. Also, it reminded them of the importance of water in the religious culture of Africa. Water appears early on in the order of creation, for without water there is no life. To plunge into the water is always to drown the old self and go through a new birth. Water purifies and regenerates. Rain, in the hands of the Creator, is blessing or punishment. According to certain tribes, it is God's saliva. Sacred baths with total immersion are central to rites of initiation. The Spirit of God inhabits each drop of water. Rivers are populated with spirits that need to be won over.

With the subject of witchcraft, we approach a clandestine reality, yet one that largely has been confirmed in North America. Just as in West Africa, we find in North America signs of good magic and signs of bad magic. Good magic is, for example, the art of using plants to cure various illnesses. In this area the slaves developed a solid reputation in the United States. Some slaves were freed because of their medical talent and services rendered. In 1751 Caesar, a slave, was freed for having agreed to reveal his remedy against poison and rattlesnake bites. Whites did not hesitate to consult these experts.

In a society in which the traditional balance was completely shattered, witchcraft found a favorable terrain. In the midst of complete confusion, the sorcerer had notoriety, for he was in much demand, since the African Americans felt vulnerable outside of their normal framework. If slavery was the fruit of the witchcraft of the whites, how could one fight against this power except by using a counter power, a counter witchcraft? Thus it was that the head of the Angolan group in Denmark Vesey's 1822 rebellion—a certain Gullah Jack, born in Africa—combined belonging to the Methodist Church and practicing witchcraft. Not only was he believed to be invulnerable to injury, but also he was thought to be able to make others invulnerable. He asked his disciples to eat only grilled corn and almonds before the battle and to place a crab's claw in their mouth so as not to be wounded. Black magic triumphed by the use of poisons that wreaked terror in the masters. In eighteenth-century Virginia at least 175 slaves were tried for poisoning. But the practice was aimed more often at other blacks than at whites. It came from a long African experience.

These elements of continuity between Africa and North America were not as powerful as those in Brazil, Haiti, or Cuba. Willy-nilly, the Catholic Church allowed a lot of syncretism, especially through the expressed value of the sacraments, the cult of the saints, and the organization of religious fraternities.

Louisiana would have a sort of voodoo in the nineteenth century. Protestantism, on the contrary, insisting on biblical teaching and interior conversion, was ill adapted to compromise. Also, the more modest size of the plantations and the small proportion of slaves born in Africa made an African continuity more difficult. Most of the slaves in the nineteenth century had known nothing other than the United States. Thus, the memory of Africa continued to diminish.

In this way there was a slow enculturation, a phenomenon of religious and cultural adaptation. The African purview did not freeze up in contact with the reality of the slave trade and slavery itself. In order to face up to the situation, the African resources were mixed in with other resources. In a certain way, the slaves had lived through the defeat of the African gods. They would be obliged to redefine themselves if they wished to survive. This redefinition took place with a particular African sensitivity. The underlying spirit came from Africa, but the concrete behaviors reveal adaptation to the American environment. In any case, the result would be a new creation, a religious and cultural innovation: the African American identity, in which the African element practically unseen on the surface lives on in the depths of the person. According to Paul E. Lovejoy,

> The Africans were not content to keep a few picturesque and symbolic "surviving" attributes, they also brought with them real concepts and living interpretations of their sad condition. . . . The condition of the slaves on the American continent was as much determined by the reinterpretation of the African concepts and institutions as by the European oppression and economy. Despite their forced migration and their enslavement, the slaves were real participants in the defining of their new Afro-American identity. In creating new communities, or in joining those already formed in the existing plantations, they necessarily brought a part of Africa with them in the Americas.[6]

We will have the occasion to confirm that. The experience of slavery also contributed to bringing together various ethnic groups, obliging them to recognize that they were on the same side because they were the victims of the same hell.

We can note here that a certain number of slaves had been touched by an encounter with Islam in West Africa. Already in the sixteenth century we have proof of the presence of black Muslims in Mexico. They would arrive in North America in the eighteenth century. A recent estimate suggests that 10 percent of Africans (that is, some thirty thousand) sent to the United States between 1711 and 1808 were Muslims. Testimonies from that time give us names, especially on the coast of Georgia. For example, there was one Salih Bilali, who was buried with his prayer carpet and Qur'an. Often the Muslims were remarkable personalities, and they were considered the most intelligent, the most cultured, and the most worthy of respect in the community of slaves. They were gladly given responsibilities on the plantations. Moreover, the black Muslims had a feeling of superiority over their blood brothers. They knew how to read. They tried to practice the pillars of the Muslim faith (notably, praying five times a day while facing east and eating beef rather than pork), but they would find it difficult to transmit their faith because of their small number and marriage with non-Muslims. In any case, no Muslim slave, to our knowledge, converted to Christianity.

The White Mission

One of the primary justifications for the Atlantic commerce in human flesh was the conversion of the pagans to Christianity. A Portuguese chronicler stated that the slavery of the body was nothing compared to the freedom given to the soul. England thought the same way, and Charles II, in 1660, requested the Council of Foreign Plantations to do everything possible to invite the Indians and the slaves to the Christian faith and to baptism, since "it being the honor of our Crowne and of the Protestant Religion that all persons of our Dominions should be taught the knowledge of God, and be made acquainted with the misteries of Salvation."[7] Local governors were to take all possible initiatives to facilitate and encourage the conversion of blacks and Indians to Christianity. They also feared the competition of Spanish or French Catholic missionaries.

Was the Church of England in a position to give orders to the American colonists? The latter had fled a world where the Anglican Church reigned as the moral arbiter. They wanted to build a new society freed from the forms of traditional religious authorities. No local government would allow itself to promote Christian religious practice. In any case, the clergy never would condemn slavery in the colonial period. The clergy themselves owned slaves. In this way, the effort would not be to abolish the institution but to improve the lot of the poor slaves by some educational projects.

Religious people tended to feel basically that blacks were "pagans" and "infidels," attached to their barbaric beliefs and practices. They were "possessed by superstition and idolatry," declared one minister. "They believe that at death they are transported to their own country to live as free men once again." They "have no idea of our holy Religion." Did they not dance to get rain? Moreover, they appeared to be intellectually limited, incapable of moral progress. In 1699 the Virginia Assembly replied to the English request, that "as to the Negroes imported here, the gross barbarity and rudeness of their manners, the variety and strangeness of their languages and the weakness and the superficiality of their spirits render impossible all progress that might come from their conversion." An Anglican minister spoke of "the incorrigible stupidity of the majority of these miserable creatures." He would make no great effort to become interested in them.

In fact, there were numerous obstacles to the evangelization of the slaves, not the least of which was the indifference or the suspicion of the slave owners. They cared more for economic profit than for spirituality. In 1685 Morgan

Godwin described perfectly the priorities of the colonists in a sermon well summarized by its title: "Trade preferr'd before Religion and Christ made to give place to Mammon."

If the planters refused religious instruction for the slaves, it was because they feared it would mean their emancipation, and the master's economic interest was more important to them than obedience to the commandment of Christ (Matthew 28:16-20). That question would quickly be answered by colonial legislation. The only freedom that Christianity would give was freedom from the slavery of sin, since the apostle Paul clearly stated that each once must remain in the condition where God's call came to him or her (1 Corinthians 7:20). By 1706 at least six colonies had passed laws denying that baptism could change anything in the status of the slave. The Virginia text (1667) "was typical of the statutes enacted expressing the hope that the masters, freed from this doubt, may more carefully endeavor the propagation of Christianity among their slaves."[8]

There remained other difficulties in the South. Religious formation takes time, and that was to the detriment of work on the plantation. Wouldn't the masters have to "free" the slaves on Sundays and holidays? The masters found it difficult to consider their Africans as full human beings. Why instruct them? It is true that the linguistic barriers would be overcome only with time and that priority would be given to the children and the slaves born on American soil. The racist attitude was barely hidden—the slaves had no right to religion because they could not be authentically human. They were beasts of burden, nothing more. If the slaves were recognized as human, would the equality of rights between masters and slaves be proclaimed? That could not be! In the end, what the master feared most was the equality of human beings that underlies the profession of the Christian faith. Security and the social order were in question here. No brotherhood, even spiritual, was possible between the oppressor and the oppressed.

Often enough, the owners believed that the acceptance of the gospel would make their slaves impudent, proud, ungovernable, and even dangerous. They would lay claim to certain rights, such as the inseparability of spouses. They would think only of their freedom and would foment rebellions. The masters also feared that the slaves would deduce from the account of Creation that all human beings are brothers and sisters in Christ and will appear as equals before the Son of Man on Judgment Day.

In response, those who preached the evangelization of the Africans were obliged to prove that Christianity would make them better slaves, happier, and more loyal. It thus was another way of condoning the institution of slavery! Christian slaves would have a sense of duty, thinking only of the good of their master, who represented God on earth. Obedience would be their primary virtue.

The difficulties did not come only from the slave owners. The region, in general, did not have a religious bent. The Southern colonists did not have the religious zeal of the *Mayflower* Pilgrims. They were far from being pillars of the church. One in twenty practiced their religion. Their moral behavior left much to be desired. If they did not take care of their own souls, how could they care for the salvation of those they did not even consider as having souls?

Clergymen were few. The Anglican priests traveled through vast territories and depended on the planters for their sustenance. We might as well say that they would not preach the revolt of the slaves! An inquiry made in 1724 at the request of the bishop of London revealed a lack of enthusiasm of Anglican priests for the evangelization of African Americans. The best among them were content simply to appeal to the conscience of the masters.

In New England, where religious life was more intense, there were fewer slaves. But the Puritans had no desire to consider Africans as their equals. Yet in this northern area, certain positive actions can be noted. The first baptism of a slave seems to date from 1641 when "a Negro woman belonging to Rev. Stoughton of Dorchester, Massachusetts, being well approved by divers years experience for sound knowledge and true godliness, was received into the Church and baptized."[9]

In 1693 Cotton Mather organized a Society of Negroes, who, with the permission of their masters, could meet each Sunday evening. In 1776, at the time of the Declaration of Independence, the majority of slaves in New England were still "pagans." It is right to evoke here the action of the Quakers through the exhortations of George Fox in 1657 and William Edmundson in 1676. Fox reminded the Quakers, "Christ died for all . . . for the swarthy and the Negroes as well as for the Whites." Edmundson urged the planters to free their slaves, for Christian freedom and physical slavery were incompatible. It would take a few decades before the Society of Friends took action.[10]

Where did the Catholics stand in this debate? During the colonial period, it would seem, the Catholic Church had more respect for the Africans than did the churches that came from the various Reformations. In the four regions where Catholic communities were found (Florida, Alabama, Maryland, and Louisiana), laws gave black slaves the right to baptism, Sunday rest, church marriage, and burial in the parish cemetery. It came to a point that the Protestant governor of Maryland, in 1745, worried about the integrated Catholic ceremonies. His coreligionists feared that the slaves might prepare insurrections during the services.

In point of fact, however, the Catholic directives met with the same difficulties as those in the Protestant milieu: the lack of ministers and the refusal of the owners. This was so much the case that in the heart of the nineteenth century, although the official position of the Catholic Church was favorable to the emancipation of slaves, many Catholics and even religious congregations owned slaves. In practice, Catholics were practically indistinguishable from their Protestant colleagues. In 1830, in Maryland, the Jesuits sold about three hundred slaves to traders in the South, not for moral reasons, but for financial motives. In Kentucky there were proportionally more Catholic slave owners than non-Catholic. They wanted to prove their perfect integration to the American social order. The slaves were perhaps equal to all other humans in the eyes of God, but not in the eyes of the church.

The first institutional effort of the Anglican Church in favor of blacks began only at the beginning of the eighteenth century with the creation, in 1701, of the Society for the Propagation of the Gospel in Foreign Lands by Thomas Bray. That was at the very time that the English colonies adopted the system of slavery! Led by the bishop of London, the society published tracts and sermons, sent missionaries and catechists, and gathered funds across England—all with the purpose of supporting the American missions. The new missionaries (353 of them in seventy years) cared especially for the white colonists, but some found the time and received permission to evangelize the slaves, especially the children, albeit with little success.[11] It must be said that a man such as Le Jau demanded two years of catechumenate and obliged the newly baptized to swear before the parish assembly that they would not seek to free themselves from obedience to their earthly masters.[12] One interesting fact is that religious instruction and general education went together in a charitable society—the Associates of Dr. Bray, organized in 1723–1734—that opened schools for the young blacks. In a church centered on the Scriptures, learning to read is of first importance. In the long run, the Africans would derive enormous profit from it. However, the association would touch only two to three thousand of the slaves, who numbered some half a million at the time of the American Revolution.

In the history of the conversion of the slaves to Christianity, the Great Awakening of 1740 marked the "dawn of a new day" (C. G. Woodson), the first period of convergence of the European and African worlds. This religious explosion, coordinated by Jonathan Edwards, reached it apex with the visits of the great preacher George Whitefield, and it drew a certain number of blacks through the power of its message of salvation, through the fervor of its spiritual expression, and by its direct appeal to the emotions and its insistence on oral expression. The Reverend Carey Allen, a Presbyterian minister, proclaimed to the slaves: "The blessed Savior died and shed his blood for you as well as for your master or any other White. He has opened wide for you the gates of heaven and invites you all to come in." In 1740 Whitefield wrote an open letter addressed to the "inhabitants of Maryland, Virginia, North and South Carolina, on the subject of their Negroes."[13] He condemned the brutality of the slave owners: "Your slaves work as hard, if not more, as the horses" and are not better treated than dogs. He was astounded that there were not more suicides among them. But their blood would cry out to heaven against their masters. Whitefield wanted to mitigate their servitude by the enlightenment of the Christian faith without contesting the existence of the institution itself.

In this context, the story of Hugh Bryan, a white planter converted by George Whitefield in 1740 at the age of forty-one, is edifying.[14] Inspired by the preaching of Whitefield, Bryan began by assailing the American clergy in a letter published in a local newspaper in South Carolina. In 1741 he assembled, in total illegality, groups of blacks. The local whites feared the worst. Bryan did nothing to allay their fears. On the contrary, he gave to his teaching an even more apocalyptic tone: "Now is the time for repentance." He prophesied the destruction of Charleston and the deliverance of the slaves. This destruction would take place "through fire and sword" and "will be executed by the Negroes before the first day of next month." Rumors spread that, with his black friends, he was stocking munitions. He was arrested at the very moment when he believed that he had been the victim of Satan in launching himself into an antislavery diatribe. But Bryan is a good example of nascent evangelism that would sap the established Anglican order on both the civil and ecclesiastical levels. This prophet, straight out of the Old Testament, reminded the slaves that freedom was at the core of the Bible's message.

Yet this first awakening remained an essentially white phenomenon. More than the Presbyterians, the Baptists and the Methodists would profit from this impetus and extend the waves of the religious revival to the western frontier, a religious awakening that would place on an equal footing slaves and masters, men and women, rich and poor alike. At the end of the eighteenth century, Baptists and Methodists were in full expansion in the South. They dared to defy the institution of slavery, with leaders such as the Methodist Francis Asbury (1745–1816). And African Americans flocked in by the hundreds. In 1786, the first year in which the Methodists distinguished between their black and white members, there were 1,890 blacks out of a total of 18,791 faithful. In 1797 there were 12,215, or about a quarter of the total membership. The same proportion is found among the Baptists, even if the latter did not keep very precise records. Charles Colcock Jones asserts that the number of black Baptists grew from eighteen thousand in 1793 to forty thousand in 1813. All these figures are proportionately weak. The first census, of 1790, found that 4 percent of the slaves in Virginia were Christians.

A catechism for blacks, published in 1787, clearly set the tone for the attitude of Christians toward them:

Q. 37. When Negroes are converted, how must they behave towards their masters?

Answer. In many places, Scripture commands them to be honest, diligent and faithful in all things, and not give impertinent answers; and even when they are whipped after having done well, to accept it with patience and to count on God for their reward. . . .

Q. 39. According to you, who is the happier person, the master or the slave?

Answer. When I get up on a cold morning and light the fire while my master is still in bed; or when I work in the sun on a hot day while my master is in the shade; then I think that he is happier than I.

Q. 40. Do you think that you are happier than he?

Answer. Yes. When I return from my work, eat my good supper, praise my Creator, go to bed without worries, sleep profoundly, and get up in the morning refreshed and strong, and hear that my master couldn't sleep, thinking about his debts and his taxes, and how he will take care of his family in food and clothing, or what he will have to do for them when they are sick—then I bless God that he has placed me in my humble situation, I feel sorry for my master, and feel that I am happier than he.

Q. 41. Then it seems that all situations are better if it is the one where God placed me?

Answer. Yes. The Scriptures say that if I am called to be a slave, I must not worry about it, for every true Christian is a free man in Christ, be he slave or free in this world.

Q. 42. How can you be free and slave at the same time?

Answer. If Christ broke the chains of sin and delivered me from the damnation of the law and the slavery to Satan, I am truly free, even if my body and my services can be under the orders of another.[15]

The nineteenth century began with a new explosion of religious revivals on the western border (Kentucky). This vast campaign of evangelization, which soon influenced each state of the young nation, used a new tool: the camp meeting. Presbyterian in origin, though quickly adopted by the Methodists and the Baptists, the camp meeting was an outdoor assembly of a great crowd for a conversion session and could last a week. A contemporary witness reported:

These assemblies are especially composed of ardent and direct preaching to which respond moans, sobs and shouts in the assembly. As long as the voice of the preacher dominated, order, (a relative order, of course) reigned in the assembly, but from the moment his voice was drowned out by the great voice of a people in distress, any exterior order ceased and a general emotion exploded everywhere. Each anguished soul raised its voice; here a convicted sinner falls to the ground and begs God's mercy, there a soul relieved of his burden of sin gives thanks to God for his mercy; elsewhere, Christians encourage their yet unconverted relatives and friends to repentance, while ministers, the natural leaders of the movement, had left the stage to bring their own exhortations and prayers from row to row of people. The most diverse scenes take place before the spectators, if there could be spectators who did not soon become actors in this great drama. One pursued by the obsessions of an awakened conscience tries to flee outside the camp but soon falls, stopped by the sovereign hand of God. Another passes almost without transition from blasphemy to prayer. In the midst of all this agitation, rise up from small groups, hymns of an incomparable sweetness, natural expressions of renewed feelings.[16]

Whites and blacks found themselves intermingled in these great "conversion fairs" (C. J. Bertrand) in which the most simple people, whatever their color, felt recognized, called, and changed. Thanks to the camp meetings and the work of the evangelists, the conversion of the slaves was hastened. Various factors came into play. Evangelical religion truly signified a renewal of the faith in the South of the United States. The mobility of the Methodist messenger and the autonomy of the Baptist preacher suited the configuration of the region. The insistence was on interior conversion, on the direct experience of repentance and regeneration; the behavior would follow. Christ died for each individual personally. The Methodist or Baptist leader excelled in visualizing and personalizing, with a maximum emotional intensity, the drama of sin and salvation, of damnation and election. "The Anglican usually taught the slaves the Ten Commandments, the Apostles' Creed and the Lord's Prayer; the revivalist preacher helped them to feel the weight of sin, to imagine the threats of Hell, and to accept Christ as their only Savior."[17] The revivalists tended to minimize the elaboration of doctrine; they sought to stir up in the simple people the experience of conversion through becoming conscious of sin. An inspired heart was more important than a full mind. Interior salvation was more important than exterior status. The number of tears shed measured the success of the service. And if a slave was called by the Spirit to give the Word, let him preach to the whites as well as to the blacks! The new missionaries did not hesitate to go into the slave quarters, to pray with the slaves and for them, to bring them the consolations of God's love through the witness of a true affection. It was the triumph of the religion of the heart.

Thus, small congregations of black Christians were born here and there. They were sometimes encouraged, sometimes tolerated, often feared. In the last case, they met in secret. It is worth noting that "in at least two towns, Petersburg, Virginia, and Savannah, Georgia, black Baptists organized churches *before* white Baptists did so."[18] With the influx of black converts in the Baptist and Methodist churches, many congregations were mixed. But blacks stayed in the rear of the building or in the balcony, when they did not remain outside the building.

As this evangelical tidal wave needed to wash far up on the land, the most lucid missionaries saw that they had take a new step in evangelization: to bring religious instruction closer to the plantations, to bring the gospel to where the slaves lived—without, of course, touching the institution of slavery itself!

Beginning in the 1830s, a complete ministry to the plantations was set in place, fostering a renewed Christian social order based on the observance of the mutual duties of master and slave. The salvation of both depended on obedience to their mutual duties. If each one kept his or her place, God would be for all. Here again the Methodists were in the vanguard. They multiplied the number of itinerant preachers, both white and black. Here are the Gospel beatitudes, revised and corrected for the good of the slave: "Blessed *are* the patient, blessed *are* the faithful, blessed *are* the cheerful, blessed *are* the submissive, blessed *are* the hardworking, and above all, blessed *are* the obedient."[19]

If we prefer a sermon, we can quote the following as a good example:

It is the good pleasure of God Almighty that has made slaves of you here, and given you nothing in this world except work and poverty to which you must submit, since it is written in His will that things are to be so. If then you wish to be free men of God, you must be good and seek to serve Him on earth. I am saying that the faults against your masters and mistresses of which you are guilty are sins committed against God himself who places in his stead your masters and mistresses over you, and expects you to serve them as you serve him. And the ministers of Jesus Christ have a duty to exhort the servants to obey their masters and to please them in all things.[20]

In order to convince the Southerners of the urgency of this mission, pamphlets, sermons, and reports were circulated. The aim of this literature is well defined in an Episcopalian text of 1823: "To show from the Scriptures of the Old and New Testament, that slavery is not forbidden by the Divine Law: and at the same time to prove the necessity of giving religious instruction to our Negroes."[21] Let us underscore the two aspects of this reasoning: the justification of slavery and the instruction of the slaves. Any remnant of bad conscience would be exorcised by this generous enterprise. New missionary societies were founded specifically for the slaves.

It was at this time that the abolitionist movement knew a growing success in the North and that the controversy about the "peculiar institution" became more acute in the churches themselves. Because in the South the abolitionist literature was as feared as an outbreak of cholera, there were hesitations about the education of the slaves. At the same time, the apologists for slavery believed that the evangelization of slaves was an elegant way to prove the good aspects of slavery. Thus the impact of the emancipation movements in the South was limited.

Yet, for all that, between 1837 and 1845 Presbyterians, Methodists, and Baptists would divide themselves along geographic lines, reflecting the division on the question of slavery. The Southern Christians would be obliged to create the society for which they would secede, a society in which the division of races would be dressed in a Christian faith that justified separation. The evangelization of the slaves could no longer be put off. Therefore, sermons to the slaves were increased on Sunday, instructions were given on certain nights of the week, and Sunday schools were organized for the children, the youth, and the adults. One aim, in particular, was to control the overly emotional character of black religious expression: "They need instruction, not emotion, understanding, not excitement: they are like a ship at sea with no one at the helm, at the mercy of the winds and carried by the current until it founders on a reef." The master and his family were frequently invited to attend the slaves' assemblies to give a good example and to create a sense of Christian community. Speech was seen as the best way to reach the slave. The wager of the missionaries, like Charles Colcock Jones and William Capers, was that the instruction of slaves would improve the morality of the blacks as well as that of the whites. The individual must be transformed, and not the social order. "The aim of the plantation mission was to create a 'biracial community' of Christian masters and slaves."[22] But the reality did not always correspond to the ideal! The converted masters were often more intransigent with their slaves. Piety did not prevent cruelty, if we are to believe many witnesses. The church only confirmed the superiority of the whites and the inferiority of the blacks.

It is important to note, however, in order to give a balanced view, that the whites who really practiced their religion were always a minority before the Civil War. In 1830 only 10 percent of the whites in Kentucky, Tennessee, Alabama, and Mississippi belonged to a Protestant denomination, and that percentage was representative of the whole nation. In regard to institutional religion, the Southerners in particular manifested apathy and sometimes hostility. In 1808 a traveler in the region noted: "The men spend their time in the pursuit of three things: all make love, most gamble, and some make money. They have nothing to do with religion, having made a pact with it and its principal article is: 'Don't disturb us and we won't disturb you.' "[23] They were more concerned with the price of cotton than with the progress of religion.

It is difficult to measure the success of this missionary program, for the slaves embraced the Christian faith first of all by the witnessing of their black brothers and sisters. The Southern Methodists were the most efficient: they went from 118,904 black members in 1846 to 209,836 in 1861 (that is, 5 percent of the black population). Black Baptists numbered more than 150,000; the Presbyterians, about 30,000; the Disciples of Christ, 10,000; and the Anglicans and the Lutherans, 1,500. DuBois estimated that there were 468,000 black Christians in the South of the United States in 1859 (12 percent of the slave population and less than 11 percent of the total black population). Christianity had become a significant reality in the slave community. The gestation had lasted 240 years.

The Christian Justification of Slavery

Violently attacked by the Northern abolitionists from 1830 on, the South would strongly defend the institution of slavery to the point of making it the distinctive aspect of the region. And religion would play a major role in the pro-slavery crusade. The Southern clergy, who were not the least of the slave owners, would establish indissoluble links among religion, morality, and slavery. And we will see what Mitchell Snay calls a "sanctification of slavery." The struggle became religious.

Until 1832, the inferiority of the black race was generally asserted in the South. And slavery was considered an economically necessary evil. Now, it would be defended as a divine blessing for an entire society, as a moral good, and as fidelity to the will of God. As the Southerners saw it, the abolitionists were attacking the very authority of God and endangered the integrity of Christianity by calling on another God, another Christ, and another Bible! The hierarchy of races would be given the aspect of a scientific proof in the 1840s and the 1850s with the development of ethnology.

The first distinctive work in this field was that of Thomas R. Dew, *Examination of the Debate of 1831 and 1832 in the Legislative Body of Virginia*. Dew promoted the biblical argument in favor of slavery, and his example was contagious: "Slavery was instituted and sanctioned by divine authority among the elect of heaven, the favored children of Israel. Abraham, the founder of this remarkable people and chosen servant of the Lord, owned hundreds of slaves. Solomon's temple, that magnificent sanctuary, was built with the hands of slaves."[24] Slavery was not an evil but a necessary stage for the human progress of the Africans, who were not ready to assume their freedom. If slavery is attested to in the Bible, it is therefore the explicit will of God. The Reverend Fred Ross writes in his book with a telling title, *Slavery Decreed by God:* "It is God who decided on slavery which must continue for the good of the slave, for that of the master, for the entire American family, until a new and better destiny is unveiled."

The biblical argument can be summarized as follows:

> We theologians and Christian statesmen from 1815 to 1865, hold that the Bible says nothing to condemn slavery as sinful, and some of us maintain that the Bible in fact commands slavery. Rooted in Noah's prophetic cursing of Ham-Canaan's descendants, slavery has been and should be practiced by God's people. Abraham, champion of faith, had many slaves. God told the Israelites to buy slaves and gave specific instructions pertaining to their service. Jesus never spoke against slavery, but used the slave image as a model for Christian conduct. Paul and Peter instructed masters and slaves in how to conduct themselves as Christians, and Paul obeyed the fugitive slave law in sending the runaway slave Onesimus back to Philemon, his master. Nowhere does the Bible condemn slavery. Either believe the Bible and support slavery. Or oppose slavery and throw out the Bible as God's authoritative Word.[25]

This argument was developed by men such as the Episcopalian bishop John Henry Hopkins, Thornton Stringfellow, and Governor James Hammond of South

Carolina, who all believed that if the Scriptures do not justify slavery, they justify nothing at all. Let us demonstrate:

THESIS 1. Slavery was divinely approved for the patriarchs.

1. Take the curse by Noah for Canaan, son of Ham (Genesis 9:24-27). The "first appearance of slavery in the bible" is "the marvelous prophecy of the Patriarch Noah" (J. H. Hopkins). In some way, God decreed the institution even before its very existence. The curse by Noah for Canaan prophesied the destiny of the black African.

2. Abraham is our pious example. Champion of the faith for all Christians, he received, owned, and wanted slaves for his children as property. Slavery is not like divorce. We cannot say that before Moses the situation was different. No, Abraham was a great slave owner. He bought slaves from Haran (Genesis 12:5), armed 318 slaves tied by birth to his house (Genesis 14:14), received slaves as a gift from Abimelech (Genesis 20:14), and wanted them as part of his property for his son Isaac (Genesis 26:13-14). Scripture says that the Lord blessed Abraham by increasing the number of his slaves (Genesis 24:35). And did not the angel order Hagar, the slave, to return to her mistress (Genesis 16:1-9)? That is clear support for the law on fugitive slaves.

3. At the time of Joseph, God approved slavery. How did Joseph save many Egyptians from famine? God commanded that Joseph buy people and land, making them slaves to the profit of Pharaoh (Genesis 47:15-25).

THESIS 2. Slavery was incorporated into the national constitution of Israel. God authorized two kinds of slavery for the life of Israel:

1. Israel could take foreigners as slaves. God commanded the Israelites to go to the slave markets of neighboring nations, buy slaves and consider them as property, and leave them as an inheritance for their descendants (Leviticus 25:44-46).

2. God provided that the Hebrews could sell themselves and their families for limited periods if they preferred slavery to freedom (Exodus 21; Leviticus 25).

THESIS 3. Slavery was recognized and approved by Jesus Christ and the apostles. Jesus and the apostles observed the cruel practice of slavery in the Roman Empire and never said a word against it. The apostles, who represented Jesus Christ, were in complete accord with Jesus, recalling even his words on the subject (1 Timothy 6:1-6).

According to the words of Governor Hammond of South Carolina:

> It is vain to look to Christ or any of his Apostles to justify such blasphemous perversions of the word of God. Although Slavery in its most revolting form was everywhere visible around them, no visionary notions of piety or philanthropy ever tempted them to gainsay the LAW, even to mitigate the cruel severity of the existing system. On the contrary, regarding Slavery as an established, as well as inevitable human condition of human society, they never hinted at such a thing as its termination on

earth, any more than "the poor may cease out over the land." . . . It is impossible, therefore, to suppose that Slavery is contrary to the will of God. It is equally absurd to say that American Slavery differs in form or principle from that of the chosen people. We accept the Bible terms as the definition of our Slavery, and its precepts as the guide of our conduct.[26]

The writings of the apostles teach us seven points about slavery:

1. The apostles approved slavery but disapproved its abuses (Ephesians 6:5-9; Colossians 3:22-25; 4:1; 1 Timothy 6:1-2; Titus 2:9-10; 1 Peter 2:18-19).

2. The apostles taught that the church does not have the authority to oppose slavery as a political system.

3. The distinctions between master and slave did not prevent faith and thus were insignificant (Galatians 3:28; 1 Corinthians 12:13; Colossians 3:11). Slave or master, as a Christian, a person had to be good in the same way.

4. Slave owners had been accepted and valued not only as members of the church but also as church leaders.

5. The apostles did not exhort Christian masters to free their slaves, but rather said that slaves must stay in their status, for the masters had a right to the work of their slaves (see 1 Corinthians 7:20-24).

6. The text of 1 Timothy 6:1-6, in which Paul declared his doctrine was based on the "sound words of our Lord Jesus Christ," is of great importance for the argument in favor of slavery. Even though people generally believed that Jesus was silent on the subject, Paul supported his remark to slave believers, asking them to honor their nonbelieving masters, by saying that his teaching reflected "the sound words of our Lord Jesus Christ." If Paul said it, it was because Jesus was not silent on the subject. Christ revealed this doctrine on slavery to Paul.

7. Finally (and this is of primary importance), the letter to Philemon about Onesimus indicated that the apostolic writings fully support slavery. For Ne-hemiah Adams, a Northerner traveling in the South, "that little writing is like a small, firm beach, where storms have beaten, but left it pure and white."[27]

THESIS 4. Slavery is a benevolent institution.

Through the practice of slavery, prisoners of war have escaped death all along the centuries, and millions of the descendants of Ham, who would otherwise have foundered in eternal ruin, have been placed under the influence of the gospel. The role of biblical morality is to mitigate the conditions of slavery; any attempt to interfere with the institution itself could lead to the extermination of the race.

That which is permitted by the Bible cannot be a moral evil, since God represents the summit of morality. Samuel Dunwody underscored this logical reasoning: "Since God is infinitely wise, just, and holy, he could not authorize a moral evil. But God authorized slavery, not only by the simple permission of his Providence, but by the express provision of his Word." An ethical teaching follows up biblical teaching, having established the correctness of human slavery, for the slave owners of the South. Robert Lewis Dabney, a Presbyterian minister from Virginia, clearly illustrated the articulation between the two stages:

> But to enjoy the advantages of this Bible argument in our favor slave holders will have to pay a price. And the price is this. They must be willing to recognize and grant in slaves those rights which are a part of our essential humanity, some of which are left without recognition or guarantee by law, and some infringed by law. These are the rights of immortal and domestic beings. If we take the ground that the power to neglect and infringe these interests is an essential part of the institutions of slavery, then it cannot be defended.[28]

Religion must blossom into morality in order to make slavery holy. The Southern clerics therefore invented a complete ethic to enlighten the conduct of the masters as regarded their slaves. This peculiar institution was an exemplary way of organizing the relation between morally responsible human beings for the good of the weaker ones. "The Lord Jesus died as much for them as for us," confessed E. T. Baird. The ideal, then, was a "mutual responsibility," interdependence, and reciprocity of rights and duties between the master and the slave. The charity of the one must echo the humility of the other. The moral behavior of the ruling class of the South would be the best answer to the arguments of the abolitionists of the North.

Thus religion helped to forge a consensus about slavery in the South of the United States by justifying human slavery through Bible interpretation, by elaborating an ethic for the master, and by engaging in efforts to bring the gospel to the slaves. It was a complete vision of the hierarchical and patriarchal society that received divine sanction. And the Southerners would risk their lives to preserve this social order.

The Answer of the Oppressed

After having looked at the development of the white Christian mission to the slaves and the biblical justification of slavery, let us examine somewhat the reasons for the conversion of the Africans to Christianity. Without minimizing divine initiative, it is important to indicate the religious sensitivity, the social motivations, and the human feelings that influenced this conversion.

It is evident that the African slaves were not immediately seduced by the religion of the whites. They did not rush in to fill the back of the Christian churches. They even resisted, in various ways, conversion to Christianity. It was because European religion appeared perverted and hypocritical to them. It was a tissue of incoherencies and contradictions. The white preacher spoke of the sanctity of marriage and the master took as concubines the beautiful black women of the plantation. "They say and they do not do." It showed a flagrant divorce between faith and lifestyle. The slaves were scandalized by it.

Autobiographical accounts often present sharp criticism of the masters' Christianity. None is more virulent than the famous one by Frederick Douglass. I will quote some of its significant passages:

> In August 1832, my master attended a Methodist assembly on the coast of the Bay, in Talbot County, and found religion. I had a feeble hope that his conversion would lead him to free his slaves and that, if he did not, it would lead him to be better in any case and more human. I was completely disappointed: it did not make him more human for his slaves and did not bring him to free them. If it had the least effect on his character, it was to make him crueler and more odious in all ways; I believe that he was much worse after than before his conversion. Before his conversion he counted on his own depravity to protect and support him in his savage cruelty. After his conversion, he had the sanction and support of religion for his cruelty towards the slaves. . . . I will cite as an example one of the numerous facts that weigh [on my master]: I saw him tie up a young cripple and hit her on her bare shoulders with a big whip, causing the warm blood to flow; to justify his bloody action, he quoted this passage of Scripture: "He who knows the will of his master and does not accomplish it will receive many lashes." . . . If I should once again fall into the chains of slavery, I would consider the fact of being a slave to a pious master as the greatest calamity that could befall me after slavery itself. . . . The bell that presides the sales of slaves and the bell that calls to worship ring together, and the bitter tears of the slave are drowned by the religious shouts of his pious owner. The growth of religion and the vigor of the slave trade go hand in hand. The slaves' prison and the church are side by side.[29]

The Christian masters had the reputation of sometimes being the cruelest. Jack White confirmed it: "Though Marster was a Mef'dis' preacher, he whip his slaves, an den drap pitch an' tuppentine on dem from a bu'nin' to'ch."[30] And Joseph Smith's wife adds: "Those who were Christians & held slaves were the hardest masters. A card-player and drunkard wouldn't flog you half to death. Well, it is something like this—the Christians will oppress you more."[31]

As soon as they had a little knowledge of the content of Christian revelation, the slaves would make a clear distinction between the Word of God and the word of the preachers preferred by their white masters. "By the law of Almighty God, I was born free," dictated Aaron Siddles, "by the law of man, a slave."[32]

The condemnation of slavery was without restriction: "We believe slavery to be a sin—always, everywhere, and only sin. Sin in itself, apart from the occasional rigors incidental to its administration, and from all those perils, liabilities, and positive inflictions to which its victims are continually exposed. Sin is the nature of the act which created it, and in the elements that constitute it. Sin because it converts persons into things; men into property; God's image into merchandise."[33]

Only the conversion of the masters could prove the reality of their faith. Otherwise, the slaves sought to hasten Judgment Day. Moses Grandy says: "During violent thunder storms, while Whites went to hide under their eider-down quilts, I often saw Negroes, young or old, go outside and raise their hands, thanking God for the coming of Judgment Day."[34]

We cannot, then, be astonished if slaves laughed at the devotions of the newly Christian blacks. They had nothing but disdain for those Africans who started to decipher the Scriptures. For them, it was simply aping the ways of the whites, and that deserved something other than an angry outburst; it rated a belly laugh.[35]

These examples help us see that there would always be a distance, not to say a chasm, between the religion of the slave and the religion of the master, for the freedom of the slave was not an integral part of the religion of the master. The slave, on the contrary, took seriously the "law of freedom" and the "exodus from Egypt." The master and the slave would never be able to communicate in the same gospel.

That is why Frederick Douglass established a radical distinction between the Christianity of the slave owners and Christianity itself: "Between the Christianity of this country and the Christianity of Christ, I recognize a considerable difference—so great a distance that, to recognize one as good, pure, and holy, it is necessary to reject the other as evil, corrupt, and perverse. To be the friend of the one is necessarily to be the enemy of the other. I love the pure, peaceful, and impartial Christianity of Christ: therefore, I hate the corrupt, partial, and hypocritical Christianity of the slave owners who whip the women and pillage the cradles of this country."[36] That which took place progressively on U.S. soil was a conflict of Christianities, an opposition of appropriations of the Christian faith.

Despite all the falsifications of the white gospel, the slaves adhered to the Christian faith in greater and greater numbers. How can we explain this conversion?

We find a first reason in the will of the whites, missionaries, and/or owners. As early as 1648 a Massachusetts law instructed: "All masters of families doe once a week (at the least) catechize their children and servants in the grounds and principles of Religion."[37] Not all missionaries were racists and not all slave owners were violent. Some masters organized times of prayer each week and brought their slaves to church. They even prayed for their Africans.[38] In the nineteenth century they built chapels and invited itinerant preachers. Certain owners were able to have a human relationship with their subordinates, a starting point for a certain complicity in the faith. Thus, a farmer, owner of slaves, confessed his moral torment to his son-in-law: "When I consider that these people [Africans] of their forefathers were born as free as my Self & that they are held in bondage by compulsion only . . . when I consider that they are human creatures Indeed with Immortal Souls capable of everlasting happiness or liable to Everlasting misery as well as our Selves, It fills my mind with horror and detestation."[39]

Certainly, the work of the missionaries and the masters was all the more efficient when they themselves believed in what they were doing. From the moment that one and the other were persuaded that religious instruction improved the master-slave relationship, served the economic interests of the plantation, and strengthened security and morality, they were able to put a certain amount of energy into the project. And results followed. In any case, white values gradually penetrated the black consciences, preparing the terrain for the confession of the Christian faith.

In my view, it would be an error to place too much emphasis on the religious imitation of the slaves. Few chose Christianity in order to please their masters. A more profound motive appears to have been the defeat of African religion. We must always remember that the American blacks arrived from Africa, where their vision of the universe was given coherence by religion.

The experience lived by the slaves, since their uprooting from their native land, was the experience of the defeat of the African god or gods. The Africans said to themselves: "If we have been uprooted, reduced to slavery, it is because the God of the whites is truly the strongest. We must conciliate this God." In the African perspective, religion is always the interplay of invisible forces, a struggle for a maximum of life. To convert to Christianity, then, would be to seek to tame the manifest power of the white God, partake of that God's power, profit from that God's life potential, and put all the trumps in one's own hand. One leaves the defeated god for the victorious God.

Be that as it may, even if African religion had lasted for a while on the soil of the United States, the situation of servitude, the dispersion of the slaves and the small size of the plantation, the distance from Mother Africa, and the increase of blacks born in North America would have ended by producing a disintegration of this religious foundation. This religion was not able to resist the erosion of the language and of the ethnic community. As the years wore on, the ancient practices lost their appeal. As they learned English, the black groups entered into the world of the whites. The phenomenon of interaction took place. Incapable of living without a religious interpretation of existence and of the world, the black community would go to the only religion available: Christianity.

Yet, as they received this new faith, the African Americans would pick and choose. They would accept what seemed familiar to them. We can assert, without fear of error, that it was the affinity of Christianity to the African religion that permitted the conversion of the black Americans to Christianity. We find this affinity in the affirmation of one Creator God, in the invisible force of grace, in the caring community, and in the recognition of religious leaders. More than an imposition by the whites, it was the similarity between the Christian religion and their traditional religion that fostered the passage to the faith of the hated master. And African beliefs still lived beneath visible Christianity.

Yet a trigger was needed: the religious awakenings of the eighteenth and nineteenth centuries. The slaves changed their attitudes because Christianity itself had changed its appearance. It no longer had the cold severity of Anglicanism, the codified ritualism of Catholicism, the obligatory reflection of the Quakers; it had donned the contagious exuberance of the Baptists and Methodists. These evangelicals had retreated in their attack on slavery as early as 1785, but it was this more accommodating attitude that gave them free access in the South and permitted them to attract the black population. Among the Baptists, the gifts of healing and prophecy were held in great honor. Speaking in tongues was less essential, but still significant, if an interpreter was there. As a place of welcome for all charisms, the community had a very strong sense of its unity and its equality. It gave a status to each person. To possess spiritual gifts did not signify a spiritual superiority. Thus a breach was made in the social order, offering an occasion for transformed relations, eliminating the distance between white and black. And the community watched the conduct of its members in all areas so that it would honor the Lord.

The principal event was the personal conversion that invited one to walk in the footsteps of Jesus. And the ministers of the revivals organized these celebrations of conversion (in which trances were not absent) in the midst of exultation and singing. All these elements were in perfect harmony with African sensitivity and experience, filling an unbearable religious vacuum. For the first time, African Americans discovered the emotional, existential, and wholeness dimensions of the white religion. Their heritage had not been destroyed but enriched: Christian conversion was the equivalent of what they had in Africa. Also, their response was immediate. In the nineteenth century, when one asked a Southern black to identify himself, he would answer: "I am a Baptist." The following remark was current throughout the region: "If a nigger ain't a Baptist, someone's been tampering with his religion."[40]

We also have some beautiful accounts of journeying in the faith. The place of the Bible, as a contact with the very Word of God, and the will to read the Bible were quite characteristic of the slave. Harriet A. Jacobs is a moving witness to that:

> I knew an old Black whose piety and confidence in God were moving. At the age of fifty-three he joined the Baptist church. He had a profound desire to learn to read. He believed that he could better serve God if he read the Bible. He came to see me and pleaded with me to teach him to read. He said that he could not pay me for he had no money, but that he would bring me beautiful fruit in season. I asked him if he knew that it was against the law and that slaves who taught others to read were whipped and imprisoned. His eyes filled with tears. "Don't worry, uncle

Fred, I told him, I could not refuse you, but I want you to know the law and that it is dangerous so that you be on your guard." He foresaw coming three times a week without raising suspicions. I chose a quiet place and I taught him the rudiments of the alphabet. Considering his age, his progress was astonishing. As soon as he could spell two syllables, he wanted to spell the words of the Bible. The happy smile that lit up his face filled my heart with joy. After a few words, he paused and said: "Dear, when I read this holy book, I feel closer to God. The white man is talented and learns easily. It is not easy for an old Black like me. I just want to read this book to know how to live; after I can die well, I am no longer afraid."[41]

The Africans thus welcomed those Christian aspects that addressed the least favored by society in warm and vibrant terms and that proposed a simple and direct program of Christian life: walking with Jesus under the eye of God. Also, on the institutional level, among the Baptists and Methodists, everything rested on the local community. The Africans thus had plenty of room for action. And their faith would gush out most spontaneously in the joy tinged with suffering in nocturnal, and often secret, assemblies. Thanks to the religious revivals and to the evangelical movements, the slaves discovered a new coherence and forged a new "sacred cosmos" integrating African and American elements. This synthesis, fashioned in the crucible of oppression, can be called "African American."

This new configuration of the faith would give birth to a new moral expression, organized around the theme of freedom. Everything that reinforced the power of the governing class was immoral. Henceforth, stealing took on a whole new meaning. Stealing from the master strengthened the slaves' self-esteem and well-being and sowed fear among the whites. On the other hand, stealing from a member of the community offended the community itself. In general, the concept of justice prevailed over the concept of equality.

One thing is certain: the converted slaves felt morally superior to their masters. They themselves belonged to a "spiritual aristocracy," according to the expression of James Baldwin. That is clear in the story told by Charlie. About thirty years after his escape, by chance he encountered his old master in the public square. Here is the conversation that took place, as told by Charlie:

"Charlie, do you remember me lacerating your back?" I said, "Yes, Mars." "Have you forgiven me?" he asked. I said, "Yes, I have forgiven you." There were a lot of people gathered around because we were a little distance apart and talking loud. . . . He asked me the next question, "How can you forgive me, Charlie?" I said, "Mars when we whip dogs we do it because we own them, it is not because we have done anything to be whipped for but we do it because we can. That is why you whipped me. I used to serve you, work for you, almost nurse you and if anything had happened to you I would have fought for you. . . . I used to drive you to church and peep through the door to see you all worship, but you aren't right yet, Master. I love you as though you never hit me a lick, for the God I serve is a God of love and I can't go to his kingdom with hate in my heart." He held out his hand to me and almost cried and said, "Charlie, come to see me and I will treat you nice. I am sorry for what I did." I said, "That's all right, Master, I done left the past behind me." I had felt the power of God and tasted His love and this had killed all the spirit of hate in my heart years before this happened. Whenever a man has been killed dead and made alive in Christ Jesus he no longer feels like he did when he was a servant of the devil. Sin kills dead but the spirit of God makes alive.[42]

If Charlie forgave, it is because he had had an experience that eliminated hate from his heart. That decisive experience was the conversion to Christ Jesus. It is important to look deeply into this often apocalyptic symbolism in order to perceive its import in the daily lives of the slaves.

The Conversion Experience

In the Methodist and Baptist experience there is a crucial event that marks the passage from unbelief to faith, from sin to grace, from darkness into light: conversion. This is a biblical term that cannot be better translated than as a "return from a detour."

For the evangelicals, salvation is expressed as being "born again." The old being has disappeared, and a new being has emerged. For this transformation, faith and repentance do not suffice. The direct and irresistible intervention of the Holy Spirit, which profoundly modifies the nature of the individual, is primary. This coming of the Spirit can be known only through an experience, for the "born again" person must be able to witness to the work of God in him or her, the gushing forth of salvation in the midst of a sinful existence.

An astounding collection of conversion accounts was put together by A. P. Watson, an anthropology student, between 1927 and 1929, from among old African Americans, especially women, and published by Clifton H. Johnson under the title *God Struck Me Dead.*[43] These accounts show a similar structure, and they belong to a coded literary genre that African Americans appropriated by listening to the whites.

Through these texts, we touch the slave community's expression as closely as by the hymns called the Negro spirituals. The affinity of the two expressions is more than astonishing. They use the same religious imagery (heaven and hell, death and life), with one difference: if all sin, saints and sinners together, only the converted can give witness to their "journey."

The evangelical's message can be summarized in a single proposition: "You must be born again." The way of the gospel is to die and to be reborn with Christ. This passage through death results in no longer fearing death, for death is behind us, already conquered by the risen Christ. In other words, it is a rite of initiation. But in Africa the initiation is a central event in the community's life, of both tribe and village. It marks the accession to personhood, for to experience it is to "become man through participating in the life of the All by the mediation of his ancestors and in communion with the others, becoming a man by transmitting the torch of this tradition to the next generation, and becoming a man by the capacity to be in harmony with all the elements of the universe."[44]

A few traces of initiation practices have been found in North America, and it is easy to understand that the slaves loved the "new birth" of death to the old identity of the oppressed and rebirth to a true and dignified humanity. They would also experience visions that would give witness to their great journey from death to life. Their ecstasies would not be escapes from reality, but celebrations of their new identity.

White Baptists had trances and visions, and blacks would not be left out of such experiences; that aspect of religion had been familiar to them from time immemorial. The stages of the vision would be the same for both: sinners feel their unworthiness (they can only be damned for eternity), and suddenly their salvation is revealed; they feel a great joy and find assurance that God is present in them. If we are to find some difference between white Baptists and black Baptists, we can say that the black religious experience accentuated the ecstatic and emotional aspects of conversion.

The vision that arose in the middle of a dream raised up by God had a determining role in the story. Indeed, it permitted a vision of oneself and of the world that transcended the physical level and created a real dissociation. It effected the passage from being the property of the master to being a member of the family of God. The encounter with God through the consciousness of a dream made of the slaves, at the same time, witnesses of and participants in the transformation of their life. It allowed them to evaluate, from a distance, the perverse institution of slavery and gave them the strength to relativize it. There existed something other than oppression. And that other status could not be revealed, except by God, in sovereign freedom and almighty action.

Let us now examine a typical conversion account, that of a former slave called Morte. It is the first account in the collection *God Struck Me Dead*. It mirrors well the principal stages of the conversion experience as lived in the black community: at first a malaise and an inability, then an intervention by God, who elates and yet, at the same time, provokes a consciousness of sin through a visit to heaven and to hell. It is a liberation that finally transforms the consciousness of self and the relationship between the slave and the master. Freed from sin and doubt, the visionary would become a preacher and an example for all.

One day while in the field plowing I heard a voice. I jumped because I thought it was my master coming to scold and whip me for plowing up some more corn. I looked but saw no one. Again the voice called, "Morte! Morte!" With this I stopped, dropped the plow, and started running, but the voice kept on speaking to me saying, "Fear not, my little one, for behold! I come to bring you a message of truth."

Everything got dark, and I was unable to stand any longer. I began to feel sick, and there was a great roaring. I tried to cry and move but was unable to do either. I looked up and saw that I was in a new world. There were plants and animals and all, even the water where I stooped down to drink, began to cry out, "I am blessed but you are damned! I am blessed but you are damned!" With this I began to pray, and a voice on the inside began to cry, "Mercy! Mercy! Mercy!"

As I prayed, an angel came and touched me, and I looked new. I looked at my hands and they were new; I looked at my feet and they were new. I looked and saw my old body suspended over a burning pit by a small web like a spider web. I again prayed, and there came a soft voice saying, "My little one, I have loved you with an everlasting love. You are this day made alive and freed from hell. You are a chosen vessel unto the Lord. Be upright before me, and I will guide you unto all truth. My grace is sufficient for you. Go, and I am with you. Preach the gospel, and I will preach with you. You are henceforth the salt of the earth."

I then began to shout and clap my hands. All the time, a voice on the inside was crying, "I am so glad! I am so glad!" About this time an angel appeared before me and said with a loud voice, "Praise God! Praise God!" I looked to the east, and there was a large throne lifted high up, and thereon sat one, even God. He looked neither to the right nor to the left. I was afraid and fell on my face. When I was still a long way off, I heard a voice from God saying, "My little one, be not afraid, for lo! Many wondrous works will I perform through thee. Go in peace, and lo! I am with you always." All this he said but opened not his mouth while speaking. Then all those about the throne shouted and said, "Amen."

I then came to myself again and shouted and rejoiced. After so long a time I recovered my real senses and realized that I had been plowing and that the horse had run off with the plow and dragged down much of the corn. I was afraid and began to pray, for I knew the master would whip me most unmercifully when he found that I had plowed up the corn.

About this time my master came down the field. I became very bold and answered him when he called me. He asked me very roughly how I came to plow up the corn, and where the horse and plow were, and why I had got along so slowly. I told him that I had been talking with God Almighty, and that it was God who had plowed up the corn. He looked at me very strangely, and suddenly I fell shouting, and I shouted and I began to preach. The words seemed to flow from my lips. When I had finished I had a deep feeling of satisfaction and no longer dreaded the whipping I knew I would get. My master looked at me and seemed to tremble. He told me to catch the horse and come on with him to the barn. I went to get the horse, stumbling down the corn rows. Here again I became weak and began to be afraid for the whipping. After I had gone some distance down the rows, I became dazed and again fell to the ground. In a vision I saw a great mound and, beside it, or at the base of it, stood the angel Gabriel. And a voice said to me, "Behold your sins as a great mountain. But they shall be rolled away. Go in peace, fearing no man, for lo! I have cut loose your stammering tongue and unstopped your deaf ears. A witness shalt thou be, and thou shalt speak to multitudes, and they shall hear. My word has gone forth, and it is power. Be strong, and lo! I am with you even until the world shall end. Amen."

I looked and the angel Gabriel lifted his hand, and my sins that had stood as a mountain, began to roll away. I saw them as they rolled over into a great pit. They fell to the bottom, and there was a great noise. I saw old Satan with a host of his angels hop from the pit, and there they began to stick out their tongues at me and make motions as if to lay hands on me and drag me back into the pit. I cried out, "Save me! Save me, Lord!" And like a flash there gathered around me a host of angels, even a great number, with their backs to me and their faces to the outer world. Then stepped one in the direction of the pit. Old Satan and his angels, growling with anger and trembling with fear, hopped back into the pit. Finally again there came a voice to me saying, "Go in peace and fear not, for lo! I will throw around you a strong arm of protection. Neither shall your oppressors be able to confound you. I will make your enemies feed you and those who despise you take you in. Rejoice and be exceedingly glad, for I have saved you through grace by faith, not of yourself but as a gift of God. Be strong and fear not. Amen."

I rose from the ground shouting and praising God. Within me there was a crying, "Holy! Holy! Holy is the Lord!"

I must have been in this trance for more than an hour. I went on to the barn and found my master there waiting for me. Again I began to tell him of my experience. I do not recall what he did to me afterwards. I felt burdened down and that preaching was my only relief. When I had finished I felt a great love in my heart that made me feel like stooping and kissing the very ground. My master sat watching and listening to me, and then he began to cry. He turned from me and said in a broken voice, "Morte, I believe you are a preacher. From now on you can preach to the people here on my place in the old shed by the creek. But tomorrow morning, Sunday, I want you to preach to my family and neighbors. So put on your best clothes and be in front of the big house early in the morning, about nine o'clock."

I was so happy that I did not know what to do. I thanked my master and then God, for I felt that he was with me. Throughout the night I went from cabin to cabin, rejoicing and spreading the news.

The next morning at the time appointed I stood up on two planks in front of the porch of the big house and, without a Bible or anything, I began to preach to my master and the people. My thoughts came so fast that I could hardly speak fast enough. My soul caught on fire, and soon I had them all in tears. I told them that God had a chosen people and that he had raised me up as an example of this matchless love. I told them that they must be born again and that their souls must be freed from the shackles of hell.

Ever since that day I have been preaching the gospel and am not a bit tired. I can tell anyone about God in the darkest hour of midnight, for it is written on my heart. Amen.[45]

In his shrewd analysis of this witness, Riggins R. Earle points out that everything is on the level of feeling, seeing, and tasting, expressions of the senses that confirm the authenticity of the conversion.[46] The first effect of the voice of God is the perception of judgment. But the Word of God reassures Morte, who finds himself in another world. He is now a "chosen vessel for the Lord," filled with the eternal love of God. A new contract can be passed between the two protagonists, a contract that has nothing to do with the rules of slavery. The divine Master is a guide and an aide: "Go, I am with you." Grace erases sin. Henceforth, Morte can be confident; he is "the salt of the earth." But now, how can one relate to the authority of the master? Morte is still afraid of the master's whip, proof that he is not yet converted deeply. Hence, the need for a second vision: the angel Gabriel shows him the mountain of his sins. Freedom comes when his sins roll into hell. He receives the gift of preaching.

The soul's journey leads through heaven and hell. It is thus that Morte can perceive the change in his being. He is delivered from the "black door of hell" and is carried to heaven. But if God can free Morte from the claws of Satan, God can also free him from the fear that his master can inspire in him. The slave, for the moment, cannot install himself in heaven; he must return to the world, filled with God's salvation. The Lord does not hesitate to use the word "oppressors," which is more politically precise than the usual term of the psalms, "enemies." The seal of Christian authenticity of these conversion accounts is the return to daily reality with the conviction of the need to morally transform that reality.

Now Morte's only motivation is the love of God. He no longer sees himself in the abasing perspective of his oppressor, but through the stimulating vision of his Creator and Savior. He is no longer afraid to face his master and tell him what happened and what God has asked of him: to preach the gospel to all. His self-contempt gives way before the consciousness of his own dignity and of his infinite value. Morte is now able to denounce the evil deeds of his master and of his family. He is a new creation. He has lived through an experience of personal transformation and community integration over which no human being has power. Emotion certainly played a large part in it, but it has ended in a new consciousness of moral responsibility.

These converts will be the agents of change in the midst of all their relationships, including those with their owners. They will live in a spiritual freedom that no prohibition will be able to tame.

Notes

1. William Stoughton, *New England's True Interest* (Cambridge [Mass.], 1670), 19.

2. John B. Boles, *Black Southerners, 1619–1869* (Lexington: University Press of Kentucky, 1984), 40.

3. Quoted in Henry Louis Gates, Jr., ed., *The Classic Slave Narratives* (New York: Mentor, 1987), 19–21.

4. Leonard E. Barrett, *Soul Force* (New York: Anchor/Doubleday, 1974), 17.

5. Rene Jaouen, "Le monothéisme dans les religions traditionnelles d'Afrique et d'ailleurs," *Mission* 6 (1999): 1, 87–88.

6. Paul E. Lovejoy, "La condition des esclaves dans les Amériques," in *La chaîne et le lien. Une vision de la traite négrière* (Paris: Unesco, 1998), 196–97.

7. Quoted in Marcus W. Jernegan, "Slavery and Conversion in the American Colonies," *American Historical Review,* April 1916, 508.

8. Ibid., 506.

9. As related by Albert J. Raboteau, *Slave Religion: The "Invisible Institution" in the Antebellum South* (New York: Oxford University Press, 1978), 108–9.

10. See Bruno Chenu, *Dieu est noir: histoire, religion et théologie des Noirs américains* (Paris: Centurion, 1977), 100–102.

11. Gayraud S. Wilmore notes that in 1750 there were only one thousand baptized slaves in Virginia out of a total of one hundred thousand in the colony.

12. Text quoted in Chenu, 105.

13. This document is found in *Three Letters from the Reverend Mr. G. Whitefield* (Philadelphia: B. Franklin, 1740), 13–16.

14. See Leigh E. Schmidt, "The Great Prophet, Hugh Bryan: Early Evangelicalism's Challenge to the Establishment and Slavery in the Colonial South," *South Carolina Historical Magazine* 87 (1986): 238.

15. *The Negro Catechism* of the Rev. Henry Patillo, South Carolina Presbyterian, published in 1787; quoted in Joseph Washington, *Anti-Blackness in English Religion* (New York: Mellen, 1984).

16. Testimony of a man named Finley, quoted in G. Swarts, *Salut par la foi et conversion brusque* (Paris: Vrin, 1931), 276–77.

17. Raboteau, *Slave Religion,* 133.

18. Ibid., 137.

19. John W. Blassingame, *The Slave Community* (New York: Oxford University Press, 1972), 63.

20. Quoted in Trevor Bowen, *Divine White Right* (New York: Harper, 1934), 110.

21. Quoted in Raboteau, *Slave Religion,* 154.

22. Ibid., 165.

23. Francis A. Cabaniss and James A. Cabaniss, "Religion in Antebellum Mississippi," *Journal of Mississippi History* 6 (1944): 200.

24. Quoted in Michel Favre, *Esclaves et planteurs* (Paris: Julliard, 1970), 244.

25. Willard M. Swartley, *Slavery, Sabbath, War, and Women* (Scottdale, Pa.: Herald, 1983), 32–33. The demonstration that follows is a reprise, slightly summarized, of pp. 33–37 of this work.

26. James H. Hammond et al., *The Pro-Slavery Argument* (Charleston, S.C.: Walker, Richards, 1852), 107–8.

27. Quoted in Olli Alho, *The Religion of the Slaves* (Helsinki: Suomalainen Tiedeakatemia, 1980), 62.

28. Quoted in Mitchell Snay, *Gospel of Disunion: Religion and Separation in the Antebellum South* (Cambridge: Cambridge University Press, 1993), 78.

29. Frederick Douglass, *Narrative of the Life of Frederick Douglass, an American Slave* (New York: Signet, 1968).

30. Quoted in James Melton, ed., *Bullwhip Days: The Slaves Remember* (New York: Weidenfeld & Nicolson, 1988), 196.

31. Quoted in John W. Blassingame, ed., *Slave Testimony: Two Centuries of Letters, Speeches, Interviews, and Autobiographies* (Baton Rouge: Louisiana State University, 1977), 411.

32. Quoted in Thomas L. Webber, *Deep Like the Rivers: Education in the Slave Quarter Community, 1831–1865* (New York: Norton, 1978), 83.

33. Text of a former slave, quoted in ibid., 84.

34. *Le récit de Moses Grandy esclave en Caroline du Nord* (Montréal: Centre de recherches Caraïbes, 1977), 41.

35. See Mechal Sobel, *Trablin' On: The Slave Journey to an Afro-Baptist Faith* (Westport, Conn.: Greenwood, 1979), 41.

36. Douglass, *Narrative,* 111.

37. Quoted in Eileen Southern, *The Music of Black Americans,* 3d ed. (New York: Norton, 1997), 175.

38. Norman R. Yetman, *Voices from Slavery* (New York: Rinehart & Winston, 1970), 167.

39. Daniel Grant to John Owen, Jr., September 3, 1790, quoted in Donald G. Mathews, *Religion in the Old South* (Chicago: University of Chicago Press, 1977), 69.

40. Quoted in Sobel, *Trablin' On,* 79.

41. Harriet A. Jacobs, *Incidents dans la vie d'une jeune esclave* (Paris: V. Hamy, 1992), 119–20.

42. Quoted in Riggins R. Earle, Jr., *Dark Symbols, Obscure Signs* (Maryknoll, N.Y.: Orbis, 1993), 68.

43. Clifton H. Johnson, ed., *God Struck Me Dead* (Philadelphia: Pilgrim, 1969).

44. Anselme T. Sanon, *Enraciner l'Évangile* (Paris: Cerf, 1981), 94.

45. Quoted in Johnson, *God Struck Me Dead,* 15–18.

46. Earle, *Dark Symbols,* 54–69.

Bibliography

Baily, David T. *Shadow on the Church: Southwestern Evangelical Religion and the Issue of Slavery, 1783–1860.* Ithaca, N.Y.: Cornell University Press, 1985.

Bruce, Dickson D. *And They All Sang Hallelujah.* Knoxville: University of Tennessee Press, 1974.

Butler, Jon. *Awash in a Sea of Faith: Christianizing the American People.* Cambridge, Mass., and London: Harvard University Press, 1990.

Clifton, Denzil T. "Anglicanism and Negro Slavery in Colonial America." *Historical Magazine of the Protestant Episcopal Church,* September 1970, 29–70.

Cornelius, Janet D. *Slave Missions and the Black Church in the Antebellum South.* Columbia: University of South Carolina Press, 1999.

Earl, Riggins R. *Dark Symbols, Obscure Signs.* Maryknoll, N.Y.: Orbis, 1993.

Fox-Genovese, Elizabeth, and Eugene D. Genovese. "The Divine Sanction of Social Order: Religious Foundations of the Southern Slave-holder's World View." *Journal of the American Academy of Religion* 55, no. 2 (1987): 211–29.

Frey, Sylvia R. "The Year of Jubilee Is Come: Black Christianity in the Plantation South in Post-Revolutionary America." In *Religion in a Revolutionary Age,* ed. Ronald Hoffman and Peter J. Albert. Charlottesville: University Press of Virginia, 1994, 87–124.

Frey, Sylvia R., and Betty Wood. *Come Shouting to Zion: African American Protestantism in the American South and British Caribbean to 1830.* Chapel Hill and London: University of North Carolina Press, 1998.

Gomez, Michael A. *Exchanging Our Country Marks: The Transformation of African Identities in the Colonial and Antebellum South.* Chapel Hill: University of North Carolina Press, 1998.

Johnson, Clifton H., ed. *God Struck Me Dead.* Philadelphia: Pilgrim, 1969.

Kay, Martin L. Michael, and Lorin Lee Cary. *Slavery in North Carolina.* Chapel Hill: University of North Carolina Press, 1995.

Loveland, Anne C. *Southern Evangelicals and the Social Order, 1800–1860.* Baton Rouge: Louisiana State University Press, 1980.

Mathews, Donald G. *Slavery and Methodism: A Chapter in American Morality, 1780–1845.* Princeton, N.J.: Princeton University Press, 1965.

———. "Charles Colcock Jones and the Southern Evangelical Crusade to Form a Biracial Community." *Journal of Southern History* 41 (1975): 299–320.

McKivigan, John R., and Mitchell Snay, eds. *Religion and the Antebellum Debate over Slavery.* Athens: University of Georgia Press, 1990.

Perdue, Charles L., Jr., et al., eds. *Weevils in the Wheat: Interviews with Virginia Ex-Slaves.* Charlottesville: University Press of Virginia, 1975.

Raboteau, Albert J. *African American Religion.* New York and Oxford: Oxford University Press, 1999.

Scherer, Lester B. *Slavery and the Churches in Early America, 1619–1819.* Grand Rapids, Mich.: Eerdmans, 1975.

Sernett, Milton C. *Black Religion and American Evangelicalism: White Protestants, Plantation Missions, and the Flowering of Negro Christianity, 1787–1865.* Metuchen, N.J.: American Theological Library Association, 1975.

Smith, Sheldon H. *In His Image, But . . .: Racism in Southern Religion, 1780–1910.* Durham, N.C.: Duke University Press, 1972.

Smith, Timothy L. "Slavery and Theology: The Emergence of Black Christian Consciousness in the Nineteenth Century." *Church History* 41 (1972): 497–512.

Snay, Mitchell. *Gospel in Disunion: Religion and Separatism in the Antebellum South.* Cambridge: Cambridge University Press, 1993.

Sobel, Mechal. *Trablin' On: The Slave Journey to an Afro-Baptist Faith.* Westport, Conn.: Greenwood, 1979.

Stringfellow, Thornton. "A Brief Examination of Scripture Testimony on the Institution of Slavery." *Richmond Religious Herald,* February 25, 1841.

Van Horne, John C. "Impediments to the Christianization and Education of Blacks in Colonial America: The Case of the Associates of Dr. Bray." *Historical Magazine of the Protestant Episcopal Church,* September 1981, 243–69.

Wilmore, Gayraud S. *Black Religion and Black Radicalism.* Garden City, N.Y.: Doubleday, 1972.

Wimberly, Edward P., and Anne Steaty Wimberly. *Liberation and Human Wholeness: The Conversion Experiences of Black People in Slavery and Freedom.* Nashville: Abingdon, 1986.

Wood, Peter H. " 'Jesus Christ Has Got Thee at Last': Afro-American Conversion as a Forgotten Chapter in Eighteenth-Century Southern Intellectual History." *Bulletin of the Center for the Study of Southern Culture and Religion* 3 (1979): 1–7.

3

"I want Jesus to walk with me."

The Faith of the Slaves

*"Among our people, in general, the Church
is the alpha and omega of all things."*
—Martin Delany
(to Frederick Douglass, February 16, 1849)

THE CHRISTIAN FAITH is not lived only in an interior dialogue between God
and the converted disciple. It is always expressed in a church. The convert is invited
to join with other believers and to celebrate with them the gift of faith and of being
loved by a merciful God. Moreover, the church does not come in after the stage
of conversion. Quite often it is because the individual has been put into contact
with a believing community that the new birth takes place.

As do all Christians, African Americans thus lived their Christianity in the
context of church. The originality of their history comes from the diversity of
church structures that the slaves experienced and gave life to. It is proper to
distinguish three types of structure:

- The participation, in one way or another, in a white church, either in the
  city or on the plantation, thereby creating the biracial church
- The founding of independent black churches
- The organization of clandestine meetings, far from the view of whites

These three types of situations called for different commitments that colored
the faith journey. In all of them, however, we find the curious phenomenon
called the "ring shout." Everywhere, also, we see the emergence of the black

preacher—a central figure of the slave community and an individual who would mark African American history to this day.

If we properly perceive the various spaces in which the black converts expressed themselves, we can attempt to describe the Christianity of the slaves. We will put that approach to the test by examining the hymns that issued from the various forms of church (especially the latter two forms): the Negro spirituals.

Biracial Worship

In the aftermath of the American Revolution, a significant number of slaves began to adhere to Christianity. Where were they found? The majority of them (an impossible to verify 60 percent has been put forward) were found in white churches that thus become biracial. We do not say "integrated," for that would be to underestimate the violence of the racial cleavage. The Mississippi Code of 1857 speaks of freedom of worship on condition that all religious services attended by blacks be supervised by at least two "discreet and respectable" whites. Yet at the same time we cannot speak of juxtaposed communities, for it is evident that the participation in the same service modified the relationship between the two groups, especially the consciousness of self that the slave population developed.

Certainly, the separation of groups—whether in the simple wooden "houses of prayer" on the plantation or in the stone churches in town—was telling: the whites sat up front, while the blacks sat at the back or on a platform set up for them. A church in Virginia went so far as to paint some pews black so that there could be no mistake. Yet this segregation was not necessarily perceived as scandalous by the slaves, for it allowed them to be in contact with the "brothers" and "sisters" from other plantations, to find the one who perhaps would become their spouse, to acquire a sense of community beyond the limits of a particular plantation. A separation of the men from the women was not rare.

More importantly, whites and blacks listened to the same Bible readings, sang the same hymns, lived through the same process of repentance and commitment. It was there that the discovery of the Word of God took place, with all the stories that struck the imagination of the slave. It was there that the revelation of a God who created all people equally and who offered the Son in sacrifice for the salvation of all took place. Of course, at the end of the common service, the slaves were subjected to special exhortation on their duty to obey their masters. But because they heard and internalized all the rest, they could take with a grain of salt the message of social control. It is certain that the African Americans would not have attended the white churches if they had heard only a long litany consecrating their oppression.

Through the biracial church, Methodist or Baptist (the dominant confessions), the slaves would discover and experience only a bit of the joy of equality. But we should not underestimate the importance of that bit, since when one was treated like a beast of burden in daily life, even a semblance of equality between the races was remarkable. And this feeling of equality was first a gift of God. The slaves learned that God does not show favoritism (Acts 10:34) and that they, as much as the masters, were "children of the Father." And that spiritual status was so much greater than the temporal one. Each slave could identify with the Suffering Servant, Jesus. Did not the history of their people resemble strangely that of Israel?

In the parish community, all received the title of "brother" or "sister," and that constituted a wonderful breach in the social hierarchy. And when a slave asked to be admitted into a particular church, the officials of the church followed the same procedures for him or her as for a white person. If the slave came from another local church, the officials communicated with that congregation, and once in possession of the answer, required no other "test of conversion."

In the registers of the First Baptist Church of Louisville, Mississippi, for the month of July 1836, we can read: "Adam, a Black brother, owned by Mr. Henry Fox, presented himself and told the church what the Lord had done for him. Satisfied, the church unanimously received him as a member and extended to him the right hand of communion. It voted to baptize him by immersion on the third Sunday of August." The following month we find exactly the same expression used for a white woman. Both were baptized in the same ceremony.

Perhaps the best example is that of disciplinary procedure. Particularly in the Baptist churches, one did not fool around with discipline. The congregation gathered regularly, often on Saturday afternoon or Saturday night, to discuss questions of morality, and the jury was the community itself. The accusations could range from intemperance to adultery. The accused could plead guilty or not guilty. If the person pleaded guilty, he or she would be punished to the extent of the sin. Often, though, the person was forgiven and was reintegrated into the community. If the accused pleaded not guilty and an inquiry proved the person's guilt, that member could be stricken from the parish registers.

The interesting thing here is that in a question implicating blacks and whites, the testimony of blacks had the same weight as that of whites. The latter were not automatically believed. We can also point out that the catalog of moral faults was the same for both groups. The accusation of adultery was most significant; it meant that the church recognized the sanctity of the slave's marriage, while the civil law did not. Evil deeds between blacks were also punished. Even if this discipline can be considered, in many ways, to have been a means of control for white domination, it nevertheless instilled a moral sense of the dignity and equality of all persons.

In these biracial churches before the Civil War, slaves were able to fulfill certain roles. Those who had evident and recognized talents could become elders, deacons, and even preachers. Almost everywhere, between 1770 and 1860, we can find black ministers who preached to mixed congregations. Often, even, while it was forbidden by law in the South to teach slaves to read and write, the churches discreetly permitted this instruction for those most apt.

Hence, the presence of blacks in the biracial churches would affect the whites. The latter would modify their views on slavery, seeking to make it more humane and feeling responsible for its "morality." They could not remain insensitive to those groups of slaves who joined the evangelical churches and manifested an edifying piety. What white person had not seen the tears of emotion trickle down the face of a black person in prayer? What white person had not been enchanted by the polyphonic melodies sung by the slaves? Even if the owners buttressed their feelings of superiority by treating their slaves as "children," this condescending label marked a certain improvement on the previous image of African slaves as savage beasts or household objects without personality. There was a limit, however; slavery would be considered a providential design of God to lead the African pagans to the knowledge of the true God. Paradoxically, the piety of the slaves would refine the arguments of the defenders of the "peculiar institution."

For the slave, the biracial church was, thus, the experience of a dignity that was beginning to take form. It "offered a spark of joy in the midst of pain, a promise of life-affirming forgiveness to soften the hopelessness of unremitting bondage, an ultimate reward in heaven for unrewarded service in this world." . . .

> Taking communion together with whites, serving as deacons or Sunday school teachers, being baptized or confirmed in the same ceremonies, even contributing their mite to the temporal upkeep of the church, could surely have been seen as symbolic ways of emphasizing their sense of self-respect and equality before God. . . . Blacks did not discover in the biracial churches an equality of treatment that spiritually transported them out of bondage, but they found in them a theology of hope and a recognition of self-worth that fared them well in their struggle to endure slavery.[1]

Nevertheless, when they would have the possibility of joining an ethnically autonomous church body, African Americans would not hesitate to leave the biracial churches. Their desire for freedom required more than the biracial churches offered.

The Independent Churches

The decision to found independent churches was not taken lightly by free blacks at the end of the eighteenth century. They would have much preferred to continue to pray with their white brothers and sisters. But patience has its limits. The African Americans would not endure humiliation and discrimination in the house of the Lord any longer. They wanted to express their faith free from all constraints, since even their preachers were kept in an inferior standing in the Methodist Church. Moreover, the whites sometimes encouraged the founding of these independent black churches. In seeing this joyous band of African Americans who soon would submerge them by becoming members of their churches, many whites became afraid, saying to themselves that it would be better to build churches than prisons to preserve the social order and (in the best scenario) believing that everyone had the right to discover salvation through a structure adapted for them. But the slave owners were more than hesitant about the new black churches.

Proof that the black Christian community had matured, the first independent churches appeared in the South on the eve of the Revolution. The sense of local freedom and democracy cherished among the Baptists was their cradle. A Baptist congregation was organized on the plantation of William Byrd III in Virginia as early as 1758. But it was the Church of Silver Bluff, in South Carolina, that claimed the honor of being the first black independent church, forming under the direction of George Liele, a slave, in 1774. Three years later, Liele and Andrew Bryan created what was to become the first African Baptist church in Savannah, Georgia. The independent churches would multiply rapidly throughout the South. They were almost all Baptist in the South, both Methodist and Baptist in the North. These churches flourished in the urban centers with free blacks at their head. In 1810 Daniel Cocker listed fifteen "African Churches" representing four denominations in ten cities. When these African Americans moved west, they brought with them their desire to found autonomous churches. Hence, in 1801 an African church was born in Lexington, Kentucky.

In reality, these churches were not truly autonomous. They were almost always supervised by whites, and even in the Baptist Church they had to be recognized by the regional assembly. Their range of freedom was thus strictly limited. From the moment that the new churches would be suspected of being the source of revolutionary agitation, at the beginning of the nineteenth century, surveillance by the whites would become even more intense. Progressively, all the rights granted to these churches would be revoked. In 1830, after the Nat Turner insurrection, the independence of the African churches would be purely nominal in the South.

The scenario for the founding of the black churches is perfectly illustrated by the history of the African Methodist Episcopal Church in Philadelphia. Under the impetus of men like Richard Allen and Absalom Jones, the St. George Methodist Church attracted more and more blacks. Plans were already in the works to organize a distinct African church, but the Methodist authorities blocked the project. At the beginning of the 1790s events accelerated when a group of blacks, headed by Allen and Jones, refused to go to the platform to pray. Richard Allen described the scene:

> We expected to take the seats over the ones we formerly occupied below, not knowing any better, we took those seats. . . . Just as we got to the seats, the elder said, "Let us pray." We had not been long upon our knees before I heard considerable scuffling and low talking. I raised my head and saw one of the trustees, H. M., having hold of the Rev. Absalom Jones, pulling

him up off his knees, and saying, "You must get up, you must not kneel here." Mr. Jones replied, "Wait until prayer is over and I will get up and trouble you no more." With that he [the trustee] beckoned to one of the other trustees, William White, to pull him up. By this time prayer was over, and we all went out of the church as a body, and they were no longer plagued with us in the Church.[2]

Absalom Jones went on to found the African Episcopal Church of St. Thomas, which was dedicated on July 17, 1794. Richard Allen would build the Church of Bethel, inaugurated on July 29, 1794. On the occasion of the opening of the Church of Bethel, a public declaration clearly specified that the founders were conscious of establishing some sort of discrimination. But this was the only way out of a situation that was considered a nuisance by whites and an insult by blacks.

As the Philadelphia story is typical, we find just about the same sequence of events in Baltimore under the direction of Daniel Cocker and in 1796 in New York, where the Methodist African Americans were called "Sionites" because of the Sion Chapel, where they first assembled.

At the outset, the two groups of "Bethelites" and "Sionites" did not intend to form new denominations. They deferred to the discernment of the bishops. The separation was necessary because of the constant problems brought up by the white Methodist authorities—the problems of ownership of the church, the right of supervision, the administration of the sacraments, and attitudes toward slavery. The African Americans, irritated by this bad faith, were obliged to draw up rules clearly stating their sole authority over their own churches. Finally, in 1816, their independence was recognized, and on April 9 the delegates of some black churches founded the African Methodist Episcopal Church. Allen was elected bishop and consecrated on April 11. In 1818 this church counted 6,748 members.

The drama lies in the fact that the new African American church bodies did not put up a common front. At one point it was believed that unity was possible between Sionites and Bethelites. But Richard Allen, who did not lack ambition, wanted the New York church to submit to his authority. The Sionites left and created their own African Methodist Episcopal Church in America. The competition, which never ceased between the two black Methodist groups, illustrates the limits of religious denominationalism among African Americans. The same effects were produced among them as among the whites. Multiplication was accomplished by division!

In any case, these churches become the first truly African American institutions in America. They were the first examples of black consciousness and separatism. In the more permissive atmosphere of the North, this founding of churches was quickly successful. In 1860 Baltimore had fifteen African churches representing five denominations. Because of growth, the churches continually had to find new locations, ordain new ministers. Blacks left the churches dominated by whites to assemble with other people of color. On the level of doctrine, these congregations innovated little. Something else was more important for them than doctrine: a way of being together in the presence of God. And on that level, African practices could once again appear.

As they appeared and grew, the independent African churches assumed multiple functions among their people. They never confined themselves to the strictly religious; or rather the religious aspect was never a separate area but instead was coextensive with the whole of black social life. The black church was a religious center, a social club, a political arena, a school for promotional activities. The disrupted life of the community restructured itself beginning with the religious assembly. I will detail these ethical, economic, educational, and political roles of the churches that made them "a nation within a nation" (E. F. Frazier) until the great migration of 1915–1916.

The ethical role of the church was greatly stressed in the revivalist groups. There was no Christian life without a personal and communal morality. Holiness was measured by the degree of honesty, modesty, temperance, and conjugal fidelity. The influence of the churches was especially strong in the area of family. We have already noted the ill effects of slavery on sexual relations. The growing community of free blacks needed a strong structure so as not to confuse freedom and license. Family life stabilized. Moreover, the church did not hesitate to excommunicate notorious sinners. In 1809 Richard Allen, Absalom Jones, and James Forten contributed to the founding of the Society of the Suppression of Vice and Immorality.

From the economic point of view, the churches were the seat of charitable societies, welfare societies, and mutual aid societies. These societies often preceded the formation of the churches, as in Philadelphia, when separate churches for blacks were unthinkable. But they functioned according to religious rituals, seeking to put into practice love of neighbor and care for the widow and the orphan. They allowed the African Americans to bury their dead with dignity—an extremely important gesture for them. They were soon transformed into insurance societies for the protection of the most poor and into savings banks. One good effect was to give experience in economic matters to a people just learning how to operate the levers of society.

Nowhere, however, was the role of the churches greater than in education. The African Americans had always fought to learn to read and write. They had to show great ingenuity to get around laws that banned slaves from learning to read and write. On that level, also, the free blacks noticed the existence of discrimination in the North as in the South, since they were sent to inferior schools. The churches therefore would have to take charge of this sector also. Each African American church had a Sunday school and often a regular school in which adults and children would take turns learning.

The abolitionist societies helped the churches to increase the number of schools. In 1834 the African Methodist Episcopal Church adopted a strong resolution on the subject. Care for education had to be a constant concern of the minister. The minister had to raise the consciousness of the parents and the congregations. Soon the motto would be "Build a church and a school." In 1856 Bishop Payne acquired the Wilberforce property, which in 1863 would become Wilberforce University, the first American university controlled by blacks.

Finally, for a long time, the church would offer to African Americans the only possible place to practice politics. We see that clearly in the debate on colonization that took place in 1816–1817, when some wanted to encourage blacks to emigrate to Africa to recover their freedom. The most important protest meeting was held at the Church of Bethel in Philadelphia in January 1817, under the direction of Richard Allen and James Forten. Besides uncovering the hidden agenda of the colonizers, the free black Christians manifested their deep solidarity with their brothers and sisters still in bondage. They preferred suffering in America with them rather than dreaming of a better situation elsewhere without them.

The black churches attacked the bastion of slavery with more difficulty. In this struggle, individuals went further than the institutions. The abolitionist movement would not have had the same vigor without the participation of free blacks of the North, notably pastors. The churches offered stopping places along the route of the Underground Railroad, the clandestine route toward the North. Occasionally, they would help slaves buy their freedom. But they would have difficulty in making a clear public stand.

The political role of the church was clearly seen in the church group itself. Indeed, the church gave its members a group consciousness, and that was not of minor importance. It was not rare to see African Americans define themselves by their church. "My nationality? Methodist." That was more than symbolic. The bosom of the church created a sense of existence, a common objective, and organized solidarity. In the end, it benefited the community. The church was a free space, sheltered from the white world, where the people rebuilt their identity and dignity. Its existence was a political statement from the black people.

To speak of politics is to speak also of responsibility. It was in the church that black leaders would have their first experience. Or rather, the first leaders of the African American community were pastors and bishops. And if ordinary Christians could not vote in the broader society, they could exercise their full rights in the church and even hold positions of responsibility. The local congregation was the political convention and the House of Representatives.

The black church was not just another institution among the black people. It was the place from which all the group's values emerged. It was the center of coordination for all social life. Its way of placing itself in the American existence involved a whole way of conceiving Christianity in which African sensibility could unfold freely.[3]

The Clandestine Prayer Meetings

The religious expression of African Americans during the time of slavery was not limited to biracial or independent churches. The latter expressed the visible face of black religion, but there was also a hidden face: secret meetings organized by the slave community for one or more plantations. These assemblies, which could coexist perfectly well with the other forms of religious services, were the fruit of a visceral need of the oppressed, were a result of the multiple interdictions imposed by the white government, especially after the Nat Turner insurrection (1831), or were the consequence of being far from a place of worship. Even the Catholic slaves held these secret assemblies in "the nineteenth-century catacombs" (Albert J. Raboteau). The slaves thus created a sacred space far from the master's house, in the woods or in the swamps, in thickets or in caves, sometimes in their huts, and established a sacred part of the night that had its own rhythm of hymns, prayer, and preaching and its own structure of ministries. This shadow religion, this "invisible institution," always threatened by the possible intervention of a patrol, was the privileged conservator of the Africans' religious identity. It was the crucible that fused the African and the Christian contributions, a place where the conversion experience was transmitted. Happily for us, African Americans spoke about these meetings.

Peter Randolph, a Virginia slave emancipated in 1847 who became a Baptist minister, told of one of these clandestine reunions:

> Not being allowed to hold meetings on the plantation, the slaves assemble in the swamps, out of reach of the patrols. They have an understanding among themselves as to the time and place of getting together. This is often done by the first one arriving breaking boughs from the trees, and bending them in the direction of the selected spot. Arrangements are then made for conducting the exercises. They first ask each other how they feel, their state of mind, etc. The male members then select a certain space, in separate groups, for their division of the meeting. They take turns preaching, and then praying and singing until they generally feel quite happy. The speaker usually begins by calling himself unworthy, and talks very slowly, until, feeling the spirit, he grows excited, and in a short time, there fall to the ground twenty or thirty men and women under its influence. Enlightened people call it excitement; but I wish the same was felt by everybody, so far as they are sincere.
>
> The slave forgets all his sufferings, except to remind the others of the past week's trials, exclaiming: "Thank God, I shall not live here always!" Then they pass from one to another, shaking hands, and bidding each other farewell, promising, should they meet no more on earth, to strive to meet in heaven, where all is joy, happiness, and liberty. As they separate, they sing a parting hymn of praise.

In some places, if the slaves are caught praying to God, they are whipped more than if they had committed a great crime. The slave owners will allow the slaves to dance, but do not want them to pray to God. Sometimes, when a slave, on being whipped, calls upon God, he is forbidden to do so, under the threat of having his throat cut, or brains blown out. . . . Sometimes the poor slave takes courage to ask his master to let him pray, and is driven away, with the answer, that if discovered praying his back will pay the bill.[4]

Thanks to this text and others, we can extract the characteristic elements of this underground church.

It clearly was a nocturnal assembly. One slave informed the others that it would begin at eleven o'clock at night and that it would be prolonged late into the night, until the morning star would appear. So much the worse if one felt more tired at work the next day. The oppressed would have lived their time of grace, a "real" meeting with "real" preaching.

The place chosen bore various names, and we don't know if we should speak of a "brush arbor" or a "hush arbor." The important thing was to find a place for oneself, far from the eyes and ears of the master and lit by only a few torches.

One delicate question was that of the noise. The owners or the patrols could not be alerted. So the slaves habitually overturned a pot or a saucepan, thinking (undoubtedly a belief of African origin) that the sound would be muffled and prevented from being heard. The slave reports tell us that, in any case, the prayers and hymns were rather whispered than proclaimed aloud. And those who went into a trance too noisily were quickly brought back to consciousness.

The participants disposed themselves in a circle on their knees around the one who directed the prayer. The service generally had three parts: prayers and hymns, an exhortation by the preacher, and the witnessing of faith and the mutual encouragement of the participants. But the presence of God was palpable, if we are to believe Simon Brown:

The people sang, prayed, "witnessed," clapped their hands, as if God was present there among them. He was not far away in heaven: he saw each one, listened to each word and promised to send his love down on them. My people was so crushed by its trials and tribulations, the heart so broken, that I saw it burst into tears like babies. . . . Yes, sir, there was no hypocrisy in these prayer meetings. There was a living faith in a just God who, one day, would hearken to the cries of these poor black children and would deliver them from their enemies. But they never said a word to the Whites about that kind of faith.[5]

The sermon, or exhortation, did not quite resemble what the slaves heard in the white churches. Its center of gravity was not the words of Paul to the slaves but his affirmation before the Areopagus of Athens: "From one ancestor he made all nations to inhabit the whole earth" (Acts 17:26). The preacher (a man or a woman) compared the slaves to the children of God in the desert to whom the Lord promised a land of milk and honey. But Charles Davenport asked himself: "But how us gwine-a take land what's already been took?"[6] In any case, the preacher spoke without restraint, in the language of the audience, telling all the stories that could magnify the power of God and the love of the Christ.

If there was a theme that dominated the expression of the invisible church, it was that of freedom. The testimony of former slaves unceasingly repeated: "We pray for freedom, to change the heart of the master, so that the day will come when blacks will be slaves only of God."

This form of black Christianity was not radically different from what was lived in the other assemblies. They had the same ingredients, the same theology, and the same ecclesiology. But the slaves here could give free expression to their emotions. They allowed themselves to criticize openly the Southern oppression and speak of the judgment to come, when those in power would be called to account. This type of meeting did not have the stamp of any particular confession. In the words of Lucretia Alexander, "You couldn't tell the difference between Baptists and Methodists. They was all Christians."[7] The women were at least as fervent as the men and did not hesitate to lead the prayers.

The sense of community was refined through such assemblies, which could regroup the adults from several plantations. Each one shared his or her concerns and listened to the trials of the others. Peter Randolph underscored that. Their hearts beat in unison in the hope of a better future.

John B. Boles expressed the social scope of these prayer meetings in this way:

> Such arenas for safe slave condemnation of the evils of slaveholding—or of a particularly oppressive owner—might have provided the occasion for catharsis that permitted slaves to deal with the most difficult moments of their bondage without recourse to forms of protest that would have been physically threatening to themselves or their loved ones. Especially when combined with a Christian gospel that offered a sense of forgiveness, that suggested one's eternal worth in the eyes of God, and that provided avenues for moral growth and leadership. The brush-arbor experience might have served as a kind of religious safety valve. Without it, there might have been more self-destructive behavior on the part of slaves or more violent protests against the worst abuses of the institution of slavery. While such protests might have brought about some reforms it more often would have resulted in violent, harsh reprisals against the dissenting slaves and the entire slave community. Brush-arbor religion might have served as the safest form of

slave protest, a kind of rebellion of the powerless that offered and essential restatement of self-worth.[8]

But the spiritual freedom lived through the celebration included the body. The clandestine service was the ideal space for collective trances and ecstasies. James Lindsay Smith stated: "The way in which we worshipped is almost indescribable. The singing was accompanied by a certain ecstasy of motion, clapping of hands, tossing of heads, which would continue without cessation for about half an hour; one would lead off in a kind of recitative style, others joining in the chorus. The old house partook of the ecstasy; it rang with their jubilant shouts, and shook in all its joints."[9]

From Shouting to the Ring Shout

A term recurs continually in the evocations of the various forms of African American religious services, especially in the plantation chapels, or houses of praise: the *shout*. This practice was organized in certain areas, notably South Carolina and further south, into a *ring shout,* the stamping of feet and clapping of hands in a circle. Shouting was individual and the ring shout was collective.

In fact, shouting arose in every celebration where blacks were free to express themselves. It was an individual and spontaneous action, born of the prayer, the singing, and especially the preaching. It was an expression of personal conversion and of the joy felt at being counted among the saved. The shouting could be verbal or nonverbal, but it was most often accompanied by interjections, clapping of hands, and skipping. It implied a temporary loss of consciousness. In any event, it was an exercise that used the body and followed no preset program. The former slaves often spoke of it concerning their parents. Thus, Isaiah Jeffries told of his mother's conversion: "When I got to be a big boy, my Ma got religion at de Camp meeting at El-Bethel. She shouted and sung fer three days, going all over de plantation and de neighbouring ones, inviting her friends to come and see her baptized and shouting and praying fer dem."[10] Martha Colquitt remembered her grandmother: "My grandma was a powerful Christian woman, and she did love to sing and shout. . . . Grandma would get to shoutin' so loud and she would make so much fuss nobody in the church could hear de preacher and she would wander off from de gallery and go downstairs and try to go down to de white folkses aisles to get to de altar where de preacher was, and dey was always lockin' her up for disturbing worship, but they never could break her from dat shoutin' and wanderin' 'round de meetin' house."[11] The shout, then, was a personal action of the believer, seized by the Spirit of God. Those who lived the experience spoke of it in these terms: "I shout because there is a fire on the inside. When I witness the truth, the fire moves on the main altar of my heart, and I can't keep still." Another said: "We children of God, shout because of that love that wells up in our bosom. It is that love which runs from heart to heart and from breast to breast. We have to cry out."[12]

I must remark that the shout was not necessarily one of joy; it could be one of sadness, such as at a funeral because of the death of a loved one. It seems that more women than men entered into a trance. That was their way of relieving tensions in the search for God, the affirmation that God comes to meet the one who seeks God. It was the "fire in the bones," the fire that enflamed the church, the tornado of the Spirit that came down on the congregation.

In the form of a ring shout, the shout becomes a group activity. We have several attestations to that in nineteenth-century newspapers. I will quote them in chronological order, even though they took place in the same period, around the time of the Civil War.

In the August 1863 issue of the *Continental Monthly,* H. G. Spaulding, a white Unitarian minister, wrote:

> After the praise meeting is over, there usually follows the very singular and impressive performance of the "Shout," or religious dance of the Negroes. Three or four, standing still, clapping their hands and beating time with their feet, commence singing in unison one of the peculiar shout melodies, while the others walk round in a ring, in single file, joining also in the song. Soon those in the ring leave off their singing, the others keeping it up with increased vigor, and strike into the shout step, observing most accurate time with the music. This step is something halfway between a shuffle and a dance, as difficult for an uninitiated person to describe as to imitate. At the end of each stanza of the song the dancers stop short with a slight stamp on the last note, and then, putting the other foot forward, proceed through the next verse. . . . They will often dance to the same song for twenty or thirty minutes, once or twice, perhaps, varying the monotony of their movement by walking for a little while and joining in the singing.[13]

The shout was a simple outburst and manifestation of religious fervor—a "rejoicing in the Lord," making a "joyful noise unto the God of their salvation."

A black teacher in the North, Charlotte Forten, lived on the islands off the east coast of the United States. She related:

> At the end of the ceremony, they all very solemnly shake hands, then, in a sort of prolonging, they have a long session of "shouting" while they sing their own hymns under the direction of Maurice, an old blind person who has a superb voice and who sings with great enthusiasm. The first session of "shouting" that we attended impressed us greatly. The big dark hall with its blackened walls; the wild, twisting dance of the *shouters;* the

crowd of somber, passionate faces, pressing around them; the silhouette of the old blind man who could barely control his movements and who had magnificent attitudes and gestures while singing; and on the whole scene the reddish glow of the pinewood fire that gave a circle of light around the hearth but that seemed to deepen and darken the shadows in the rest of the room, the whole gave a wild, strange and striking tableau that is difficult to forget.[14]

The most precise description that we have is found in the May 30, 1867, edition of the journal *The Nation:*

The true "shout" takes place on Sundays or on "praise"-night through the week, and either in the praise-house or in some cabin in which a regular religious meeting has been held. Very likely more than half the population of the plantation is gathered together. . . . The benches are pushed back to the wall when the formal meeting is over, and old and young, men and women, sprucely-dressed young men, grotesquely half-clad field hands— the women generally with gay handkerchiefs twisted about their heads and with short skirts—boys with tattered shirts and men's trousers, young girls barefooted, all stand up in the middle of the floor, and when the "sperichil" is struck up, begin first walking and by and by shuffling round, one after the other, in a ring. The foot is hardly taken from the floor, and the progression is mainly due to a jerking, hitching motion, which agitates the entire shouter, and soon brings out streams of perspiration. Sometimes they dance silently, sometimes as they shuffle they sing the chorus of the spiritual, and sometimes the song is itself also sung by the dancers. But more frequently a band, composed of some of the best singers and of tired shouters, stand at the side of the room to "base" the others, singing the body of the song and clapping their hands together or on the knees. Song and dance are alike extremely energetic, and often, when the shout lasts into the middle of the night, the monotonous thud, thud of the feet prevents sleep within half a mile of the praise-house.[15]

Let us try to assemble the characteristics of this special dance:
• Three different roles can be identified: the singer, those who give the basic rhythm, and the dancers (that is, the rest of the participants).
• "The dance is born of the rhythmic chanting that accompanies it, that is the corporal expression; the dancers participate in the singing, intermittently; a musical dialogue is established between the singer and the dancers."[16]
• The dancers moved single file in a circle, almost always counter-clockwise.

- The slip step was used. The feet were never to cross or leave the floor. But the entire body was involved in the dance.
- The singing was monotone. The meaning was less in the words than in the action.
- There was an increasing acceleration of the singing and the dancing, and it was in this way that the participants entered into a trance and ecstasy. For the aim was possession by the Spirit, a sign of the reality of conversion. It was not rare to see people fall to the floor, "struck down by God." According to the phrase of Jon Michael Spencer, "the rhythm provided the pulse and the Holy Spirit, the impulse."[17]

Here, then, we have a religious rite that intertwined the personal and community dimensions and served as a spiritual event.

The reaction of the whites to this sacred dance was often negative. For them, this kind of frolic had no spiritual dimension; it was the cult of unbridled emotion. The reward was the whip or contempt. In Louisiana, Catholic priests prohibited the shout. The story is told that a master promised new boots to his slave if he did not "shout" during the service. During the second half of the service, the old man could not keep still any longer; he leapt up and announced: "Boots or no boots, I gwine to shout today."[18]

But the resistance of certain African Americans was just as strong. The severe judgment of the black bishop Daniel Alexander Payne is often quoted. In his *Recollections* of 1888, he considered this dance, which he discovered in a clandestine meeting a dozen years before, as "ridiculous and pagan" and immediately ordered the pastor to have it cease immediately. For him, such a practice was a shame for blacks and a blot on the Christian name. The young leader replied to him that sinners could not be converted without a ring. Bishop Payne was disconsolate: "By the ignorant masses . . . it was considered the essence of religion."[19] Before Payne, Richard Allen had rejected these practices. The Baptists, however, never objected to them.

What was the origin of this round of slip steps? Opinions diverge. The eighteenth-century Methodists knew the physical expression of religious fervor, and the First Awakening did not lack them. At the camp meetings, the trance phenomenon took hold of whites as well as blacks. The only difference was that blacks did not stop and did not seem to tire. In 1807 Jesse Lee, a Georgia evangelist, remarked: "The first day of the meeting, we had a gentle and comfortable movement of the spirit of the Lord among us; and at night it was much more powerful than before, and the meeting was kept up all night without intermission. However, before day the white people retired, and the meeting was continued by the black people."[20] And the slaves found that the whites were quite inexperienced in the matter of trances.

We must, then, look to West Africa to find the roots of this "danced religion."

Some suggest that the word *shout* comes from the Arab word *saut,* which means "to walk" or "to run here and there." A similar African ritual used in the cult of the ancestors was not transplanted as such, but it lent its gestures to Christian worship. The emotional explosion focused on the meaning proposed by American Protestantism: salvation in Christ, along with recognition of the work of God in history, personally and collectively. The shout was, then, a Christian celebration in an African costume.

The High Status of the Black Preacher

At the crossroads of all the religious expressions of the oppressed community we find an important personage: the preacher. He gives the key to all that goes on in the world of the slaves. The judgment of W. E. B. DuBois is famous: "Three things characterized this religion of the slave—the Preacher, the Music, and the Frenzy. The Preacher is the most unique personality developed by the Negro on American soil. A leader, a politician, an orator, a 'boss,' an intriguer, and idealist, —all these he is, and ever, too, the center of a group of men, now twenty, now a thousand in number."[21] In more theological terms, Howard Thurman recognized: "The ante-bellum Negro preacher was the greatest single factor in determining the spiritual destiny of the slave community. He it was who gave to the masses of his fellows a point of view that became for them a veritable Door of Hope. His ministry was greatly restricted as to movement, function, and opportunities of leadership, but he himself was blessed with one important insight: he was convinced that every human being was a child of God. This belief included the slave as well as the master."[22]

Undoubtedly, we can refer here to the African priest even if there was no marked continuity between the African priest and the black Christian minister. Both were conscious of the mysterious forces at work in the universe. Both had the same sense of the oral tradition and musical rhythm. Both profusely used stories, parables, and proverbs. Both were sufficiently near their people to grasp spontaneously their expectations.

These black preachers, who were found especially in the South, did not follow any course of training. Very often they were self-ordained; or rather it was the direct call of God that had consecrated them. They felt themselves invested with a mission to preach. The Reverend Reed, a former slave, told us that fervently: "I am no mathematician, no biologist, neither grammarian, but when it comes to handling the Bible, I knocks down verbs, break up prepositions and jumps over adjectives. Now I tell you something—I am a God-sent man."[23] It seems that the natural leaders of the black community were spontaneously drawn to this task. They knew perfectly well that it was the way to prestige as well as to service to the black people.

These men, possessed of their interior investiture, were often feared in the South. The owners were suspicious of them. They believed that under the cover of religion the preachers harbored hidden designs. They were liars, robbers, and troublemakers. They wanted to install a black government. Yet it was not rare to find blacks preaching to white congregations in the South as well as in the North. Some slaves won their freedom because of their oratorical talents. In Virginia, between 1770 and 1780, we can count no fewer than six African American preachers serving white churches. Of course, this success among whites increased their prestige among their fellow blacks even more. The whites listened to them!

We need to distinguish between the eighteenth and nineteenth centuries because the situation was more liberal in the eighteenth century, more restrictive in the nineteenth. On the honor roll of the eighteenth century, we must cite the famous "Black Harry"—Harry Hoosier—who spread the good Word throughout the United States with the Methodist bishop Francis Asbury. By some, he was considered the greatest preacher of his time, but he never rose above the status of preacher, for white Methodists had no desire to share power with blacks (they would ordain the first black deacons in 1800). He did not know how to read or write, but he knew how to address a white audience. While Asbury brought him along to preach especially to blacks, Harry's success among the whites disturbed the bishop.

In reality, there was not just one model of preacher. Milton C. Sernett clearly distinguished four types of leaders among the African Americans of the South:[24]

- The ministers who took an active role in the evangelization of the South at the end of the eighteenth century. They were officially recognized by the ecclesiastical authorities and preached to mixed assemblies. Often knowing how to read and write, they had all the attributes of a minister of the church. Working mostly in the city, they saw their activities severely diminished and strictly controlled in the South after the revolts of Prosser and Vesey. They virtually disappeared after 1830, except where they were supervised, as in Alabama, by five slave owners.

- The deacons, or exhorters, who were the assistants of the white missionary on the level of the plantations. Between the visits of the evangelist, these men and women took charge of the community, led the prayer, and watched over the morality of the group. Their lack of education did not prevent them from having an acute evangelistic sense and great piety. But they were closely watched by the local white authorities.

- The inspired, who exercised a prophetic mission without ecclesiastical approval. Nat Turner was one of them. These apocalyptic preachers were the most dangerous for the social order. They feared nothing and no one.

- The leaders of voodoo cults and the sorcerers. This last type existed outside the Christian orbit.

Today we are sure that a certain number of women participated in the ministry of the Word, on the basis of a call from God and a personal charism. But they must not have been afraid of defying the establishment. One of the first names recalled is that of Elizabeth, born a slave in Maryland in 1766. At age twelve, she had a vision. At forty, she received a direct call to preach, but the teachers of religion in the area told her that there was nothing in the Scriptures to authorize such practices. So she organized meetings of women in Baltimore before launching an itinerant ministry. Jarena Lee, one of the "daughters of thunder," was the first to react, in 1811, against the restrictions placed upon preaching by women: "If the man can preach because the Savior died for him, why not the woman, since he died for her also?" The official acceptance of the ordination of women would take place only at the end of the nineteenth and the beginning of the twentieth centuries. The first black denomination to ordain a woman (Julia Foote), in 1895, would be the African Methodist Episcopal Church of Sion. In clandestine meetings, however, women did not wait for the blessing of the authorities, and they nourished the faith and hope of the black community.

The African Americans have always preferred a black preacher from their own people, whatever his or her denominational category. "Only a Negro can move a Negro," the saying goes.[25] Anthony Dawson of North Carolina recounted: "Most of the time we had white preachers, but when we had a Negro, it was heaven."[26] The slaves clearly perceived the difference between the white sermons and the black sermons. Nancy Williams had her own way of expressing it: "The old white preacher had the habit of speaking with his tongue to say nothing at all, but Jesus told us slaves to speak with our hearts."

This was a difference that was particularly remarked upon when there were no white ears around. But it was also a difference that said something about the rhythm and the music of the word, the intonation of the voice, as practiced by black versus white preachers.

The black sermon is as much a question of music as of the spoken word. It leads into a rhythm that has a crescendo causing one enter into the mystery that emerges into a collective exultation. That rhythmical word touches the heart of the community, and the community begins to dance its emotions. The sermon is a collective celebration, a dialogued religious experience in which each person is transported beyond himself or herself. The community expresses its approval and communes with the given word. It is not rare that the sermon leads to a hymn. Certain witnesses hold that the spirituals were born of a sermon in a sort of natural extension. The Spirit dances and sings in the collective body of the faithful.

To consider only the text is to mutilate the event that is the sermon of the black preacher—the manner is all! True preachers, besides, do not burden themselves with a completely written text. They depend on an outline and on the response of the assembly to their words. They value the words that have a direct impact on their audience and use them as a refrain. They purposely modulate the intensity their voice. They know the Bible stories by heart and they can express them with a poetic imagery that is easily remembered. They let their imagination wander under the impulsion of the text. The authentic sermon is the one that seizes the audience's heart, in a constant dialogue between the pastor and the congregation. The listeners encourage the witness of God: "Preach, brother, preach!" "Go on!" "Oh yes! How true!" As they recognizes their own vital problems, the congregation express their approval to commune even more with the preached word. When the pastor asserts, "Jesus will lead us," the people of the congregation confess: "I'm got my hand in my Jesus' hand."[27]

The art of preaching, through this interaction, lies in the progression of the collective emotion. The traditional sermon leads into a sort of sacred trance in which the preacher and the assembly mix their voices in a paroxysm of exultation that is, for each of them, the experience of heaven, the experience of communion with the Spirit in the here and now.

Such a style of preaching draws deeply from the preachers' heart. If they want to move the emotions of their congregation, they have to put into play their own feelings, organize them around a biblical text, and draw the attention of the assembly like a magnet by everything they do. The congregation must see what they see. The preacher is the principal actor in a decisive drama, that of the meeting of God with people. Preachers are the mediators of the power of the Spirit among their congregation. With a gesture, an inflection of the voice, they can lead their people from joy to ecstasy, from exuberance to hysteria. There lives in them a fire that wants only to spread and to burn.

The content of the sermon, evidently, is not secondary. Of course, the slave owners preferred that the preacher recommend patience here below to obtain a reward in heaven. But was not speaking of a transcendent order called heaven an invitation to call into question the legitimacy of the present institutions that deprived the children of God of their dignity? And was it not subversive to teach that all of humanity, in its ethnic diversity, descends from Adam and Eve? The black ministers sought to preach a gospel of freedom. But their margin of maneuver was small and they often walked a tightrope, desiring to be accepted by both whites and blacks. The Reverend Anderson Edwards recognized the two facets of his preaching: "Till freedom, I had to preach what they told me to. Master [Gaud] made me preach to the other niggers that the Good Book say that if niggers obey their master, they would go to Heaven. I knew that there was something better for them, but I did daresn't tell them so, 'lest I done it on the sly. That, I did lots. I told the niggers—but not so the Master could hear it—that, if they keep praying, the Lord would hear their prayers and set them free."[28]

Prophets of Almighty God, the preachers did their best to give the slaves the "courage to be," to reassure them of who they were before God, and to destroy any divine basis for slavery. It was a truly revolutionary enterprise, but one that could not lead to any immediate overthrow. The Day of the Lord would come sooner or later—the Christian slaves had an unshakable certainty of that, a certainty that defied any human institution. They did not call upon an earthly messiah; God would suffice for the task, and we reach God through faith. The religious service was the contemplation of the action of God, the moment when one places one's burden in God's hands, when one dreams of a better world, when optimism overcomes daily despair, and when the feeling of inferiority is replaced by a sense of spiritual equality.

To assume this religious role as the leader of a people was to assume a political role. The Africans did not know our Western distinction of religion and politics and never separated these areas. For them it was natural that the religious leader was also their social leader. That is why the preachers were there to establish abolitionist societies, to guarantee the stages of the Underground Railroad, to organize schools and universities. In black history, the pulpit has not been far from the political platform.

The Christian Religion of the Slaves

Though at the time of their arrival in North America nothing would have caused the slaves to expect it, religion would progressively become the most characteristic element, the central axis, and indeed the womb of African American culture. And surprisingly, that religion would be the religion of the master: the Christian religion.

Of course, we can't lose sight of the numbers. The black community did not convert as a bloc. The official statistics in 1860 put the percentage of Christian slaves at 12 percent. But it also seems clear that Christian influence extended well beyond the duly registered Christians.

Despite the slaves' belonging to different confessions, the Christian identity among them was seen as singular: they were the black church. The slaves truly had the feeling of belonging to just one Christian movement—a movement in which similarities far outweighed the differences. Indeed, although the Baptist and Methodist currents were the strongest, the collective consciousness did not pay much attention to particular confessions.

Did the conversion of the slaves to Christianity mark the disappearance of African religion? We have underscored that African religion was present at the beginning of the slave experience, and it remained so as long as the Christian religion maintained its foreign character and offered a justification of the unjustifiable: slavery. The slaves, however, were not able to recreate in North America a coherent religious system based on African religion. The ancestral lands were far away and the dispersion of the Africans on small isolated plantations did not permit effective communication among them. Their traditional view of the world progressively deteriorated. The dimension of magic was perhaps the one that resisted decay longest, because it was used to counter tragic wrongs in the new environment. Christianity filled the void the slaves felt, especially from the moment when it was expressed in a liturgical style reminiscent of the African exuberance and prodigality, widening the confined space within which the slave dwelled.

African Americans would accept the expressions of Christianity while reinterpreting some of its elements. A subtle negotiation was at work here, and we know only the later results in the clandestine church or in the independent black churches that formed. But religion would always be the envelope of human and cosmic existence. There was only one world fusing together the visible and the invisible, and that world became African-Christian. "The originality of African-American Christianity, then, lies neither in its African elements, nor in its Christian elements, but in its unique and creative synthesis of both."[29]

The evocation of African sensitivity should not, however, minimize the importance of what was borrowed from white culture. It surely was European Christianity that the African Americans accepted. And if they were not always sensitive to the subtleties of dogma, their expression of the faith was completely in line with what the Protestant revivals had valued: strong biblical roots, insistence on personal conversion, a God who is first and foremost a Savior, and a human being who is first and foremost a sinner. The names of their independent churches would always have, at the same time as their African character, a link with the white Christian tradition.

Because of its dependence on the gospel, black Christianity often has been accused of having a strong accent of pietism. It deeply involves the individual. The attention is turned toward another world, the present world being only a vale of tears. Heaven will console all the sorrows of the earth. Is it, then, a Christianity of escape, of compensation, of unwinding stress? Some celebrations can make us think so. This religion of the heart leaves the oppressive system intact because we must love our enemies.

At the same time, it is not difficult to demonstrate that the acceptance of the Christian faith allowed the slaves to strengthen their will to resist. As early as 1774, slaves in Massachusetts proclaimed the incompatibility of Christianity and slavery: "We have in common with other men a natural right to our freedoms without being deprived of them by our fellow man. . . . There is a great number of us sencear members of the Church of Christ."[30]

In 1779 two African slaves addressed a petition to the General Assembly of Connecticut: "Reason and Revelation unite to declare that we are creatures of this God who made of one blood and of one paternity all the nations of the earth; we see by our own reflection that we have the same faculties as our masters and that there is nothing to lead us to believe or suspect that we are more obliged to serve them as they, us, and the more we consider the question, the more we are convinced of our right to be free . . . and we cannot be convinced that we were made to be slaves."[31]

And we must not forget that in the nineteenth century it was the black church that supported all the insurrectional ferment. It furnished the place to assemble, circulated the information, and constituted the basic network.

We will look only at the example of Nat Turner. Apocalyptic visionary and charismatic leader, he led an insurrection that created a great panic in Southampton County, Virginia, and that claimed sixty white victims in a twenty-four-hour period and two hundred black victims in reprisal. It was the bloodiest revolt in the history of American slavery.

Nat Turner of Virginia was a prophet. From the first years of his life, he felt the impulse of the Spirit, "the one who spoke to the Prophets of old."[32] (We will see the continual interaction of the Spirit and of Christ in his vocation as a revolutionary.) Nat was marked out as special by his grandmother, "who was very religious," and by his master, "who belonged to the Church." He commented: "To a mind like mine, restless, inquisitive, and observant of everything that was passing, it is easy to suppose that religion was the subject to which it would be directed." He consecrated much of his time to prayer. The way others responded to him made him consider himself a superior being, with a subtle intelligence, called to a unique destiny. "Having soon discovered to be great, I must appear so, and so studiously avoided mixing in society, and wrapped myself in mystery, devoting my time to fasting and prayer."

As an adult, "hearing the Scriptures commented on at meetings [undoubtedly Methodist], I was struck with that particular passage which says: 'Seek ye the kingdom of heaven and all things shall be added unto you.' I reflected much on this passage and prayed daily for light on the subject. As I was praying one day at my plough, the Spirit spoke to me, saying: 'Seek ye the kingdom of heaven and all things shall be added unto you.' "After this revelation, Nat Turner continued to pray and received confirmation that he was "ordained for some great purpose in the hands of the Almighty." The events that unfolded reinforced him in that feeling. His household companions sincerely believed that his wisdom came from God.

At about twenty-one, Nat succeeded in escaping from his plantation. He spent thirty days in the woods but then—to the astonishment of the other slaves—returned to his master. He explained: "The reason for my return was, that the Spirit appeared to me and said I had my wishes directed to the things of the world, and not to the kingdom of heaven, and that I should return to the service of my earthly master." Immediately, the other slaves turned away from him.

"About this time I had a vision—and I saw white spirits and black spirits engaged in battle—and the sun was darkened—the thunder rolled in the skies and blood flowed in streams—and I heard a voice saying: 'Such is your luck, such you are called to see, and let it come rough or smooth, you must surely bear it.' " It was indeed the announcement of racial violence to come, an apocalyptic battle. As much as possible, Nat kept away from his companions "in the avowed purpose of serving the Spirit more fully."

Henceforth the visionary would seek to attain "true holiness." He received "true knowledge of faith." He had become perfect. The Spirit never ceased to accompany him. He saw the lights coming out of the "Savior's hands, stretched forth from east to west as they were extended on the cross on Calvary for redemption of sinners." He said: "Shortly afterward, while laboring in the field, I discovered drops of blood on the corn, as though it were dew from heaven."

The meaning of these miracles was evident for the prophet: "For as the blood of Christ had been shed on this earth, and had ascended to heaven for the salvation of sinners, and was now returning to earth again in the form of dew; and as the leaves on the trees bore the impression of the figures I had seen in the heavens, it was plain to me that the Saviour was about to lay down the yoke he had borne for the sins of men, and the great day of judgment was at hand." A new vision called Nat Turner to be baptized. He received that rite, but not without difficulty, for his faith does not appear to have been very orthodox. He had a power of vision and of healing that exceeded the accepted limits. Certain whites consider him a sorcerer. But he continued the ministry of preaching on the plantations.

On May 12, 1828, at the age of thirty-one, Turner received a decisive illumination: "I heard a loud noise in the heavens, and the Spirit instantly appeared to me and said the Serpent was loosened and Christ had laid down the yoke he had borne for the sins of men, and that I should take it on and fight against the Serpent, for the time was fast approaching when the first should be last and the last should be first."

The matter at hand was the combat against the serpent of slavery in the name of Christ. The African Americans, the combatants of the final hour, would overturn the social situation: the first would be last (Matthew 20:16; Mark 10:31). The visionary now awaited the heavenly sign that would indicate to him the beginning of the struggle against the slave system. It would come in the month of August 1831. The meeting he held on August 21 took on the appearance of a Last Supper before the ultimate battle and the final judgment.

Turner's rebellion was short-lived, and he himself was arrested and brought to trial. When Thomas R. Gray, Turner's lawyer, asked him if he had any regrets, if he had not made a mistake, Nat Turner replied: "Was not Christ crucified?" He saw himself as a black Christ dying for his brothers and sisters of color. He had been baptized in the Spirit, had borne the yoke; now he awaited crucifixion. Ironically, the name of the Virginia town where he was hanged on November 11, 1831, was Jerusalem. His vocation had been that of a synthesis of the Old Testament prophet and of the Jesus of the Last Judgment. His Christ was the horseman of the apocalypse (Revelation 19:11-16). He would be regarded by many of his fellow African Americans as a legendary hero and the instigator of the first war against slavery (the second being the Civil War).

This example of the African American struggle reveals the apocalyptic dimension of the slaves' Christianity. For those in chains, Revelation is one of the fundamental books of the New Testament because it is the realization of hope. The judgment of God hangs over history and reveals that evil will not have the last word. Certainly it established a great distance between the masters and the slaves. It was in the assurance of the judgment of God on their enemies that the African Americans found the energy for a multifaceted and yet always dangerous struggle.

Yet if black Christianity is as much a dynamic of conversion as it is a yeast of struggle, it is because it is a place of affirmation, recognition, and identification. Against all odds, Christianity allowed the slaves to recognize their humanity. It was the place where they were able to feel themselves exist as persons and as a people because it was God who decreed their identity and their dignity. Thanks to the Bible stories, the Africans recovered their confidence in life, preserved their moral health, and discovered a future. Their existence no longer could be defined only by the master's whip; there was another reality, another scale of values, and another world. And the strength of the gospel brought into existence a "people of God," a coherent community who knew there were limits to submission.

In this experience of faith, there was especially God—a loving God who was near and active. Far from being an obscure force of the universe, God was the familiar support, the attentive Parent. Where evil abounded, God made good superabundant. One could appeal to God, and God would respond. The African Americans existed as a people from the moment they could call themselves "people of God." It was in finding God that they found themselves and acquired an unbeatable freedom. What good fortune it was to count in the eyes of God and to be created in God's image and likeness! The great joy of the slaves, which made relative their present suffering, was to belong to the family of God, to be "children of God." God does not discriminate among persons: all are brothers and sisters in Christ.

Recognized by Almighty God, the African Americans now had the strength to assert themselves before humans. And in the universe of slavery, one did not assert oneself without opposing other. One had to put up with the implacable white hegemony, but at the same time one could create areas of survival and expression. Faith put up a protective shell that the continual aggression of the whites could slide off. Beyond Protestant individualism, it wove, among the African Americans, ties that strengthened their sense of community and their ethnic pride. It gave especially an invincible hope in the final triumph of justice.

We must abandon the opposition between a Christianity of resignation and a Christianity of rebellion, between a pragmatism that adjusts to a situation and a prophetic stance that contests it. The Christian faith is first of all a condition for survival, a form of hope. Eugene D. Genovese, an artist on the subject, recognizes it well:

> Afro-Americans accepted Christianity's celebration of the individual soul and turned it into a weapon of personal and community survival. But their apparent indifference to sin, not to be confused with an indifference to injustice or wrongdoing, guaranteed retention of the collective, life-affirming quality of the African tradition and thus also became a weapon for personal and community survival. The slaves refashioned the Christianity they had embraced; they conquered the religion of those who had conquered them. . . . The slaves developed an Afro-American and Christian humanism that affirmed joy in life in the face of every trial.[33]

The new faith allowed them to maintain a distance from the white world. There was a Master above the master. All the cultural and religious expressions contributed to create an area of freedom, an alternative. Lawrence W. Levine says as much in the conclusion of a study of black religion:

> The slaves' expressive arts and sacred beliefs were more than merely a series of outlets or strategies; they were instruments of life, of sanity, of health, and of self-respect. Slave music, slave religion, slave folk beliefs— the entire sacred world of the black slaves—created the necessary space between the slaves and their owners and were the means of preventing legal slavery from becoming spiritual slavery. In addition to the world of the masters which the slave inhabited and accommodated to, as they had to, they created and maintained a world apart which they shared with each other and which remained their own domain, free of control of those who ruled the earth.[34]

Is Christianity, so defined, a syncretism? Surely it is, if we remove from this term the pejorative connotations it has received in current theological vocabulary. There is syncretism as soon as there is a meeting of two religious traditions and a new religious structure comes from one of those traditions. The black people lived through this meeting of their traditional religion with white Christianity in an environment of oppression. Christianity was the dominant tradition that organized the new belief system. But black Christianity remains marked by African sensitivity, even on the level of the synthesis. It is a Christianity of authenticity and liberation, of affirmation and exuberance, that is able to resist the pressure of despair and dehumanization.

We will be able to confirm everything I have written about the Christian religion of the slaves through a precise and concrete example: the Negro spirituals. The songs of the slaves were, indeed, at the center of African American life in the nineteenth century. They are at the summit of religious expression.

Notes

1. John B. Boles, *Masters and Slaves in the House of the Lord: Race and Religion in the American South, 1740–1870* (Lexington: University Press of Kentucky, 1988), 14.

2. Quoted in Eileen Southern, *Histoire de la musique noire américaine* (Paris: Buchet/Chastel, 1976), 72.

3. I have described a typical service in *Dieu est noir: histoire, religion et théologie des Noirs américains* (Paris: Centurion, 1977), 144–50.

4. Quoted in Milton C. Sernett, ed., *Afro-American Religious History: A Documentary Witness* (Durham, N.C.: Duke University Press, 1985), 67–68.

5. Quoted in William J. Faulkner, *The Days When the Animals Talked* (Chicago: Follett, 1977), 54.

6. Quoted in Norman R. Yetman, ed., *Voices from Slavery* (New York and San Francisco: Holt, Rinehart & Winston, 1970), 75.

7. Quoted in ibid., 13.

8. John B. Boles, *The Irony of Southern Religion* (New York: Peter Lang, 1994), 50–51.

9. James L. Smith, *The Autobiography of James L. Smith* (Norwich, Conn.: Bulletin, 1881), 27.

10. Quoted in George Rawick, ed., *The American Slave: A Composite Autobiography*, 19 vols. (Westport, Conn.: Greenwood, 1972–1979), 3:19.

11. Quoted in ibid., 12:247.

12. The two last quotations are from Clifton H. Johnson, ed., *God Struck Me Dead* (Philadelphia: Pilgrim, 1969), 11.

13. H. G. Spaulding, "Under the Palmetto," *Continental Monthly* 4 (August 1863): 196–97.

14. Quoted in Michel Favre, *Esclaves et planteurs* (Paris: Julliard, 1970), 128.

15. *The Nation* 4 (May 30, 1867): 432–33.

16. Guy-Claude Balmir, *Du chant au poème. Essai de littérature sur le chant et la poésie populaire des Noirs américains* (Paris: Payot, 1982), 46.

17. Jon Michael Spencer, *Protest and Praise: Sacred Music of Black Religion* (Minneapolis: Fortress, 1990), 143.

18. Rawick, ed., *The American Slave* 2:135.

19. Daniel Alexander Payne, *Recollections of Seventy Years* (Nashville: A.M.E. Sunday School Union, 1888), 253–55.

20. Quoted in Howard Thurman, *Deep River and The Negro Spiritual Speaks of Life and Death* (Richmond, Ind.: Friends United Press, 1975), 11.

21. W. E. B. Du Bois, *The Souls of Black Folk* (Chicago: McClurg, 1969), 171.

22. Thurman, *Deep River,* 11.

23. Quoted in Fisk University Social Sciences Institute, *Unwritten History of Slavery* (Nashville: Fisk University Social Sciences Institute, 1945), 20.

24. Milton C. Sernett, *Black Religion and American Evangelicalism, 1787–1865* (Metuchen, N.J.: American Theological Library Association, 1975), 93–101.

25. Quoted in "The Religious Life of the Negro Slave," *Harper's New Monthly Magazine,* 1863, 677.

26. Quoted in Norman R. Yetman, ed., *Life under the "Peculiar Institution": Selections from the Slave Narrative Collection* (New York: Holt, Rinehart & Winston, 1970), 95.

27. Quoted in Balmir, *Du chant au poème,* 85.

28. Quoted in James Mellon, ed., *Bullwhip Days: The Slaves Remember* (New York: Weidenfeld & Nicolson, 1988), 191.

29. Charles Joyner, " 'Believer I Know': The Emergence of African American Christianity," in *African American Christianity: Essays in History,* ed. Paul E. Johnson (Berkeley: University of California Press, 1994), 37.

30. Quoted in Albert J. Raboteau, *Slave Religion: The "Invisible Institution" in the Antebellum South* (New York: Oxford University Press, 1978), 290.

31. Quoted in Vincent Harding, *There Is a River* (New York: Harcourt Brace Jovanovich, 1981), 43.

32. This quotation and the following ones are taken from *The Confessions of Nat Turner, the Leader of the Late Insurrection in Southampton, Va. As Fully and Voluntarily Made to Thomas R. Gray* (Richmond, Va.: Gray, 1832), 7–22. They seem trustworthy.

33. Eugene D. Genovese, *Roll, Jordan, Roll: The World the Slaves Made* (New York: Pantheon, 1974), 212.

34. Lawrence W. Levine, *Black Culture and Black Consciousness: Afro-American Folk Thought from Slavery to Freedom* (New York: Oxford University Press, 1977), 80.

Bibliography

Alho, Olli. *The Religion of the Slaves: A Study of the Religious Tradition and Behavior of Plantation Slaves in the United States, 1830–1865.* Helsinki: Suomalainen Tiedeakatemia, 1980.

Balmir, Guy-Claude. *Du chant au poème.* Paris: Payot, 1982.

Blassingame, John W. *The Slave Community: Plantation Life in the Antebellum South,* rev. ed. New York: Oxford University Press, 1979.

Boles, John B. *The Irony of Southern Religion.* New York: Peter Lang, 1994.

———. *Masters and Slaves in the House of the Lord: Race and Religion in the American South, 1740–1870.* Lexington: University Press of Kentucky, 1988.

———. "Slaves in Biracial Protestant Churches." In *Varieties of Southern Religious Experience,* ed. Samuel S. Hill. Baton Rouge and London: Louisiana State University Press, 1988, 95–114.

Clarke, Erskine. *Wrestlin' Jacob: A Portrait of Religion in the Old South.* Atlanta: Knox, 1979.

Coleman, William E., Jr. "A Study of African American Slave Narratives as a Source for a Contemporary, Constructive Black Theology." Ph.D. Diss., University of California, Berkeley, 1993.

Costen, Melva Wilson. *African American Christian Worship.* Nashville: Abingdon, 1993.

Creel, Margaret Washington. *"A Peculiar People": Slave Religion and Community Culture among the Gullahs.* New York: New York University Press, 1988.

Dixie, Quinton H., and Cornel West, eds. *The Courage to Hope: From Black Suffering to Human Redemption.* Boston: Beacon, 1999.

Fulop, Timothy E., and Albert J. Raboteau, eds. *African American Religion: Interpretive Essays in History and Culture.* New York and London: Routledge, 1997.

Hopkins, Dwight N. *Down, Up, and Over: Slave Religion and Black Theology.* Minneapolis: Fortress, 2000.

———. *Shoes That Fit Our Feet: Sources for a Constructive Black Theology.* Maryknoll, N.Y.: Orbis, 1993.

Hopkins, Dwight N., and George Cummings. *Cut Loose Your Stammering Tongue: Black Theology in the Slave Narratives.* Maryknoll, N.Y.: Orbis, 1991.

Jones, Norrece T. *Born a Child of Freedom, Yet a Slave.* Hanover, N.H., and London: University Press of New England, 1990.

Joyner, Charles. " 'Believer I Know': The Emergence of African American Christianity." In *African American Christianity: Essays in History,* ed. Paul E. Johnson. Berkeley: University of California Press, 1994, 18–46.

Mathews, Donald G. *Religion in the Old South.* Chicago: University of Chicago Press, 1977.

Oates, Stephen B. *The Fires of Jubilee: Nat Turner's Rebellion.* New York: Harper & Row, 1975.

Raboteau, Albert J. "The Slave Church in the Era of the American Revolution." In *Slavery and Freedom in the Age of the American Revolution,* ed. Ira Berlin and Ronald Hoffman. Charlottesville: University Press of Virginia, 1983.

———. *Slave Religion: The "Invisible Institution" in the Antebellum South.* New York: Oxford University Press, 1978.

Rawick, George P., ed. *From Sundown to Sunup: The Making of Black Community.* Vol. 1 of *The American Slave: A Composite Biography.* Westport, Conn.: Greenwood, 1972.

Sernett, Milton C. *Afro-American Religious History: A Documentary Witness.* Durham, N.C.: Duke University Press, 1985.

Simpson, Robert. "The Shout and Shouting in Slave Religion of the United States." *The Southern Quarterly* 23, no. 3 (spring 1985): 34–47.

Stuckey, Sterling. *Slave Culture: Nationalist Theory and the Foundations of Black America.* New York: Oxford University Press, 1987.

Webber, Thomas L. *Deep Like Rivers: Education in the Slave Quarter Community.* New York: Norton, 1978.

4

"All God's chillun got a song."

What Is a Spiritual?

"The Spirit will not come without a song."
—African saying

IN THE AFRICAN AMERICAN RELIGIOUS SERVICE, whatever its particular context, everything begins and ends with music. A religious service without music simply does not exist, for the Spirit comes on the wings of a spiritual. The pedagogy of the liturgical experience goes from the spoken word to the song, from the song to exultation. While prayer, witnessing, and preaching (the other fundamental ingredients of the African American service) are calls to the community by an individual, the song is the immediate context of the community's experience of God where each individual is thrust into the exultation of all.

In order to understand the proper nature of the African American religious hymn in the era of slavery, one must note the importance of music in Africa. At the same time, we also should not underestimate the influence of European Protestant hymnology, which set the tone for the evangelical revivals. The slaves sang in the cotton fields, in their cabins, and in the churches. The spiritual would be an expression of Christian faith confronted with the distress of slavery and set to music, with a double fertilization from Africa and Europe. Even if the spiritual was a synthesis, it was a solidly original creation to the point of becoming the primary contribution of the American black to world Christianity. In it we discover "one of the most subtle meetings of the European and African cultures."[1] Syncretism was surpassed through a new creation that went beyond its obvious sources.

Song in West Africa

Obviously, we do not have recordings of African music from the time of the slave trade. We are not deprived, however, of all information, thanks to the quality of the oral tradition: today's practices are rooted in past centuries. We have, especially, the accounts of the first explorers to Africa, who noted details that concern us directly.

The first report comes from Richard Jobson, an English captain who visited Gambia from 1620 to 1621 to evaluate its commercial potential. On his return he wrote: "There is without doubt, no people on earth more naturally affected to the sound of musicke than these people; which the principal persons do hold as an ornament of their state, so as when wee come to see them their musicke will seldom be wanting."[2] And Olaudah Equiano, in his autobiography, recognized: "We are almost a nation of dancers, musicians, and poets. Every great event, such as a triumphant return from battle, or other cause of public rejoicing, is celebrated in public dances, which are accompanied with songs and music suited to the occasion."[3] Despite the diversity of peoples in Africa, it would seem that we can speak of a homogeneity of style in African songs.

What appears then, as expressed by Equiano, is the connection of the song to the dance, of the audible and the visual. I have already underlined the central place of dance in African religion as a "danced religion" (A. Métraux). Dance is, at the same time, a means of expression, of recreation, and of communication. The aim is not to amuse, but to underscore each event in the life of the family or the tribe, whether it might have a bellicose or peaceful connotation. Dancing in a circle is the more usual practice, with (sometimes) a couple or an individual dancing in the center. Using the total flexibility of the body, it can end in a trance.

In Africa, musical expression does not ignore instruments, notably strings and most importantly the drum. The drum is made from a hollowed-out tree trunk and the skin of a leopard or a sheep. It is struck with the palm of the hand and not with sticks. It sustains rhythm and transmits messages concerning the relationships among people or with the invisible world. That is why the North American planters quickly became suspicious of it. The Virginia colony had already banned the use of the drum by 1676.

The first characteristic of African chant, affecting the body directly, is the rhythm, or rather the crisscrossing of different rhythms, called polyrhythms. Rhythm in African singing is what melody is to European singing. Africans love to do syncopation, rendering more and more complex the best-known melody to create a sort of tonal mosaic. They vary the inflections and use a vastly extended vocal register. They do not hesitate to overlap different voices with a great art of counterpoint. The effect produced leads to a kind of enchantment. The felt emotion has to grow.

Also typical is the call-response structure with the alternation, or even partial superposition, of a soloist (or group of singers) and a multivoiced choir. The repetitive and unchanging response of the choir gives a solid base for the improvisations of the soloist. But it is the soloist who leads the singing, embellishing the basic melody and adapting the text to the circumstances. Thus there is a balance between tradition and innovation, antiphony and improvisation. The art of improvisation is such that it is sometimes difficult to recognize the original song, for the soloists, creating in the moment, have recourse to special effects such as falsettos, shouts, grunts, and guttural sounds.

Mungo Park, the explorer, transcribed the song the cotton weavers had improvised while giving him shelter for the night:

> The winds roared, and the rains fell,
> The poor white man, weak and tired,
> Came to sit at the foot of our tree.
> He doesn't have a mother to bring him milk,
> No wife to grind his corn.

> *Chorus:*
> Let us pity the white man
> No mother has he to bring him milk,
> No wife to grind his corn.[4]

In African music, no one remains outside of the singing; the assembly participates spontaneously by clapping their hands and stamping their feet while swaying their bodies. They transform acoustic stimulation into kinetic energy. As John Lovell remarks: "The African rarely plays *for* someone as Westerners do; he usually plays *with* someone. An inactive audience to a musical performance simply does not exist. Song is the bond of fellowship between men and tribes; music is the essential part of the African's inmost being. It has the power to liberate him fully."[5] It ensures the socialization of all. Everybody sings.

The aim of African music has always been to translate daily and spiritual experiences into sounds: cradle songs, reflective songs, historical epic songs, fertility songs, celebration songs, and songs of death and bereavement. It is modeled on the life of the community, and often the words are improvised according to the situation. It brings to the surface the most intimate aspects of the black soul, the oral culture of an ethnic group. It is the means of transmission of the collective memory from generation to generation. But the tradition is never frozen in time, because the improvisation imagines the sounds and the words that best reflect what is felt at the moment itself.

We cannot be surprised, then, that hardly had they been embarked on the slave ships when the slaves began to sing about their plight. "[The slaves on the ship] sang songs of painful lamentation. . . . They sang songs that expressed their fear of being beaten, of lacking food, especially African food, and never seeing their homeland again."[6]

The Evolution of Religious Chant in White Churches

Though it has at times been the source of conflicts and even schisms, music has always been a vital element for Christian worship in North America. Two traditions that issued from the sixteenth-century Reformation had the greatest influence: that of Calvin in Geneva and that of Wesley. The latter, influenced by the Moravian Brethren, returned to the Lutheran heritage. We know that Martin Luther had insisted on singing in the assemblies.

While Ulrich Zwingli did not extol music in the liturgical service, John Calvin was as vigorous as Luther in introducing biblical chant in the language of the people. Reacting against the Latin liturgy, he decided to limit the singing to the psalms and to a few fundamental texts of the Scriptures, such as the Ten Commandments. His inspiration was his experience in Strasbourg, where the psalms had been highlighted. The Geneva Psalter of 1542, which was revised a few times, became the model for most of the Reformed churches. Theodore Beza and Clément Marot made a versified edition in 1562 using music by Louis Bourgeois. The churches of England and Scotland adopted the psalmody of Calvin rather than the hymnody of Luther.

It was this heritage of versified psalms that the Anglicans and Puritans brought to North America. The first book published in North America (1640) was the famous *Bay Psalm Book*, a psalter that did not have a musical notation, so that it was necessary to learn the melody and memorize it. It was the choir director's duty to intone the psalm and give the tone. The method called "lining out" was explained by the Reverend John Cotton in a 1647 treatise: "It will be a necessary helpe, that the lines of the Psalme, be openly read beforehand, line after line, or two lines together, that so they who want either books or skill to reade, may know what is to be sung, and joyne with the rest in the dutie of singing."[7] The principal cantor, who stood facing the assembly, therefore would read the verse or verses before giving the tone and singing loudly and clearly enough to lead the rest of the faithful. The chant was very slow and performed in a monotone, each syllable marked by a whole note and often more. We can cite the example of the versified version of Psalm 19:

> The heavens doe declare
> The majesty of God:
> lso the firmament shews forth
> His handy-work abroad.

Day speaks to day, knowledge
night hath to night declar'd.
There neither speach nor language is,
where their voyce is not heard.[8]

Since the psalms are addressed to God rather than to Christ, as the flowering
of Jewish piety, during the eighteenth century we see an evolution in religious
music with the passage from the psalms to hymns.

The great reformer was Isaac Watts. Born in Southampton in 1674, young
Isaac showed early signs of musical talent. Having become an independent
minister (that is, a moderate Calvinist who avoided doctrinal quarrels), he
published his first work in 1707, *Hymns and Spiritual Songs,* which was the
hymnbook that marked the history of British Christianity most profoundly. It was
reedited in Boston in 1839. It contained, first of all, hymns that were paraphrases
of Scripture, especially from the New Testament, plus 110 hymns on religious
subjects without a direct relationship with scriptural texts, and finally a few hymns
for the celebration of the Lord's Supper. Here is what Psalm 19 becomes under
Watts's poetic pen:

1. God of the morning, at whose voice
The cheerful sun makes haste to rise,
And like a giant doth rejoice
To run his journey through the skies.

2. From the fair chambers of the east
The circuit of his race begins,
And without weariness or rest
Round the whole earth he flies and shines.

3. O like the sun may I fulfill
Th' appointed Duties of the Day,
With ready Mind and active Will
March on and keep my heavenly way.

4. But I shall rove and lose the Race,
If God my Sun should disappear,
And leave me in this World's wild Maze
To follow every wand'ring Star.[9]

In 1719 Watts published his *Psalms of David Imitated,* which also became very
popular. He did not use all the psalms, but he took care to transform them into
Christian hymns. He filled them with the language and themes of the New

Testament. Throughout his compositions Watts sought to express an evangelical faith in poetic terms. His melodies are much more alluring than those used in the classic psalters. However, the first reaction of the official churches was negative. So much so, in fact, that Christians would sing the hymns of Watts outside of the churches. The Church of England would never approve Watts's work. Only in 1861 would a first collection of hymns appear in that church. The American Anglicans, however, would accept the style of hymns more quickly. A rift was, in general, quite clear: the progressives of the evangelical wing adopted the hymns of Watts, while the traditionalists resisted them. During the awakenings, which followed the visit of Whitefield to North America in 1740, some Presbyterian parishes were divided on the question of hymns. Only in the nineteenth century would a climate of peace prevail on this issue.

Admirers of Watts, the Wesley brothers used his hymns in the Methodist communities, and they would develop their own creations. It was in Savannah, Georgia, that John and Charles Wesley compiled the first book of hymns ever made in an Anglican church, and they published it in 1737 in Charleston, South Carolina. In this collection of seventy hymns, thirty-five were by Dr. Watts. The Wesleys published a total of fifty-six hymnals, with a growing proportion of the collections being Charles Wesley's compositions. In his lifetime he would write some six thousand hymns. The two brothers were influenced by the Moravian Brethren, a Christian group of German origin, whom they met on the ship carrying them to North America. They were attracted to the Moravians' sentimental approach to Jesus. They would then write texts that emphasized the themes of expiation, of the need for Christian perfection, and of the continuing role of the Holy Spirit. In general, the hymns of Charles Wesley are less ecumenical and less elegant than those of Watts. The music, however, is more varied and often of excellent quality, with the use of music by composers such as George Handel.

The hymn, then, triumphed in the nineteenth century. Its style, however, would be modified again in the melting pot of the famous camp meetings, those mass interracial assemblies in which fervor was expressed in emotions and exultation. With an unlettered population, everything had to be simple and direct, using secular music and attractive refrains that everyone could learn quickly. The text paraphrased biblical passages, and the refrain consisted especially of multiple alleluias or similar expressions of praise. To distinguish them from hymns and psalms, the new songs, which were never longer than a few verses, were called "spiritual songs." They were characterized by the choir (which sang verses, while all sang the refrain), the use of popular melodies, and free verses that referred to daily experience as well as to the Scriptures. There were even "errant verses" that had enormous success among the participants and that could be grafted onto various compositions. In his 1801 collection Richard Allen gave a few examples:

Halleluia to the Lamb,
Who has purchased our pardon;
We will praise him again
When we pass over the Jordan.

There's glory, there's glory in my soul;
Come, mourners, see salvation roll.

Firm united let us be,
In the bonds of charity;
As a band of brothers join'd,
Loving God and all mankind.[10]

The black slaves were not simply passive witnesses of this musical evolution; they were often its initiators and propagators, as we will now see.

When the Slaves Began to Sing

More than any other manifestation of the Africans' culture, their music crossed the Atlantic, and the slaves would fill their various activities with song, whether pleasant or painful. A former slave, Vinnie Brunson, explained this:

De nigger used to sing to nearly everything he did. Hit wuz jes' de way he 'spressed his feelin's, and hit made him relieved. If he wuz happy, hit made him happier; if he wuz sad, hit made him feel better. An' so he jes' naturally sings his feelin's.

De timber nigger, he sings as he cuts de logs, 'an keeps de time wid his axe. Women sing as dey bend over de washtub. De cotton choppers sing as dey chops de cotton. De mother sings as she rocks her baby to sleep. An' dey all sing in de meetin's, an' at de baptizin's, an' at de funerals.

Singin' is de nigger's mos' joy an' dey mos' comfort. When dey needs all dese things, de sing 'bout de joys in de nex' world and' de trouble in dis. Dey first jes' sung de 'ligious songs. Den, dey commenced to sing 'bout de life here. An' when dey sung of bofe, dey called dem de "spirituals." De ole way to sing dem was to keep time wid de clappin' of de han's an' pattin' of de feet. Dey sing dem in different ways fur different occasions. At a meetin', when dey shouts, dey sing joyful, an' when dey sing de same song at a funeral, dey sing hit slow and moanful. When dey sing de same song in de fiel's, hit is sung quickly, if dey workin' fas'. If dey is tired, hit is sung slow. If hit is sung at Christmas, den hit is sung gay an' happy.[11]

The masters encouraged their slaves to sing at work, for it produced a better rhythm of labor. For the slaves, it was a way to think about something else, to keep up their morale, and to strengthen the cohesion of the group. The brothers John and Alan Lomax described a scene in which the slaves attacked a rocky soil rhythmically with a song more or less improvised under the watchful eye of the foreman (the leader of the song):

The hot southern sun glistens on the shiny brown muscles of a group of workers. Over the shoulders of the singers, the pickaxes arc like rainbows. As the tools penetrate the soil, the men give a deep guttural grunt; their contained force passes into the handles of their tools, and they relax their bodies in preparation for the next blow. The song leader now begins, the handle of his pickaxe whirling between his palms, the point blazing in the sun: "Take this hammer—Ugh!"

The men grunt as their pickaxes bite into the stony soil together. They join their voices to the words of the leader, following them, one in harmony, another in saying the words, yet another mumbling them between his teeth, while another shouts out in a high and thin falsetto over the voices of his companions. At the last syllable, the picks come down again, bite anew into a piece of rock, and again, a grunt is exhaled with their breath: "Go bring it to the boss—Ugh!"

The picks all whirl at the same time in the sunlight and coming down once again, they resound in concert in the soil, with the possible exception of two or three of them which rebound once or twice in a sort of syncopation. When the soloist comes to the third "Go bring it to the boss," he holds on the word "boss" as long as he can, looks in the direction of the master and smiles broadly; his companions hide their laughter and relax for a moment for they know he is giving them a bit of rest; then bam! the steel bites into the rocky soil and all the team shouts so loudly at the last phrase that the hill sends back an echo.[12]

Caustic humor was never absent from these songs. For proof of this observation, I will give only the evocation of the "mistress of the big house" compared to the black "mammy," and the labor of the slave under the strict discipline of the master, in the following lyric:

Missus in de big house,
Mammy in de yard.
Missus holdin' her white hands,
Mammy workin' hard,
Mammy workin' hard,
Mammy workin' hard.
Missus holdin' her white hands,
Mammy workin' hard.

Ol' marse ridin' all time,
Niggers workin' 'roun'.
Marse sleepin' day time,
Niggers diggin' in de groun',
Niggers diggin' in de groun',
Niggers diggin' in de groun'.
Marse sleepin' day time,
Niggers diggin' in de groun'.[13]

The song carries an acid judgment on a situation of inequality and exploitation.

Of course, the slaves sang as they returned to their quarters. In 1853 a traveler in South Carolina was surprised to hear a nocturnal clamor: "Suddenly one [a slave] raised such a sound as I had never heard before, a long, loud musical shout, rising and falling, and breaking into falsetto, his voice ringing through the woods in the clear frosty night air, like a bugle call. As he finished, the melody was caught up by another, and then, another, and then, by several in chorus."[14]

Through all these musical manifestations, a communal identity was built up. The slaves did not have a wide choice of means to recognize each other in the diversity of their origins and grow into belonging to a community of destiny. But song was one of them. It allowed the group to exist, and to last, on the basis of a common identity that was forged by the creativity of vocal expression.

The whites did not take long to recognize the vocal aptitudes of their slaves. They then would seek to convert them to Christianity through music, for it was music that attracted them over and above anything else in the religious experience. And we will find in the evolution of the attitudes of African Americans the three stages of psalmody, hymn singing, and camp-meeting songs.

It was first of all the Anglicans who introduced the African Americans to the practice of lining out the psalm chant following a choir leader. This repetitive practice suited perfectly a population who did not know how to read or to decipher written music. And especially it strangely resembled the call-response of traditional African singing. In their correspondence for the years 1745 to 1751, some New York missionaries revealed that the "chant of a psalm produces a good effect: it attracted many Negroes to apply themselves more to the study of reading." In 1756 Samuel Davies, a Presbyterian pastor, wrote from Virginia: "A number of them [blacks] spent the whole night in my kitchen, and sometimes when I would awaken at around two or three in the morning, a torrent of sacred harmonies filled my room and transported my soul to Heaven. . . . I cannot but observe that the *Negroes,* above all the Human Species that I ever knew, have an Ear for Musick, and a kind of extatic Delight in Psalmody."[15]

Also, the whites entrusted to blacks the teaching of music in certain schools in the North. In 1768 William Knox observed: "The Negroes in general have an ear for musick, and might without much trouble be taught to sing hymns, which would be the pleasantest way of instructing them, and bringing them speedily to offer praise to God."[16] In 1784 Bishop Porteus of London even invited the clergy to compose new hymns bearing in mind the musical traditions of the slaves. These hymns were to have short texts with melodies that approximated as much as possible those that the slaves themselves sang every day.

We must acknowledge that the slaves loved the hymns of Dr. Watts, which offered them a biblical and poetic imagery in which God blessed the poor and delivered the captives. The message would not be forgotten. It is rather ironic to remark that one of the favorite hymns of blacks in the eighteenth century (and one that remains a favorite), "Amazing Grace," was composed by an Englishman who, before his conversion, had participated in the slave trade for six years as the captain of a slave ship.

In 1801, in answer to the needs of the black Christian community, Richard Allen published a *Collection of Spiritual Songs and Hymns*. It contained fifty-four hymns, without music, of which some were by Isaac Watts and the Wesley brothers, while others were chosen from among the more popular Methodist and Baptist hymns. It is interesting to note that already in the second edition in the same year, Allen added ten hymns that he had composed. He also modified the texts of the previously selected fifty-four hymns—he replaced complicated words and phrases by simpler expressions and added refrains to the usual stanzas. Thus African sensitivity was at work in a corpus of European texts. This made Elizabeth Kilham, a southern teacher, remark: "Watts and Newton will never recognize their works through the transformations they have had at the hands of their Black admirers."[17]

But the experience that would foster, at the same time, the massive conversion of the slaves and their musical creativity was that of the camp meeting of the Second Awakening. In that effervescent celebration of Christian salvation the children of Africa would rediscover their roots while assimilating the colorful and down-to-earth language of the evangelical preachers. There is abundant testimony on the strong presence of blacks in the singing. After having attended a camp meeting in Georgia, the Swedish novelist Frederika Bremer wrote: "What a magnificent choir! It probably came from the Black part of the assembly, for it was three times more numerous than that of the Whites, and their voices are naturally pure and beautiful. . . . The Black tents overflowed with religious fervor, each one at a different stage. One group intoned, in a remarkable way, the *Spiritual, Canaan.* . . . At five thirty the next morning, we could still hear from all sides, the hymns of the Blacks."[18] According to another witness of the participation of the slaves, coming this time from Pennsylvania: "Their shouts and hymns had such a force that the singing of the Whites was often drowned out by the echoes and the reverberations of the tumultuous voices of the colored."

This vocal effervescence did not please everyone. And we know of the bitter remarks of the Methodist John F. Watson, in 1819, who denounced as evil the influence of blacks on Methodist practices.

We have too, a growing evil, in the practice of singing in our places of public and society worship, *merry airs,* adapted from old *songs,* to hymns of our composing: often miserable as poetry, and senseless as matter, and most frequently composed and first sung by the illiterate *blacks* of the society. . . . Here ought to be considered too, a most exceptionable error, which has the tolerance of at least the rulers of our camp meetings. In the *blacks'* quarter, the coloured people get together, and sing for hours together, short scraps of disjointed affirmations, pledges, or prayers, lengthened out with long repetition *choruses.* These are all sung in the merry chorus-manner of the southern harvest field, or husking frolic method of the slave blacks. . . . With every word so sung, they have a sinking of one or other leg of the body alternately; producing an audible sound of the feet at every step, and as manifest as the steps of actual Negro dancing in Virginia, &c. If some, in the meantime sit, they strike the sounds alternately on each thigh. What in the name of religion, can countenance or tolerate such gross perversions of true religion! but the evil is only occasionally condemned, and the example has already visibly affected the manners of some whites. From this cause, I have known in some camp meetings, from 50 to 60 people crowd into one tent, after the public devotions had closed, and these continue the whole night, singing tune after tune, (though with occasional episodes of prayer) scarce one of which was in our hymn books.[19]

The spontaneity of the slaves found emulators, and the tabernacle songs showed African influences, such as syncopation, altered notes (*mi* flat, *ti* flat, the blues notes), the use of minor keys, the improvisation of couplets, melodies borrowed from popular songs and easily remembered airs, and the use of running verses that could fit all circumstances.[20] And on the last day of the camp meeting, the slaves would not hesitate to engage in a gigantic ring shout.

It is not surprising that a white report of 1856 would say: "The only musical population of this country are the Negroes of the South. . . . Might not our countrymen all learn a lesson from these simple children of Africa? We are a silent and reserved people. . . . Let us not be ashamed to learn the art of happiness from the poor bondman at the South. . . . If [the slaves'] love of music which is inborn in them, could be inbred in us, it would do much to lighten the anxiety and care which brood on every face and weigh on every heart."[21]

The Birth of a Spiritual

At what moment can we baptize a black song a Negro spiritual? The term does not appear before the Civil War, and it undoubtedly comes from the common expression "spiritual song" in Colossians 3:16. However, from the moment the African Americans adapted to their own sensitivity the singing of the psalms and hymns—that is from 1760, when the hymns of Watts were taught to the slaves in Virginia—the spiritual was in gestation. It would take a long period of interaction with the music and texts of the white churches for the Negro spiritual to affirm its own personality.

What is certain is that we cannot find the precise moment when the black religious chant was transformed into the form of a spiritual. The first versions were never written and were lost in the night of slavery. The best witnesses that we can gather come from European visitors in the region. They heard the slaves sing, and sometimes create, an original melody during a religious service.

One of the oldest records goes back to the middle of the eighteenth century. During the visit of one of the Wesleys to America, the assembly was so numerous that the slaves had to leave their usual balcony and listen to the preacher from outside the church. After the sermon, those who felt a strong desire for conversion were invited to go up to the altar. An old black woman named Mary was so moved that she went into the church, approached the altar, and expressed a great desire to become a member of that church. She was refused, and since she was so insistent, she was counseled to join one of the black churches in the neighborhood. In tears Mary went back through the church muttering: "One of these days, I will tell God how you treated me." Witnessing the scene, the blacks outside began to sing:

Oh, Mary, don't you weep,
Don't you mourn,
Pharaoh's army got drowned.[22]

Among whites, it was common to say that blacks accepted their condition through their songs. But that was not paying proper attention to what was really being expressed.

Without a doubt, the creation of the independent black churches and the holding of clandestine meetings would greatly foster the emergence of the spiritual. It was from the moment that they conducted their own religious services that the African Americans would modulate their hymns according to their own needs.

In 1811 a Russian traveler, Paul Svinine, visited the temple of the African Methodist Church in Philadelphia. He noted: "At the end of every psalm the entire congregation, men and women alike, sang verses in a loud, shrill monotone. This lasted about half an hour. When the preacher ceased reading, all turned toward the door, fell on their knees, bowed their heads to the ground and set up an agonizing, heart-rending moaning. Afterwards, the minister resumed the reading of the psalter and when he had finished sat down on a chair; then all rose and began chanting psalms in chorus, the men and women alternating, a procedure which lasted some twenty minutes."[23] There are two things to point out about this report: the choral response of the faithful to the reading of each psalm and the alternating chant by the men and women. The Africans have always loved responsorial chant, and they give themselves to it totally with "heart-rending" lamentations.

While visiting the United States in 1833–1841, Henry Russell, an English musician, observed the transformation of a psalm tone in a black church in Vicksburg, Virginia: "When the minister gave out his own version of the Psalm, the choir commenced singing so rapidly that the original tune absolutely ceased to exist . . . in fact, the fine old psalm Tune became thoroughly transformed into a kind of Negro melody; and so sudden was the transformation, by accelerating the time, that, for a moment, I fancied that not only the choir but the little congregation intended to get up a dance as part of the service."[24] This statement underscores the fact that the black singing was based on existing music but modified the rhythm to harmonize it with the African tempo.

In the years from 1850 to 1860, evidence for this would increase, which undoubtedly denotes the coming to maturity of black compositions. In 1850 Frederika Bremer, the writer, attended a service in the African Methodist church of Cincinnati, Ohio:

I found fervor and life in this church. The church was overflowing with faithful, the assembly was singing hymns of their own composition. The singing rose and bounded as a melodious torrent, and the hands, feet and elbows of the faithful rocked in unison with the voices, demonstrating obvious pleasure and enchantment. . . . The hymns and psalms that the Negroes had themselves composed have a particularly naïve, childlike character, filled with imagery and life. Here is an example of their popular church hymns:

> What ship is this that's landed at the shore?
> > Oh, glory halleluiah!
> > It's the old ship of Zion, halleluiah,
> > It's the old ship of Zion, halleluiah,
> Is the mast all sure, and the timber all sound?
> > Oh, glory halleluiah!
> > She's built of gospel timber, halleluiah!
> > She's built, &c.
>
> What kind of men does she have on board?
> > Oh, glory halleluiah!
> > They're all true-hearted soldiers, halleluiah!
> > They're all, &c.
>
> What kind of captain does she have on board?
> > Oh, glory halleluiah!
> > King Jesus is the Captain, halleluiah,
> > King Jesus, &c.

> Do you think she will be able to land us on the shore?
> Oh, glory halleluiah!
> I think she will be able, halleluiah.
> I think, &c.

> She has landed over thousands, and can land as many more.
> Oh, glory halleluiah!" &c., &c.

After the singing of the hymns, which was not led by any organ or musical instruments whatever, but which arose like burning melodious sighs from the breasts of the congregation, the preacher mounted the pulpit.[25]

During the Civil War, James McKim asked a free black man from the Sea Islands where the black songs came from. His answer was eloquent: "Dey make'em, sah.' . . . I'll tell you, it's dis way. My master call me up, and order me a short peck of corn and a hundred lash. My friends see it and is sorry for me. When dey come to de praise-meeting dat night dey sing about it. Some's very good singers and know how; and dey work it in—work it in, you know, till de get it right; and dat's de way."[26]

That statement is confirmed by a former slave, Jeannette Robinson Murphy:

We, the old folks, we composed them [the spirituals] in an instant. . . . The notes are right for you, but for us they are a mystery. . . . On the Lord's Day, we were all in the house of prayer and the White preacher was explaining the Scripture and read what Ezekiel had said: "The dry bones will live again." And, dear, the Lord all brilliant appeared in those pages and revived my old black heart, and I jumped here and there and shouting and singing and tapping my feet, and the others caught my words and I sang them on an old prayer Melody from Africa that I had heard them sing, and the others took them and repeated them, and continued to add to them and it became a *Spiritual*.[27]

The slaves often said: "The Lord puts every word in our mouths because we are ignorant."[28]

At the beginning of the twentieth century, Nathalie Curtis Burlin witnessed the birth of a spiritual at a prayer meeting in rural Virginia, on a hot Sunday in July.[29] All the assembly was in prayer and in the midst of the more and more intense buzz of supplications when suddenly, like an electric vibration, a lamentation arose in a musical rhythm. From one corner of the assembly, a voice improvised a response; the other voices entered into the cadence. Progressively, a song was formed that was not the work of an individual in particular, but was the composition of the whole prayer community.

In her fundamental study of American black music, Eileen Southern underscores that it is practically impossible to identify the author of a spiritual and to find its original form. The song is a stone, polished by the river of oral tradition. It is modified according to circumstances. Also, this type of music is particularly difficult to transcribe. James Weldon Johnson, the poet, sought to celebrate those unknown authors who gave us these little masterpieces:

> O black and unknown bards of long ago,
> How came your lips to touch the sacred fire?
> How, in your darkness, did you come to know
> The power and beauty of the minstrel's lyre?
> Who first from midst of his bonds lifted his eyes?
> Who first from out of the still watch, lone and long,
> Feeling the ancient faith of prophets rise
> Within his dark-kept soul, burst into song?[30]

The black communities that wanted to express themselves through singing had three possibilities: embellishing an already existing song, combining elements of various hymns to create new ones, or composing an entirely new hymn. African tradition impels one to adopt the first solution. It loves to multiply variations on a theme. The spirituals, however, are often of the second variety—they regroup verses of Scripture and expressions taken from Protestant hymns, notably those of Dr. Watts. Let me give as an example one of the favorite hymns of the slaves in the collection of Watts, "When I Will Be Able to Read My Name" (no. 26 in Allen's collection). Here is the text:

> When I can read my title clear
>   To mansions in the skies,
> I'll bid farewell to ev'ry fear,
>   And wipe my weeping eyes.
>
> Should earth against my soul engage,
>   And hellish darts be hurl'd,
> Then I can smile at Satan's rage
>   And face a frowning world.
>
> Let care, like a wild deluge come,
>   And storms of sorrow fall;
> May I but safely reach my home,
>   My God, my heav'n, my all.
>
> There shall I bathe my weary soul,
>   In seas of heav'nly rest,

> And not a wave of trouble roll
>   Across my peaceful breast.[31]

It inspired this spiritual:

> Good Lord, in the mansions above,
> Good Lord, in the mansions above,
> My Lord, I hope to meet my Jesus
> In the mansions above.
>
> My Lord, I've had so many crosses,
> And trials here below;
> My Lord, I hope to meet you,
> In the mansions above.
>
> Fight on, my brother,
> For the mansions above;
> For I hope to meet my Jesus there,
> In the mansions above.[32]

From that example, we can easily see the phenomenon of transcription and adaptation. The description of this world is much more concrete and depicts, straightforwardly, the traumatizing experience of slavery. Yet we must not forget that two-thirds of the spirituals have no white parallels. And the texts are closer than the music.

The spirituals thus are more the product of a community's consciousness than that of an individual's talent. They give witness to a collective creativity that one or another unknown poet has put into form at a given moment. But they are first of all a community re-creation that uses the materials at hand. This inventiveness can take place in a church, but it also can arise in the fields, in the woods, in huts at night. It can be stimulated by all kinds of circumstances: the death of a loved one, the cruelty of the master, the sale of friends, the separation of a couple, a successful celebration, the proximity of emancipation, the loneliness of old age. "The *spiritual* is the community in rhythm, swinging to the movement of life."[33]

And the spiritual never has a definitive form. The community remodels it unceasingly according to the events and its moods. It thus is never at a loss. We have many versions of the same spiritual, for the community cannot freeze its inspiration at one moment; it always feels free to create new verses and new tones. During the same celebration, the same hymn was heard sung on six different tones. It is not surprising, then, that Lovell was able to count more than six thousand of them![34] Most of those that we know took shape between 1830 and 1860, the golden age of the spirituals.

A Syncretistic, or Crossbred, Phenomenon

If I must synthesize the definition of the Negro spiritual at this point in the study, I would say that it is a popular religious song born of the meeting of an African sensitivity with European music found in the very specific context of oppressive slavery. It is an African musical expression adapted to the American situation under the influence of Protestant hymnology. In this cultural interpenetration, it is the original product of the black American community, the "burning lava from the entrails of oppressed men and women" (J. Ki-Zerbo).

The song is African not only in its form but also in its essence:

The great characteristic of black singing is the rhythm—a complex, syncopated rhythm, underscored by the clapping of hands and the tapping of feet. Sudden shouts arise with overlaps between soloist and choir. The rhythm of the body accompanies the rhythm of the singing. The pieces are as much played as they are sung. There is often a form of dance (that is, the ring shout). We can say that it is the rhythm that holds together all the elements of musical expression.

The most common structure is the call-response between two partners: a soloist and a group, or two groups. This dialogue form allows the participation of a greater number. And they are not afraid to repeat the phrase that carries the most weight or systematically use a refrain.

The most frequently used scale is the pentatonic, which gives a joyful vivacity and tonality to the singing. Certain songs that are used for funerals play on only two words.

One aspect that defines this type of chant is improvisation, because to sing a spiritual is to participate in a creative event. That makes the transcription difficult. William Allen underlines this in his collection: "What makes it all the harder to unravel a thread of melody out of this strange network is that, like birds, they [that is, the black singers] seem not infrequently to strike sounds that cannot be precisely represented by the gamut, and abound in 'slides from one note to another and turns and cadences not in articulated notes.' "[35] Throat-clearing sounds, howls, invocations, and vibratos—the panoply of ornamentation is wide open.

Can we speak of polyphony? Eileen Southern tries to be more precise:

The slave songs were not typically sung in unison, despite evidence to the contrary in the music sources, where most of the songs are written down as melodies. And yet the term *polyphonic,* in its true meaning, hardly applies to the singing, for the slaves did not believe themselves to be singing different melodies at the same time. Perhaps the best descriptive word is *heterophony,* in that singers followed the lead melody for the most part but allowed themselves to wander away from it when its tones were too high, or when the text called for special emphasis, or simply when their whims indicated the need for more variety.[36]

The concept of religion expressed by the spirituals has evident African consonances: the absence of a cleavage between the sacred and the profane, the accent on daily experience, the proximity of spiritual forces, the progressive entry into the phenomenon of possession by the Spirit. The singing is not reserved for worship, but can color all daily activities. We can say that the spiritual has been the privileged conservatory of the African Americans' ancestral culture.

The spiritual is also European in both form and essence:

The white song furnished, first, a common language so that the African Americans could express themselves together and understand each other. It is rare to find African terms inserted into these spirituals.[37]

The black slaves liked the melodies and texts of Dr. Watts. That was the foundation from which they began to freely express their inspiration.

The slaves were even more attracted by the evangelical hymns of the camp meetings, for these manifested a true proximity to the African experience: a complex rhythmic structure, strong percussion, and the use of syncopation. As these assemblies were interracial, there occurred a mutual influence on the level of the singing. Many witnesses stressed the fact that the slaves submerged these assemblies with what we might call a "torrent of sacred harmony." The sharing of the same religious experience provoked similar reactions because people from the most disadvantaged classes came together.

The religious language came exclusively from the Bible, and it no longer referred to a Creator God or to the African spirits, but to the God of Jesus Christ. It is very difficult to find the tiniest allusion to African religion in the spirituals.

At the same time, we must not set aside the differences between the white spiritual and the black spiritual. Lawrence W. Levine tried to give a balanced judgment:

From those few analyses of white spirituals that exist it is possible to hypothesize tentatively that while white spiritual songs shared a number of textual characteristics with their black counterparts—a sense of community, a frequent use of martial imagery, the depiction of Heaven as a place containing many of those joys denied in this world, an emphasis on the need to prepare oneself for the coming glory, and a tendency to dwell upon the imminent and permanent reunion of loved ones in death— there were significant differences in content and emphasis. White spirituals seem to have been informed by a more pervasive otherworldliness, a more marked rejection of the temporal present, and a tendency to concentrate upon Jesus, which were never typical of black spirituals, while they lacked much of the vivid Biblical imagery, the compelling sense of identification with the Children of Israel, and the tendency to dwell incessantly upon and relive the stories of the Old Testament that characterized the religious songs of the slaves.[38]

Yet in the confrontation between the African sources and the European influences, we must not forget the importance of the concrete situation of slavery. It was the experience of humiliation that gave rise to the cry of pain and hope that is the spiritual. The song was the slaves' daily experience set to music. It expressed what could not be said in direct language, for it was wholly directed toward freedom. The God of the masters was converted to the task of emancipating those in chains, on a foundation of biblical symbolism. The slaves found that their hymns showed "more religion than those in books."[39] It was a question of relativizing oppression and setting up another scale of values. The song thus was an instrument of resistance, a way of saving one's soul.

We can, then, speak of the Negro spiritual as a syncretistic, or crossbred, phenomenon. As such, it was the most significant artistic creation of the slaves. It allowed them, in the secrecy of their assemblies, to create a synthesis of their vision of the world and of their experience of God. The European influence did not turn them away from themselves; it furnished them with a language and the tools for an original creation. For the spiritual cannot be strictly identified with any of the influences that brought it about. It went beyond them because of the depths of the black soul. And through this depth, it acquired a universality that causes it to be recognized throughout the world as a unique musical jewel, imitated but never equaled. This music is the honor of humanity because it is the cry of the conscience.

Henceforth, to know the black American people, one must know their religious songs. They are the psalms of a people in exile who lament, implore, praise, and thank God in the midst of their struggle. They create the free space of an oppressed people who forever refuse to put their heart in chains. Once again, they prove that the body can be slashed but that the soul cannot be destroyed. They are the Bible set to music by illiterate people marked and purified by trials. They are the revenge of humanity when people believe that they have been made lower than dirt. They are the spiritual armor of a wounded but never despairing people. And they do not preach a doctrine, but tell a story—simple, edifying, and exemplary. Through them, it is an entire community that affirms its existence before God and before humanity.

The History of the Interpretation of the Spirituals

Until the Civil War, no collection of spirituals was made. There are only occasional allusions to them in reports of people who traveled through the South or in autobiographies of former slaves written for the abolitionist movement. A man as remarkable as Frederick Douglass made reference to the religious songs of the slaves in his autobiography, published in 1845. He evoked "these simple and apparently incoherent songs" with "strong, long and profound accents" that "breathed the prayer and complaint of souls suffering the most cruel anguish. Each voice was a witness against slavery and a prayer that God would deliver us from our chains. . . ."

I often found myself in tears listening to them."[40] He also invited his readers to go and listen to them on the Southern plantations.

It was during the Civil War that the people of the North would become more interested in the cultural expression of the African Americans, precisely in order to support their emancipation. Young people then discovered the spirituals through "war contraband"—slaves who had found themselves free on the plantations because their masters had gone to the war front. The first song published with its music was "Go Down, Moses," at first in Virginia by the *National Anti-Slavery Standard* (October 12, 1861), then with all its verses in the *New York Tribune* (December 21, 1861).

In 1862 Lucy McKim Garrison, a nineteen-year-old woman, did a more systematic study in the Sea Islands, off the coast of South Carolina, where slaves were allowed to be more autonomous. At first she published two songs, "Poor Rosy, Poor Gal" and "Roll, Jordan, Roll." With friends, William Francis Allen and Charles Pickard Ware, she was at the origin of the first volume of spirituals, published under the title *Slave Songs of the United States* (1867). The collection had not been easy to prepare because of the musical genre. The authors explained it thus:

> There is no singing in *parts,* as we understand it, and yet no two appear to be singing the same thing—the leading singer starts the words of each verse, often improvising, and the others, who "base" him, as it is called, strike in with the refrain, or even join in the solo, when the words are familiar. When the "base" begins, the leader often stops, leaving the rest of his words to be guessed at, or it may be they are taken up by one of the other singers. And the "basers" themselves seem to follow their own whims, beginning when they please and leaving off when they please, striking an octave above or below (in case they have pitched the tune too low or too high), or hitting some other note that chords, so as to produce the effect of a marvelous complication and variety, and yet with the most perfect time, and rarely with any discord.[41]

The collection did not attract much attention. The volume was quickly forgotten and would not be attributed its true worth until the 1930s.

In that same year, 1867, Colonel Thomas Higginson, of the first regiment to include emancipated blacks fighting the Confederates, published a well-received article in *The Atlantic Monthly* entitled "Negro Spirituals."[42] This Unitarian minister and abolitionist described the "stifled voice of a race free at last." He transcribed as well as he could the thirty-seven songs heard at night around the campfires during a shout. For him, these songs stimulated courage and connected to heaven. A young drummer had already confided to him that "Lord" in the text was a code word for "the Yankees."

It was only with the concerts of the Fisk University choirs, beginning in 1867, that the spirituals would acquire notoriety, with the risk of being interpreted in an "arranged" musical form and with an "approved" text. The particular sensitivity of the slaves began to deviate and disappear.

If we do an overview of a century of interpretation of the spirituals (1875–1975), we discover a fluctuation between a mainly religious interpretation and a mainly social interpretation, between an insistence on despair and an insistence on hope. On the one hand, we find men like W. E. B. DuBois and Howard Thurman. On the other, we can mention John Lovell and Miles Mark Fisher. A certain balance between the two interpretations is found in James H. Cone, in 1972, even though he places the black songs in the context of a global project of liberation.

The first serious study of the spirituals was that of W. E. B. DuBois at the end of his book *The Souls of Black Folk* (1903). He wrote: "The music of Negro religion is that plaintive rhythmic melody, with its touching minor cadences which, despite caricature and defilement, still remains the most original and beautiful expression of human life and longing yet born on American soil. Sprung from the African forests, where its counterpart can still be heard, it was adapted, changed, and intensified by the tragic soul-life of the slave, until, under the stress of law and whip, it became the one true expression of a people's sorrow, despair, and hope."[43]

DuBois's last chapter, "Of the Sorrow Songs," examines thoroughly the meaning of the spirituals. For him, "the popular Black song—the rhythmic cry of the slave—today represents not only the only American music, but also the most beautiful expression of human experience born on these ocean shores." It constitutes "the greatest gift of the Black people." DuBois insisted on the poignant dimensions of these songs. It was the music of an unhappy people, of disappointed children; "they tell of death and suffering and unvoiced anger longing toward a truer world."[44] "Of nearly all the songs, however, the music is distinctly sorrowful."[45] The shadow of fear covered the intimate thoughts as well as the social relations of the slaves. Yet they had no fear of death. "Through all the sorrow of the Sorrow Songs there breathes a hope—a faith in the ultimate justice of things. The minor cadences of despair change often to triumph and calm confidence. Sometimes it is faith in life, sometimes a faith in death, sometimes assurance of boundless justice in some fair world beyond. But whichever it is, the meaning is always clear: that sometime, somewhere, men will judge men by their souls and not by their skins."[46]

Benjamin Mays, a sociologist, was the first to analyze the spirituals in theological categories, in his book *The God of the Negro* (1938). He very much underscored the compensatory role of God at the end of time. The spirituals manifest an absolute confidence in God, who will make straight in the next world what was twisted in this world. They gave a certain psychological comfort to the slave, who was convinced that the oppression would not last eternally. In this perspective, the notions of heaven, hell, and the judgment come first. The person who has obeyed the will of God will be received into God's glory; the one who has done evil will be condemned to hell. The slaves' vision was focused on the other world. Nothing motivated slaves to fight to eliminate the source of the evils that befell them. This world was passing. For the complete realization of desires that cannot be experienced here below, one must turn to heaven. Generally speaking, the spirituals kept the slaves in submission, humility, and obedience. They didn't have to combat oppression, but rather needed to place their burden at the feet of the Lord, who heals the wounded heart. At the end, God will render justice.

Poet, mystic, and theologian Howard Thurman was one of the great black religious figures of the twentieth century. He deeply influenced Martin Luther King, Jr. After the end of the war, in 1945, he published two short books—*Deep River* (1945) and *The Negro Spiritual Speaks of Life and Death* (1947)—that sought to restore the memory of the spirituals for the young blacks who despised these songs of the slaves. For Thurman, these songs were "the voice, sometimes strident, sometimes muted and weary, of a people for whom the cup of suffering overflowed in haunting overtones of majesty, beauty and power! For many years it has been a growing conviction with me that the clue to the meaning of the spirituals is to be found in religious experience and spiritual discernment."[47] For the slaves who were at the origin of these songs, "the awareness of the presence of a God who was personal, intimate and active was the central fact of life and around it all the details of life and destiny were integrated."[48] "The center of focus was beyond themselves in a God who was a companion to them in their miseries even as he enabled them to transcend their miseries."[49]

In his first article, in 1939, John Lovell already rejected a specifically other-worldly religious reading of the spirituals. In his opinion, the spiritual is "essentially social," an excellent means of revealing the resistance of the slaves and their earthly aspirations. Three themes run through these songs: the slaves' desire for a concrete freedom, the slaves' aspiration for justice that would call to account those who oppressed them, and the slaves' strategy to attain a better future, a land of freedom.

The first form of resistance of the slave was mental rather than physical and sought an earthly rather than heavenly salvation. Lovell did not hesitate to write: "The idea that they put all their eggs in the basket of heaven after death is absurd."[50] The biblical terms must be deciphered, for they depict in fact the historical conditions of slavery and the will to change the existing social order.

In the same vein is the collection of slave songs put together by Miles Mark Fisher (1953). He insisted on the quality of the information given in the spirituals as being more African than European. "Actually, no one Spiritual in its primary form reflected interest in anything other than a full life here and now."[51] Through the medium of music, these songs "tell how Negroes attempted to spread brotherhood by the sword, took flight to 'better' territory when possible, became pacific in the United States, and laid hold on another world as a last resort."[52]

James H. Cone, a great theologian, in his book *The Spirituals and the Blues* (1972), attempted to keep a middle position between the religious and the social interpretations. His background for this reading was the Black Power movement, the struggle for recognition of black dignity separate from the white world. For Cone, the heart of the spiritual was the desire for freedom, for this song was born from the experience of servitude and resistance. God cannot want such a condition for God's children. Thus "the divine *liberation* of the oppressed is the central theological concept in the black spirituals."[53] Its rootedness in black history and the perception of the contradiction between an alienating present caused by people and a shining future through God's action are a condition for the correct interpretation of these songs, for "Black history is a spiritual."[54] For this reason, we will take up the message of the spirituals by analyzing how they echo the daily experience of slavery.

Notes

1. Guy-Claude Balmir, *Du chant au poème. Essai de littérature sur le chant et la poésie populaire des Noirs américains* (Paris: Payot, 1982), 26.

2. Quoted in Eileen Southern, *The Music of Black Americans,* 3d ed. (New York: Norton, 1997), 5.

3. Quoted in Henry Louis Gates, Jr., *The Classic Slave Narratives* (New York: Mentor, 1987), 14.

4. Quoted in Southern, *Music of Black Americans,* 1.

5. John Lovell, *Black Song: The Forge and the Flame* (New York: Macmillan, 1972), 337.

6. Ecroyd Claxon, *Minutes of Evidence . . . Respecting the Slave Trade,* 34, 14-16.

7. Quoted in Southern, *Music of Black Americans,* 29.

8. Quoted in ibid., 30.

9. Quoted in ibid., 34.

10. Quoted in ibid., 83.

11. Quoted in James Mellon, ed., *Bullwhip Days: The Slaves Remember* (New York: Weidenfeld & Nicolson, 1988), 144–45.

12. John A. Lomax and Alan Lomax, eds., *Folk Song: U.S.A.* (New York: Grosset & Dunlap, 1947), 293–94.

13. Quoted in H. Odum and G. Johnson, *Negro Workaday Songs* (Chapel Hill: University of North Carolina Press, 1926), 117.

14. Frederick Law Olmsted, *A Journey in the Seaboard Slave States* (New York: Dix & Edwards, 1856), 2:19.

15. Quoted in Dena J. Epstein, *Sinful Tunes and Spirituals* (Urbana: University of Illinois Press, 1977), 104.

16. William Knox, *Three Tracts Respecting the Conversation and Instruction of the Free Indians and Negro Slaves in the Colonies. Addressed to the Venerable Society for Propagation of the Gospel in Foreign Parts* (London: n.p., 1768), 39.

17. Elizabeth Kilham, *Sketches in Color,* vol. 6 of *The Negro and His Folklore,* ed. Bruce Jackson (Austin: University of Texas Press, 1967), 123.

18. Frederika Bremer, *The Homes of the New World: Impressions of America,* 2 vols. (New York: Harper & Brothers, 1853), 1:1.

19. Quoted in Eileen Southern, ed., *Readings in Black American Music* (New York: Norton, 1971), 62–64.

20. Robert Sacré, *Les Negro Spirituals et les Gospel Songs* (Paris: PUF, 1993), 11.

21. Quoted in Ronald Rodane, "Denoting Difference: The Writing of the Slave Spirituals," *Critical Inquiry* (spring 1996): 520.

22. The story is told by the great preacher C. L. Franklin, the father of Aretha Franklin, the singer.

23. Quoted in Southern, *Music of Black Americans,* 78–79.

24. Henry Russell, *Cheer! Boys, Cheer! Memories of Man and Music* (London: MacQueen/Hastings, 1895); quoted in Portia K. Maultsby, "Afro-American Music, 1619–1861" (Ph.D. diss., University of Wisconsin, 1974), 169.

25. Bremer, *Homes of the New World,* 2:158–59.

26. Quoted in William Francis Allen, Charles Pickard Ware, and Lucy McKim Garrison, *Slave Songs of the United States* (Bedford: Applewood, 1867), L. XVIII.

27. Jeannette Robinson Murphy, "The Survival of African Music in America," *Popular Science Monthly,* 1899, 662.

28. M. V. Bales, "Some Negro Folk Songs of Texas," in *Follow de Drinkin' Gou'd,* ed. James Dobie (Austin: Texas Folklore Society, 1928), 85.

29. Nathalie C. Burlin, "Negro Music at Birth," *Musical Quarterly* 5, no. 1, 86–89.

30. James Weldon Johnson, *Fifty Years and Other Poems* (New York: AMS), 6–7.

31. Eileen Southern, *Histoire de la musique noire américaine* (Paris: Buchet-Castel, 1976), 177.

32. Ibid., 177–78.

33. James H. Cone, *The Spirituals and the Blues: An Interpretation* (New York: Seabury, 1972), 33.

34. Lovell, *Black Song,* 19.

35. Southern, *Music of Black Americans,* quoting *Slave Songs* by William Allen.

36. Ibid., 198.

37. There are none in our selection of spirituals (appendix 1). For a nonreligious song that has some, see John Blasingame, *The Slave Community: Plantation Life in the Antebellum South,* 2d ed. (New York: Oxford University Press, 1979), 34.

38. Lawrence W. Levine, *Black Culture and Black Consciousness* (New York: Oxford University Press, 1977), 23.

39. James B. Sellers, *Slavery in Alabama* (University: University of Alabama Press, 1950), 300.

40. Frederick Douglass, *Narative of the Life of Frederick Douglass, an American Slave* (New York: Signet, 1968), x.

41. William F. Allen, Charles P. Ware, and Lucy McKim Garrison, *Slave Songs of the United States* (1867; reprint, Bedford, Mass.: Applewood, 1995).

42. Thomas W. Higginson, "Negro Spirituals," *Atlantic Monthly,* June 1867, 685–94.

43. W. E. B. DuBois, *The Souls of Black Folk* (1903; reprint, New York and Toronto: Signet, 1969), 212.

44. Ibid., 267.

45. Ibid., 270.

46. Ibid., 274.

47. Howard Thurman, *Deep River and The Negro Spiritual Speaks of Life and Death* (Richmond, Ind.: Friends United Press, 1975), 12.

48. Ibid., 38.

49. Ibid., 41.

50. John Lovell, "The Social Implications of the Negro Spiritual," in *The Social Implications of Early Negro Music in the United States,* ed. Bernard Katz (New York: Arno, 1969), 132–36.

51. Miles Mark Fisher, *Negro Slave Songs in the United States* (New York: Citadel, 1953), 137.

52. Ibid., 183.

53. Cone, *The Spirituals,* 34.

54. Ibid., 33.

Bibliography

Allen, William Francis, Charles Pickard Ware, and Lucy McKim Garrison. *Slave Songs of the United States*. 1867.

Balmir, Guy-Claude. *Du chant au poème. Essai de littérature sur le chant et la poésie populaire des Noirs américains*. Paris: Payot, 1982.

Brown, Joseph A. *To Stand on the Rock: Meditations on Black Catholic Identity*. Maryknoll, N.Y.: Orbis, 1990.

Chase, Gilbert. *America's Music: From the Pilgrims to the Present*. 2d ed. New York: McGraw-Hill, 1966.

Cleveland Public Library. *Index to Negro Spirituals*. Rev. ed. Chicago: Center for Black Music Research, 1991.

Cone, James H. *"Les Negro-Spirituals. Une interprétation théologique."* *Concilium* 222 (1989): 51–62.

———. *The Spirituals and the Blues: An Interpretation*. New York: Seabury, 1972.

Conkin, Paul K. *The Uneasy Center: Reformed Christianity in Antebellum America*. Chapel Hill and London: University of North Carolina Press, 1995.

Cruz, John. *Culture and the Margins: The Black Spiritual and the Rise of American Cultural Interpretation*. Princeton, N.J.: Princeton University Press, 1999.

Dixon, Christa. *Wesen und Wandel geistlicher Volkslieder: Negro Spirituals*. Wuppertal: Jugunddienst-Verlag, 1967.

———. *Negro Spirituals: From Bible to Folksong*. Philadelphia: Fortress, 1976.

DuBois, W. E. B. *The Souls of Black Folk*. Chicago: McClurg, 1903.

Esptein, Dena J. *Sinful Tunes and Spirituals: Black Folk Music to the Civil War*. Urbana: University of Illinois Press, 1977.

Floyd, Samuel A., Jr. *The Power of Black Music: Interpreting Its History from Africa to the United States*. New York: Oxford University Press, 1995.

Johnson, James W., and J. Rosamond Johnson. *The Book of American Negro Spirituals*. New York: Viking, 1925.

Jones, Arthur C. *Wade in the Water: The Wisdom of the Spirituals*. Maryknoll, N.Y.: Orbis, 1993.

Lead Me, Guide Me: The African American Catholic Hymnal. Chicago: G.I.A., 1987.

Katz, Bernard, ed. *The Social Implications of Early Negro Music in the United States*. New York: Arno, 1969.

Kirk-Duggan, Cheryl A. *Exorcising Evil: A Womanist Perspective on the Spirituals*. Maryknoll, N.Y.: Orbis, 1997.

Lehmann, Theo. *Negro Spirituals: Geschichte und Theologie*. Berlin: Eckart-Verlag, 1965.

Levine, Lawrence W. *Black Culture and Black Consciousness: Afro-American Folk Thought from Slavery to Freedom*. New York: Oxford University Press, 1977.

———. "Slave Songs and Slave Consciousness: An Exploration of Neglected Sources." In *Anonymous Americans: Explorations in Nineteenth-Century Social History*, ed. Tamara K. Hareven. Englewood Cliffs, N.J.: Prentice-Hall, 1971, 99–130.

Lorenz, Ellen Jane. *Glory, Hallelujah! The Story of the Camp-Meeting Spiritual*. Nashville: Abingdon, 1990.

Lovell, John. *Black Song: The Forge and the Flame*. New York: Macmillan, 1972.

McClain, William B. *Come Sunday: The Liturgy of Zion*. Nashville: Abingdon, 1990.

Martin, Denis-Constant. "Filiation or Innovation? Some Hypotheses to Overcome the Dilemma of Afro-American Music's Origins." *Black Music Research Journal* 11, no. 1 (spring 1991): 19–38.

———. *Le gospel afro-américain. Des spirituals au rap religieux*. Paris: Cité de la musique/Actes Sud, 1998.

Mathews, Donald H. "The Spiritual: A Narrative Interpretation of African American Religion." Ph.D. diss., University of Chicago, 1992.

Maultsby, Portia K. "Afro-American Religious Music, 1619–1861." Ph.D. diss., University of Wisconsin, 1974.

———. "The Use of Performance of Hymnody, Spirituals, and Gospels in the Black Church." *The Journal of the Interdenominational Theological Center* (fall 1986–spring 1987): 141–59.

Newman, Richard. *Go Down, Moses: A Celebration of the African American Spiritual.* New York: Potter, 1998.

Peters, Erskine, ed. *Lyrics of the Afro-American Spiritual: A Documentary Collection.* Westport, Conn.: Greenwood, 1993.

Proctor, Henry Hugh. "The Theology of the Songs of the Southern Slave." *The Journal of Black Sacred Music* (spring 1998): 51–63.

Ronado, Ronald. "Denoting Difference: The Writing of the Slave Spirituals." *Critical Inquiry* 22 (spring 1996): 506–44.

Sacré, Robert. *Les Negro Spirituals et les Gospel Songs.* Paris: PUF, 1993.

Songs of Zion. Nashville: Abingdon, 1981.

Southern, Eileen. *The Music of Black Americans.* 3d ed. New York: Norton, 1997.

Spencer, Jon Michael. *Protest and Praise: Sacred Music of Black Religion.* Minneapolis: Fortress, 1990.

Thurman, Howard. *Deep River and The Negro Spiritual Speaks of Life and Death.* Richmond, Va.: Friends United Press, 1975.

Walker, Wyatt Tee. *"Somebody's Calling My Name": Black Sacred Music and Social Change,* Valley Forge, Pa.: Judson, 1979.

Warren, Gwendolin Sims. *Ev'ry Time I Feel the Spirit.* New York: Holt, 1997.

White, John. "Veiled Testimony: Negro Spirituals and the Slave Experience." *Journal of American Studies* (1983): 251–63.

Wilson-Dickson, Andrew. *Histoire de la musique chrétienne.* Paris: Brépols, 1994.

Work, John W. *American Negro Songs: 230 Folk Songs and Spirituals, Religious and Secular.* Mineola, N.Y.: Dover, 1998.

5

"Oh freedom, oh freedom, oh freedom over me."

From Suffering to Deliverance

*"I told the niggers—but not so
the Master could hear it—
that if they keep praying, the Lord
would hear their prayers and set them free."*
—Anderson Edwards, former slave

ONE'S FIRST CONTACT with the text of the spirituals can give the disagreeable impression of a purely spiritual discourse in which the soul expresses its desire for heaven and passes over in silence the daily life of the body on earth. The song seems to be in another world, where the conversation is with Jesus and God, no longer with the master and the boss. The slaves thus appear to have maintained an imaginary universe to console themselves for the distress they felt under the lead mantle of slavery.

It's a misleading impression! On the one hand, this impression is misleading because, in the black community, there is no opposition between the sacred and the profane, but rather a continuity that places spiritual realities in the world of daily experience. The figures in sacred history of whom the believer sings have the same reality as the members of the planters' oligarchy. And on the other hand, the impression is misleading because the spirituals do not proclaim only religious convictions but instead evoke the whole of the life of the slaves, the whole scope of their situations and feelings. They contain the chronicle of the life of the oppressed in all its dimensions. As Benjamin Mays wrote:

These songs are the expressions of the restriction and dominations which their creators experienced in the world about them. They represent the soul-life of the people. They embody the joy and sorrow, the hope and despair, the pathos and aspiration of the newly transplanted people; and through them the race was able to endure suffering and survive. Clearly the Negro Spirituals are not songs of hate; they are not songs of revenge. They are songs neither of war nor of conquest. They are songs of the soil and of the soul.[1]

Indeed, it was not always possible to hold together the soil and the soul, to name in direct terms the infamy and the dehumanization. So the African Americans would use two types of expressions that allowed them to steer clear of a bald designation of the facts and of their cruelty: (1) references to the biblical story, with its enormous narrative resources; and (2) double entendre, in which the spiritual expression masks a concrete meaning. The slave often had to go forward wearing a mask in nineteenth-century U.S. society. But it is not difficult to perceive the slave's deeper feelings. The spirituals transcribed into music the great aspiration of the slave community: the passage from slavery to freedom, from suffering to deliverance. But this transition was to come through belonging to a community that by the grace of God is the church. The theology of the black song is first and foremost that of its movement.

Accursed Slavery

Slavery is rarely the principal and explicit theme of a spiritual. It is most often indicated by allusions or by metaphors. Yet how can we not be unsettled by the following song? *(Note: the numbers in parentheses correspond to the numbers in appendix 1 of spirituals.)*

> Lord, how come me here?
> I wish I never wuz born.
>
> Dere ain't no freedom here.
> I wish I never wuz born.
>
> Dey treat me so mean here.
> I wish I never wuz born.
>
> Dey sol' my chillun away.
> I wish I never wuz born. (119)

One of the most unbearable moments of the slaves' journey, as the text above expresses, was the sale at auction. The following song echoes the anguish of a child and his or her mother:

Mother, is master going to sell us tomorrow?
Yes, yes, yes!
O, watch and pray!

Going to sell us down in Georgia?
Yes, yes, yes!
O, watch and pray!

Farewell, mother, I must lebe you.
Yes, yes, yes!
O, watch and pray!

Mother, don't grieve after me.
No, no, no!
O, watch and pray!

Mother, I'll meet you in Heaven.
Yes, my child!
O, watch and pray! (127)

In this "inimical," "hostile" (88) world full of "snares" (107), "full of scandal-ous things" ("Keep in de Middle ob de Road"), that of the oppression of slavery, the African Americans would use the vocabulary of war or of a storm. For some, the situation was surely that of "a battlefield," of a war in progress.

Going to take my breastplate, sword and shield,
And march out boldly in the field. (57)

If the slave sang, it was with "a sword in ma han' " (168). But for the moment the slave was in the "dungeon," in chains (209). The slave felt committed to a "holy war" ("I Thank You, Lord"). And the slave would remain in the field until the end of the war ("I'm Goin' t' Stay in de Battlefiel' ").

For others, a storm warning was to be proclaimed. The wind blew in violent squalls, and the rains drenched the slave to the skin. One didn't know if one should speak of "the heat of the day," of the "hot furnace," or of "the dark of the night." Yet the thunderstorm rumbled: "I've Been in de Storm So Long" (94):

That trouble it comes like a gloomy cloud,
Gather thick, and thunder loud. (162)

One must bear the shock (199). And that which could be only a temporary trial seemed never ending. It was even longer than one could have imagined (103), and the slaves asked themselves: "How long?" (71). But this "winter" would finally end ("Winter Will Soon Be Over"). The slaves' feelings would play with a whole gamut of words that tried to circumscribe an exhausting experience: *misfortune, sorrow, trial, burden,* and *cross.* Two texts place these words in succession:

> In my trials . . . when the shades of life are falling . . .
> In my sorrows . . . when my heart within is aching . . .
> In my troubles . . . when my life becomes a burden. (84)

> Lord, I'm bearin' heavy burdens . . .
> Lord, I'm climbin' high mountains, . . .
> Lord, I'm standin' hard trials. ("Tryin' to Get Home")

Slavery was the "cemetery of the spirit" (Henri Bibb, former slave).

A "child of misery" (195), the slave was at times on the verge of despair. Everyone was down on the slave ("Down on Me"), scorned the slave (93), and placed the slave lower than dirt. No improvement of the slave's status seemed to be on the horizon. "Burdened with grief" (92), the slave was completely down.

> Poor me! Poor me!
> Trouble will bury me down. ("Po' Me")

> Oh, wretched man that I am.
> I am bowed down with a burden of woe. ("Who Shall Deliver
>   Po' Me?")

> My knee bones am aching,
> My body's rackin' with pain.[2]

> I am a poor pilgrim of sorrow
> I'm tossed in this wide world alone,
> No hope have I for tomorrow. (19)

There remained tears:

> Sometimes I feel like
> A moanin' dove
> Sometimes I feel like
> A moanin' dove
> Wring my han's an'
> Cry, cry, cry,
> Wring my han's an'
> Cry, cry. ("Wring My Hands and Cry")

The worst situation was that there was no one to confide in: "Nobody knows de trouble I've seen" (134). It was the experience of deep solitude. The spirituals express that experience in various ways. Because the separation of families was such a dramatic, though common, experience, the slave was an orphan, with an unfathomable sadness of heart. The slave no longer had brothers, sisters, father, or mother:

> My mother is gone,
> Ain't but me one;
> Oh, Lord, ain't but me one. ("Ain't but Me One")

> Sometimes I feel like a motherless chile,
> A long ways from home. (176)

> Lord, I can't stay here by myself, by myself.
> My mother has gone and left me here,
> My father has gone and left me here,
> I'm going to weep like a willow
> And mourn like a dove. . . .
> Yes, I am a poor little motherless child. (120)

The solitude was that of the stranger in an inhospitable land:

> I'm a poor, wayfaring stranger,
> While journeying through this world of woe. (87)

It is not surprising, then, that the slave knew highs and lows and was close to foundering from one moment to the next:

> Sometimes I'm up, sometimes I'm down, oh, yes, Lord,
> Sometimes I'm almost to the ground, oh, yes, Lord. (134; see
>   also 77, 182, 195)

It was trauma to the extent that the slave had to recognize "that nobody knows who I am" ("Nobody Knows Who I Am"). The feelings of the slave expressed a great weariness, the antechamber of death:

> I'm troubled in mind,
> If Jesus don't help me, I surely will die. (92)

It cannot be said, then, that the spirituals avoid mentioning the situation of the slave. They do not hide the repercussions on the slave of living through an unbearable drama. The testimony of Frederick Douglass is characteristic: "These songs are at the origin of the first vague notion I had of the dehumanizing character of slavery."[3]

Yet the context of slavery could be expressed indirectly through aspects of biblical history that evoke similar situations. The selection of biblical stories would be significant, especially the way of expressing without identifying the present context.

In fact, the biblical code is not very complicated. The land where the "peculiar institution" reigned, essentially the South of the United States, was Egypt, Babylon, or hell. The slave owner was designated by the personages of Pharaoh, the Egyptians, or Satan. The Ohio River, the road to freedom, became the Jordan. The Atlantic Ocean took on the color of the Red Sea. Africa, Canada, or the North of the United States was called the Promised Land, Canaan, or heaven. And the African Americans identified themselves perfectly with the Israelites and with all the children of God:

> We has a hard time.
> Don't God's children have a hard time? ("We Has a Hard Time")

One experience common to the Old and the New Testaments allows us to name the life of the slaves: the desert. It is, first of all, the place of trials and sin. "This world's a wilderness of woe" (99). It has to be set on fire (see 162). But it is also the place of the meeting with the Lord, and one will not be able to leave it without depending on him ("Come Out de Wilderness").

Among the biblical events of the Old Testament, only four metaphors for American slavery will be cited here: (1) the situation of the Israelites in Egypt, (2) Daniel in the lions' den, (3) Jonah in the whale, and (4) the Hebrew children in the furnace. In the next chapter we will visit the use of the whole of Bible by the spirituals' creators.

The slaves were living the same situation as the children of Israel.

> When Israel was in Egypt's land . . .
> Oppressed so hard they could not stand . . . (50)

Pharaoh's army resembled the slave owners' patrols that pursued fugitives night and day. But the biblical reference demonstrates that, with divine intervention, one could escape.

The lions' den where Daniel was thrown is a magnificent metaphor and was honored in various songs (20, 32, 65). I choose the one that establishes the most direct link with the situation of yesterday and that of today, extending it with two other biblical examples:

> Oh-o Lord, Daniel's in de lion's den
> Come he'p him in a hurry,
>
> Oh-o Lord, Daniel's ain't got no frien'
> Come frien' him in a hurry,

Oh-o Lord, won't you ease my trubblin' min'
Come ease it in a hurry,

Oh-o Lord, you know I ain't got no frien'
Come frien' me in a hurry,

Oh-o Lord, Jonah in de belly ob de whale
Come he'p him in a hurry,

Oh-o Lord, t'ree Hebrew chillun in de firy furnace
Come he'p em in a hurry. ("Daniel in de Lion's Den")

It appears more difficult to find comparable situations in the New Testament because that portion of the Bible less often evokes collective realities. Yet the symbolism of the blind man on the side of the road had meaning in the slaves' situation:

The blind man stood on the road and cried,
Cryin' oh my Lord, save-a me. . . .
Cryin': "Help me, O Lawd, if you please,"
Cryin': "O Lawd, show me de way." (186)

It clearly was a new vision of reality and a new way that the slave wanted to find. But the song does not mention that. It ends with the same supplication as in the beginning. There was no immediate, miraculous answer from God.

The poor wretches did not hesitate to apply to themselves the situations of need that the Son of Man mentioned as occurring on Judgment Day (Matthew 25:31-46):

1. I'm a beggar, don't drive me away,
Lord, you know I am poor,
But I'm knocking at your door.
Please don't drive me away.

2. I love you, don't drive me away. . . .

3. I am motherless, don't drive me away. . . .

4. I am afflicted, don't drive me away. . . .

5. I am needy, don't drive me away. . . . ("Don't Drive Me Away")

The Gospel text allowed the enslaved community to give a name to its true situation.

The slave would converse with God "about all these outrages and all these humiliations" ("I Will Tell God How You Treated Me"; see also 75, 155, 173, 175). The believer was convinced that God had pronounced a definitive judgment about slavery: "The time that's been will be no more!" (185). But how would the slave behave in such a painful situation? Did the slave have the means to react, flee, fight? The songs evoke the gamut of possible or tolerable reactions.

An Unequal Struggle

If the slaves had one priority, it was to not lose their identity, to not allow their personality to dissolve under the lashes of the master. Where violence reigned, they would try to introduce conscience. And it is wondrous to see how the slaves did not want to gain heaven before having accomplished their duty on earth. Like Joshua, they would not leave as long as their task was not over (see 118).

Resistance came from the very heart of the person:

> I shall not be moved,
> Like a tree planted by the water,
> I shall not be moved.
>
> When my cross is heavy,
> I shall not be moved. (82)

There is no fatigue possible where there is faith:

> I ain't got weary yet,
> I've been in the wilderness a mighty long time,
> And I ain't got weary yet. (73)

At the same time, the slaves were sure that time is short in this earthly life (see 3). The refuge is called Jesus:

> Steal away, steal away,
> Steal away to Jesus!
> Steal away, steal away home,
> I ain't got long to stay here. (179)

The famous "Steal Away," with its apocalyptic scenes, is a kind of exaltation of flight. The Underground Railroad was also a common theme of the double entendre spirituals that served as rallying songs. Frederick Douglass enlightens us on this strategy: "At certain moments, we had an extraordinary spiritedness, we sang hymns, we shouted for joy, on a tone that was almost as triumphant as if we were already secure in a land of freedom. An attentive observer would have been able to see in the repetition of 'O Canaan, sweet Canaan, I'm goin' to the land of Canaan' something more than the hope to reach heaven. In it we expressed our hope to reach the North and the North was our Canaan."[4]

But it was not always possible to dream of other horizons and put into place a plan of escape from the prison of the South. So a song would give rules for the daily life of the slave:

> I'm goin' t' stay in de battle fiel' til I die;
> I'm goin' t' watch, fight an' pray, til I die.
> ("I'm Goin' t' Stay in de Battle Fiel'")

Those three verbs—watch, fight, and pray—are important. First of all, there had to be observation and vigilance, for one had to profit from all the chinks in the system. If daytime was the domain of the owner, night was the kingdom of the slave. It was only prudent to avoid offering to the master reasons to be harsh. If the environment was implacable, it was not totalitarian.

In fact, it is not mostly in their songs that the slaves proclaimed their forms of resistance. They did not want to attract attention in this way. But since it was a privileged expression of religion, the spiritual contributed, like religion, to affirming the identity of the black slave. After all, humanity of each person is the marvelous gift of the Creator God, a gift that no human being can change. Every personal and collective action of the slaves thus would seek to limit the omnipotence of the whites as well as the underhanded actions of Satan. Questioned by an inquiry committee in 1863, Robert Smalls, a former slave, lifted the veil on the common attitude:

Q. Do the masters know anything of the secret life of the colored people?
A. No, sir; one life they show their masters and another life they don't show.[5]

And the slaves were careful not to betray the activities of their brothers and sisters. By all possible means, fugitives were protected, and the slave quarters rejoiced in their success.

The ordinary Christian knew perfectly well the place God allotted to him or her:

> I'm a soljuh in the Army of thuh Lawd.
> I'll live again in the Army of thuh Lawd.
> I've had a bad time in the Army of thuh Lawd.
> I'm fightin' faw mah rights in the Army of thuh Lawd.
> ("I'm a Soldier in the Army of the Lord")

Where the exploiter spoke only of duties, the exploited knew they had rights to claim: first of all, the right to exist; then, the right to a decent life. Justice could not be profitable for only one group.

But the best weapon for the unarmed, without a doubt, was prayer. It was on the "praying ground" that the slaves discovered their new faith (see "Poor Sinner, Fare You Well"). And they had an intense need for prayer:

> It's me, it's me, it's me, O Lord.
> Standing in the need of pray'r.
>
> 1. Not my brother, not my sister, but it's me, O Lord. . . .
>
> 2. Not my father, not my mother . . .
>
> 3. Not the preacher, not the deacon . . .
>
> 4. Not the stranger, not my neighbor . . . (178)

The experience of the slave trade was that of the silence of God. And it is in the context of the slave ships that we can understand the song "I Couldn't Hear Nobody Pray" (76).

The slaves did not forget the promise of Jesus: "Where two or three are gathered in my name, I am there among them" (Matthew 18:20). Hence the insistent plea:

> Kum ba yah, my Lord, Kum ba yah! . . .
> Someone's praying, Lord, Kum ba yah! (113)

Prayer was the key to the kingdom of God:

> Prayer is the key of Heaven,
> Faith unlocks the door;
> I know that. (153)

Jesus recommended that one never stop praying:

> I prayed all day; I prayed all night,
> My head got sprinkled wid duh midnight dew. (70)

Ah, if only the sinner, and especially the exploiter, could begin to pray! As long as the slaves had the "breath to pray" ("I Love the Lord"), they asked God to not allow their hearts to be filled with despair.

> Prayer makes the darkest cloud withdraw,
> Prayer climbed the ladder Jacob saw.
>   ("God Got Plenty o' Room")

For the Lord promised to fulfill the prayers of God's children ("Holy, Holy, You Promised to Answer Prayer"). One must, then, stay on one's knees (45).

That is what Jacob, a courageous slave in Maryland, understood: he prayed three times a day regardless of the work he was assigned or the time of day. One day his master pointed a revolver at him and threatened to blow his brains out if he did not stop praying. According to the teller of this story: "Jacob would finish his prayer and then tell his master to shoot in welcome—your loss will be my gain—I have two masters one on earth and one in heaven—master Jesus in heaven, and master Saunders on earth. I have a soul and a body; the body belongs to you, Master Saunders, and the soul to master Jesus. Jesus says men ought always to pray, but you will not pray, neither do you want to have me pray."[6] This simplified anthropology is subversive!

Whatever the attitude of the slave, more combative or more reserved, there is one requirement that flows through most of the spirituals: movement, displacement, and traveling. The true enemy was the status quo, and God detests nothing more than getting accustomed to oppression. Therefore, we are going to explore minutely the symbolism of movement, which is not without objectives even if these could not be expressed directly.

The Exaltation of Movement

To speak of movement is to believe, with crazy hope, that the situation is not frozen, that social status is not unchangeable. A different future is possible. Nothing would express better the transitional quality of the situation. Tomorrow will be another day, if God is at our side.

The main idea that comes out of many spirituals is that life is a journey. Of course, the final end is pointed out through faith, and the believer thinks he or she is not far from the "shore" (44). But it is important to encourage the traveler who feels weary:

> Let us cheer the weary traveler
> Along the heavenly way. ("Let Us Cheer the Weary Traveler")

The same song, however, underscores that the road is filled with trials:

> And if you meet with crosses
> And trials along the way,
> Just keep your trust in Jesus
> And don't forget to pray.

Meanwhile, traveling companions are welcome:

> 1. I am seekin' for a city . . .
> For a city into de heaven . . .
> Oh, bredren, trabbel wid me. . . .
> 2. We will trabbel on together . . .
> Gwine to war agin de debbel . . .
> Gwine to pull down Satan's kingdom. (75)

The journey is not an easy one. It is constantly troubled by the attacks of Satan, the symbol of exploitation. One must not be overcome by weariness (36) and should travel as lightly as possible (157).

The journey takes on the aspect of a pilgrimage, for it is made in the company of Jesus. But his presence does not make it less rough:

> I want Jesus to walk with me
> All along my pilgrim journey,
> Lord, I want Jesus to walk with me.
>
> In my trials, Lord, walk with me
> When my heart is almost breaking,
> Lord, I want Jesus to walk with me. (84)

The slaves' path was like a manifestation of both the unity of a community and mutual encouragement:

> Oh, walk togedder, children, don't you get weary,
> Dere's a great camp-meetin' in de Promised Land. (197)

In the end it is the Lord who makes the way (200).

The image of life is sometimes that of climbing. And it is in that perspective that the biblical image of Jacob's ladder is used:

> 1. We are climbin' Jacob's ladder,
> Soldier(s) of the cross.
>
> 2. Ev'ry round goes higher 'n' higher.
> Soldier(s) of the cross. (100; see also 189)

The climb is not only physical; it is also social, economic, and spiritual. It affords a higher standard of living. And the ladder can become a mountain:

> Climbin' up d' mountain, children,
> Didn't come here for to stay. (20)

And if this mountain has a name, it is Mount Zion (Isaiah 2:3; Revelation 14:1).

The obsession to escape that gripped the slaves caused them to see life as a race:

> I'm runnin' on, I'm runnin' on,
> I done left this world behind;
> I done crossed the separatin' line,
> I done left this world behind. ("I'm Runnin' On")

The allusion to escape is clear. But the adventure was not over when fugitives left the plantation. They had to avoid the patrols that would hasten to return them to their owner, with a warning punishment in store. Here is a popular song that has no religious dimensions, but it expresses well the situation:

> Run, nigger, run, de patroller ketch you,
> Run, nigger, run, it's almos' day;
> Dat niggger run, dat nigger flew,
> Dat nigger tore his shirt in two;
> Dat nigger, he said, don't ketch me,
> But get dat nigger behind de tree;
> Dat nigger cried, dat nigger lied,
> Dat nigger shook his old fat side,
> Run, nigger, run, it's almos' day.
>
> Over de hill and down de holler,
> Patroller ketch nigger by de collar;
> Dat nigger run, dat nigger flew,
> Dat nigger tore his pants in two.
> Run, nigger, run, de patroller git you,
> Run, nigger, run, de patroller come;
> Watch, nigger, watch, de patroller trick you;
> Watch, nigger, watch, he got a big gun.[7]

The fugitives could not let themselves be distracted on the way:

> You'd better run, run, run-a-run
> You better run, run, run-a-run
> You'd better run to the city of refuge
> You'd better run, run, run. ("Yo' Better Run, Run, Run")

The story of Mary of Magdala running after discovering the large stone moved from the entrance of the tomb of Jesus (John 20:2) inspired a people buried in the tomb of slavery:

> Run, Mary, run.
> Oh, run, Mary, run,
> I know the other world is not like this. (162)

For this pilgrimage, this climb, or this race, many roads, streets, and paths are needed. And the spirituals are not stingy in expressing directly the symbolism of the roadway. There are roads that go down and are filled with unbelievers (187).

There are roads that rise up to the heavenly Jerusalem but are terribly demanding in terms of conversion and behavior.

> Dark and thorny is de pathway
> Where de pilgrim makes his ways;
> But beyond dis vale of sorrow
> Lie de fields of endless days.[8]

In a traditional song, those who take the Underground Railroad are counseled to follow Ursa Major, which has the form of a gourd:

> Follow the drinkin' gourd!
> Follow the drinkin' gourd.
> For the old man is awaitin'
> For to carry you to freedom,
> If you follow the drinkin' gourd.
>
> When the sun comes back
> And the first quail calls,
> Follow the drinkin' gourd.
> For the old man is awaitin'
> For to carry you to freedom
> If you follow the drinkin' gourd. ("Follow the Drinkin' Gourd")

As the horizontal flight is filled with perils, the slaves did not hesitate to take to the less dangerous airways, metaphorically speaking. The same spiritual that invites people to travel together (197) also invites the traveler to go it alone to reach the Promised Land. It is an invitation to be more angel than devil. One spiritual is called "Now Let Me Fly" and refers to flight to Mount Zion (137).

But all this traveling requires a means of locomotion, for the slaves could not be limited by their capacity to walk. Thus we find references to chariots, a train, a ship, and wings. Most of these images have solid biblical bases, though not all of them do.

The image of the chariot is directly out of the story about the ascension of the prophet Elijah. "As they [Elijah and Elisha] continued walking and talking, a chariot of fire and horses of fire separated the two of them, and Elijah ascended in a whirlwind into heaven" (2 Kings 2:11). No fewer than eleven spirituals mention this chariot in the title, and twenty-four do so in the text. The best known is "Swing Low, Sweet Chariot," which declares, "Swing low, sweet chariot, comin' for to carry me home" (182). It is a chariot that comes from heaven and that brings the passenger to heaven:

> Good news! The chariot's coming

And I don't want it to leave me behind. (56)

The size of the chariot is apparently extraordinary:

> Oh, de good ole chariot passing by. . . .
> She jarred de earth an' shook de sky. (146)

It is a chariot "of gold," pulled by twelve horses "white as milk." The front wheels are moved by God's grace and the back ones by faith ("Little Children, Then Won't You Be Glad").

The train, a more modern means of transportation, was even more popular in spirituals than the chariot. It did not arrive in America before 1820 and was not implanted in the South until the 1830s, but its speed and power, its smoke, its schedules, its noise, its capacity to transport a large number of passengers, and its implicit democracy fascinated the slaves. Here is the complete text of "Get on Board, Children" (47). It is also called "Gospel Train."

> *Refrain:*
> Get on board, children,
> For there's room for many a more.

> 1. The Gospel train is coming,
> I hear it jus' at hand,
> I hear the car wheels moving,
> And rumbling thro' the land.

> 2. I hear the bell and whistle,
> The coming round the curve;
> She's playing all her steam an' pow'r
> An' strainin' ev'ry nerve.

> 3. No signal for another train
> To follow on her line,
> O sinner, you're forever lost,
> If once you're left behind.

> 4. This is the Christian banner,
> The motto's new and old,
> Salvation and repentance
> Are burnished there in gold.

> 5. She's nearing now the station,
> O sinner, don't be vain,
> But come and get your ticket,
> And be ready for the train.

6. The fare is cheap an' all can go,
The rich an' poor are there,
No second class aboard the train,
No diff'rence in the fare.

7. There's Moses, Noah and Abraham,
And all the prophets, too,
Our friends in Christ are all on board,
O, what a heavenly crew.

8. We soon shall reach the station,
O, how we then shall sing,
With all the heavenly army,
We'll make the welcome ring.

9. We'll shout o'er all our sorrows,
And sing forever more,
With Christ and all His army,
On that celestial shore.

This "little black train" is "bound for glory." And it does not carry the mockers, the cigar smokers, or the sleepers. It carries only "the virtuous." There is no need for baggage. But what is extraordinary is that the physically handicapped will not be left off:

I may be blind an' cannot see
But I'll meet you at the station
When the train comes along.

I may be lame an' cannot walk
But I'll meet you at the station
When the train comes along. ("When the Train Comes Along")

It expresses how determined the oppressed were.

The ship reflects another experience, since the slaves (either they or their ancestors) had to live through the "black passage" across the Atlantic and also since the South faces the sea. Furthermore, a certain number of slaves were seamen or boatmen. That means of transportation would allow them to express the movement of Christian life:

I set my foot on the Gospel ship,
And the ship it began to sail,
It landed me over on Canaan's shore,
And I'll never come back any more. (32; see also 37, 199)
'Tis the old ship of Zion

Git on board.

1. It has landed many a thousand . . .

2. Ain't no danger in de water . . .

5. It will take you home to Glory . . . (193)

However, contrary to the assertion of this last song, the sea is not always calm. The message has to be completed by verses from another hymn:

> We are on the ocean sailing,
> and awhile must face the stormy blast,
> but if Jesus is our captain,
> we will make the port at last. ("Move Along")

When the river is broad, it is necessary to use a boat. But we never know if we stand before the Red Sea, the Jordan, or the Atlantic Ocean!

The gospel ship does not replace Noah's ark, which allowed "two of every kind" of animal to be saved (Genesis 6:20). A spiritual describes it in these terms:

> De ol'ark's a-moverin' an' I'm goin' home. . . .
> Ol' ark she reel, ol' ark she rock,
> Ol' ark she landed on de mountaintop. (28)

Yet since they have to meet also "in the middle of the air" (38), the slaves will need a good pair of wings:

> Oh, give me wings,
> Oh, good Lord, give me wings,
> Oh, good Lord, give me wings to move along.
>   ("Oh, Give Me Wings for to Move Along")
>
> Lawd, I want two wings to fly away.
>   ("Lawd, I Want Two Wings")

The best example of wings we can find in creation are eagle's wings. God used that metaphor to express the loving designs God had for people: "You have seen . . . how I bore you on eagles' wings and brought you to myself" (Exodus 19:4). God resembles the eagle that "takes them [its young] up, and bears them aloft on its pinions" (Deuteronomy 32:11). With these wings, the believer will be able to fly to paradise.

Sometimes I feel like

A eagle in the air,
Spread my wings an'
Fly, fly. ("Wring My Hands and Cry")

"The wings of a dove" will also do in remembrance of the end of the Flood.

While the aim of the journey was always precisely understood in the heart of the slaves, they knew that they had to be patient. It was not by the wave of a magic wand that they would be able leave their prison. Each step in the right direction counted and had to be valued. That is the meaning of this spiritual:

Keep a-inching along
Jesus will come by and by.
Continue a-inching along, like a poor inchworm
Jesus will come by and by. (108)

The ladder is climbed rung by rung. Constancy is the daily equivalent of valor. In order to give themselves courage, the slaves believed that they were almost done toiling ("Mos' Done Toilin' Here") and traveling.

Human Community and Christian Community

As we become acquainted with the texts of the religious songs of the slaves, we must be struck by the dominance of the first person singular: the spiritual is expressed by the "I." It shows the will to express personhood, for oppression is a machine that eliminates individuality, and therefore survival is possible only in the restructuring of the personality. Of course, conversion to Christianity always gives more weight to the name of the believer.

To believe only in an added personal worth to isolated individuals would be to ignore African sensitivity. The "I" is also a communitarian word, the expression of a collective consciousness. The feelings expressed are shared feelings. And American history teaches us that the slaves in their quarters rapidly organized themselves on the foundation of the nuclear family: the parents and the children, with eventually a grandparent, an uncle, or an aunt.

The drama of servitude reached a peak in the separation of the members of a family. It could happen on the occasion of a death, but it also occurred by a sale at auction. A spiritual expresses it with the classic distinction of body and soul:

Good-bye, brothers, good-bye, sisters,
If I don't see you anymore;
I'll see you in Heaven
In the blessed kingdom,
If I don't see you anymore.
We'll part in the body,

> We'll meet in the spirit,
> If I don't see you anymore. ("Good-bye, Brothers")

The mother was the central figure in the family, for it was she who transmitted life, educated the children, introduced them to religion, and furnished a haven of security and tranquillity. Nothing was more terrible than to become "a motherless child." The slaves often mentioned the way the mother introduced her children to all the things of life. Thus James Adams said: "What religious instruction I received on the plantation was from my mother." Josiah Henson remembered that his mother was "a good mother to us, a woman of deep piety, anxious above all things to touch our hearts with a sense of religion. . . . I remember seeing her often on her knees."[9]

On the other hand, the role of the father seems to have been more in the background. But his role grew with the age of the children. He sought to improve the conditions for the family by cultivating a piece of land or by keeping a poultry yard, when that was feasible. The more skillful made furniture. Fathers taught their sons to hunt and fish and transmitted to them what they received through oral tradition or from their own experience.

Some former slaves evoked the delicate love that united their parents: "My mother just rejoiced in him. Whenever he sat down to talk, she just sat and looked and listened. She would never cross him for anything. If they went to church together she always waited for him to interpret what the preacher had said or what he thought was the will of God."[10]

Some songs would echo these strong family ties. They spoke of relations as "brothers," "sisters," and "children." It is still the same in the black community today.

> You are my brother, so give me your hand. . . .
>
> My lovin' brother . . . my lovin' sister,
> When the world's on fire,
> Don't you want Christ's bosom
> To be your pillow? ("Rock of Ages")

The great event in heaven will be the reunion of the family, with "my dear old father" and "my dear old mother" (180). It will be a sort of return to paradise in which each one will be able to rejoice in the tree of life.

> O, brother, O, sister,
> You got a right, I got a right,
> We all got a right to the tree of life. (209)

In the turmoil of this world, everything possible had to be done to maintain the cohesion of the group: "Oh, walk togedder, children, don't you get weary"

(197). It was only together that the slaves would be able to resist the violence of the storm, the whims of the overseer, "to not turn around" or not go back (4). Cooperation with the oppressor was forbidden. They were warned: "Keep the straight and narrow way" ("Don't You Let Nobody Turn You 'Round"). The slaves often had the impression of walking on a tightrope.

The collective experience sometimes took on the aspect of an army troop, but the conditions to belong to it were strict:

> We want no cowards in our band,
> That will their colors fly,
> We call for valiant-hearted men,
> That are not afraid to die. (17)

The circle of family and friends had to be widened even more, and those in need were not to be forgotten. One song establishes a surprising list:

> Lord, help the poor and needy,
> In this land, in this land,
> Lord, help the poor and needy,
> In this land, in this land.
>
> Lord, help the widows and the orphans,
> Lord, help the motherless children,
> Lord, help the hypocrite members,
> Lord, help the long tongue liars. ("In This Land")

If the slaves could constitute a people, it was because they were the people of God, the people born of God, and God constantly sustained that identity. The community existed because God carried it. It was a community that found its fulfillment by becoming a church, a community of faith, prayer, and song in which the people had the experience of religion as a precious "treasure," ("Religion Is a Fortune") a "blooming rose" (99), a "morning star" ("The Religion That My Lord Gave Me").

The first gift of God was to "change the name" of the slave. Slaves were no longer named by the exploiter but by the Lord. The sign of belonging to "good" religion was the changing of the name—guarantee of a new identity. The change was made in a dialogue with Christ:

> Ah tol' Jesus it would be all right, if He changed mah name.
> Jesus tol' me ah would have to live humble, if He changed mah name.
> Jesus tol' me that the world would be 'gainst me, if He changed mah name.

But ah tol' Jesus, it would be all right, if He changed mah name.
(16)

Sometimes the angels of heaven were given the task of giving the new name ("The Angels in Heaven Have Changed My Name"). And it was essential that this name be written. The baptismal name, sign of a rebirth, became the important one in the eyes of the slave; it was the guarantee of happiness on earth as in heaven:

I got a new name over in Zion,
Well, it's mine, mine, mine,
I declare it's mine. ("I Got a New Name")

But the name change had to be the exterior sign of an interior conversion:

You may be a white man,
White as the drifting snow,
If you soul ain't been converted,
To hell you're sure to go. (129)

All the changes previously expressed can be interpreted as a conversion experience that allowed one to leave the old self and receive a new self in Christ. This experience was expressed in vivid imagery:

I sweep my house with the gospel broom. (3)

Master Jesus gave me a little broom,
To sweep my heart clean. (42)

We find other expressions from conversion accounts:

Looked at my hands, and they looked new,
Looked at my feet and they did too. ("O Lamb, Beautiful
Lamb")

The slaves expressed their firm resolve:

1. Lord, I want to be a Christian in-a my heart . . .

2. Lord, I want to be more holy in-a my heart . . .

3. Lord, I don't want to be like Judas in-a my heart . . .

4. Lord, I just want to be like Jesus in-a my heart. (121)

All human beings are given a decisive choice: Jesus or Judas. It is this desire for conversion that the slaves wanted to live out by participating in the "great camp meeting" of the religious awakenings. These camp meetings are evoked in the hymns even if the expression designates both the celebration on earth and the celebration in heaven, the public meeting and the secret meeting:

> Dar's a big camp-meetin' in de kingdom, Lord. (106)

> Dere's a great camp-meetin' in de Promised Land. (197)

> Get you ready, there's a meeting here tonight,
> Come along, there's a meeting here tonight.

> Camp-meeting down in the wilderness. . . .
> I know it's among the Methodes'. (190)

What was going to happen at these meetings? The believers would give themselves to prayer, singing, preaching, and a shout:

> We're sure to hab a little shout tonight,
> For I love to shout, I love to sing,
> I love to praise my Hebbenly King. (67; see also 113, 143, 168)

One spiritual, and only one, speaks of the celebration of the Eucharist, for that ceremony was never frequent in American Protestant churches:[11]

> Let us break bread together on our knees . . .
> Let us drink wine together on our knees. (116)

The Christian was the one who always confronted the world on his or her knees, that is, with an attitude of humility and prayer.

Because they received the faith at the time of the evangelical awakenings, the African Americans mentioned only the Methodist and Baptist churches in the spirituals, with a preference for the Methodists:

> My father says it is the bes', . . .
> To live an' die a Methodes'. (190)

One song presents both the Methodists and the Baptists in the same way, but quickly adds:

> While marching on the road,
> A-hunting for a home,

> You better stop your differences
> And travel on to God. (59)

One is tempted to ask, "What differences?" The text does not elaborate. But in other places we can find the evocation of competition:

> The Baptists, they go by water,
> The Methodists, they go by land,
> But when they get to Heaven
> They'll shake each others hand. ("Don't You Let Nobody Turn You 'Round")

Everyone should be able to count on his or her "brother":

> We may not belong to the same denomination . . .
> But if you take me by my han' an' lead me home to my Lord,
> You're my brother, so give me your han'.
> ("You're My Brother So Give Me Your Han' ")

It is not church affiliation that guarantees salvation:

> You may be a good Baptist,
> And a good Methodist as well,
> But if you ain't the pure in heart
> Your soul is bound for Hell. ("Don't You Let Nobody Turn You 'Round")

In each community the roles were well defined: the preacher, the deacon, and the elder (84; see also 125). They each had a right to a couplet. But the church can live only with the solidarity of all, according to Paul's body of Christ imagery:

> Ah, well, de toe bone connected wid de foot bone,
> De foot bone connected wid de ankle bone,
> De ankle bone connected wid de leg bone,
> De leg bone connected wid de knee bone,
> De knee bone connected wid de thigh bone. (39)

God's flock must not disperse itself, much less get lost, but rather it must strengthen its solidarity. The great enemy is sin. Thus the church must be purified of all those who do evil:

> Let the church roll on, my Lord,
> You can put the Devil out, my Lord,
> Let the Church roll on, my Lord.

> If there's preachers in the church, my Lord,
> An they're not living right, my Lord;
> Just turn the preachers out, my Lord,
> And let the church roll on.
>
> If there's members in the church, my Lord,
> And they're not living right, my Lord;
> You can put the members out, my Lord,
> And let the church roll on.
>
> If there's liars in the church, my Lord,
> And they're not living right, my Lord . . .
> If there's sinners in the church, my Lord, . . .
> Just put the sinners out. (115)

If need be, it was God who would put the preachers, the deacons, and the members of the church on the right path ("God's Goin' to Straighten Them"). Meanwhile, hypocrites got a deservedly vitriolic description:

> You call yourself a church member,
> You hold your head so high,
> You praise God with your glitt'ring tongue,
> But you leave all your heart behind. (138)
>
> Meet dat Hypocrite on de street,
> First thing he do is to show his teeth.
> Nex' thing he do is to tell a lie,
> An' de bes' thing to do is to pass him by. (137)

It is enough to look away. What God expects of the one called and converted is a beautiful witness before the world: "My soul is a witness for my Lord" (204).

That witness was to be given every day of the week: "on Monday, on Tuesday, on Wednesday, on Thursday, on Friday and on Saturday" ("I'm a Everyday Witness"). Even in extreme situations, the Christian has a mission.

The Actual Experience of Freedom

If the slaves endured the inhuman condition imposed on them, if they sought by every means to escape the South, if they fostered in themselves an unexpected dynamism, if they fostered solidarity with their brothers and sisters, it was because only one passion lived in them: freedom. Their entire being strained toward this pearl of a great price, this happiness that seemed to be hundreds of miles from their daily servitude. They could never spend too much time imagining it or especially too much time in prayer asking for it. Who, in fact, could be content with the status of a slave for an entire life? It was a curse from all points of view. One day an African American confessed that desire to his master, who asked him if the slaves spoke of freedom among themselves: "Dat's all dey talk, master—dat's all, sir."[12]

In order to understand the extraordinary fascination with this desire for freedom, this inextinguishable internal fire, it suffices to hear Aaron tell the following story:

> A poor slave, on his death bed, pleaded with his master to give him freedom before dying: "I want to die free, master." His master replied that he would die soon, what would that freedom give him? "O master, I want to die free." He said to the slave: "You are free." "But write it down, master, I want to see it on paper." At his urgent request, the master wrote that he was free; the slave took the paper with a trembling hand, looked at it with a smile and exclaimed: "Oh, how beautiful it is! Oh, how beautiful it is!" and shortly after went to sleep in the arms of death.[13]

The African Americans had the ineradicable conviction that they were created to be free. Freedom is the very stuff of true humanity. Slavery abases the chained person to the level of beasts of burden. Charlie Moses testified: "God Almighty never meant for human beings to be like animals. Us niggers has a soul an' a heart an' a mine. We are not like a dog or a horse. . . . I prays to the Lord for us to be free always. That's the way God Almighty wants it."[14] Thomas Likers, a former slave, agreed completely: "As soon as I came to the age of maturity, and could think for myself, I came to the conclusion that God never meant me for a slave. & that I should be a fool if I didn't take my liberty if I got the chance."[15] No one intends to die in Egypt ("I Never Intend to Die in Egypt Land").

Because of the brutality of the slave system, the slaves would have to distinguish between the freedom possible in the here and now and freedom in capital letters, total freedom. Faith taught them not to reason in terms of all or nothing. True, freedom is a whole, but the present partial freedom is not to be minimized, even if it calls for more.

The present experience of freedom is not an illusion. It can be expressed simply in these words: the body is enslaved, the soul is free. And nothing would prevent the slave from being among the elect:

> You may beat upon my body,
> But you cannot harm my soul;
> I will join the forty thousand by and by.

> You may sell my Children to Georgy
> But you cannot harm their souls;
> They will join the forty thousand by and by.[16]

The most astounding illustration of this is found in "Oh, Freedom":

> Oh, freedom,
> Oh, freedom,
> Oh, freedom over me!

> An' befo' I'd be a slave,
> I'll be buried in my grave,
> An' go home to my Lord an' be free. (143)

The African Americans realized very quickly that legal slavery could not be transformed into spiritual slavery. A great part of themselves was out of reach of the master's whip and of physical degradation. There was an interior place where the slaves were never enslaved, where they could allow themselves to defy the Constitution of the United States as well as the rampant racism of the churches. It was better to die than to give up personal dignity.

This freedom is patently the fruit of the action of Jesus and conversion to the gospel:

> I am free,
> I am free, my Lord,
> I am free,
> I'm washed by the blood of the Lamb. (74)

And so one can sing:

> I woke up this morning with my mind
> Stayed on freedom. ("My Mind Stayed on Freedom")

Christian life gives a healing that reestablishes the totality of the believer's personality:

> There is a balm in Gilead,
> To make the wounded whole;
> There is a balm in Gilead,
> To heal the sin-sick soul.

> Sometimes I feel discouraged
> And think my work's in vain,
> But then the Holy Spirit
> Revives my soul again. (8)

The wonder of this text is that it reshapes in the affirmative what the prophet Jeremiah had expressed as a question: "Is there no balm in Gilead? Is there no physician there?" (Jeremiah 8:22). The oppressed blacks were certain of the healing brought about by faith in the gospel.

> Jesus' blood done make me whole,
> Since I touched the hem of his garment,
> Jesus' blood done make me whole. (101)

If the soul, filled by the "amazing grace" of God ("Amazing Grace"), was out of reach of the claws of exploitation, it would give itself a free space: religious services. It was in the prayer meeting that the black community would experience a freedom that always surpassed that which it would be able to write in history. The seed of freedom was planted in each slave's heart, and its growth would be irresistible, for the Spirit of the Lord calls to sing, to shout, to preach, to pray (89).

In the religious service, singing was a kind of group therapy. It was right to answer the call:

> Over my head I hear music in the air
> There must be a God somewhere. (151)

Music leads the way to the discovery of God. And this God is a God who has the power to establish a kingdom of freedom:

> I'm gonna sing till the power of the Lord comes down,
> Lift up your head, don't be afraid
> I'm gonna sing till the power of the Lord comes down. (169)

The slave felt gifted by the miraculous power of Jesus:

> Jesus make de dumb to speak, . . .
> Jesus made de cripple walk, . . .
> Jesus give de blind his sight, . . .
> No man can hinder me. ("No Man Can Hinder Me")

The prayer was not turned toward another world that would be the joy-filled alternative to this one; it was a cry for help from the pit of distress of this world, for its radical transformation: "Save me now."

Also, the biblical figures called upon in the spirituals, such as Moses, David, Jonah, and Daniel, gave witness to an earthly freedom. Thus the slave could ask:

> Oh my Lord delivered Daniel,
> O Daniel, O Daniel,
> Oh my Lord delivered Daniel,

O why not deliver me too? (138)

In one sense, the oppressors were already defeated, deprived of any future, because they did not represent the sense of history desired by God's will: "Didn't old Pharaoh get los' in de Red Sea?" (33). And in a juxtaposition of the events of the Exodus and of the cross:

> Oh, Mary, don't you weep, don't you mourn,
> Pharaoh's army got drowned. (145)

The slave community was convinced that God would not delay in "setting this world on fire" and would render justice to the innocent.

The partial deposits of full freedom would become even more tangible with the Civil War. During this war tension mounted, and a black woman did not hesitate to sing in a camp-meeting, in December 1862, as a parody of "Go Down, Moses":

> Go down, Abraham
> Away down in Dixie's land;
> Tell Jeff Davis
> To let my people go.

Emancipation would correspond to the biblical year of Jubilee, which was traditionally observed by the abolition of debts and of servitude:

> The master runs away! Ha, ha!
> Blackie stays! Ho, ho!
> It must be the coming of the Kingdom
> And the year of Jubilee.[17]

> Slavery chain done broke at last,
> Going to praise God till I die. (173)

> This is the day of jubilee. . . .
> The Lord has set his people free. (57)

In the following spiritual, the "today" is rich in meaning relative to the recent past:

> Tain't no mo' sellin today
> Tain't no mo hirin' today
> Tain't no mo' pulling off shirts today
> It's stomp down freedom today.
> Stomp it down! ("Stomp It Down")

The Fulfillment of Emancipation

Human emancipations are only partial liberations, and the aftermath is not always joyful. Only God can give full freedom in the kingdom as an unearned gift and gracious fulfillment. The vision of the slave carries all the way there:

> I know I have another building,
> I know it's not made with hands, O brethren;
> I want to go to Heaven and I want to go right,
> O, I want to go to Heaven all robed in white.
> ("I Have Another Building")

But the space of perfect freedom is distant. And another obstacle presents itself—a river to cross, most often designated by the biblical name of the Jordan.

> Oh, wasn't dat a wide riber, Riber ob Jordan, Lord,
> Wide riber, dere's one more riber to cross. (146)

> Deep river, my home is over Jordan;
> Deep river, I want to cross over into campground. (27)

One must then "be ready" on the shore (83). And the crossing requires a total personal commitment:

> When you reach the River Jordan,
> You got to cross it by yourself;
> No one may cross it with you,
> You got to cross it by yourself. (184)

Only the sanctified can cross. But angels come to the aid of those who aspire to freedom:

> I looked over Jordan, an' what did I see,
> Comin' for to carry me home?
> A band of angels comin' after me,
> Comin' for to carry me home. (182)

This help is not superfluous, for:

> Jordan River is chilly and cold,
> Chills the body but not the soul. (40)

The slave finds strength in the presence of Jesus: "Jesus is sitting on the waterside" (102). Just hearing the flow of the river gives peace:

> Roll, Jordan, roll, roll, Jordan, roll,
> I want to go to heaven when I die
> To hear Jordan roll. (160)

Imitating the gesture of Moses separating the waters of the Red Sea, the believers stretch their rod and come across (162). Only then, on the other side of the river, can they cry out, as later Martin Luther King, Jr., did at the end of his most famous speech:[18]

> Free at last, free at last,
> Thank God a'mighty, I'm free at last. (46)

This new land of freedom, in its ever-present double sense (social and spiritual), is the land of "never again," of the final end of slavery. And the humiliated people expressed the new freedom in a poetic manner:

> 1. No more rain fall for wet you, Hallelu, hallelu. . . .
>
> 2. No more sun shine for burn you. . . .
>
> 3. No more parting in de kingdom. . . .
>
> 5. Every day shall be Sunday. (136)

Or in a very realistic way:

> No more auction block for me. . . .
> No more peck o' corn for me. . . .
> No more driver's lash for me. . . .
> No more pint o' salt for me. . . .
> No more hundred lash for me. . . .
> No more mistress' call for me. (124)
>
> I ain't going to study war no more. (180)

This freedom is the new "Promised Land" (137, 197, 207) or the "mountain-top" (132, 57). In any case, it is a synonym for eternal rest. The person who has lived under the regime of forced labor will be able to "sit down" (172) and will have nothing to do (205). Then will the words of Jesus in the Gospel (Matthew 11:28) be fulfilled:

> Come to Me, ye who are hard opprest;
> Lay your head gently upon my breast;
> Come to Me, and I will give you rest. (23; see also 166)

We might well ask ourselves if, at the end of this journey, the slaves expressed feelings of vengeance toward those who crushed them. The black community was perfectly conscious of the hypocrisy of the masters, as I have already underscored in passing. They believed that God would render justice, and the judgment was described and set to music in numerous spirituals. We can only be astounded by the slaves' capacity to forgive, following the example of their true Master, as this song shows:

> Come slave trader, come in too;
> The Lord's got a pardon here for you;
> You shall join the forty thousand by and by.[19]

In the end, the slave trader did not know what he was doing. And while the black Christians hated the sin, they tried to love the sinner. They proved here again their humanity according to the heart of God.

Notes

1. Benjamin Mays, *The Negro's God as Reflected in His Literature* (Boston: Chapman & Grimes, 1938), 19.

2. Quoted by Anderson Edwards, a former slave. See Albert J. Raboteau, *Slave Religion* (Oxford and New York: Oxford University Press, 1978), 218.

3. Frederick Douglass, *The Life of Frederick Douglass, an American Slave* (New York: Signet, 1968), x.

4. Frederick Douglass, *Life and Times of Frederick Douglass* (1892; reprint, New York: Collier, 1962), 159.

5. Quoted in Arna Bontemps, introduction to *Five Black Lives* (Middletown, Conn.: Wesleyan University Press, 1971).

6. Quoted in John B. Blassingame, ed., *Slave Testimony: Two Centuries of Letters, Speeches, Interviews, and Autobiographies* (Baton Rouge: Louisiana State University, 1977), 377.

7. Quoted in James Mellon, ed., *Bullwhip Days: The Slaves Remember* (New York: Weidenfeld & Nicolson, 1988), 139–40.

8. This was the rallying cry of Harriet Tubman. Quoted in Sarah Bradford, *Harriet: The Moses of Her People* (New York: Lockwood, 1886), 37.

9. Quoted in Thomas I. Webber, *Deep Like the Rivers* (New York: Norton, 1978), 162.

10. Quoted in ibid., 173.

11. Erskine Clark recounts how Communion took place in the Presbyterian Church of Charleston, South Carolina, beginning in 1814, in *Wrestlin' Jacob* (Atlanta: John Knox, 1979), 133–34. The spiritual apparently alludes to a celebration in an independent church. Thus, the First African Baptist Church of Savannah, in 1850, celebrated the Lord's Supper "once every three months."

12. Quoted in Harold Courlander, *A Treasury of Afro-American Folklore* (New York: Marlowe, 1976), 275.

13. *The Light and Truth of Slavery: Aaron's History* (Worcester, Mass.: 1843), 8.

14. Quoted in Mellon, *Bullwhip Days,* 146.

15. Quoted in Blassingame, *Slave Testimony,* 395.

16. Slave song published in 1855; quoted in Eileen Southern, *The Music of Black Americans,* 3d ed. (New York: Norton, 1997).

17. Quoted in Leon F. Litwack, "Free at Last," in *Anonymous Americans: Explorations in*

Nineteenth-Century Social History, ed. Tamara K. Hareven (Englewood Cliffs, N.J.: Prentice-Hall, 1971), 131.

18. King gave the speech "I Have a Dream" on August 28, 1963, in Washington, D.C. Both the French and English texts are in Martin Luther King, Jr., *Je fais un rêve* (Paris: Bayard, 1988), 62–75.

19. Another couplet of the song quoted in note 16.

Bibliography

Marbury, Carl. "Hebrews and Spirituals: Soulful Expressions of Freedom." In *God and Human Freedom: A Festschrift in Honor of Howard Thurman,* ed. H. J. Young. Richmond, Ind.: Friends United Press, 1983, 75–94.

Pinn, Anthony B. *Why, Lord? Suffering and Evil in Black Theology.* New York: Continuum, 1995.

Sinclair, Bryan T. "Merging Streams: The Importance of the River in the Slaves' Religious World." *Journal of Religious Thought* 53.2–54.1 (1997): 1–19.

6

"Didn't old Pharaoh get los'?"

A Bible with an Exodus Flavor

"Your statutes have been my songs
wherever I make my home."
—Psalm 119:54

"HOLY BIBLE, holy Bible, holy Bible, book divine, book divine" ("Holy Bible").
As she attended a slave's funeral, in 1839, Fanny Kemble (a slave owner herself)
noted the text of this spiritual. It shows clearly what we could call, without
exaggeration, the cult of the Bible in the black Christian community. Very early,
the Africans had discovered the importance of the sacred book among the whites.
Their first reaction had been one of suspicion and rejection. Through the
evangelical preachers, they discovered, with new eyes, the power of the Bible. The
message of the Scriptures, especially in the Old Testament accounts, coincided
completely with the expectations of the slaves: they revealed that the Creator God
was a liberating God, that this God had created humankind to be free, and that
God wanted to wrest people from all forms of servitude.

The Scriptures thus would become the "Good Book," the only reference book,
the one in which the oppressed community would discover a compassionate God,
a suffering Christ, and a history flowing in the direction of justice. This book
speaks the truth:

> Now take your Bible, an' read it through;
> An' ebery word you'll find is true. (67)

What pagans needed most was a Bible ("De Po' Heathens Are Dyin' "), for it would bring them to the fulfillment of their humanity. The slaves manifested a frantic desire to learn to read because they wanted to possess the Word of God in the text.

It is not unimportant that the Bible the slaves came in contact with was the King James Version. Begun in 1604 by a group of forty-seven specialists and published in 1611, this translation is famous for its literary and poetic qualities. The slaves jumped into it with delectation, selecting passages according to their own sensitivities. Scripture would furnish a language for those who were experiencing a religious upheaval. It offered images to those whose horizon was limited to a plantation. The Bible constituted, especially, a world compatible with their daily universe, for it was, at the same time, that universe's extension and its critic. While the white world showed multiple examples of enemy figures and transformed human relations into relations of power and exclusion, the biblical world showed multiple relations of friendliness to the pariahs of society. The spirituals were born through the fertility of Scripture. The Word of God began to sing in the midst of the black community by furnishing the text. We have here another proof that the statement of Gregory the Great is true: "Scripture grows with those who read it."

The center of gravity of the black reading of the Bible would shift to the Exodus account, and we can safely assert that they would see all of Scripture through this liberating filter. This privileged Bible story, however, would not obscure the other pages of the Old and New Testaments. With as much objectivity as possible, I will show this with the texts we have. I will leave the more direct designation of God and Jesus for the next stage.

The Drama of the World

The beginning of the Book—that is, the text of Genesis—is an extraordinary meditation on the adventures of the one type of being created in the image and the likeness of God: humans. In the stories of the early humans we learn about good and evil, responsibility, fall from grace, violence, sin, alliance, forgiveness, and struggle. All the important human situations are already in place, and the slave was not insensitive to the stakes involved in these first pages of the Bible. Adam and Eve, Noah and the patriarchs were, for the slave, familiar figures.

In fact, one spiritual retells the first Creation story with a certain humor. It begins with the text of Ezekiel 37, which is about dry bones that return to life with the breath of God:

> 1. De Lawd, He thought He'd make a man, . . .
> Made 'im outa mud an' a han'ful o' san'.

> 2. Thought He'd make a woman, too,
> Didn' know 'xactly what to do.

3. Took a rib from Adam's side,
Made Miss Eve for to be his bride.

4. Put um in a garden fine and fair,
Tole um to eat whatever was there.

5. But to one tree they mus' not go,
Must leave de apples dere to grow.

6. Sarpint quoiled around a chunk,
At Miss Eve his eye he wunk.

7. First she took a little pull,
Then she filled her apron full.

8. Adam took a little slice,
Smack his lips an' say 'twas nice.

9. De Lord He spoke with a 'ponstrous voice,
Shook de world to its very jois'.

10. "Stole my apples, I believe."
"No, Marse Lord, I 'spec' it was Eve."

11. "Out of this garden you must git,
Earn yo' livin' by yo' sweat."

12. He put an angel at de do',
Tol' um never come dere no mo'.

13. Of this tale there is no mo',
Eve et the apple and Adam de co'. (31)

And one song is not tender for Eve:

Eve disobeyed,
She broke the alliance,
And we have to pay her debt.[1]

Elsewhere temptation is presented as an ever-present situation:

Old Satan tempted Eve,
And Eve, she tempted Adam;
And that's why the sinner has to pray so hard
To get his sins forgiven. (59)

But the most striking situation for the mind of the slave was the one in which God looked for the man, who hid after eating the forbidden fruit (Genesis 3:7-13):

> First time God called Adam,
> Adam refused to answer,
> Adam's in the garden laying low;
> Second time God called Adam,
> Adam refused to answer,
> Adam's in the garden laying low.
> Eve, where is Adam,
> O, Eve, where is Adam?
> Lord, Adam's in the garden pinning leaves. (1)

Another spiritual underscores, however, that Adam finally answered: "An' Adam said: 'Hear me, Lord' " (55). It is of no use to flee God, since God is the ultimate Judge.

We again find this dimension of judgment in the story of Noah and the Flood. Some people believed that Noah was a "foolish man" because he built the ark on dry land, but he was in fact a "just man" because he obeyed God. God really wanted to destroy a wicked world and recreate a purified world. For the community trapped in slavery, the story of the Flood was one of hope: their exploitation would not last eternally. Noah's ark therefore was popular among the slaves:

> God told Norah to build the ark
> Three hundred cubits long,
> Fifty cubits wide,
> And thirty cubits high.
> Oh! Norah, go build the ark,
> Just like the Lord command. ("Oh! Norah, Go Build the Ark")

In fact, this construction project involved both Noah and the Lord. God was the architect and Noah was the builder. It was the salvation of creation that was at stake through them:

> They knocked at the window and they knocked at the door,
> They shouted: "Oh, Noah, please take me aboard."
> Noah shouted back: "You are full of sin,
> The Lord has the key and I can't let you in." ("Didn't It Rain")

It began to rain for forty days and forty nights:

> When it begun to rain,
> Women and children begun to scream.

It rain all day and it rain all night,
It rain 'til mountain top was out of sight. (141)

The sinner went mad in the Flood.

The Genesis story says: "At the end of forty days Noah opened the window of the ark that he had made" (Genesis 8:6). He first let out a crow and then a dove "to see if the waters had subsided from the surface of the ground" (verse 8). "The dove found no place to set its foot," but seven days later it came back "and there in its beak was a freshly plucked olive leaf" (verse 11). The scene struck the imagination of the African Americans, for the dove was the harbinger of a world rid of slavery:

> Open the window, Noah!
> Open the window,
> Let the dove come in.
>
> The little dove flew in the window and mourned,
> Open the window,
> Let the dove come in.
>
> The little dove brought back the olive leaf,
> Open the window,
> Let the dove come in. (150)

The olive leaf was "an assurance of heavenly love" ("Show Me the Way"). And the poor slave would like to have the dove's wings to find a place of freedom:

> Lord, I wisht I had wings like Norah's dove,
> Norah's dove.
> I would fly way to heav'n and be at rest,
> Be at rest. ("Lord, I Wish I Had Wings Like Norah's Dove")

At the end of the Flood, God sent "the sign of the rainbow," saying: "No more water but fire next time" (141). The Bible text clearly states God's point of view: "I have set my bow in the clouds, and it shall be a sign of the covenant between me and the earth. . . . When the bow is in the clouds, I will see it and remember the everlasting covenant between God and every living creature of all flesh that is on the earth" (Genesis 9:13, 16). The meaning of the story of the Flood is not the destruction of the world, but the deliverance of Noah and his family.

Various other patriarchs of Bible history are mentioned on occasion. For example, "Father Abraham" is in the glory of God, as seen in the Gospel parable of the poor man Lazarus (Luke 16:19-31). When the poor man died, he was carried by angels to "the bosom of Abraham" (verse 22). And the spiritual pleads:

> Rock o' my soul in de bosom of Abraham,
> Lord, rock o' my soul. (159; see also 43)

The sacrifice of Isaac and the sale of Joseph get scant attention in the spirituals (see 43). Esau is presented as an "experienced hunter" who "sold his birthright for a bowl of thin broth" ("Sen' Dem Angels Down"). On the other hand, Jacob got favored treatment because two episodes fascinated the slaves: Jacob's dream, in which the patriarch saw a ladder placed on the earth but whose top touched the sky (Genesis 28:12), and the struggle of Jacob with the angel at Jabbok (Genesis 32:23-33).

Jacob's ladder connected earth and heaven. It was, then, a symbol of the passage from the world of human beings to the world of God. The angels were no longer in the picture because it was the human being who was directly concerned and who had to show determination in climbing to the heavenly kingdom:

> I want's to climb up Jacob's ladder
> But I cyan' until I mek muh peace wid de Lawd. ("I Want to
>   Climb Up Jacob's Ladder")

At the top of the ladder, the meeting with Jesus and with deceased parents takes place. But to make progress in the right direction, one must struggle, and therein lies the point of the nocturnal struggle between Jacob and the angel of God.

The dialogue between the two combatants is recorded:

> 'Rastlin' Jacob, let me go,
> I will not let you go. (154)

The stake is nothing less than God's blessing (Genesis 32:27). The slaves found in this text a model for their own struggle:

> All night
> Wrastlin' Jacob's all night
> All night till de break ob day.
> O we will wrastle
> Wrastle al de night till de break ob day. ("All Night")

> I hold my brudder wid a tremblin' han',
> De Lord will bless my soul
> Wrastl' on Jacob, day is a-breakin',
> Wrastl' on Jacob, oh he would not let him go. ("I Hold My
>   Brudder wid a Tremblin' Han' ")

The struggle between the adversaries took place at night and required a long vigil.

One must last in this struggle by relying on one's brothers and sisters. But dawn will come as a blessing of the Lord, for it brings freedom or the kingdom of God (which, for the slave, were the same reality). Those who held fast in the terrible battle would receive a new name.

The Symbols of Exodus

With the story of the Exodus, we are at the core of the black church's faith. No other text had so much attraction for the black believer. We do not talk about interest, because that can be fleeting, but of fascination. A chaplain in the Union Army had seen it in 1864 among the freedmen: "There is no part of the Bible with which they are so familiar as the story of the deliverance of Israel. Moses is their ideal of all that is high, and noble, and perfect, in man. I think they have been accustomed to regard Christ not so much in the light of a *spiritual* Deliverer, as that of a second Moses who would eventually lead *them* out of their prison-house of bondage."[2] Although whites considered America a new Promised Land, a new Israel, blacks knew full well that in reality it was Egypt, a land of oppression that would suffer the worst calamities if it did not free the children of Africa.

Even before the general emancipation of 1865, the African Americans believed they were going through an experience similar to that of Exodus. In 1808 Absalom Jones, an African American preacher, interpreted in that sense the official suppression of the slave trade; it was a providential happening comparable to the Exodus from Egypt. The parallel was even more striking with the Civil War. And as soon as a strong personality emerged from the black community, he or she was called a "black Moses." That appellation was given to Harriet Tubman, Booker T. Washington, Marcus Garvey, and Martin Luther King, Jr.

As soon as it began, black Christian preaching took the Exodus as its central theme, not to say its only theme. Charles Davenport, a former slave, expressed it this way: "Us niggers didn't have no secret meetin's. All us had was church meetin's in arbor out in de woods. De preachers 'ud exhort us dat us was de chillun o' Israel in de wilderness an' de Lawd done sont us to take dis lan' o' milk an' honey."[3] They were not to cease praying for freedom, and God would finally hear the cries of the people (compare Exodus 3:7).

What did the slaves find in the Exodus? Here is their way of summarizing the decisive event of the history of Israel that would illuminate their own history:

> God sends Moses to tell Pharaoh to free the enslaved Hebrews. Punishing the Egyptians and hardening the heart of Pharaoh, God, through Moses, directs a prodigious drama that intensifies with the death of the first-born of the Egyptians. Grieving for the death of his first-born child, Pharaoh gives freedom to the Hebrews. Later, the heart of Pharaoh is hardened anew and pursues the Hebrews with his chariots to enslave them again. Facing the sea and with Pharaoh gaining rapidly on them, the children

of Jacob feel trapped. "Moses said to the people: 'Do not be afraid. Stand firm and you will see the deliverance the Lord will bring you today. . . . The Lord will fight for you; you need only be still' " (Exodus 14:12-14). God ordered Moses to lift over the water his staff of deliverance. The waters parted. The children of Jacob, carrying the bones of Joseph, crossed over, on the journey to the Promised Land. The army of Pharaoh was drowned and the children of the Hebrews knew that their God was the Almighty God of deliverance.[4]

Two spirituals suffice to encompass the Exodus event. The first, and best known, is considered to be the "national anthem" of the black people: "Go Down, Moses." It has twenty-five couplets in its official version. The first twenty were already present in the *New York Tribune* publication of 1861. It is not difficult to see that the five last couplets are rather far removed from the Exodus theme. Here is the 1861 text:

Refrain:
Go down, Moses,
'Way down in Egypt land,
Tell ol' Pharaoh,
Let my people go!

1. When Israel was in Egypt's land,
   Let my people go.
   Oppressed so hard they could not stand,
   Let my people go.

2. Thus saith the Lord, bold Moses said . . .
   If not, I'll smite your first-born dead. . . .

3. No more shall they in bondage toil . . .
   Let them come out with Egypt's spoil. . . .

4. When Israel out of Egypt came . . .
   And left the proud oppressive land. . . .

5. O, 'twas a dark and dismal night . . .
   When Moses led the Israelites. . . .

6. 'Twas good ole Moses and Aaron, too . . .
   'Twas they that led the armies through. . . .

7. The Lord told Moses what to do . . .
   To lead the children of Israel through. . . .

8. O come along, Moses, you'll not get lost . . .
Stretch out your rod and come across. . . .

9. As Israel stood by the waterside . . .
At the command of God it did divide. . . .

10. When they had reached the other shore . . .
They sang a song of triumph o'er. . . .

11. Pharaoh said he would go across . . .
But Pharaoh and his host were lost. . . .

12. O, Moses, the cloud shall cleave the way . . .
A fire by night, a shade by day. . . .

13. You'll not get lost in the wilderness . . .
With a lighted candle in your breast. . . .

14. Jordan shall stand up, like a wall . . .
And the walls of Jericho shall fall. . . .

15. Your foes shall not before you stand . . .
And you'll possess fair Canaan's land. . . .

16. 'Twas just about harvest time . . .
When Joshua led his host divine. . . .

17. O let us all from bondage flee . . .
And let us all in Christ be free. . . .

18. We need not always weep and moan . . .
And wear the slavery chains forlorn. . . .

19. This world's a wilderness of woe . . .
O, let us on to Canaan go. . . .

20. What a beautiful morning that will be . . .
When time breaks up in eternity. (50)

We have gone through the whole itinerary from Egypt to the Promised Land, and it is with the liberating role of Christ and the perspective of eternity that the song ends. Christ is the one who has the power to anticipate in history the heavenly emancipation. The message of this spiritual, a hymn to freedom couched in biblical terms, was so clear that singing it was banned on certain plantations, for "Exodus is the clearest Old Testament example of both the sensitivity for God to the oppressed and of the destruction of the oppressors."[5]

The other song based on Exodus is more centered on the defeat of Pharaoh:

Didn't old Pharaoh get los', get los', get los'.
Didn't old Pharaoh get los' in de Red Sea, true believer,
  O Red Sea?

De Lord said unto Moses "Go unto
Pharaoh now,
For I have hardened Pharaoh's heart
To me he will not bow." (33)

The central figure in this biblical epic is surely that of Moses, who often took on messianic aspects. Few spirituals are specifically about him, but he is often mentioned. We see him at the head of his army (196). He received the law that God etched in his heart ("My Lord's Goin' Move This Wicked Race"). We find "brother Moses" in the kingdom (106). It was in his heart that God had written the law ("He Had to Run"). He was the model of the "man of God" ("Witness for the Lord").

Moses does not totally eclipse Joshua, the one who took the city of Jericho (Joshua 6). The event is well recalled:

Joshuway was the son of Nun,
He prayed for God to stop the sun,
The sun it stopped at the hour of seven,
The ram horn blowed,
God heard it in Heaven. ("I Can't Stay Away")

The tumbling down of the walls of Jericho was a powerful evocation of the desired crumbling of the walls of slavery. It proclaimed that the Promised Land was not out of reach for a courageous community that put total faith in God. The musical summary of the biblical narrative reaches the apex of art:

Joshua fit de battle of Jericho;
An' de walls come tumblin' down.

You may talk about yo' king of Gideon,
You may talk about yo' man of Saul;
Dere's none like good ol' Joshua
At de battle of Jericho.

Up to de walls of Jericho
He marched with spear in han';
"Go blow dem ram horns," Joshua cried,
"Cause de battle am in my han'."

Den de lam' ram sheep horns began to blow,

Trumpets began to soun';
Joshua commanded the chillun to shout
An' de walls come tumblin' down. (104)

From just after the conquest of Canaan, another figure attracted the African Americans: Samson. He was "the strongest man that ever lived on earth" and he slaughtered a thousand Philistines ("He Had to Run"). How could they not linger on his exploits (Judges 13–16)?

Stop an' let me tell you what Samson done,
He looked at the lion an' de lion run,
But Samson killed that lion dead
And the bees made honey in the lion's head.

Samson burned up a field of corn,
They looked for Samson but he was gone.
A-so many formed a plot,
It wasn't many days 'fore he was caught.

They bound him with a rope and, while walking along,
He looked down and saw an old jawbone,
He moved his arms, the rope snap like thread,
When he got through killin', three thousand was dead.
    ("Samson")

The refrain of this spiritual is, at the same time, an allusion to the final scene of the life of Samson (the collapse of the temple on the Philistines) and a call to mobilization of the slaves:

He said, "An' if I had'n my way,
I'd tear this buildin' down."

But the last refrain states differently:

He said, "And now I got my way,
And I'll tear this buildin' down."

That building can only be the edifice of slavery. And the oppressed express a great confidence in the future.

In the same theme of victory, we must cite David the musician. The African Americans especially recalled the meeting between David and Goliath—a powerful symbol for those who did not have the same weapons as their oppressors.

Lit'le David play on yo' harp, Hallelu, hallelu,

Lit'le David play on yo' harp, Hallelu.

Lit'le David was a shepherd boy;
He killed Goliath an' shouted fo' joy. (118)

The Prophets of Liberation

The third group of Old Testament figures who are evoked by the spirituals are the prophets. Frequently, we find references to Elijah, Ezekiel, Jonah, Daniel and the Hebrew children, and Job. However, Isaiah and Jeremiah, whose books are the largest among the Old Testament prophets, are little mentioned by the slaves. This is proof (if we needed any) that the new Christians were selective in their choice of books from the biblical library. The choice gives added value to their selected passages.

We have already had occasion to speak about Elijah's chariot of fire (2 Kings 2:11). The slave never tired of saying:

> Rock, chariot, I told you to rock!
> Judgment goin' to find me! ("Rock, Chariot, I Told You to Rock")

> Elijah, rock, shout, shout;
> Elijah, rock, coming up Lord. ("Elijah, Rock")

And as there can be no chariot without wheels, Ezekiel's wheels fascinated the slave. The Bible text expresses it this way: "As I looked at the living creatures, I saw a wheel on the earth beside the living creatures, one for each of the four of them. . . . The four had the same form, their construction being something like a wheel within a wheel" (Ezekiel 1:15-16). This intersection of the wheels stimulated the imagination of the black community:

> Ezek'el saw de wheel
> 'Way up in de middle o' de air,
> De big wheel run by faith,
> De little wheel run by de grace o'God,
> A wheel in a wheel
> 'Way in de middle o' de air. (41)

The coupling of faith and grace expresses perfectly the collaboration of God and humanity on the journey for the salvation of humanity. Sometimes the coupling is faith and love, following good theological logic. But one spiritual gives a different meaning to the text:

> De big wheel represent God Himself
> An' de little wheel represent Jesus Christ. ("Sweet Hebben")

Finally, it was in their heart that the slaves found a "little wheel": "There is a little wheel that turns in my heart." And that discovery filled the oppressed with joy to the point that they entered into a trance (29). It was the wheel of religion, moaning, praying, shouting, crying, and laughing ("Ezekiel's Wheel").

The other text selected from Ezekiel was that of the dry bones (Ezekiel 37):

> God called Ezekiel by His word:
> "Go down and prophesy!"
> "Yes, Lord!"
> Ezekiel prophesied by the power of God,
> Commanded de bones to rise. (39)

The human being, reduced to nothing, can return to life and strength to confront adversity, certain of divine help.

Another symbolic representation of the annihilation endured in slavery was the belly of the whale where Jonah found himself. In its own popular and humorous way, the following song tells the epic of the little prophet. It is a kind of shortened sermon, with its main point being the importance of listening to the word of God:

> Jonah was a man called by a word of God to go
> And to preach the Gospel in a sinful land.
> But he boarded a ship and tried to escape and it met
> A storm in the middle of the sea.
>
> The Lord made waves just to roll so high,
> The boat began to sink and all began to shout.
> So they pulled Jonah from the hold
> And threw him in the water to lighten the load.
>
> The Lord then made a whale very long and wide;
> Lord, Lord, what a fish!
> It swallowed Jonah whole;
> Lord, Lord, what a fish!
>
> Jonah began to pray in the belly of the whale. . . .
> He repented of his sins like a man in jail. . . .
>
> Now Jonah must have been a very wicked man, he must have
>   been a sinner. . . .
> Because when the whale swallowed him, it didn't like its dinner. . . .
>
> Well, it swam round and round in the ocean feeling very sick. . . .
> And after three days, it had to free him. . . .
> So the whale spit him out on dry land. . . .

And he began to preach like a just man. . . .

So the people abandoned their sins when they heard him in town. . . .
So when you hear the call, don't turn away from the Gospel.[6]

The first chapters of Daniel were among the most savored by the slaves. They chose four episodes in particular: the vision of the stone that breaks off from the mountain without anyone's intervention (Daniel 2:31-45), the story of the three young men in the furnace, the writing on the wall (chapter 5), and Daniel in the lions' den (chapter 6).

Since the story of the stone is not well known, it is good to be reminded of its context. We are in Babylon. King Nebuchadnezzar has dreams, but he does not know how to interpret them. He asks the magicians of the realm to divine their meaning without his explaining what he saw. The trial is impossible, and all the wise men will be massacred. It is then that Daniel intervenes. The mystery of the dream of Nebuchadnezzar is revealed to him in a night vision. The king saw a great and beautiful statue. "As you looked on, a stone was cut out, not by human hands, and it struck the statue on its feet of clay and broke them in pieces. . . . But the stone that struck the statue became a great mountain and filled the whole earth" (Daniel 2:34-35). That is the dream. What, then, is its interpretation? The stone signifies a kingdom "that shall never be destroyed, nor shall this kingdom be left to another people." It shall "crush" all the previous kingdoms, "and it shall stand forever" (verse 44).

Here is how a spiritual expresses the key to the text:

Daniel saw the stone hewn out of the mountain,
Tearing down the kingdom of this world.

Have you seen that stone,
Tearing down the kingdom of this world?

You'd better seek that stone. . . .

Jesus was the stone. (24)

We see here a typically Christian reading of the Old Testament. The stone is essentially a sign, a prophecy of Jesus Christ. And the days of the kingdom of this world are short.

Right from the start, Daniel had Hebrew companions who had been given the imposed names of Shadrach, Meshach, and Abednego (Daniel 1:7). After his personal success in the service of King Nebuchadnezzar, Daniel had them selected to serve in the province of Babylon. But the Chaldeans denounced them before the king because they did not adore the statue that had been set up. Nebuchadnezzar had them thrown into a furnace. Can there be a better metaphor for slavery?

> Hebrew children in de fiery furnace.
> And dey begin to pray
> And de good Lawd smote dat fire out. . . .
> Lawd, wasn't dat a mighty day! (20)

Daniel 5 tells the story of a mysterious writing on the wall of the royal palace by a man's hand while King Belshazzar was in the middle of a drinking orgy. No one except Daniel could decipher it. Three words needed to be understood: "MENE, God has numbered the days of your kingdom and brought it to an end; TEKEL, you have been weighed on the scales and found wanting; PERES, your kingdom is divided and given to the Medes and Persians" (verses 26-28). At least three spirituals rejoice in this writing on the wall, for it signaled the defeat and the judgment of the present world. The end of oppression was decreed by God Almighty.

Could we doubt it? It suffices that we read the following episode of the Book of Daniel in which the one who adores the true God is thrown into the lion's den:

> Daniel in de lion's den,
> Oh de angel lock de lion's jaws.
> Oh how-a could Daniel pray!
> Daniel pray three times a day. ("Daniel in de Lion's Den")

The slaves began to pray:

> Oh-o Lord, Daniel's in de lion's den,
> Come he'p him in a hurry. (another version)

But the slaves never lose sight of their own situation:

> Oh my Lord delivered Daniel,
> O why not deliver me? (138)

Let us end our journey through the Old Testament with the figure of Job. One song echoes the first chapter of Job:

> Err, Job! All your sheeps an' servants burned,
> The Lord hath given
> An' the Lord has taken away,
> Blessed be the name of the Lord.
>
> Err, Job! All your camels is gone. . . .
> The Lord hath given. . . .
> Err, Job! All your chilluns is dead. . . .

> Job's wife said—"Curse God and die."
> Job said the Lord hath given
> An' the Lord has taken away,
> Blessed be the name of the Lord. ("Err, Job!")

This song shows how conscious the slave community was of the intensity of its trials. The temptation to curse God lurked, but only the unfathomable will of God was important. Each person journeyed on in the mystery of God's designs. God knew what God was doing, even when God's behavior confused the slaves and stripped them of everything.

We would not want to end this journey through the Old Testament without insisting on how the slaves felt they were contemporaries of these persons who lived in very different periods of history. On the train of the gospel, there were "Moses, Noah, and Abraham, and all the prophets" (47). These formed a kind of celestial court into which the convert was introduced. And especially, they gave strong examples of how to behave in the harsh situation of servitude.

But the most important fact is that all through this history of highs and lows, of defeats and victories, God remained the same.

> When Moses an' his soldiers f'om Egypt's lan' did flee,
> His enemies were in behin' him, an' in front of him de sea.
> God raised de waters like a wall, an' opened up de way,
> An' de God dat lived in Moses' time is jus' de same today. . . .
>
> Daniel faithful to his God, would not bow down to men,
> An' by God's enemy he was hurled into de lion's den,
> God locked de lion's jaw we read, an' robbed him of his prey,
> An' de God dat lived in Daniel's time is jus' de same today. (65)

The Men of the Gospel

The New Testament is essentially the proclamation of the good news concerning Jesus Christ, Son of God and Savior. Jesus is at the center of the narrative and of the message, and everything has meaning through him. His presence illuminates all the writings of the primitive church. The gospel is a person.

Apart from Jesus, the other New Testament figures do not have the same status as the heroes of the Old Testament. In this abridged Gospel that is the spirituals, it is interesting to seek out the characters who were chosen for attention through popular tradition. Of course, there are the disciples, but there are also key figures such as Nicodemus and Lazarus and even some characters from parables.

The profile of John the Baptist, Christ's forerunner, seems to have been the object of a debate. It was most probably to avoid too harsh a word in the call to conversion:

> Some say that John the Baptist was nothin' but a Jew,
> But the Holy Bible tells us that John was a preacher too. (111)

Despite the African Americans' experience of being marginalized and being made
to feel inferior, over time an anti-Jewish sentiment grew up among some African
Americans in urban centers. It would become widespread only after the great
migration to the North, at the beginning of the twentieth century.

   While baptism is the decisive event of Christian conversion, especially in the
Baptist churches, the baptism practiced by John allowed the new believer to express
his or her expectations:

> In the river of Jordan John baptized,
> How I long to be baptized,
> In the river of Jordan John baptized
> Unto the dying Lamb. ("Pray On")

   The apostle Peter is mentioned a few times because his work as a fisherman
brought him close to the condition lived by the slave. His vocation is evoked:

> Peter on de Sea o' Galilee, . . .
> Take yo' net an' foller me. ("My Lord Says He's Gwineter Rain
>   Down Fire")

But it was Peter's trial of faith that most spoke to the heart of the believer:

> Peter walked upon the sea,
> And Jesus told him, "Come to me." ("Come down, My Lord")

It would not do to underestimate Peter's qualities as a preacher, for it would be
difficult to imitate him (8). He was especially an example of a good shepherd, and
it was to him that Jesus said, "Peter, if you love me, feed my sheep" (210). The
African American felt called to a greater love.

   In a Christianity centered on conversion, Nicodemus had a special place, for
"Christ tol' Nicodemus, he mu' be born again" (91), and he asked himself how
that can be done ("My Lord's Goin' Move This Wicked Race"). And everything
that had to do with healing and the resurrection acquired a particular force. The
scenes with the blind men prove it:

> The blind man stood on the road and cried,
> Cryin', oh my Lord, save-a me. (186)

> Blind man lying at the pool.
> Lying there to be healed. . . .

Crying: O Lord save me. . . .
Save my weary soul. (10)

The African Americans identified directly with such a person, as also with the apostle Thomas, "who doubts," Judas, "who steals," and Pilate, "who washes his hands" (see 38).

If there are two blind men in the spirituals, there are also two Lazaruses in the Gospels: that of the parable in Luke 16, and the brother of Martha and Mary. In a spiritual the distance between the Lazarus of the parable and the slave of the nineteenth century is erased:

Poor man Lazarus, poor as I, Don't you see? . . .
When he died he foun' a home on high.
He had a home in-a dat Rock, Don't you see?

Rich man, Dives, He lived so well, Don't you see? . . .
When he died he foun' a home in Hell,
He had no home in-a dat Rock, Don't you see? (78)

The community also cried out, "I want to die as Lazarus died," for his death brought a resurrection "in the bosom of Abraham." And what happened to the brother of Martha and Mary could happen again today for the children of God:

Oh, He raise-a poor Lazarus, Raise him up,
He raise him from de dead, I tol' ye so,
While many were standin' by,
Jesus loosen' de man from under de groun',
An' tell him: "Go prophesy." (144)

The return of the prodigal son is also told, following closely the narrative of Luke ("I Believe I'll Go Back Home"). Stephen, the first martyr of the primitive Christian community, is praised for the firmness of his faith and of his spirit ("Plenty Good Room"). And the last man to have a place in the spirituals' list of those who carried the gospel is none other than the apostle Paul. But it is surprising that the evocation of Paul does not correspond at all to the path of his personal destiny. His conversion did not inspire the unknown bards, who avoided quoting his concept of the relationship between masters and slaves. Only one event in the life of Paul is evoked in the spirituals: his arrest in Philippi.

Paul and Silas, bound in jail,
Sing God's praises both night and day. (11)

The two men's roles are sometimes shared—one sings and the other prays ("I Ain't

Gwine Grief Muh Lawd No Mo' " or "All Night"). But in any case, the composer appropriated the situation for himself:

> Paul and Silas, put in jail, all the night,
> And who shall deliver po' me!
>
> Oh, they prayed so loud that the jailer couldn't sleep,
> And who shall deliver po' me!
>
> The prison door opened wide,
> And who shall deliver po' me!
>
> The jailer asked Paul what to do . . .
> Convert yourself to me and be baptized.
> ("Who Shall Deliver Po' Me")

The Women of the Gospel

If for the moment we leave aside Mary the mother of Jesus, the female space in the spirituals, as far as the New Testament goes, is dominated by the sisters of Lazarus—Martha and Mary—and by Mary Magdalene. In my selection of 210 songs, twelve texts evoke one or the other of these women in the context of resurrection, be it that of Lazarus or that of Jesus. Even then it is not always easy to make a distinction between the two circumstances, as can be seen in the following refrain:

> Oh, Mary don't you weep, don't you mourn,
> Pharaoh's army got drowned. (145)

What is more significant here is that this spiritual links the Christ of the resurrection to the God of the Exodus. The same power of God at work in liberating the children of Israel from Egypt was also at work in liberating Jesus from death. The liberation the Bible speaks of is at the same time social and spiritual, the end of oppression as well as the end of death. The spirituals repeat over and over that the time of tears "under the weeping willow" is over and that the dawn of a new day is at hand.

Mary Magdalene's run on Easter morning (John 20:2) impressed the slave.

> Run, Mary, run,
> I know the other world is not like this. (162)

The race to the tomb is turned into a race to the disciples to announce the meeting place in Galilee ("Oh, Mary, Oh, Marthy"), and thus the race toward the kingdom of God. For Mary is already present in the kingdom: she wears a gold chain on whose rings are inscribed the name of Jesus; she welcomes guests to the table of the celestial banquet; she sings the praise of the Lamb. With Martha, she rings the bells of the New Jerusalem. It is as much as to say that these women were the first messengers of the resurrection, and at the same time prophets and disciples, and that all women after them must have a recognized place in the Christian community.

As we are still awaiting the definitive return of the Lord, it is important to stay awake and keep one's lamp lit. The parable of the ten virgins in Matthew 25 (verses 1-13) inspired a few songs, the most symbolic among them being the following:

> Don't let him catch you with your work undone.
> He is coming again so soon.
> Be ready when he come.
>
> Don't be like them foolish virgins when he come.
> He is coming again so soon.
>
> Five was wise and five was foolish when he come.
> He is coming again so soon.
>
> Have oil in de vessels when de Bridegroom come.
>
> Have your lamp trimmed and burning when he come.
> Go meet him when he come. ("Be Ready When He Come")

The Words of the Sermon on the Mount

The discourse of Jesus preferred by the slaves was the Sermon on the Mount. This collection of wisdom sayings contains strong teachings that give a code of behavior for one's whole life. "Take Matthew 5 and read the whole chapter; it is a guide for Christians, and it tells them what they must do."

To my knowledge, four of these texts were set to music. First, "You are the light of the world" (Matthew 5:14) yielded the following:

> Hold out yo' light you heav'n boun' soldier.
> Let yo' light shine aroun' de world. ("Hold Out Yo' Light")
>
> O Christians, hold up yo' light.
> Hold yo' light till the heaven doors close. ("Hold Up Yo' Light")

Also, God's providence that allows the birds to neither sow nor reap (Matthew 6:26) and the word about the foxes and the Son of Man (8:20) are evoked together:

> De foxes have a hole, an' de birdies have a nest,
> De Son of man he dun no where to lay de weary head.
> Jehovia, halleluja, de Lord is perwide. ("Foxes Have Holes")

But the slave is not always so sure of God's attention:

> The foxes have holes in the ground
> And the birds have nests in the air
> And everything has a hiding place
> But we poor sinners have none. ("Ain't Dat Hard Trials")

A gentler version of the same text distinguishes between Christians and sinners, reserving a better place for believers:

> The foxes, they have holes in the ground,
> The birds have nests in the air,
> The Christians have a hiding place,
> But sinners ain't got nowhere. (59)

The slave was conscious of the existence of sin. We have proof of this in the use of the metaphor of the mote and the beam. There were a lot of weaknesses in the interpersonal relationships in the oppressed community. The originality of the spiritual consists in speaking about the beam of the "sister" where the Gospel speaks only of the mote of the "brother" (Matthew 7:3). The change possibly indicates the difficulty of maintaining a relationship of equality between men and women in the slave community:

> I saw the beam in my sister's eye,
> Couldn't see the beam in mine;
> You'd better leave your sister's door,
> Go keep your own door clean. (81)

The only solution, individual and collective, consists in "building on the rock" (Matthew 7:24-27). The image underscores the necessity of a solid rooting in the faith, for the rock is Christ:

> I build my house upon de rock, O yes, Lord!
> No wind no storm can blow 'em down, O yes, Lord! ("March On")

That house is halfway between heaven and earth, and it is at the moment of death that one will really arrive there. But it demonstrates that the oppressed were never totally domiciled on their plantation. Their true address was elsewhere.

Notes

1. Quoted in John Lomax and Alan Lomax, eds., *American Ballads and Folk Songs* (New York: Macmillan, 1947), 597.

2. W. G. Kephart, letter dated May 9, 1864, quoted in Albert J. Raboteau, *A Fire in the Bones* (Boston: Beacon, 1995), 33.

3. Quoted in James Mellon, ed., *Bullwhip Days: The Slaves Remember* (New York: Weidenfeld & Nicolson, 1988), 377.

4. Josiah Young, ""L'Exode, paradigme pour la théologie noire," *Concilium* 209 (1987): 114.

5. Ibid.

6. Text sung by Louis Armstrong; quoted in Theo Lehmann, *Negro Spirituals: Geschichte und Theologie* (Berlin: Eckart-Verlag, 1965), 381, n 150.

Bibliography

Cannon, Katie Geneva. "Slave Ideology and Biblical Interpretation." *Semeia* 47 (1989): 9–19.

Gilkes, Cheryl Towsend. " 'Go and Tell Mary and Martha': The Spirituals, Biblical Options for Women, and Cultural Tensions in the African American Religious Experience." *Social Compass* 43, no. 4 (1996): 563–81.

Kabasele Mukenge, André. "Figures Bibliques dans les Negro-spirituals. Un exemple de lecture contextuelle de la Bible." *Revue africaine de théologie* 18 (1994): 83–102.

Wimbusch, Vincent L. "The Bible and African Americans: An Outline of and Interpretative History." In *Stony the Road We Trod: African American Biblical Interpretation,* ed. Cain Hope Felder. Minneapolis: Fortress, 1991, 81–97.

Young, Josiah. "L'Exode, paradigme pour la théologie noire." *Concilium* 209 (1987): 113–21.

7

"He's got the whole world in his hands."

The Almighty God and Jesus Crucified

"God struck me dead with his power."
—a former slave

THE ABUNDANCE AND THE RICHNESS of biblical references in spirituals should not lead us to believe that God was an immediately evident being for the black American slaves. Certainly, they came from a land where the Creator God was in the background of everything in daily life. But their confrontation with the inexplicable reality of slavery did not only create believers. The Reverend Joshua Boucher recounted the following conversation between a pastor and a slave somewhere in the South:

> —Have you any religion?
> —No, sir.
> —Don't you want religion?
> —No, sir.
> —Don't you love God?
> —What, me love God who made me with a black skin and white man to whip me![1]

In 1839 Daniel Alexander Payne, a bishop of the African Methodist Episcopal Methodist Church, reflected on the causes of the unbelief of the slaves:

These slaves are sensible of the oppression exercised by their masters; and they see these masters on the Lord's Day worshipping in his holy sanctuary. They hear their masters professing Christianity; they see their masters preaching the gospel; they hear these masters praying in their families, and they know that oppression and slavery are inconsistent with the Christian religion; therefore they scoff at religion itself—mock their masters, and distrust both the goodness and justice of God. Yet I have known them even to question his existence. I speak not of what others have told me, but of what *I have both seen and heard from the slaves themselves*.[2]

In the hands of slavers, the religion of Christ often took on the worst hypocrisy. Frederick Douglass, during the struggle for the abolition of slavery, thundered against the Christian religion as revised by the white masters:

For my part, I would say: long live unbelief! long live atheism! long live anything! Rather than the Gospel preached by these churchmen. They make of religion an instrument of tyranny and barbaric cruelty. . . . It is a religion for the oppressors, the tyrants, the robbers of men, assassins. . . . A religion that favors the rich against the poor, that exalts the proud over the humble; that divides humanity into two classes, the tyrants and the slaves; that tells the man in chains: "Remain in your estate" and to the oppressor: "Continue to oppress."[3]

A certain number of blacks believed that there was no God, for God never would have allowed the whites to perpetrate so many crimes over so many years. It is difficult to evaluate the number of these atheists.

Meanwhile, the spirituals are songs of faith. They consider God to be the ultimate goal in the journey of faith, but they are not theological treatises. For example, even though they follow Scripture closely, they never use the word "Trinity." Do they speak of God as the African God or as the Christian God? It is often difficult to tell if a text speaks to God the Father or to Christ. Just think of the use of the term "Lord," which can be used for the Father of Jesus or for Jesus himself. I will attempt, however, to give a profile of God and a profile of Jesus through the expressions used in these songs. The dossier is particularly abundant, especially when we consider the passion of Jesus. For the slave, music and song constituted proofs of the existence of God: "There must be a God somewhere" (151). Which God is it?

The Almighty God

The answer is in the omnipotence of God (see 46, 195), of God's active sovereignty, of God's greatness. But first of all, we must be conscious of and account for God's being different from the changing condition of humanity:

> God is a God! God don't never change!
> God is a God an' He always will be God! (53)

The Letter to the Ephesians tells us about the width, the length, the height, and the depth of the plan of God (3:18). One song uses these dimensions to evoke the incommensurability of God:

> Mah God is so high, yuh can't get over Him;
> He's so low, yuh can't get under Him;
> He's so wide, yuh can't get aroun' Him;
> Yuh mus' come in by an' through de Lam'. (123)

One must confess the immensity of God before giving God a more familiar face. The slaves always knew how to keep in balance the distance and the proximity of the One who is the master of history.

Five faces of God can be discerned in the spirituals. They mark the trajectory that goes from the birth of the world to its final end. God is first of all the One who creates and cares for creation. It is this One who calls people and brings them to freedom. In all circumstances, God comforts poor human beings and heeds their prayers. Finally, God will render justice on judgment day.

If black preaching spoke admirably about Creation,[4] black music is less expansive on the subject. In the spiritual I have already quoted (53), we find two beautiful stanzas about God's creation as both a past and a permanent activity:

> He made the sun to shine by day,
> He made the sun to show the way,
> He made the stars to show their light,
> He made the moon to shine by night. . . .
>
> The earth is His footstool an' heav'n His throne,
> The whole creation all His own,
> His love and power will prevail,
> His promises will never fail. (53)

But the praise of creation is expressed with even more insistence and sensitivity:

> He's got the whole world in His hands,
> He's got the big, round world in His hands. . . .
>
> He's got the wind and the rain in His hands. . . .
>
> He's got the little baby. . . .
> He's got you and me, sister. (64)

Certain versions do not hesitate to add that God also holds the "gambler," the "liar," and the "dice shooter." But the ones we think about, without explicit mention, are the earthly owners: their power was strictly limited through God's sovereignty. The community of captives felt itself to be the object of a special providence of God, or else it would not have been able to triumph over the enormous obstacles in its path.

The relationship of humankind to God is a relationship of origin. The human being is born of God, as the spiritual proclaims: "I been bawn of God" ("No Condemnation in My Soul"), and thus has the privilege of being a "child of God" and destined to commune with God. "I know de Lord has laid his hands on me" (79).

But it is also a relationship of knowledge, as in Psalm 139: "Oh, he sees all you do, he hears all you say" ("My Lord's a-Writing All the Time"). It is impossible to hide far from God's face (135). "God knows the secret of each heart." "My Lord is sitting in his Kingdom, His eyes are upon me."

The creature is invited to behave in a way worthy of his or her Creator, that is, to be moral and responsible.

The God who creates is also the God who speaks and who calls. This call can resonate at the moment of death, but it is first and foremost a call to conversion in the context of the religious service or of daily life:

> Hush, Hush, somebody's callin' mah name
> Oh mah Lawd, what shall I do? (72)

It is God looking for Adam, God waking Samuel from his sleep. It is the Lord who seeks witnesses, and the Lord needs mediators of the Lord's Word. God's call is "loud and strong," but no one can answer for you: "You got to answer by yourself" (184). Slaves were willing to be used by their true Master ("I Wanta Live So God Can Use Me"). This call takes on special importance in an apocalyptic work that has political connotations:

> My Lord calls me,
> He calls me by the thunder;
> De trumpet sounds within-a my soul:
> I ain't got long to stay here. (179)

In fidelity to the Bible, the Word of God is action—freeing action. We rediscover the Exodus theme, the acts of the prophets, the stories in the Book of Daniel. God delivered the children of Israel from the land of slavery, Daniel from the lions' den, Jonah from the belly of the whale. The hand of God has been at work in all the historic liberations. And God's past actions are the guarantee of present and future actions, since God "don't never change" (53). God has a special interest in Africa, according to the word of the psalm that, in the understanding of the slaves, announces Africa's salvation: "Let Ethiopia hasten to stretch out its hands to God" (Psalm 68:31).

Furthermore, in the spirituals, we discover an Almighty God with the aspect of a "mighty man of war" (170).

> My God He is a Man—a Man of war,
>   An' de Lawd God is His name.
> He tole Noah to build an ark,
>   By his holy plan;
> He tole Moses to lead the chillun,
>   From Egypt to the Promised Lan'. ("My God Is a Man of War")

The battle took place in the slaves' day "at the black door of Hell" ("Rock-er Ma Soul")—a transparent allusion to slavery. And the Civil War was already a strong experience of freedom:

> Oh! Praise an' tanks! De Lord he come
>   To set de people free;
> An' massa tink it day ob doom,
>   And we ob jubilee.
> De Lord dat heap de Red Sea waves,
>   He jus' as strong as den;
> He say de word: we la' night slaves
>   To-day, de Lord's freemen.
>   De yams will grow, de cotton blow,
>   We'll hab de rice an' corn;
>   Oh! nebber you fear, if nebber you hear
>   De driver blow his horn.
>
> We pray de Lord he gib us signs
>   Dat some day we be free;
> De Norf wind tell it to de pines,
>   De wild duck to de sea;
> We think it when de church-bell ring,
>   We dream it in de dream;
> De rice-bird mean it when he sing,
>   De yams will grow. . . .
>
> We know de promise nebber fail,
>   And nebber lie de word;
> So like de 'postles in de jail,

> We waited for de Lord;
> An' now he open ebery door,
>   An' trow away de key;
> He tink we lub him so before,
>   We lub him better free.
>   De yam will grow. . . .[5]

The emancipation would be even more complete with entry into the kingdom of God:

> We'll soon be free . . .
> When de Lord will call us home.
> My brudder, how long . . .
> 'Fore we done sufferin' here? ("We'll Soon Be Free")

Confidence is the order of the day, since it is the Lord who "has made the way" (200). In a world that turns awry and is in dire need of a revolution, God is a stable support and a true comfort.

> My God is a rock in a weary land, weary land,
> In a weary land.
> My God is a rock in a weary land,
> And a shelter in the time of storm! (128)

The imagery is sometimes daring: "Let thy bosom be my pillah" ("Hide-a-Me"). For the poor person knows quite well that, separated from father and mother, he or she cannot "stay here by myself" (120).

All those who suffer oppression speak to God in prayer: "Lord, I need you now" (94); "Kum ba yah" (113); "It's me, it's me, it's me, O Lord, standin' in need of pray'r" (178).

The need is individual. And prayer comes through song: "I'm gonna sing till the power of the Lord comes down" (169).

The attitude of the supplicant is expressed in biblical terms:

> Father I stretch my hands to Thee,
> No other help I know;
> If Thou withdraw Thyself from me,
> Ah, wither shall I go?

> Author of faith! To Thee I lift
> My weary longing eyes;
> O let me now receive that gift!
> My soul without it dies. ("Father I Stretch My Hands to Thee")

To put that type of prayer in context, listen to the account of a slave named Stroyer in the Deep South:

> When I went home to father and mother, I said to them, "Mr. Young is whipping me too much now; I shall not stand it, I shall fight him." Father said to me, "You must not do that, because if you do he will say that your mother and I advised you to do it, and it will make it hard for your mother and me, as well as for yourself. You must do as I told you, my son; do your work the best you can, and do not say anything. . . . I can do nothing more than pray to the Lord to hasten the time when these things shall be done away; that is all I can do. . . ." When the time came for us to go to bed, we all knelt down in family prayer, as was our custom; father's prayer seemed more real to me that night than ever before, especially in the words, "Lord, hasten the time when these children shall be their own free men and women." My faith in father's prayer made me think that the Lord would answer him at the farthest in two or three weeks, but it was fully six years before it came, and father had been dead two years before the war.[6]

> Even if God delays sometimes, it is God who hears and fulfills
>   the prayer (209).

> Oh, my Good Lord's done been here!
> Blessed my soul and gone away. (129)

Unless the soul is truly "anchored in de Lord" (132), so many causes impel it to let itself go and "sink down" (see 109).

A few times already we have seen that God the Father has a particularly important role at the end of history. That is when we will join him on his throne of glory. He will have rendered the ultimate judgment, in all justice:

> We have a just God to plead-a our cause,
> We are the people of God.
> He sits in the Heaven and he answers prayer. ("Come Along,
>   Moses")

On earth there is no way we can escape the Almighty's attention. "Dere's no hidin' place down dere" (135). God writes down everything that happens because he is "a-writin' all de time" (130). But faith chases fear from the heart of the disinherited:

> Soon-a will be done with the troubles of the world,
> Goin' home to live with God. (177)

Life then will be an eternal praise of God, for "the gift of God is eternal life" ("De Gif' of Gawd Is Eternal Life"). God's glory will be the clothing of the believer.

> Long befo' the flyin' clouds,
>   Befo' the heavens above,
> Befo' creation evuh was made,
>   He had redeemin's love. ("My God Is a Man of War")

When God comes, it is always for salvation.

The knowledge of God can remain purely intellectual. So the slaves quickly specified: "It ain't enough to talk about God, you've got to feel him moving on the altar of your heart." Having a relationship with God cannot fail to commit the whole person and make him or her vibrate to the same divine beat.

The Person of Jesus

To go from God the Father to God the Son is not simple, since the spirituals do not demonstrate a reflective Trinitarian theology. Only rarely is Jesus designated as the "only Son" or as the "darlin' Son" (129). To my knowledge, only one text speaks of the Father-Son relationship:

> The Father looked at His Son an' smiled,
> The Son did look at-a Him. (18)

The actions of the two are expressed in similar terms, indicating the difficulty the black community had in distinguishing them clearly:

> The Father saved my soul from hell
> And the Son freed me from sin. (18)

Even if we have spoken of the massive presence of the Old Testament and of its heroes, we must not conclude that Jesus is absent from, or rarely present in, the spirituals. While references to Christ are not highly developed in the spirituals, an analysis of 494 spirituals by Olli Alho indicates that "Jesus" (a more musical name than "Christ") is mentioned in 174 of them.[7] And we will see that the Son of God made flesh is given a multitude of titles and that the four great moments of his life—his birth, ministry, passion, and resurrection—are all well accounted for. In a few words, the spiritual "Amen" summarizes his life:

> See the little baby,
> Lying in a manger,
> On Christmas morning.
>
> See Him at the temple,

> Talking to the elders,
> How they marveled at His wisdom.
>
> See Him in the garden,
> Praying to His father,
> As Judas betrays Him.
>
> See Him on Calvary,
> Dying for our sins,
> But he rose on Easter. (7)

The implication of the slave in the life of Jesus would always be a characteristic of the black song: "Oh, I don't know nothing. I can't read a word. But, oh! I read Jesus in my heart, just as you read him in de book."[8]

To completely identify Jesus, the spirituals use three levels of titles: titles of glory, combat titles, and intimate names. Jesus is, at the same time, the Savior, the Warrior, and the Friend.

Two titles of honor emerge most strongly: "Savior" (eleven times in our selection) and "King" (twelve times). One song expresses it most solemnly:

> He is King of kings, he is Lord of lords,
> Jesus Christ, the first and last, no one works like him. (62)

Whatever Jesus did he brought to perfection. "That Jesus hath done all things well" (14). A fugitive slave, Josiah Henson, told how he was struck by this message of salvation he received from the mouth of a white preacher in Maryland:

With insistence, the preacher repeated the words: "for all men." This good news, this salvation was not for the benefit of a select few. They were for the slave as well as for the master, for the poor as well as for the rich, for the persecuted, the afflicted, the captive; even for me among the rest, a poor despised creature ill-treated, considered by the other to be incapable of anything but unpaid work—yet physically and mentally degrading. Oh! The joy and the sweetness of the feeling to know that one is loved! I would have wanted to die of joy at that moment, and I kept repeating to myself: "The compassionate Savior from whom I heard the words: 'he loves me,' He looks down on me from heaven, He died to save my soul and He will welcome me in Heaven." I was transported with sweet joy. I felt I could see a glorious being, in a cloud of splendor, smiling from above. In complete contrast to the experience I had felt of scorn and brutality from my earthly master, I was strutting under the benevolent smile of this heavenly Being. I thought: "He will be my refuge, He will dry all the tears from my eyes. Now I can endure anything; nothing will appear difficult for me after that." I was sure that if only master Riley knew him, he would not live such a coarse, evil and cruel life. Drowning in the beauty of divine love, I loved my enemies and prayed for those who had treated me cruelly.[9]

The poor sinner was "washed by the blood of the Lamb" (74). Jesus even made the sinner "white" (74). Jesus is the presence of life. He is the true Master, who replaces the false master of the plantation. He is the "governor of the nations" (181):

> Jesus is de ruler,
> He rule ma soul.
> He rule de hebben.
> He rule de sinner.
> He rule little David.
> He rule ole Goliath.[10]

Jesus is present everywhere: "Everywhere I go, my Lord, somebody's talking about Jesus."[11] Christ's victory over sin and death is strongly underscored. This "King Emmanuel" is a "mighty 'manuel" (110). All power is in his hand. As much as God, he can be considered "a mighty solid Rock" (198). We can take refuge in him in the storm (170, 78).

But if Jesus is King, it is not only because he is seated comfortably on a throne of glory; it is also because he gives battle daily against the forces of evil. In the past, he "broke the Roman kingdom down" (62). Now this gallant warrior appears as the horseman of the apocalypse (Revelation 6:2; 19:11). He leads his troops "on a horse white as milk." That is why the faithful encouraged him in his punitive expedition: "Ride on, King Jesus" (156).

The battle was against Satan, symbol of evil and oppression. The believer gave witness from his or her own experience:

> When I was lyin' at hell's dark door,
> No one to pity po' me,
> Massa Jesus He come ridin' by,
> An' bought my liberty. (122)

> King Jesus, he was so strong (ter), my Lord,
> That he jarred down the walls of hell. ("Little Children, Then
>   Won't You Be Glad")

Jesus is the stone mentioned by Daniel that "tear[s] down the kingdom of this world" (24; see Daniel 2:45). The same event can be expressed in more poetic terms:

> The walls of my house were made of brick

> With steel in the middle,
> King Jesus stood and fought in the blood
> And conquered until he fell.[12]

It is surprising that some texts present Jesus in a role that the Old Testament attributes to Moses. The figure of Jesus is superimposed on that of Moses and in some way completes him.[13] Hence, Jesus delivers his people from slavery, leads them across the desert, and makes them cross the Jordan. A new Moses and a new Joshua, King Jesus is the captain of a ship that sails toward the Promised Land ("The Ship of Zion"). The tomb of Jesus is compared to the closing of the Red Sea:

> Oh, Mary, don't you weep, don't you mourn,
> Pharaoh's army got drowned. (145)

And Calvary is compared to Egypt:

> Jesus Christ had died for me.
> Far away in the land of Egypt,
> Jesus Christ gave me freedom,
> Far away in the land of Egypt.

If this Jesus bears a strong resemblance to Moses, the freedom that he gives concerns the soul as well as the enslaved body. The theme of spiritual liberation certainly is not absent, in imitation of all the hymns inspired by pietism and heard in the churches of the South:

> I think it was about twelve o'clock,
> When Jesus led me to the rock;
> I remember the day, I know the time,
> Jesus freed this soul of mine;
> My head got wet with the midnight dew,
> The morning star was witness too. (153)

> I'm a chile of God wid my soul set free.
> For Christ hab bought my liberty.[14]

Slaves suffered much from being sold by the masters; now it was Jesus who bought them in a completely different transaction. As the soul cannot be separated from the body, complete freedom is historically inevitable, indissoluble on earth and in heaven, personal and collective:

> Now no more weary trav'lin'

> 'Cause my Jesus set-a me free
> An' dere's no more auction block for me
> Since He give me liberty. (173)
>
> O, shout my sister, for you are free,
> For Christ has brought you liberty. (188)

It was he who raised Lazarus from the dead. Thus "Uncle Lawson" was able to give an answer to Frederick Douglass, who could not see how to get out of slavery for life: "The Lord want to make you free, my dear; everything is possible with him. . . . 'Ask and it shall be given unto you.' If you want freedom, ask it from the Lord in faith, and he will give it to you."[15] Christ's time on earth sowed liberty. Although he went up to heaven, he left behind freedom for humankind ("Can't You Live Humble").

These titles of glory and victory could lead one to believe that the relationship with Jesus is accompanied by military marches played on a mighty organ. But that would be forgetting the intimate relationship established between Jesus and the slave. King Jesus is first of all a friend, a confidant, "my Jesus" (5, 37, 76). That perspective brings new images:

> Sweet Jesus, sweet Jesus,
> He's the Lily of the Valley,
> He's the Bright and Morning Star.
> Sweet Jesus, sweet Jesus,
> He's the Fairest of ten thousand to my soul. (181; see also 68, 183)

And the poor slave did not hesitate to "roll in Jesus' arms" (see 161). Here was a friend on whom one could count, "my only friend" (112), my "dearest friend" (163), "my bosom friend" (21). Jesus continues to be the companion right to the end of the road, no matter how difficult the way. And the prayer becomes insistent:

> I want Jesus to walk with me
> All along my pilgrim journey,
> Lord, I want Jesus to walk with me. (84)

But Jesus was already waiting there on the roadside:

> I heard the voice of Jesus say:
> "Come unto me and rest (and rest);
> Lay down, thou weary one, lay down
> Thy head upon my breast."
> With pitying eyes the Prince of Peace

Beheld our helpless grief (our grief);
He saw, and O amazing love!
He came to our relief! (166)

Happiness consists in walking as closely to Jesus as possible:

Just a closer walk with Thee,
Grant it, Jesus, is my plea,
Daily walking close to Thee,
Let it be, dear Lord, let it be.

I am weak and Thou art strong;
Jesus, keep me from all wrong;
I'll be satisfied as long,
As I walk, let me walk close to Thee. (107)

And so Jesus was a counselor, a comforter, and a confidant who stayed very close:

O, a little talk wid Jesus, makes it right, all right;
Lord, troubles of ev'ry kind,
Thank God, I'll always find,
Dat a little talk wid Jesus makes it right.
    ("A Little Talk Wid Jesus Makes It Right")

The invention of the telephone allowed for a different expression of the same idea:

Oh, Jesus is on the main line;
Tell Him what you want.[16]

Only Jesus knows "de trouble I've seen" (134). He listens all day long to hear the sinner pray (111). He knocks at the door (174), calling each one by name (72). So we must not give up: "Oh, you got Jesus, hold him fast" (146).

A newly freed slave asserted, as he told of the brutality he had endured: "If I didn't know Jesus Christ, I go crazy all dese years . . . ! Jesus is my trust. He keep heart right. If I do right, Jesus take me. When he send for me, if I can on'ly meet him, I satisfied. Distress and hard labor drive me to Christ. So heart-broken, tired, heart all fall down inside!"[17]

This relationship can be expressed as that of the shepherd and his flock: "Jesus carries de young lambs in his bosom" (157). He leads the old sheep to calm waters (Psalm 23:2). But then a lamb goes astray:

Oh! Shepherd, your lamb gone astray,

> Oh, come and go with me.
> ("Oh, Shepherd, Your Lamb Gone Astray")

The problem can be even bigger if "the sheep all gone astray" ("Shepherd, Where'd You Lose Your Sheep?"). Singers asked, don't "you hear the lambs crying" (210)? The slaves prayed that someday the sheep would come back, and they sang alleluia when the lost sheep was found (35).

Following Peter's example after the resurrection, the believer shouted:

> Lord, I love Thee, Thou dost know; . . .
> O give me grace to love Thee more. (210)

The slaves found joy only when they made more room in their heart for the Lord (90). And they wanted that love to be a reality for all human beings:

> Is there anybody here who loves my Jesus?
> Anybody here who loves my Lord?
> I want to know if you love my Jesus;
> I want to know if you love my Lord. (99)

The slave became a missionary for salvation through Jesus:

> Come to Jesus,
> Come to Jesus just now. . . .
> He will save you. . . .
> He is able. . . .
> He is willing. . . .
> He will hear you. . . .
> He will forgive you. . . .
> He will cleanse you. . . .
> Only trust Him. (22)

Love invites imitation, and the slaves very much wanted to "be like Jesus" in their heart (121).

You will have noticed that in this list of the qualities ascribed to Jesus, from the most solemn qualities to the most familiar qualities, Jesus is never presented as "black." That claim of "blackness" for God and for Jesus would appear only at the end of the nineteenth century with Bishop Henry McNeal Turner.18 And this theme would be developed in the twentieth century by visionaries such as Marcus Garvey, by Muslims such as Elijah Muhammad, and by theologians of the 1960s such as James H. Cone.

The Celebration of Christmas

On the North American calendar, Christmas held a prominent place. But it was celebrated more as a pagan festival than as a Christian feast, and above all it was considered the great annual holiday. Solomon Northup witnessed to this: "The Christmas holidays constitute the only respite accorded to the slave during a year of incessant labor. Epps gave us three days—others four, five or six, according to their generosity. It was the only event that the slave awaited with at least a little interest and pleasure."[19] The celebration was marked by a great meal that could gather the personnel of a few plantations. "Christmas Day! Oh, what a time us niggers did have dat day! Marse Lordnorth and Marse Alec give us evvything you could name to eat: cake of all kinds, fresh meat, lightbread, turkeys, chickens, ducks, geese, and all kinds of wild game."[20] It was all was well washed down with whiskey and other types of alcohol! After the meal, the Christmas ball took place, where the black musicians could show off their talent with the banjo or the violin. Sometimes there were even fireworks in the evening.

It is not surprising, then, that the list of Christmas spirituals is limited. Couplets on the theme are late additions to preexisting refrains (see "Go, Tell It on de Mountain" [52]). Our selection has five songs centered on the birth of Christ (52, 126, 158, 167, 171). If we add five other, less important texts, we will have seen all the possible documentation. But thanks to this regrouping, we can reconstitute the infancy narratives of the Gospels according to the African Americans.

First of all, the news is expressed simply, even though the event has a directly emotional content:

> Sister Mary had-a but one child,
> Born in Bethlehem,
> And-a every time-a that baby cried,
> She's-a rocked him in a weary land. (171)

This news had to be proclaimed everywhere:

> Go tell it on the mountain,
> Over the hills and ev'rywhere;
> Go tell it on the mountain
> That Jesus Christ is born. (52)

The slaves, who were the poor, were immediately attentive to the conditions of this birth:

> Away in a manger, no crib for a bed,
> The little Lord Jesus laid down his sweet head;
> The stars in the bright sky looked down where he lay,

The little Lord Jesus asleep on the hay. ("Away in a Manger")

Fortunately, there was a star to show the way:

> Behold that star!
> Behold that star up yonder.
> Behold that star,
> That star of Bethlehem.
> There was no room found in the inn,
> For Him who was born free from sin. ("Behold That Star!")

The shepherds would be alerted without delay and give to the event the popular context it deserved:

> While shepherds kept their watching
> O'er silent flocks by night,
> Behold throughout the heavens
> There shone a holy light.
>
> The shepherds feared and trembled
> When lo! above the earth
> Rang out the angel chorus
> That hailed our Savior's birth. (52)

They were invited to follow the sign of the star:

> There's a star in the East on Christmas morn,
> Rise up, shepherd, and follow,
> It will lead to the place where the Christ was born,
> Rise up, shepherd, and follow. (158)

One question that preoccupied the slaves was one's name, as I have already underscored (in chapter 5). The community paid particular attention to the name because the name was always significant for the identity of the person and for his or her place in history. So they put the question to Mary:

> O Mary, what will you call this beautiful child?
> Some call him a thing, I believe I'll call him Jesus.
> Some call him a thing, I believe I'll call him Emmanuel. ("Glory
>   to the Newborn King")

Curiously enough, the slaves were interested in the month when Jesus was born. There was a choice to be made, and the Lord chose "the last month of the year," "the twenty-fifth day of December." Underscoring the date undoubtedly expressed the idea that the coming of Jesus took place at the end of the year as the fulfillment of time. With this birth, new times begin. Or perhaps the slaves wanted to accentuate again the humility of the birth, with Christ choosing the last of the months since he would act as a brother to the least of the human family.

The journey of the Magi, and its consequences, was followed with interest by the community of the oppressed:

> Oh, three wise men to Jerusalem came.
> They traveled very far.
> They said: "Where is he born King of the Jews,
> For we have-a seen his star."
>
> King Herod's heart was troubled.
> He marveled but his face was grim.
> He said: "Tell me where the Child may be found,
> I'll go and worship him."
>
> An angel appeared to Joseph,
> And gave him-a this-a command:
> "Arise ye, take-a your wife and child,
> Go flee into Egypt land."
>
> For yonder comes old Herod,
> A wicked man and bold.
> He's slayin' all the children,
> From six to eight days old. (171)

When the slaves sang such a song, they knew full well who Herod was and that the massacre of the innocents was not a drama only of the past. Their way of appropriating for themselves the Christmas event is clear in the following text:

> Poor little Jesus boy,
> Made him to be born in a manger
> World treated him so mean
> Treats me mean too.[21]

Jesus could not expect an easy life:

> O, poor little Jesus,
> This world gonna break Your heart.
> There'll be no place to lay Your head, my Lord. ("O, Poor Little Jesus")

Then we find Jesus at the age of twelve among the teachers in the temple of Jerusalem:

> "Lit'l Boy, how ole are you?"
> "Sir, I'm only twelfe years old."
>
> 1. This Lit'le Boy had them to remember
> That he was born on the 25th of December.
> Lawyers and doctors were amazed,
> And had to give the Lit'le Boy the praise.
>
> 2. Lawyers and doctors stood and wondered,
> As though they had been struck by thunder.
> Then they decided while they wondered,
> That all mankind must come under. ("Lit'le Boy, How Ole Are You?")

The point of view expressed in this spiritual is not quite that of the Evangelist Luke, but it shows the faith of the slave community in the cosmic power of the Christ.

The Ministry of Jesus

We have already had occasion to discover the Gospel figures, men and women, who are mentioned in the spirituals. Also, I have commented on the various facets of the relationship of the slave to the person of Jesus. Now, I would like to discover the manner in which the earthly ministry of Jesus is told in the spirituals.

Two verbs summarize perfectly this public ministry: Jesus preached and healed. The Christian slaves considered themselves bound to the words of their true Master and were fascinated by the power of healing that emanated from Jesus. They were not unaware of the prophetic preaching of Jesus in the synagogue of Nazareth:

> When [Jesus] came to Nazareth, where he had been brought up, he went to the synagogue on the sabbath day, as was his custom. He stood up to read, and the scroll of the prophet Isaiah was given to him. He unrolled the scroll and found the place where it was written:
>
> > "The Spirit of the Lord is upon me,
> > because he has anointed me
> > to bring good news to the poor.
> > He has sent me to proclaim release to the captives
> > and recovery of sight to the blind,
> > to let the oppressed go free,
> > to proclaim the year of the Lord's favor."

And he rolled up the scroll, gave it back to the attendant, and sat down. The eyes of all in the synagogue were fixed on him. Then he began to say to them, "Today this scripture has been fulfilled in your hearing." (Luke 4:16-21)

In response, the slaves confessed absolutely:

> Jesus on the mountain
> Preachin' to the po'
> Never heard such a sermon
> In all my life befo'. ("Lawd, I Want Two Wings")
>
> Did eber you see de like befo', . . .
> King Jesus preachin' to de po'? (79)

We notice particularly the words "to the poor." The content of the preaching is love—the love that gives to the one who practices it his or her true status as a child of God and a disciple of Christ.

But the extraordinary thing about Jesus is that he did what he said. His word was effective, giving fullness of life:

> He give heal unto de sick, Yes, He did,
> He give sight unto de blin', I know He did,
> He done 'able de cripple to walk,
> Oh, He raise de dead from under de groun'
> An' give dem permission to talk. (144; see also 17)

For those who were subject to some infirmity, just one gesture sufficed—to touch "the hem of His garment" (101) in imitation of the "woman who had been suffering from hemorrhages" (Matthew 9:20). From then on, it would no longer be possible to feel, to cry, to walk, to talk, to sing as before. The inner self had been truly transformed. What a wondrous thing it was!

"Jesus do most anything," one spiritual says ("No Man Can Hinder Me"). The word "most" prevents it from being an absolute assertion. The statement thus reflects the belief that Christ was practically invincible. Yet the cross stood in the way, and it was in the drama of the Passion that black American music would reach the apex of expression.

The Passion of Our Lord Jesus Christ

A black woman, born in 1845, having endured separation from her father and mother through their auction, gave witness to a vision that comforted her:

My mother say she didn't know a soul. All de time she'd be prayin' to de
Lord. She'd take us chillum to de woods to pick up firewood, and we'd
turn around to see her down on her knees behind a stump, aprayin'. We'd
see her wipin' her eyes wid de corner of her apron, first one eye, then de
other, as we come along back. Den back in de house, down on her knees,
she'd be aprayin'. One night, she say she been down on her knees aprayin'
an' dat when she got up, she looked out de door and dere she saw comin'
down out de elements a man, pure white and shining. He got right before
her door, and come and stand right to her feet, and say, "Sarah, Sarah,
Sarah!."—"Yes, Sir."—"What is you frettin' 'bout so?"—Sir, I'm a stranger
here, parted from my husband, with five little chillun and not a morsel
of bread."—"You say you're parted from your husband? You're not parted
from your husband. You're jest over a little slash of water. Suppose you
had to undergo what I had to. I was nailed to the Cross on Mount Calvary.
And here I am today. Who do you put your trust in?" My mother say
after dat, everything just flow, just as easy.[22]

The slaves would never suffer as much as Jesus. If Jesus triumphed over his terrible
trial, the slaves could live through their daily harassment by putting it into perspective.

A number of spirituals follow the way of Jesus' cross, step by step. The slaves
did not tire of contemplating the crucified one. Why? Because the life of Jesus
strangely resembled their own lives. The slaves began to identify with Jesus. The
cross of Jesus and the cross of the slave would finally become one cross. Faith and
life experience were fused.

I begin the commentary of the Passion with the first stage, the Last Supper:

> Jesus was a-sittin' at the last Passover,
> John, he rested upon His shoulder,
> Jesus said one word that seemed to blight,
> He said, "One of you goin' to betray me tonight."
> Mark cried out,
> "Lord, is it I?"
> James cried out,
> "Lord, is it I?"
> Then Jesus said, "A-look an' see,
> Him dat dip in-a de dish-a wid me."
> My time is come,
> My time is come,
> Oh, my time is come! ("My Time Is Come")

There is no allusion to the institution of the Eucharist or to Jesus' ministry;
everything is centered on the betrayal.

The following step is the agony in the Garden of Gethsemane:

> Then Jesus with His disciples Simon Peter
> And others went into the Garden,
> Jesus said to them,
> "Tarry ye here, while I go and pray."
> Then when Jesus on returning
> Found His disciples asleep,
> He said: "Simon! Simon! Sleepest thou?
> Simon! Could'st thou not watch one hour?
> But the flesh is weak,
> My time is come." ("My Time Is Come")

One spiritual allows for a more personal reflection of Jesus:

> Dark was the night and cold the ground
> On which the Lord was laid;
> His sweat like drops of blood ran down,
> In agony he prayed,
> "Am I born to die,
> Am I born to die,
> Am I born to die,
> To lay this body down?
>
> "Father, remove this bitter cup,
> If such Thy sacred will,
> If not, content to drink it up,
> Thy pleasure to fulfill."
>
> Go to the garden, sinner, see
> Those precious drops there flow,
> The heavy load He bore for thee,
> For there He lie so low. ("Am I Born to Die?")

Next, the troop sent by the high priests and the elders of the people (Matthew 26:47) arrived. They arrested Jesus:

> They led my Lord away,
> Oh, tell me where to find Him. (191)

Here is the longer version of "He Nevuh Said a Mumbalin' Word" (see 63):

> 1. O they took my blessed Lawd

An' he never said a mumblin' word,
Not a word, not a word, not a word.

2. They led Him before Pilate's bar. . . .

3. O they bound him with a purple cord. . . .

4. O they plaited him with a crown o' thorn. . . .

5. O they put it on His head. . . .

6. An' the blood came streamin' down. . . .

7. An' dey judged him all night long. . . .

8. An' dey whipped Him up the hill. . . .

9. An' dey nailed Him to the cross. . . .

10. An' de blood came tricklin' down. . . .

11. An' de stars refused to shine. . . .

12. O wasn't that a pity an' a shame! . . .

While the Western church emphasized the last words of Jesus, the black church insisted on his silence.

No detail of the Passion escaped the attention of the slave—for example, the whip and the hammer:

> Dey whipp'd Him up an dey whipp'd Him down. . . .
> Dey whipp'd dat man all over town. (202)

> Those cruel people! Those cruel people hammering!
> Hammering! Hammering! . . .
> You hear the hammer ringing. (58)

Jesus was the victim of the most intentional violence: he was "licked with violence" ("Look-a How Dey Done Muh Lawd"). The spectacle leaves no one indifferent:

> They nail my Jesus down,
> They put on Him the crown of thorns,
> O see my Jesus hangin' high!
> He look so pale an' bleed so free:
> O don't you think it was a shame,
> He hung three hours in dreadful pain.

In reality, Jesus was not totally silent on the cross, "the cruel tree." Black tradition notes first the word of the crucified to the apostle John. But this word, placing his mother in the care of the beloved disciple, had a particular resonance with the experience of slavery—no one wanted his mother to be present during his suffering and his torment. Jesus would want to spare his mother the sight of her son in his agony. Here is the stunning transposition:

> I think I heard Him say,
> When he was strugglin' up the hill,
> I think I heard Him say,
> "Take my mother home."
>
> I think I heard Him say,
> When dey was spittin in His face,
> "Then I'll die easy,
> Take my mother home."
>
> I think I heard Him say,
> When dey was rafflin' off His clothes,
> I think I heard Him say,
> "Take my mother home." ("Take My Mother Home")

The other words of Christ at the crucifixion were not completely forgotten:

> *Refrain:*
> Calvary,
> Surely He died on Calvary.
>
> 1. Ev'ry time I think about Jesus
> Surely He died on Calvary.
>
> 2. Don't you hear the hammer ringing?
>
> 3. Don't you hear Him calling His Father?
>
> 4. Don't you hear Him say, "It is finished"? (15)

Another impressive fact in this death is the blood—the blood that flowed and the blood that saves:

> 1. I know it was the blood for me.
> One day when I was lost,
> Jesus dies on the cross.
> I know it was the blood for me.

2. It was my Savior's blood for me. . . .

3. The blood came streaming down for me. . . .

4. He suffered, bled, and died for me. (80; see also 184)

The spear piercing Jesus' side was part of the tragedy of the shedding of his blood:

> When Jesus was hangin' on de cross
> An' de Jews wuz standin' round
> One picked up de sword and plunged it in his side
> And de blood came tricklin' down.
> ("I Lub Muh Blessed Saviour")

The shepherd had become the Lamb of God, who offered his life for the multitude. "He hung His head and died" (63). And the whole of creation mourned the death of Jesus:

> The sun rose, my dear friends,
> And it recognized Jesus hanging on the cross.
> Just as soon as the sun recognized its Maker,
> Why, it clothed itself in sack clothing and went down,
> Oh, went down in mournin'! ("The Man of Calvary")

At each step on the way of the cross, the slaves saw themselves as the crucified. They were not only Simon of Cyrene, the black man who helped the crucified; they recognized their own face in that of Jesus, their own condition of abasement in that of Jesus. They communed fully with the Suffering Servant because through their experience they knew what suffering was all about. The slaves thus were moved in their inmost depths. The suffering of Jesus was no ordinary suffering; it was the suffering of the innocent one who was made sport of, who was abandoned and became an apparent failure, who had offered love and been rejected. If Jesus endured everything for the slave's salvation, then the slave could endure everything for Jesus.

The Christian faith stems from Calvary. It is inescapable. We must accompany Jesus in his sacrifice if we want to be sure of his presence at our side today.

> Were you there when the crucified my Lord?
> Oh! Sometimes it causes me to tremble, tremble, tremble.
> Were you there when they crucified my Lord?
>
> Were you there when the nailed Him to the tree?
> Oh! . . .
>
> Were you there when the pierced Him in the side?

Oh! . . .

Were you there when the sun refused to shine?
Oh! . . .

Were you there when they laid Him in the tomb?
Oh! . . . (201)

It is to be where Christ is so that he will be where we are. It is to be "soldiers of
the cross" (100). It is to endure the worst humiliations without flinching.

James Weldon Johnson, the poet, placed "Were You There?" in the context of
the oral tradition:

> The words of this powerful *Spiritual,* that makes us grimace with shame
> and grow in responsibility, seem to belong to a catalogue of succinct
> formulas in which the Gospel accounts of the passion of Jesus were
> crystallized by the faith of many believers who identified themselves with
> this passion. The couplets are so concise and carefully honed in their
> formulation of the most important moments of this profoundly moving
> story that they could easily be learned by heart or memorized and thus
> reappear every time someone intoned a song on the crucifixion or the
> resurrection that had about the same rhythmic motif.[23]

John Lovell, on the other hand, underscored the interplay of the "you" and
the "me" in this hymn and added: "The setting, the phrasing, the powerful
momentum of this poem surely make it one of the great poems of all time. Every
great wrong, it says, is committed under the eyes of frightened or uncaring people.
For the wrongs of humankind, the finger points at us all. We are all guilty. We are
guilty not so much because of what we do, as what we allow to happen. And
without a doubt, the slave singer was including the slavery of human flesh in the
bill of indictment."[24]

Identifying with the suffering Christ, the slaves did not hesitate to speak of
their own cross in the singular or in the plural. I must "Shoulder up mah cross"
(2) if one day I want to exchange it for the crown of the kingdom. And the
imitation of Christ includes the way of dying:

> I want to die like-a Jesus die,
> And he die wid a free good will. ("Lord, Remember Me")

Jesus went to his death freely. All believers must do the same. One slave expresses
it in a precise manner: "I tracked him by his drops of blood, and every drop he
dropped in love."[25]

We can end this way of the cross with the words of Marguerite Yourcenar:

"From this total identification with the pain of God are produced these poems that attain the poignant dignity of the ancient liturgical 'sequences.' "[26]

The Angel of the Resurrection

Death, however, is not the last word in the story of Jesus. That is so, for one thing, because Jesus' death has a salutary effect for the whole of humanity:

> Jesus died for every man.
>
> He died for yo', He died for me,
> He died t' set po' sinner free.
>
> He died for de rich, He died for de po'
> He ain't comin' here t' die no mo'.
>
> He died for de blind, He died for de lame,
> He bore de pain an' all de blame. (13)

Second, Jesus' death is not the last word because he died once and for all and he has passed through to the other side of death: "He died one time, He'll die no mo' " ("Cruel Jews").

It is interesting to note that some communities could not endure these songs being centered only on the Passion and that they later added a triumphant couplet on the resurrection. A typical example of this is "Were You There?" (201). After a certain number of years, there appeared a last verse that has two versions: "Were you there when he rose up from the dead?" and "Were you there when they rolled the stone away?" Also, Mary had to stop weeping because:

> He bow'd His head to die no more,
> He rose from the dead,
> He's coming again on the Judgment Day. ("Weepin' Mary")

The descent into hell, the passage where Jesus goes down into the abyss of desolation, is mentioned at least once:

> He went right down to hell,
> He said, "Peter I got de Keys
> Of death an' de grave."
> Grave, where yo' victory?
>> ("Look-a How Dey Done Muh Lawd"; compare 1 Corinthians
>> 15:55 and Revelation 1:18)

This is certain:

The cold grave could not hold Him,
nor death's cold iron band. (61)

Jesus "removed the sting of death and robbed the grave of her victory."[27]

The meditation of the black community focused a while on the tomb and on the deliverance from the tomb:

Twas on one Sunday morning
Just 'bout de break of day.

An Angel came down from Heaven
And rolled de stone away.

John and Peter came a-running,
And found an' empty tomb.

Mary and Martha came weeping
And lo! Their Lord had gone. ("Twas on One Sunday Morning")

Another spiritual expands on these events:

De angel roll de stone away,
Twas on a bright an' shiny morn
When de trumpet begin to soun'
De angel roll de stone away.

1. Sister Mary came a-runnin'
At de break o' day,
Brought de news f'om heaben
De stone done roll away.

2. I'm lookin' for my Saviour,
Tell me where he lay,
High up on de mountain,
De stone done roll away.

3. De soljas dere a plenty
Standin' by de do'
But dey could not hinder
De stone done roll away.

4. Pilate an' his wise men
Didn't know what to say
De miracle was on dem
De stone done roll away. ("De Angel Roll de Stone Away")

Everything took place in the night, in God's great silence: "Chillun, did you hear when Jesus rose?" (18).

Mary's run received special treatment, for it expressed dynamic faith:

> O run, Mary, run, Hallelu, hallelu!
> It was early in de mornin', Hallelu.
> Dat she went to de sepulcher.
> And de Lord, he wasn't da.
> But she saw a man a-comin.
> And she thought it was de gardener.
> But he say: "O touch me not
> For I am not yet ascended.
> But tell to my disciples
> Dat de Lord he is arisen."
> So, run, run, Mary, run. ("O Run, Mary, Run")

From now on, the news of the resurrection would be at the center of the Christian good news: "Yes, Jesus is risen from the dead." A spiritual introduces the chain of witnesses in music:

> In-a this-a band we have sweet music:
> Jesus is risen from the dead.
>
> Go, tell Mary and Martha,
> "Yes, Jesus is risen from the dead."
>
> Go, tell John an' Peter. . . .
>
> Go, tell doubting Thomas. . . .
>
> Go, tell Paul and Silas. . . .
>
> Go, tell all th' Apostles. . . .
>
> Go, tell ev'rybody:
> "Yes, Jesus is risen from the dead." ("Jesus Is Risen from the Dead")

When it came to the resurrection, as with the Passion, the slaves did not distance themselves from the event. In Christ, they also passed from death to life:

> I'm so glad,
> I've been in the grave an' rose again.
> I'll tell you how I love the Lord. ("I'm So Glad")

If the angel rolled away the stone, if Jesus left the tomb, the black people had acquired the certainty that they would not forever remain in the tomb of slavery. The groaning was over! The resurrection was at the same time victory over sin, the defeat of death, and the conquest of freedom. It gave the assurance that the black community was from now on in the hands of the Lord of life and freedom. The Lord "shall bear his children home" ("He Rose").

At the end of this long journey in the footsteps of Jesus, we come to the conclusion that Jesus gave himself to the slave community by means of three basic experiences: proximity, efficacy, and identification.

Jesus was near. Within reach through prayer and song, Jesus was always the one who walked with the oppressed. And we should not suspect that the humanity of Jesus was the only consideration. For the black community, the divinity of Christ was never more profoundly expressed than in his human qualities during his trials. One must be from God in order to be so human.

If we bear in mind the warrior images found in various spirituals, we see Jesus as a second Moses, a Messiah King. He heals, he frees, and he triumphs. To discover Christ is to learn that he has already vanquished sin and death. And it was in the traces of his work of liberation that the slaves recognized "Master Jesus." He is what he does.

Finally the people, living under the yoke of slavery, identified themselves with Jesus. For the prophet of Galilee had known the same trials. He had descended into hell. Everybody could see in his face their own features, their own Calvary. And this revelation was discovered with the emotion of an intense communion.

And the Spirit?

Did the black Americans succeed in passing from the African spirits that take possession of their initiates to the Holy Spirit, the fire in the hearts of Christian believers? If in African religion there is no inkling of the coming to earth of the Son of God, the notion of spirit—the invisible force—is everywhere present. And the slaves would be as sensitive to the Spirit as God's action in the Old Testament as to the Spirit of Jesus revealed in the New Testament.

In black tradition, the Spirit is a fire. The Spirit "falls" on the assembled community to make it burn with love and justice. As we saw in the shout of the clandestine assemblies, the people allowed themselves to be submerged, shaken by the presence of the Spirit. Also, the slaves would say with legitimate pride: "The whites have the Book. We have the Spirit." This was an effervescent Spirit who left traces of passage in the heart and in the body. This was a Spirit who caused the slaves to shout out their pain and dance with joy and who caused them to enter into a collective trance. In this way a community was forged that was capable of resisting the evils of the time. This was the Spirit of Pentecost:

> When Peter was preaching at Pentecost,
> He was endowed with the Holy Ghost. (85)

But in the city of Jerusalem, it was the entire people who, on that day, received the Spirit ("Time Is Drawin' Nigh").

According to the spirituals, the Christian can do nothing as long as the Spirit is not present. The Spirit is the life of God, who gives life to humanity:

> I'm goin' to wait till de Holy Ghost come.
> I'm goin' to sing till de Holy Ghost come.
> I'm going to watch till de Holy Ghost come.
> I'm goin' to pray till de Holy Ghost come. ("I'm Goin' to Wait
> Till de Holy Ghost Come")

The Spirit, furthermore, is a "heavenly breeze" that God sends to those who implore God:

> If you want to seize this heavenly breeze,
> God sown in the valley on your knees;
> Bend your knee upon the earth
> And ask God to convert you.

The Spirit was God's agent in the depths of history, fashioning from the inside the events and the persons. This Spirit was found in Zion, and the Spirit became the slaves as Jesus become theirs ("I Found Jesus over in Zion"). A former slave told how the Spirit became the force of his courage: "In slavery times, my master whipped me terribly, especially when he knew I was praying. He was determined to whip the Spirit out of me, but he never could, for the more he whipped me, the more the Spirit made me happy to be whipped."[28]

From now on, Christian life would be defined by possession of the Holy Spirit. Conversion was identified by "the baptism in the Spirit" ("Time Is Drawin' Nigh"), which allowed the person to take the initiative in his or her own life. One of the bonds that is best attested to in the spirituals is that of the Spirit of prayer, reflecting Romans 8:

> If you hear me prayin',
> That ain't nothin' but love.
> That must be the Holy Ghost. ("When You Feel Like Moaning")

> Ev'ry time I feel the Spirit moving in my heart,
> I will pray. (40)

Faith is also an interior "feeling," and the "feeling" of the black community distinguished it from any other community in the world. That "feeling" emerged into emotion and exultation, a personal and collective joy (see 197).

One must, then, allow oneself to be moved by the Spirit. One must obey the Spirit and not the lackeys of white power:

> I'm gonna sing (shout, preach, pray)
> when the Spirit says a-sing,
> And obey the Spirit of the Lord. (89)

It is in this fidelity that the believer found true comfort:

> Sometimes I feel discouraged
> And think my work's in vain,
> But then the Holy Spirit
> Revives my soul again. (8)

The Spirit filled the heart with love. It was the Spirit who witnessed to the good behavior of the believer:

> God knows I am a Christian,
> God knows I'm not ashamed.
> Well, the Holy Ghost is my witness.[29]

Even if they fall short of elaborating a rigorous system of doctrine, the spirituals speak of God, of Jesus, and of the Spirit from a profound religious experience, a true interior rendering of relationship with the Lord of history. The slaves were not content to repeat the catechism they had received. Beginning with their life experience, they fashioned a new vision of the action of God in history. More than ever before, the Almighty was on the side of the powerless and of the innocent victims, and God would find the way out of a closed situation. All idolatry of human power is a negation of Christian faith.

Even before the final emancipation, faith allowed the slaves to discover a stunning serenity. In getting close to God, the slaves backed away from suffering and humiliation. The slaves then felt peace, joy, and love—feelings that had appeared to be humanly impossible.

> I've got peace like a river in my soul. . . .
> I've got joy like a fountain in my soul. . . .
> I've got love like an ocean in my soul. (96)

Notes

1. Quoted in Olli Alho, *The Religion of the Slaves* (Helsinki: Suomalainen Tiedeakatemia, 1980), 146.

2. Quoted in Douglas C. Strange, "Document: Bishop Daniel Alexander Payne's Protestation of American Slavery," *Journal of Negro History* (January 1967): 63.

3. Quoted in Carter G. Woodson, ed., *Negro Orators and Their Orations* (Washington, D.C.: Associated, 1925), 215.

4. See the poem (sermon in verse) "The Creation" in James Weldon Johnson, *God's Trombones* (Paris: Épi, 1960), 15–19.

5. Quoted in A. M. French, *Slavery in South Carolina and the Ex-Slaves* (New York: 1862), 22–23.

6. Jacob Stroyer, *My Life in the South*, rev. ed. (Salem, Mass.: Salem Observer Book and Job Print, 1885), 22–24.

7. Alho, *Religion of the Slaves.*

8. Quoted in Albert J. Raboteau, *Slave Religion* (New York: Oxford University Press, 1978), 242.

9. Josiah Henson, *Truth Stranger than Fiction: Father Henson's Story of His Own Life* (Boston: Jewett, 1858), 26–29.

10. Quoted in E. A. McIlhenny, *Befo' de War Spirituals* (Boston: Christopher, 1933), 49.

11. Cited in Harold Courlander, *A Treasury of Afro-American Folklore* (New York: Marlowe, 1976), 326.

12. Charles S. Johnson et al., eds., *Fisk University's Unwritten History of Slavery: Autobiographical Accounts of Negro Ex-Slaves* (Nashville: Social Science Institute, Fisk University, 1945), 124–25.

13. See couplet 17 of "Go Down, Moses," spiritual 50 in appendix 1.

14. Quoted in James H. Cone, *God of the Oppressed* (New York: Seabury, 1975), 152.

15. Frederick Douglass, *Life and Times of Frederick Douglass* (1892; reprint, New York: Collier, 1962), 91.

16. Quoted in Harold A. Carter, *The Prayer Tradition of Black People* (Valley Forge, Pa.: Judson, 1976), 68.

17. Quoted in French, *Slavery in South Carolina*, 183.

18. See Bruno Chenu, *Dieu est noir: histoire, religion et théologie des Noirs américains* (Paris: Centurion, 1977), 139–40.

19. Solomon Northup, *Twelve Years a Slave: Narrative of Solomon Northup* (Auburn, N.Y.: Derby and Miller, 1853).

20. Quoted in James Mellon, ed., *Bullwhip Days: The Slaves Remember* (New York: Weidenfeld & Nicolson, 1988), 10.

21. Quoted in Cecil W. Cone, *The Identity Crisis in Black Theology* (Nashville: AMEC, 1975), 37.

22. Quoted in George P. Rawick, *The American Slave: A Composite Biography,* 19 vols. (Westport, Conn.: Greenwood, 1972–1979), 2:181.

23. James Weldon Johnson, ed., *The Book of American Negro Spirituals* (1925; reprint, New York: Viking, 1969).

24. John Lovell, *Black Song* (New York: Macmillan, 1972), 304.

25. Johnson, *American Negro Spirituals*, 9.

26. Marguerite Yourcenar, *Fleuve profond, sombre rivière* (Paris: Gallimard, 1964), 40.

27. Quoted in Clifton H. Johnson, ed., *God Struck Me Dead* (Philadelphia: Pilgrim, 1969), 101.

28. Quoted in *American Missionary,* 2d ser., 11 (May 1862): 102.

29. Quoted in Courlander, *Afro-American Folklore*, 337.

Bibliography

Baldwin, Lewis V. "Deliverance to the Captives: Images of Jesus Christ in the Minds of Afro-American Slaves." *Journal of Religious Studies* (1985): 27–45.

Douglas, Kelly Brown. *The Black Christ*. Maryknoll, N.Y.: Orbis, 1994.

8

"City called heaven."

Destination: Heaven

"The last will be first."
—Mark 10:31

IF THERE IS A MAJOR TENSION that cuts across the Negro spirituals, it is the tension between the here below and the hereafter. I have attempted to show the consistency of the here below in chapter 5. But the biblical setting (chapter 6), and especially the manner of speaking about God and Jesus (chapter 7), direct attention to an invisible world even more real than the visible world. Not only does the mystery of the invisible overshadow each moment of history and judge it, but also it offers an extraordinarily profound vision of the future. Reality is not circumscribed in the vital time line that extends from birth to death. There is life after life, fulfillment or punishment. And the spirituals speak abundantly of that antithetical pair, heaven and hell, without placing them on the same footing. Hope is crystallized in the word *heaven.*

Of course, in all the talk about heaven, one must never forget the presence of a double meaning—the religious terms are also a code to express the desire for emancipation. Heaven has the colors of the North of the United States. At the same time as we consider the importance of this political strategy, we must not reduce the evocation of the ultimate destiny of humankind to their earthly pilgrimage. Heaven does not consist only of freedom in life; it also designates the definitive wedding of God and God's people in a city that is not built by human hands, fulfilling the personal and collective aspirations of the human being.

We are now going to peruse the discourse on death and the "after death." It is the narrow door of death that permits entry into eternity as promised by God and so ardently desired by the slave. But beware of taking the wrong path at the crossroads of final destiny! One must be ready for the hour of judgment.

The Cult of the Dead

No African practice has been so fully observed and analyzed as that which encompasses death and the dead. Ethnologists (among whom Louis-Vincent Thomas is of the first rank[1]) have been able to pierce through the mystery of a ritual honed by the centuries. Thanks to them, we can discern the African heritage of the slaves in the United States.

In black Africa, as elsewhere, death is always painful, for it indicates a journey without return, marks the breaking up of relationships, and involves a loss of vital energy. The one who has died has gone away, and we fear he or she might leave us misfortune in exchange. Hence the importance of ritual purification to undo the power of death. Often the realm of death is reached by crossing a river with the help of a boat whose pilot has to be paid with money. That is why parents and friends place money in the coffin of the deceased.

Opinions among Africans vary on the mode and conditions of life in the realm of the dead. For some, there is continuity; it is the same life as that on earth. For others, it is a life marked by superior faculties because those who have gone live with the spirits. In any case, insofar as the new abode is permanent, it is called "the house": "The person has gone home."[2] God has nothing to do with it; God exists on another level.

In the African perspective, then, it is of first importance to clarify the causes of a death. The event cannot go unexplained. And since God is not responsible, one has to seek the answer on the human level. Thus people do not hesitate to speak to the deceased and ask him or her to explain. The African particularly fears evil spells. It is necessary to work out the best relationship possible with those who have left us, because they have gone to the village of the ancestors. The funeral rites are there to appease the deceased by showing them the interest we have in them and to recreate the unity of the community by respecting the taboos.

Evidently, the ideal is to arrive at the status of ancestor. There are certain conditions for that: wisdom, physical integrity, moral rectitude, and good relations with the members of the clan. At that point, the deceased become mediators of life for those who remain on earth. They maintain a strong involvement in human affairs, representing the memory of the society, the authority of tradition, and the source of fertility. They call attention to themselves through dreams. It is through the ancestors that the three great goods are obtained: life, land, and culture. "Birth, harvests and social order are controlled by their goodwill."[3] One must show interest in them through offerings, prayers, and sacrifices. The important thing is that life triumph through successive trials.

Because of this cultural heritage (even though we do not find clear traces of a cult of the ancestors among them), the African Americans gave particular attention to death and surrounded the funeral with special care. John Jasper, a black preacher, underscored that: "There was one thing which the Negro greatly insisted upon and which not even the most hard-hearted of masters were willing to deny them. They could not bear that their dead be put away without a funeral."[4] Death was the most important rite of passage.

Yet funerals were not necessarily a priority for the owners. For the owners, work came before anything else. And especially, the whites feared that this type of celebration could become an ideal time for a conspiracy. Already in 1687, one area in Virginia banned public funerals for slaves. A few years earlier, colonial legislators had stated that "the frequent assemblies of a considerable number of Black slaves under the pretext of funerals are considered dangerous." In the eighteenth century, the city of New York disallowed funerals at night. That fear was well founded, since the Gabriel Prosser rebellion of 1800 was stirred up on the occasion of a child's funeral.

The legislation was not especially favorable to slave funerals, but a certain number of owners had a deeper understanding of the gesture their slaves wanted to make. They plainly regretted the death of their better servants and they were sometimes sensitive to the grief of the survivors and furnished them the necessities for a decent funeral: wood for a coffin (many slaves had to be content with just a blanket) and a plot of land for the tomb. Some slaves even had the privilege of being buried in the same manner and in the same cemetery as the whites. It was a rather ambiguous privilege that did not meet with unanimous approval among the slaves.[5]

Along the coasts of Georgia and South Carolina, especially, we find traces of the funeral practices of the slave community. Olli Alho was able to trace six distinct phases in the rites practiced in that region: (1) the preparation of the corpse and the precautions taken concerning his or her immediate entourage, (2) the death vigil, (3) the funeral procession, (4) the burial, (5) the rites for the well-being of the soul of the deceased in the next world, and (6) the funeral sermon.[6]

The preparation of the body consisted of washing it and dressing it before placing it in the coffin. Sometimes coins were placed on the eyes to prevent them from opening, and salt was placed on the stomach to purify it. The mirrors in the hut were turned toward the wall, and the body was never left alone.

The funeral vigil, which according to popular belief was attended by the spirit of the deceased, was an occasion for the slaves of the plantation, and eventually those of the neighborhood, to say good-bye to the deceased and to console the family and friends. The deceased would be asked not to take with him or her other members of the family. Most of the songs sung would be spirituals, and the mourners would not hesitate to have a session of collective trance (shouting). At midnight there would be a pause in the singing and praying, for a light meal, but the vigil would continue into the second half of the night, often until early morning.

The body would be buried in the local cemetery, for the soul could not be allowed to wander in the area. As for the funeral procession, it would take place at night, the participants carrying torches and all the while singing hymns. At the entrance to the cemetery, permission to enter would be asked of the soul of the deceased. Upon arrival at the tomb, which was oriented east to west, the coffin would be placed in the earth, the head at the west end so that the eyes were turned toward Africa and the rising sun. A short prayer meeting would be held there, with a reading from the Bible and a sermon. Most often, the sermon would be pronounced by a slave, for some of them specialized in that function. Each slave would approach the tomb with a handful of dirt that he or she would throw on the casket as a farewell gesture.

The funeral cortege would leave the tomb in procession. Some believed that the spirit of the deceased accompanied the procession, while most believed that it remained in the tomb. Pottery and glasses were broken to symbolize the destruction of the body by death. To steal them would be violating a taboo. The return of the spirit of the deceased to haunt the house of the living had to be avoided at all cost, and he or she had to be helped to attain the status of ancestor.

As a matter of fact, this first burial was considered only temporary because it had to be hurried in order to avoid the decomposition of the body in the humid heat of the South. A few weeks later, a second funeral would take place, and this one would be more solemn, gathering the entire black community in memory of one or more deceased. It was then that the true funeral sermon would be delivered.

What was the meaning of this long ritual? The numerous spirituals created for this occasion uncover the complexity of the relationship with death, for to place the accent on death can be a way of exalting another life just as much as it can be a way of softening death.

Just like all other human beings, the slave felt the violence of death. It came without warning. It cut the flower in full bloom ("Death Is Awful"). It was represented either in the form of a man or in the form of a horseman.

> O Master Death
> Is a very small man,
> He goes from door to door;
> He kills some souls
> And wounds others.
>
> Behold, I saw a white horse, behold, I saw a black,
> He that sat on him had a pair of scales;
> And I looked and beheld a pale horse,

His name that sat on him was Death,
And Hell followed with him.
   ("When I'm Dead, Don't You Grieve after Me")

Death ain't nothin' but a robber, don't you see.
Death came to my house, he didn't stay long,
I looked in the bed an' my mother was gone. (25)

Death's go'n'ter lay his col', icy hands on me. (26)

It is normal that the first feeling toward death be repulsion:

O death is frightful,
Give me another year.

For death is everywhere:

There is a man who goes around taking names,
He took my mother's name
And left my heart in pain.
There is a man who goes around taking names,
O, death is the man who takes names.[7]

The only consolation is knowing that death takes rich and poor alike:

Ef salvation wuz a thing money could buy
Den de rich would live an' de po' would die.

But ah'm so glad God fix it so,
Dat de rich mus' die jes' as well as de po'![8]

Because of their servitude, the slaves had a real sense of the proximity of death.
It could come at any time:

Before this time another year, I may be gone,
Out in some lonely graveyard,
O, Lord, how long? (9)

O bye and bye, bye and bye,
I'm goin' to lay down dis heavy load. (14)

Soon one mawnin' death come creepin' in yo' room.
("Soon One Mawnin' Death Come Creepin' in Yo' Room")

And the image of ice is in the mind of the poet:

> My mother's broke the ice and gone,
> O, Lord, how long?
>
> By the grace of God I'll follow on,
> O, Lord, how long? (9)

In any case, life is passing: "I feel like my time ain't long" (77). Without knowing it, we are perhaps at the last instant of our life: "This may be your last time, I don't know" ("This May Be Your Last Time").

The important thing is to be ready. And the call to vigilance is portrayed with humor. Two texts prove it:

> Death went out to the sinner's house,
> (Said) come and go with me.
> Sinner cried out, I'm not ready to go,
> I ain't got no travellin' shoes.
>
> Death went down to the gambler's house,
> Called him come and go with me.
> The gambler cried out I'm not ready to go,
> I ain't go no travellin' shoes. ("Got No Travellin' Shoes")
>
> Sinner man lay sick in bed,
> Death come a-knockin' at de do';
> Says he, "Go 'way, Death, come in Doctor.
> I ain't ready to go."
>
> Christian man lay sick in bed,
> Death come a-knockin' at de do';
> Says he, "Come in Death, go 'way Doctor.
> Ise ready to go."[9]

The slaves heard the hammers banging on their coffins and the wheels of the hearse on the way to the cemetery ("The Hammers Keep Ringing"). These were all free warnings. The sinner's problem, according to the wonderful expression of a spiritual, was "Yo' bed's too short" ("O, Sinner"). Because they were exploited, and also because people in the service of others in the kingdom are generous, the African Americans did not always have the time to think about death: "Ain't got time to die" (5).

According to a myth that is far more ancient than Christianity, death is like a river (in the case of the spirituals, the Jordan) that must be crossed. To be conscious of the reality of death is thus to stand on the riverbank, for "dere's one more riber to cross" (146). And someone will help the "traveler" to cross:

> When my feeble life is o'er,
> Time for me will be no more;
> Guide me gently, safely o'er,
> To Thy kingdom shore. (107)

The slaves wanted to proclaim loudly that they were not afraid to die ("I Am Not Afraid to Die"), that is, insofar as they called on their Lord Jesus:

> Oh, when I come to die,
> Give me Jesus.
> You may have all this world,
> Give me Jesus. (48)

> When I'm dyin', Lord, remember me. (34)

But it was, in fact, Jesus who would call the slave by name ("Soon, One Mawnin' Death Come Creepin' in Yo' Room"). For God remained the master of the situation: God was the one who told death to go down to earth to bring the servant of God home ("Go Down, Death"). The poor wretch then would have every reason to dispel anxiety:

> I want to die easy when I die;
> Shout salvation as I fly,
> You needn't mind my dying,
> Jesus goin' to make up my dying bed. ("Jesus Goin' a-Make Up
>   My Dyin' Bed)

> In my dying room I know,
> Somebody is going to cry,
> All I ask you to do for me,
> Just close my dying eyes (Ibid.)

> Who will go down into the grave with me
> When I die?
> Jesus will go down into the grave with me.

> Who will sing that last hymn
> When I die?
> Jesus will sing that last hymn.

> Who will say that last prayer

When I die?
Jesus will say that last prayer. ("When I Die")

During the Civil War, Thomas Wentworth Higginson, the commander of the first regiment of freed slaves, was particularly impressed by the following song:

I know moon-rise, I know star-rise,
Lay dis body down.
I walk in de moonlight, I walk in de starlight,
To lay dis body down.
I'll walk in de graveyard, I'll walk through de graveyard,
To lay dis body down.
I'll lie in de grave and stretch out my arms;
Lay dis body down. (114)

Higginson paused at the line "I'll lie in de grave and stretch out my arms" and noted, "Never, it seems to me, since man first lived and suffered, was his infinite longing for peace uttered more plaintively that in that line."[10]

Angels had a role in the event since they would do what was necessary to carry the deceased to the kingdom of God:

Dig my grave long an' narrow,
Make my coffin long an' strong.
Bright angels to my feet,
Bright angels to my head,
Bright angels to carry me when I'm dead.
Oh my little soul goin' shine, shine,
Oh my little soul goin' shine like a star.[11]

Dig my grave wid a silver spade,
Angels lookin' at me. ("Angels Lookin' at Me")

The burial was another occasion to shout the glory of God and ring the bells of Jerusalem ("The Graveyard"). The "alleluia" was absolutely required here ("Now We Take This Feeble Body").

When you hear that I'm going to die,
I don't want anyone to cry.
All I ask of my friends
Is to ring this bell.

When you see me this way,

I don't want you to be alarmed,
For I want to see King Jesus coming
To fold my dying arms.[12]

Christ conquered death once and for all:

O didn't Jesus rule Death in His arms,
Yes, rule Death in His arms,
On the other side of Jordan,
Ah! rule Death in His arms. ("Rule Death in His Arms")

The true destination of the human being is the other side of the Jordan. If we don't meet the slave at the hearth in the evening, it is because he or she has gone "to walk and talk with Jesus," "to sit at the welcome table," "to drink and nevah get thirsty" ("When I'm Gone"). It is because "the gift of God is eternal life" ("De Gif' of Gawd Is Eternal Life").

The Struggle against Satan to Avoid Hell

In the conversion accounts, which often describe a visit to the invisible world, hell is always present. We have seen that in the witnesses I have quoted:[13] Morte sees his "old body over a hot furnace, suspended by something that resembled a small spider web." This furnace is also a big hole in which sins and sinners are cast.

The spirituals allude also to the "dark door" of hell (122). They know well that "hell is deep and dark despair" ("O Sinner Man").

Oh, hell is deep an' hell is wide,
Oh, hell ain't got no bottom or side.[14]

Such is the eternal destiny of the sinner (135). One must take care not to get too close to it:

When I was a sinner
I loved my distance well,
But when I came to find myself,
I was hanging over Hell (187).

Some converts found themselves, in a vision, "at the greedy jaws of hell," and there they met the devil: "I saw the devil, a terrible clubfooted man, with red eyes like fire. I called upon God to deliver me from that place, for the weeping and gnashing of teeth was awful. I saw a big wheel that seemed full of souls, and as it turned the cry of 'Woe! Woe! Woe!' was pitiful."[15]

In the same way, the spirituals personalize hell in the figure of Satan. He is a figure that is not at all imaginary, abstract, or invented, but rather is one who interferes constantly in human affairs:

> I went down in de valley to pray,
> I met ol' Satan on de way.
> What do you think he said to me,
> "You're too young to pray an' too young to die."
>   ("Oh, Yes! Oh, Yes! Wait 'til I Git on My Robe")

In black tradition, the devil is no less real than you and me. He is the very incarnation of sin, the one who roams unceasingly around human beings to drag them into the flames of hell. In order to understand his role, we must go back to the Creation stories:

> Old Satan tempted Eve,
> And Eve, she tempted Adam;
> And that's why the sinner has to pray so hard
> To get his sins forgiven. (59)

From this success, Satan draws his conclusions too rapidly:

> Old Satan thinks he'll get us all, Yes, my Lord!
> Because in Adam, we did fall, Yes, my Lord![16]

At the beginning of the nineteenth century, a legend was current in North Carolina according to which the devil tried to imitate the creation of Adam. Not having enough clay, he went to the swamp, took a bit of mud, and used thick, curly moss to make the hair. When he examined his work, he was so disgusted that he gave it a kick in the shins and punched the nose, thus giving to the black race their physical attributes.[17] In this way, the discrimination received a religious sanction!

In any case, Satan pursues his existence in the human world in the form of a serpent:

> Old Satan just like a snake in the grass,
> He always in some Christian's path.[18]

> Ol' Satan's like a snake in the grass,
> Waitin' to bite you as you pass. ("Chilly Water")

> Oh! Satan is a snake in the grass,
> If you don't take care, he'll get you at the end.
>   ("Hard to Rise Again")

More rarely, he takes on the aspect of a greyhound:

> Ol' Satan's like an ol' greyhoun'
> Runnin' dem sinners roun' an' roun'.[19]

The hounds of hell, in a pack, are always at the heels of those who believe and pray. But the best definition of Satan is still to assert that he is a liar and a conjurer:

> The Devil am a liar and a conjurer too,
> If you don't look out, he'll conjure you through.
>   ("Hard to Rise Again")

The figure of a sorcerer for Satan has no biblical roots but clearly constitutes an African remembrance. Satan is the prince of the night, always preparing some evil deed. This malfeasance often is expressed in the image of shoes for the slaves, who often had to go barefoot:

> The Devil is a maker, Lord!
> O' brass shoes, Lord!
> And if you don't mind, Lord!
> Children he'll slip them on you! ("Way Up on de Mountain")

> Ol' Satan wears a club-foot shoe, . . .
> If you don' min' he'll slip it on you. (41)

> Ol' Satan's got slippery ol' shoe
> And if you don't mind he will slip it on you. ("Chilly Water")

That symbolic gesture refers to the possession of the one who does only evil. We can ask ourselves if the slaves gave themselves a good conscience too easily by attributing their own poor behavior to a creature outside of themselves. But this objectification of evil was undoubtedly necessary to establish a personal balance.

Satan's favorite sports seem to have been shooting and throwing stones. Examples:

> Ole Satan shot his ball at me
> Dun got over at las'
> He missed ma soul an' cotch ma sin. ("Tone de Bell")

> Old Satan shot one ball at me,
> Been blind but now I see. ("Been Blind but Now I See")

We can readily see that this restoration of sight is more a case of a new spiritual lucidity than of a physical healing.

> Ole Satan is a busy ole man,

He roll stones in my way. (21)

The devil is always on the rampage (50), in the world as well as in the church, since we find him even in the "amen corner" (105), that is, in the midst of the most exuberant Christians. His designs don't fool anyone:

> Old Satan's mighty busy,
> He follows me night an' day,
> An' ev'ry time I go to pray,
> I find him in my way.
>
> Now don't you mind old Satan,
> Wid all his temptin' charms,
> He wants to steal your soul away,
> An' fol' you in his arms. (122)

Satan, however, has illusions about his power. But if you keep your mind "stayed on Jesus" (206), he can't catch you. For it is a kind of race between Satan and the believer:

> I an' Satan had a race,
> Win de race agin de course. . . .
> Satan tell me to my face . . .
> He will break my kingdom down. ("I an' Satan Had a Race")

It is then that, in the same song, Jesus intervenes:

> Jesus whispers in my ear,
> He will build it up again.

The action of Jesus is the exact opposite of that of Satan. As the devil rolls stones in the way, Jesus removes them. And human life becomes the arena of a kind of celestial tourney between two horsemen, one on a milk-white horse, Jesus, and the other on an iron-gray horse, Satan ("I Am Not Afraid to Die").

How can we assure the victory of Jesus? First of all, by prayer. We have already noted that Satan tried to prevent the slaves from praying. But the believer knows that well.

> Old Satan tremble when he sees, . . .
> The weakest saints upon their knees.
>   ("God's Got Plenty o' Room")

Second, by living the gospel. It is the Christian who must chase away sin:

> If you want to see Old Satan run,
> Just pull de trigger o' de gospel gun.[20]

> The Bible is our engineer
> That's what Satan's a-grumbling about.
> It points the way to heav'n so clear,
> That's what Satan's a-grumbling about. ("That's What Satan's
>   a-Grumbling About")

Such actions set Satan's camp on fire:

> Fier, my Saviour, Fier,
> Satan's camp a-fire;
> Fier, believer, fier,
> Satan's camp a-fire. (164)

The nocturnal celebrations have that as an objective:

> I come dis night to sing an' pray,
> Oh, yes, to drive ol' Satan away. (Oh, Yes! Oh, Yes! Wait 'til I Git
>   on My Robe)

Also, Satan's anger doesn't ease off:

> Ol' Satan's mad, an' I'm glad,
> He missed de soul he thought he had. ("Lead Me to the Rock";
>   compare 133)

Once rid of Satan, we can express a little humor:

> Ole Satan thought he had a mighty aim;
> He missed my soul and caught my sins.
> He took my sins upon his back;
> Went muttering and grumbling down to hell.[21]

Indeed, the believer is destined for the glory of heaven and not to the decadence of hell. He or she is destined for freedom:

> Ole Satan t'ought he had me fas'
> Dun got over at las'
> But I broke his chain an' got free at las'. ("Tone de Bell")

Once in heaven, the believer will be able to tell how he or she was able to avoid the gates of hell ("I Am Bound for the Promised Land"):

> Ole Satan's church is here below,
> Up to God's free church I hope to go.[22]

Satan must return to his natural habitat:

> He's in hell an' he cain' get out.
> Ol' Satan's a-settin' on a red-hot seat,
> A-coolin' his head an' a-warmin' his feet.[23]

Satan's final defeat can be celebrated every day:

> Oh, shout, you Christians, you're gaining ground,
> Done with the sin and sorrow;
> We'll shout old Satan's kingdom down,
> Done with the sin and sorrow.[24]

At the same time, slavery is a daily experience of hell ("This Old World's a Hell to Me"), and it is only beyond that trial that one will find consolation:

> My body is feeble and suffering
> But it served the master well.
> I will land in heaven,
> Having already gone through hell.[25]

The Colors of Heaven

The spirituals have a great veneration for the Bible, for God, and for Jesus. But the most dominant theme in them by far is that of heaven. In the selection I have made of 210 songs, seventy-four (more than a third) speak directly of this ultimate perspective. Superficial commentators could conclude that here is proof we are in the presence of an alienating religion! The enslaved people looked to the next world in order to forget for a time their present miseries, and this outlook removed any desire to revolt.

That, of course, is really what the whites wanted to instill in the minds of poor blacks: "Be good to de massa an' missus, don't steal dey chickens an' eggs, an' when you die dey will carry you to Heaven."[26] The slaves were told of the beauty of the heavenly city, but the whites were careful not to give the impression that racial relations in heaven would be under the sign of equality. Frank Roberson gives an account of a white minister's sermon: "You slaves will go to heaven if you are good, but don't ever think that you will be close to your mistress and master. No! No!

there will be a wall between you; but there will be holes in it that will permit you to look out and see your mistress as she passes by."[27] Therefore, there would be a "black heaven" that would, so to speak, be a "kitchen heaven."

Were the slaves fooled by this biased discourse? Not at all! They reasoned thus: "There must be two separate heavens—no, this could not be true, because there is only one God. God cannot be divided in this way. I have it! I am having my hell now—when I die I shall have my heaven. The master is having his heaven now; when he dies he shall have his hell."[28] And so they sang: "Heaven, heaven, everybody talking about heaven ain't goin' dere" (6).

For those who were exploited, heaven was the antithesis of earth, the counterimage of the present experience. It asserted in a positive way what the condition of slavery expressed negatively. "Dar's no more slave in de kingdom" (106).

In the spirituals, the vocabulary of heaven is rich, using both Christian terms and terms from common human experience. The most usual word for heaven is "home" (examples: 19, 23, 42, 78, 87, 144, 194). So heaven is a familial and welcoming place. Other common expressions are "another building" or "bright mansions above" (97; compare John 14:2). The image of "green pastures" (139), though appearing only once in the Bible (Psalm 23:2), had great success in the black cultural tradition. Along with the belief that there was a river to cross (the Jordan), heaven becomes the "other shore" (44, 87) or the "celestial shore" (47). We are also still close to biblical language when Canaan is spoken of (12, 32) as well as the Promised Land (27, 55, 69, 137, 197) and Jerusalem (50, 75, 85). We also find the classic terms of "paradise," "the Kingdom" (106) and the "Glory" (86, 111, 193). But we discover the flavor of the African Americans' discovery of Christianity through two other synonyms: the camp meeting and the "great association" (189). When they spoke of "the Church above," "a better day," and the "world above," the meaning was always heaven. The difference on the vertical axis is never too marked.

In order to be somewhat systematic about the preaching on heaven, I will organize it according to five themes. Heaven is at the same time (1) the place of humanity, (2) the haven of a family reunited, (3) the throne of God and of Christ, (4) the creation of a new world, and (5) the reward of the elect. These five meanings of heaven constitute a sort of circle that begins with humankind and returns to humankind, because for the slave, to speak of heaven was to speak first of all about the destiny of the human being.

The initial assertion is perhaps that "my soul is a heaven born" and not for the earth (46). It is only in heaven that people can really be themselves and blossom in freedom and equality.

But the slave first had to be recognized as a person. The value as a person—the opposite of slavery's degradation—would be expressed by the opulence of the slave's new clothing: the robe, the belt, the shoes, the stockings. Everything the slaves lacked in earthly life would be supplied with finery in heaven as symbols of the joy offered by God:

> I got shoes, you got shoes,
> All God's chillun got shoes;
> When I get to heaven, goin' to put on my shoes,
> Goin' to walk all over God's heaven.
>
> I got a robe, you got a robe,
> All God's chillun got a robe;
> When I get to heaven, goin' to put on my robe,
> Goin' to shout all over God's heaven. (6)

There would even be a "walking cane" ("Hand Me Down My Silver Trumpet"). As the songs of the blessed resound in the heavens, the elect would be given a harp (2), a trumpet, and even a bell. The talents of each one would be fully recognized. Travel no longer would be a problem because a pair of wings would also be given (56). But the most explicit sign of the new dignity of the person would be the "starry crown" (56, 106, 142, 180; see also 27, 117, 130).

This recognition of the person is expressed in a dialogue between God and a woman:

> "Sit down, chile."
> "Good Lord, I can't sit down."
> "What is de matter, chile?"
> "Oh, you know what you promise me.
> "Good Lord, my long white robe (my starry crown, my golden
>   shoes, my angel wings)."
> "Run, Angel, an' git a robe an' let her try it on." ("Lord, Is Dis
>   Hebben?")

What a joy it would be to see "my long white robe come down to my toes" ("I'm on My Journey Home")! All the garments would be shining; they would "be more brilliant than the brightest sun" ("I'm Going to Join the Heavenly Choir").

But there can be no human dignity without freedom. Uncle Silas understood that well. Beverly Jones, a former slave from Virginia, told his story:

> The Reverend Johnson, he was praying and we, the slaves, we were
> sitting there, and we were sleeping and fanning ourselves with oak
> branches and Father Silas, an old black, stood up in the first row of
> the slaves' bench, and he stopped the Reverend Johnson: "Will we, the
> slaves, be free in Heaven?" asked Father Silas. The preacher stopped
> and he looked at Silas as if he wanted to kill him, because no one has
> the right to say anything, except "Amen," while he is preaching. He

waited a minute, yes, all the while looking at Silas without flinching, and did not answer. "Are we going to be freed, we the slaves, when we get to Heaven?" shouted Silas. The old white man, he got out his handkerchief and wiped the sweat off his face: "Jesus said, 'Come to me all you who are without sin, and I will give you salvation.' " "Will he give us freedom with salvation?" asked old Silas. "The Lord gives and the Lord takes away and the one who is without sin, will have eternal life," said the preacher. Then he continued to preach, quickly and without paying any more attention to Silas. But Silas refused to sit down during the whole rest of the sermon, yes, and he never went back to church, because he died before there was another service; I suppose he found out if he will be free sooner than he expected.[29]

The spiritual clearly affirms that:

> I'll be buried in my grave,
> An' go home to my Lord an' be free. (143)

In the presence of God we can sing in truth:

> Free at last, free at last,
> Thank God a'mighty, I'm free at last. (46)

This freedom is expressed, for example, in the possibility to "choose ma seat" ("Comin' Down de Line") and to walk about the city of God without fearing the intervention of a patrol or of the hateful police.

This new world would give witness to an equality unknown during life on earth, for "all God's chillun got a robe, shoes, a harp." There would be no division between the haves and the have-nots. All would enjoy the same happiness, the same fullness, and the same song.

Slavery had broken so many family ties that one of the slaves' first definitions of heaven was the reunion of the family and the realization, perhaps for the first time, of an extended family (19, 87, 106). Already on the auction block, the adults were accustomed to say goodbye with the phrase "I'll meet you in Heaven" (see 127).

> Want to see my mother when I die,
> Want to see my father when I die,
> Want to see my sister when I die.
>   ("Want to Go to Heaven When I Die")

It is interesting to note the order in which the family members are mentioned: the mother first, then the sister and the brother, and only after them the father.

That underscores how much the black family (yesterday mostly, though the situation is not so much different today) was "carried" by the mother. There is sometimes a contrast in the manner in which the two parents are mentioned:

> My mother has reached that pure glory,
> My father's still walkin' in sin. (19)

Beyond the family, friends are mentioned (38), as well as the members of the church, and the hope was to be reunited with them all in the kingdom of God. Together, they would enjoy the company of two specifically chosen biblical figures: Abraham (because of the parable of the poor Lazarus) and sister Mary (a synthesis of all the Marys of the Gospels). The time for reconciliation would come at death.

Human beings recover their dignity and their family only by the grace of God, around the "throne of God" (43). Heaven is eminently God's place:

> Lord, is dis hebben,
> Oh Lord, is dis hebben,
> Lord, is dis hebben,
> Have I got here at las'? ("Lord, Is Dis Hebben?")

The most ardent desire of the slave was now to be fulfilled: "[I'm] goin' home to live with God" (177), "[I] gwine to live wid God forever" (197).

God always takes the initiative to call: "My name is called and I must go" ("I Heard from Heaven To-day"). But the most original aspect of heaven in the spirituals is the familiarity—one could say friendship—that is established between the citizen of heaven and the Master of the place:

> Me and God goin' to de graveyard field.
> We gwine to stand and talk like you and me.
> Me and my God gwine to do as we please.
> Gwine to argue with the Father and chatter with the Son.
>   ("Me and God")

The poor slaves would, of course, tell the Father of all the problems they had in their earthly existence. And the list would be long.

The conversation would be even more considerable with the "darlin' Son" (129), for heaven is presented as the true home of Jesus, the place where "I can shake the hand of my Lord." The perfect meeting with Christ, the definitive vision "face to face," is in heaven. What a joy it would be for the slaves to reunite with all their friends and with Jesus, to sit at his side, and to place at his feet the crown of glory (27)!

> Good Lord, in the manshans above,

> I hope to meet my Jesus in the manshans above.
>
> My Lord, I've had many crosses and trials here below,
> My Lord, I hope to meet you, in de manshans above.
> Fight on, my brudder, for de manshans above,
> For I hope to meet my Jesus dere, in de manshans above.
>   ("Good Lord, in the Mansions Above")

To go to heaven is always to go to Jesus (2, 36), "the bleedin' lam'" ("Goin' to Heaven"), "King Jesus sittin' on the throne" (156).

God could not be present in all God's majesty without the angelic court. It was they who would accompany the pilgrimage to heaven with their hymns (67).

> I looked over Jordan, an' what did I see
> comin' for to carry me home?
> A band of angels comin' after me,
> comin' for to carry me home. (182)

The desire of the believer was to join the band of angels, to "stand where the angels stand," in the adoration and praise of the only Lord, "to eat, to cry and to sleep" as they do ("I Want to Go to Heaven").

If heaven is a place where personal relationships are everything, we must not forget that it is also the visualization of a new world, often described as a city: the New Jerusalem.

> I've heard of a city called heaven,
> I've started to make it my home. (19; compare 75)

The description of this marvelous city is taken from the Book of Revelation:

> Oh! what a beautiful city,
> Twelve gates-a to the city-a, Hallelu!
>
> Three gates in-a de east, Three gates in-a de west,
> Three gates in-a de north, And three gates in-a de south,
> Making it twelve gates-a to de city-a, Hallelu!
>   (147; compare Revelation 21:12)

In this city, where the bells ring (152), the streets are covered with gold and the doors with pearls (50, 156). It is a place where there is only beauty:

> I want to be ready
> To walk in Jerusalem just like John. (85)

In this new world, the celebration—"the celebration of love"—is eternal. It takes on the biblical form of a great banquet:

> I'm go'n'ter set down at de welcome table, some o' dese days. . . .
> I'm go'n'ter feast on milk an' honey. . . .
> I'm go'n'ter drink from de golden fountain. (175)

> Mary set her table
> In spite of all her foes;
> King Jesus sat at the center place
> An' cups did overflow. (18)

The notion of time is transformed. Heaven is everlasting: "The Sabbath has no end" ("Sabbath Has No End"); "Every day shall be Sunday" (136); "It will always be hello! And never goodbye!"[30]

The evocation of the Sabbath introduces the dimension of rest. Slaves living in the South of the United States had only the Christmas holiday as time off; the summer was totally given over to the harvest. But in heaven the oppressed would at last be able to "lay their burden down" (see 49). And God would have another dialogue with a sister freshly arrived home:

> Oh, sit down, sister, sit down!
> I know you're tired,
> Sit down!
> 'Cause you come a long way,
> Sit down, chile! Sit down!
> An' rest a little while.
> Oh, you come a long way,
> An' you had hard trials,
> An' I know you're tired
> Sit down, chile!
> Sit down, an' res' a lit'le while.
> Tell me what you're waitin' for.
> I'm a waitin' for my mother
> 'Cause I want to tell her howdy. ("Sit Down, Chile"; compare 172)

Solomon Northup told of one of his companions in slavery who did not have very clear ideas on the distinction between the spiritual life and the corporeal life. "His idea of the joys of heaven was simply rest, the rest that is expressed so perfectly in these lines from a melancholic singer":

> I don't expect a paradise up there;
> Except care for an oppressed land,

The only heaven that I desire
Is rest, eternal rest.[31]

To express it as a paradox: heaven is a negation of the negation. All the afflictions of life on earth are ended and make room for joy and peace:

In my Father's House there ain't no trouble up there,
Nothing but Joy! Joy! Joy!

In my Father's House there ain't no sickness up there,
Nothing but Joy! Joy! Joy!

In my Father's House there ain't no dying up there,
Nothing but Joy! Joy! Joy!

In my Father's House there ain't no weeping up there,
Nothing but Joy! Joy! Joy. ("In My Father's House")

The same positive experience will be had in confrontation with the evildoers on earth:

There are no liars there
In my Father's house;
Oh, there is peace, peace everywhere.
There are no gamblers there
In my Father's house . . .
There are no card players there.[32]

The principal occupation no longer would be prayer, but shouting for joy (197) and singing a new song. Because there would be no work, there would be no more weariness.

The slave's conscience was bothered by only one fact: the number of the elect is limited, while the love of God is universal ("Roll On"). How can the tension between election and universality be resolved? John's vision in Revelation (5:11-12) struck the community's imagination:

John saw de holy number
Settin' on de golden altar.
Worthy is the Lamb. (103)

But the myriads of myriads become a more precise number in Revelation 7:4: "John saw the hundred forty-four thousand."

So the slave immediately presented his or her request: "Tell John not to call de roll till I git dere" ("John Saw de Number"). The slave absolutely had to join the "holy number." The concrete sign would be the inscription of the slave's name in the book of life (106). The angels would take charge of that task: "The angels in heaven will write my name" ("De Angels in Heb'n Gwineter Write My Name").

This self-interested proceeding, however, did not express a will to exclude others. The slaves never stopped meditating on the words of Jesus in the Gospel of John: "In my Father's house there are many dwelling places" (14:2). So they would sing on every tone that "there's plenty good room" in the kingdom:

> There's plenty good room . . . in my Father's Kingdom. . . .
> Just choose your seat and sit down.
>
> O brother, don't stay away, O sister, don't stay away,
> For my Lord says dere is room enough,
> Room enough in Heaven for us all. (30)

Only the sinners had cause to worry, for Jesus could shut the door on them. The slaves asked themselves about the presence or absence of their masters in heaven, but Christ "cast not out none dat come by faith" ("My Lord, What Shall I Do?"), inhabited by "Christian love" ("Got My Letter").

The theme of heaven definitely was a way of expressing the transcendence that inhabits the present as well as the future. It broadened the vision of reality in limiting earth and in affirming God's action in history, which can only flow in the direction of justice and of freedom. It especially gave flesh to the hope that awakened the capacity of the slaves to resist the dehumanization of servitude and sharpened their desire for a radically transformed world. God has the last word.

This is clearly expressed in an African American folk tale in which John, a slave, prays to God:

> Every night, before going to bed, John prayed. In his prayer, he asked God to come get him and take him straight to heaven. He did not even want to take the time to die. He wanted the Lord to take him as he was there, with his boots, stockings and all. He got on his knees and said: "Lord, once again it's your humble servant who kneels and bows before you, and my heart is lower than my knees and my knees are in a lonely valley, and with tears I beg for mercy if there is still time to get mercy. Lord, I implore you in the most humble way that I know to give me the joy to come in your fiery chariot and carry me to your heaven of immortal glory. Come, Lord, you know how life is hard. Massa makes me work so hard and doesn't leave me time to rest. So, come, Lord, with peace in one hand and forgiveness in the other, and tear me away from this sinful world. I'm weary, I want to go home."[33]

Judgment Day

The spirituals' evocation of heaven often has the sweet colors of family reunions or of friendship with Jesus. But the dramatic pages of Revelation also attracted the black Christians. The daily conflict between good and evil becomes a gigantic epic in the visions attributed to the apostle John. The grand apocalyptic spectacle carries a definitive message: injustice will not triumph. Already, in his regimental camp, Colonel Thomas Higginson noticed that Revelation, along with "the books of Moses" (the Pentateuch), constituted the Bible of the African Americans.[34] And the slaves did not forget the texts that evoke the end of the world in the Gospels (Matthew 24–25; Mark 13; Luke 21).

Revelation describes the scene at the breaking of the sixth seal like this: "The sun became black as sackcloth, the full moon became like blood, and the stars of the sky fell to the earth" (6:12-13). A spiritual echoed the text in this way:

> The moon run down in a purple stream,
> The sun forbear to shine,
> And every star disappear,
> King Jesus shall be mine. (32)

The prophecy of Jesus in Matthew—"As the lightning comes from the east and flashes as far as the west, so will be the coming of the Son of Man" (24:27)—is echoed in various ways:

> The wind blows east, and the wind blows west,
> It blows like the judgment day. (32)
>
> Dere's fire in de eas' an' fire in de wes',
> Sen' dem angels down. (133)

It is truly the end of the world, the end of this unjust and crushing world, that is described. The drama begins in the morning:

> My Lord, what a mornin', when de stars begin to fall.
>
> You'll hear de trumpet sound, to wake de nations underground,
> Lookin' to my God's right hand, when de stars begin to fall. (131)

The general resurrection will take place in this cosmic uproar, and then God will judge the whole of humanity. The spirituals that describe this final event seek the conversion of sinners and call all persons to take heed.

One song gives a general picture of the upheaval of the world. It is proper to quote fully "In Dat Great Gittin' Up Mornin' ":

I'm a-goin' to tell you 'bout de comin' of the Savior,
Fare you well, fare you well.

Refrain:
In dat great gitin'up mornin',
Fare you well, Fare you well.

1. Dere's a better day a-comin',
Fare you well, Fare you well;
O preacher, fol' yo' Bible,
Fare...
Prayer maker, pray no mo'
For the las' soul's converted.

2. Dat de time shall be no longer. . . .
For judgment day is comin'. . . .
Den you hear de sinner sayin'. . . .
Down I'm rollin', down I'm rollin'. . . .

3. De Lord spoke to Gabriel. . . .
Go look behin' de altar. . . .
Take down de silvah trumpet. . . .
Blow yo' trumpet, Gabriel. . . .

4. Lord, how loud should I blow it. . . .
Blow it right calm an' easy. . . .
Do not alarm my people. . . .
Tell 'em to come to judgment. . . .

5. Gabriel blow yo' trumpet. . . .
Lord, how loud shall I blow it. . . .
Loud as seven peals of thunder. . . .
Wake de livin' nations. . . .

6. Place one foot upon de dry lan'. . . .
Place de other on de sea. . . .
Den you'll see de coffins bustin'. . . .
See de dry bones come a creepin'. . . .

7. Hell shall be uncapp'd an' burnin'. . . .
Den de dragon shall be loosen'd. . . .
Where you runnin' po' sinner. . . .

8. Den you'll see po' sinners risin'. . . .
Den you'll see de worl' on fiah. . . .
See de moon a bleedin'. . . .

See de stars a fallin'. . . .

9. See de elements a meltin'. . . .
See de forked lightnin'. . . .
Den you'll cry out for cold water. . . .
While de Christians shout in glory. . . .

10. Sayin' Amen to yo' damnation. . . .
No mercy for po' sinner. . . .
Hear de rumblin' of de thunder. . . .
Earth shall reel an' totter. . . .

11. Den you'll see de Christians risin'. . . .
Den you'll see de righteous marchin'. . . .
See dem marchin' home to Heab'n. . . .
Den you'll see my Jesus comin'. . . .

12. Wid all His holy angels. . . .
Take de righteous home to glory. . . .
Dere dey live wid God forever. . . .
On de right hand side of my Saviour. (98)

In this epic scene, we find all the obligatory stages of the end of time: history stops; God calls Gabriel; Gabriel blows his trumpet; the dead rise; hell opens; the world burns; the sinners and the just go to their respective destinies.

The reality of the Last Judgment was an absolute certainty for the slave. No one can escape it, especially not sinners who lose their way on muddy roads. The trumpet sounds for everyone, and God will sort them out.

Oh a sad day is a-comin' soon
Where the saints and the sinners
Will fall to the right and left.
Are you ready for Judgment Day?[35]

The allusion to the parable of the separation of the sheep and the goats in Matthew 25 is clear. Elsewhere, it will be the separation of the wheat and the tares ("God's Gonna Separate the Wheat from the Tares").

The God of judgment is often portrayed in the spirituals as an angry God who inspires a terrible fear: "No one can resist when my God is angry."[36] But it is the "poor sinner" especially who is fearful:

O, po' sinner, O, now is yo' time, O, po' sinner, O,
What yo' gwine to do when yo' lamp burn down? (202)

Even if the sinners try to flee to the mountains, they will not avoid the call from God. And they will not stop "hollering" at the bar of judgment ("Blow, Gabriel").

Since God "sees all you do, he hears all you say" (130), each person has to take responsibility for his or her own actions. The spirituals insist on it:

> You got to cross the test of judgment,
> You got to cross it for yourself,
> O, no one can cross it in your place,
> You got to cross it for yourself. ("You Got to Cross It for
> Yourself"; compare 184)

Prayer is still the best way to prepare for it (141, 162).

But fear is not the dominant feeling in the spirituals, for Satan is "bound" by a chain and "cast into the fire" ("Mighty Day"). Much more often, it is joy that bursts out. The convert has complete confidence, for he or she holds "the key to the Kingdom":

> Where shall I be when de first trumpet soun',
> Where shall I be when it soun' so loud,
> When it soun' so loud till it wake up de dead? . . .
> Gwine to try on ma robe when de firs' trumpet soun'. (203)

> And I will shout and I will dance,
> And I'll get up early in the morning;
> Oh! my friends, my friends! I'll be there on time
> When old Gabriel blows his horn.[37]

And it was through this judgment that the slaves would reveal their true identity:

> Oh, no one knows who I am,
> Until Judgment morning.[38]

And they would receive their reward:

> The man who loves to serve the Lord,
> When death shall shake this frame,
> He shall receive his just reward,
> When death shall shake this frame.[39]

Each one would reap what he or she has sown:

> It makes no difference is you black or white,
> What you been doing in the middle of de night
> Gwine be drug out in de broad day light. ("Blow, Gabriel")

But the notion of judgment must not hide the joy of the Jubilee, which marks the return of Christ (144). It gives access to the biggest tree in paradise (11). And the right acquired by the faithful believer who has gone through the trial of slavery is precisely the right to enjoy fullness of life, or what we call eternal life:

> You got a right, I got a right,
> We all got a right to de tree of life. (209)

Notes

1. See Louis-Vincent Thomas, *La mort africaine* (Paris: Payot, 1982).

2. John Mbiti, *Religions et philosophie africaines* (Yaoundé, Cameroon: Clé, 1972), 166.

3. Thomas, *La mort africaine,* 251.

4. Quoted in David R. Roediger, " 'And Die in Dixie': Funerals, Death, and Heaven in the Slave Community, 1700–1865," *Massachusetts Review* (spring 1981): 163.

5. A slave named George was informed by his master that he would be buried in a good coffin and placed next to the earthly remains of his owner, in the same vault. George's reaction was rather mixed: "I like to have good coffin when I die, but I 'fraid, massa, when de debbil come take your body, he make mistake, and get mine." The anecdote is told by Albert J. Raboteau, *Slave Religion* (New York: Oxford University Press, 1978), 292.

6. Olli Alho, *The Religion of the Slaves* (Helsinki: Suomalainen Tiedeakatemia, 1980), 159–63.

7. Quoted in Clarence C. White, *Forty Negro Spirituals* (Bryn Mawr, Pa.: Presser, 1927), 58–59.

8. Quoted in John Lomax and Alan Lomax, eds., *American Ballads and Folk Songs* (New York: Macmillan, 1947), 610.

9. Quoted in ibid., 602.

10. Quoted in Milton C. Sernett, ed., *Afro-American Religious History: A Documentary Witness* (Durham, N.C.: Duke University Press, 1985), 120.

11. Quoted in H. E. Krehbiel, *Afro-American Folksongs* (New York: Schirmer, 1914), 104.

12. Quoted in Lomax and Lomax, *Ballads and Folk Songs,* 60.

13. See pp. 53–55.

14. Quoted in Lomax and Lomax, *Ballads and Folk Songs,* 590.

15. Quoted in Clifton H. Johnson, *God Struck Me Dead* (Philadelphia: Pilgrim, 1969), 121.

16. Quoted in J. B. T. Marsh, *The Story of the Jubilee Singers, with Their Songs* (London: Hodder & Stoughton, 1877), 215.

17. Told by Lawrence W. Levine, *Black Culture and Black Consciousness* (New York: Oxford University Press, 1977), 84.

18. Quoted in Christa Dixon, *Wesen und Wandel geistlicher Volkslieder: Negro Spirituals* (Wuppertal: Jugenddienst-Verlag, 1967), 220.

19. Quoted in Lomax and Lomax, *Ballads and Folk Songs,* 589.

20. Quoted in G. C. Balmir, *Du chant au poème* (Paris: Payot, 1982), 170.

21. Quoted in Thomas L. Webber, *Deep Like the Rivers: Education in the Slave Quarter Community, 1831–1865* (New York: Norton, 1978), 127–28.

22. Quoted in Harriet A. Jacobs, *Incidents dans la vie d'une jeune esclave* (Paris: V. Hamy, 1992), 117.

23. Quoted in Lomax and Lomax, *Ballads and Folk Songs,* 590.

24. Quoted in Marsh, *Jubilee Singers,* 148.

25. Quoted in Elma Stuckley, *The Big Gate* (Chicago: Precedent, 1976), 21.

26. Lewis V. Baldwin, " 'A Home in Dat Rock': Afro-American Folk Sources and Slave Visions of Heaven and Hell," *Journal of Religious Thought* 41, no. 1 (spring–summer 1984): 40.

27. Ibid.

28. Howard Thurman, *Deep River and The Negro Spiritual Speaks of Life and Death* (Richmond, Ind.: Friend United Press, 1975), 43.

29. Quoted in Virginia Writers' Project, *The Negro in Virginia,* (New York: Hastings House, 1940), 109.

30. From the song by Mahalia Jackson, "Move On Up a Little Higher."

31. Solomon Northup, *Twelve Years a Slave: Narrative of Solomon Northup* (Auburn, N.Y.: Derby and Miller, 1853).

32. Quoted in Carl Sandburg, *The American Songbag* (New York: Harcourt Brace, 1927), 483.

33. Roger D. Abrahams, ed., "John the Black and John the White," in *Afro-American Folktales: Stories from Black Tradition in the New World* (New York: Pantheon, 1985).

34. Cited in Sernett, *Afro-American Religious History,* 117.

35. Quoted in E. A. McIlhenny, *Befo' De War Spirituals* (Boston: Christopher, 1933), 53.

36. Quoted in ibid., 194.

37. Quoted in E. C. Perrow, "Songs and Rhythms from the South," *Journal of American Folklore* 26 (1913): 160–61.

38. Quoted in John Wesley Work, *Folk Song of the American Negro* (Nashville: Press of Fisk University, 1915), 98.

39. Quoted in Henry Hugh Proctor, "The Theology of the Songs of the Southern Slave," *Journal of Black Sacred Music* (spring 1988): 61.

Bibliography

Baldwin, Lewis V. " 'A Home in Dat Rock': Afro-American Folk-Sources and Slave Visions of Heaven and Hell." *Journal of Religious Thought* 41, no. 1 (spring–summer 1984): 38–57.

Byrd, James Preston, Jr. "The Slave Spiritual as Apocalyptic Discourse." *Perspectives in Religious Studies* (summer 1992): 199–216.

Cone, James H. *"La signification du ciel dans les Negro-Spirituals." Concilium* 143 (1979): 77–91.

Roediger, David R. " 'And Die in Dixie': Funerals, Death, and Heaven in the Slave Community, 1700–1865." *Massachusetts Review* (spring 1981): 163–83.

Conclusion

SINCE ITS BEGINNING as a refrain hummed in the slave quarters of South Carolina, the spiritual has become a song of choice found in all latitudes. Not only have the artists and choirs of black America crisscrossed the planet, but also a multitude of men and women have recognized themselves in this musical genre and have translated into their own languages the words of these old hymns. The spiritual has crossed all borders, bringing a fresh breeze of dignity and freedom for the oppressed of the earth, for it is a universal parable of human existence. And who can deny its influence on the development of a music that has triumphed in the twentieth and twenty-first centuries under the generic term of "jazz"? According to the analysis of James H. Cone, the blues is nothing other than "secular Spirituals."[1]

When he arrived in the United States in the autumn of 1892 as director of the National Conservatory of New York, the Czech composer Antonín Dvořák immediately became interested in the music of the African Americans and invited his American colleagues to draw from this treasure of popular melodies. In 1893 he declared:

> I am convinced that the future music of this country must be based on what are called the Negro melodies. They must constitute the true foundation of any serious and original school of composition in the United States. . . .They are the folklore songs of America and your

composers must turn to them. All the great musicians have borrowed from the most popular songs.... I find in these Negro melodies everything that is necessary to found a great and noble school of music. They are moving, tender, passionate, melancholic, solemn, religious, daring, joyful, gay, and everything you want.[2]

His well-known *New World Symphony* borrows a number of its themes from Negro spirituals. For him, popular music was like a rare flower growing amid weeds: people passed over it and trampled it until someone with an attentive mind singled it out and showed its value.

Coming from an entirely different scene, but no less a lover of music, the young Lutheran pastor Dietrich Bonhoeffer was struck, in 1930 and 1931, by the services in the black churches of Harlem. He spent a sabbatical year at the great Protestant seminary of New York, Union Theological Seminary, and dedicated his Sundays to visiting the churches of the black quarter. His biographer tells how he collected recordings of the spirituals and how he made them known to the seminarians of the Confessing Church at Finkenwalde. He believed that he had found much more of the Christianity of the Reformation in black piety than in the white churches.[3]

Dvořák and Bonhoeffer are but two examples chosen among a thousand to show how the spiritual has spread far and wide.[4] But such an international success must not lead us to forget the concrete roots, the precise meaning of these songs. This book has had no other ambition than to shed as much light as possible on the text and the context. It is the particular context of the spiritual's birth that creates the universality of its message. We have here the phenomenon of a popular expression that arose from a constant interaction with an oppressive environment. These poignant psalms of human suffering are also irresistible hymns of Christian hope. The spiritual breaks chains because it celebrates a God of ebony who never abandons God's people. The dignity of the human person comes from the communion lived in song with his or her brothers and sisters and with God. The words of the Acts of the Apostles are at the heart of the faith of the black experience: "God shows no partiality, but in every nation anyone who fears him and does what is right is acceptable to him" (Acts 10:34-35). Deliverance was but a matter of time for the American slaves, and it was already at work in the heart of the believer who refused to allow his or her soul to be enslaved. Even if the body was a prisoner, the soul was free.

In the end, the spiritual was one of the wombs of black identity in the last two centuries. It nourished the language of prayer and furnished the language of the struggle as well as the language that allows African Americans to reread and grasp their own history. We now understand better that "Black history is a Spiritual."[5]

Since we are in the framework of religion, we find no distinction between the song and the prayer in the black community. The singing gives a form to the prayer, and the prayer internalizes the song. There are not two different levels, but one way only of expressing the personal and community experience. The proof of this is found in the prayer of an old grieving woman in 1867:

O Father Almighty, O sweet Jesus, most glorified King, will you be so pleased to come dis way and put your eye on dese poor mourners? O sweet Jesus, ain't you the Daniel God? Didn't you deliber de tree [three] chillun from the fiery furnis'? Didn't you heah [hear] Jonah cry in de belly ub de whale? O, if dere be one seekin' mourner here dis afternoon, if dere be one sinkin' Peter, if dere be one weepin' Mary, if dere be one doubtin' Thomas, won't you be pleased to come and deliber 'em? Won't you mount your Gospel hoss, an' ride roun' de souls of dese yere mourners, and say, "Go in peace and sin no moah?" Don't you be so pleased to come wid de love in one han' and de fan in de odder an', to fan away doubts? Won't you be so pleased to shake dese here souls over hell, an' not let 'em fall in! (Amen.)[6]

Yet the spirituals' most astounding aspect is the impact they have had on the social and political struggles of African Americans. That became clear during the civil rights movement led by Martin Luther King, Jr., between 1955 and 1968. What occurred at that time was not only the rediscovery of the old Negro spirituals but also their actualization and their adaptation to a nonviolent struggle against segregation. The history of the movement was even told by means of these songs.[7] Some spirituals did not even need to be revised, for they declared "Ain't gonna let nobody turn me 'round" (4) or "Free at last, free at last, thank God Almighty, we're free at last" (46, put in the plural). Yet others were rewritten to reflect the situation. For example: "This little light of mine, I'm going to let it shine" (192) was endowed with new couplets:

We have gotten the light of freedom, we will make it shine,
In the south, we will make it shine . . .
Go tell Chief Pritchett [the Albany police chief], we will make it
  shine . . .
All in jail, we will make it shine.

Another example: "If you don't see me praying here" becomes:

If you don't see me at the back of the bus,
And you don't find me anywhere,
Go to the front of the bus,
You'll see me sitting there.

Andrew Young, a companion of King, commented on the role of music during this modern epic: "Somehow, through the music, a great secret was discovered: that black people, otherwise cowed, discouraged, and faced with innumerable and insuperable obstacles, could transcend all those difficulties and forge a new determination, a new faith and strength. . . . Music was the gift of the people to themselves, a bottomless reservoir of spiritual power."[8] For Martin Luther King, Jr., the songs were the "soul of the Movement" because they always ended on a note of hope.[9]

If the spirituals helped to mobilize the black people in the cause of justice, they allow an even greater account of the odyssey of the African American community. It is still a biblical imagery that enhances the telling of the secular adventure. It is a religious language that expresses the political aims. It is a vision of faith that determines the future. James Baldwin, the novelist (previously a preacher), is the principal witness to that, as he gave his first novel the title of a spiritual: *Go Tell It on the Mountain* (1952). The apocalyptic vision of his hero and alter ego is a reading of black history seen through the prism of the spirituals. His poetic evocation is the best conclusion for us:

> [John] opened his eyes on the morning, and found them, in the light of the morning, rejoicing for him. The trembling he had known in darkness had been the echo of their joyful feet—these feet, bloodstained forever, and washed in many rivers—they moved on the bloody road forever, with no continuing city, but seeking one to come: a city out of time, not made with hands, but eternal in the heavens. No power could hold this army back, no water disperse them, no fire consume them. One day they would compel the earth to heave upward, and surrender the waiting dead. They sang, where the lion waited, the fire cried, and where blood ran down:
> *My soul, don't you be uneasy!*
> They wandered in the valley forever; and they smote the rock, forever; and the waters sprang, perpetually, in the perpetual desert. They cried unto the Lord forever, and lifted up their eyes forever, they were cast down forever, and He lifted them up forever. No, the fire could not hurt them, and yes, the lion's jaws were stopped; the serpent was not their master, the grave was not their resting-place, the earth was not their home. Job bore them witness, and Abraham was their father, Moses had elected to suffer with them rather than glory in sin for a season. Shadrach, Meshach, and Abednego had gone before them into the fire, their grief had been sung by David, and Jeremiah had wept for them. Ezekiel had prophesied upon them, these scattered bones, these slain, and in the fullness of time, the prophet, John, had come out of the wilderness, crying that the promise was for them. They were encompassed in a very cloud of witnesses: Judas, who had betrayed the Lord; Thomas, who had doubted Him; Peter, who

had trembled at the crowing of a cock; Stephen, who had been stoned; Paul, who had been bound; the blind man crying in the dusty road, the dead man rising from the grave. And they looked unto Jesus, the author and the finisher of their faith, running with patience the race He had set before them; they endured the cross, and they despised the shame, and waited to join Him, one day, in glory, at the right hand of the Father.[10]

Such is the history of the black people of America—forever and ever.

Notes

1. James H. Cone, *The Spirituals and the Blues: An Interpretation* (New York: Seabury, 1972), 108.

2. *The Musical Record* (1893): 13.

3. Eberhard Bethge, *Dietrich Bonhoeffer* (Genève: Labor et Fides; Paris: Centurion, 1969), 128.

4. John Lovell, in his book *Black Song*, devoted 180 pages to the spiritual as a "world phenomenon," showing how it has been seen in each country in the world.

5. Cone, *Spirituals and the Blues*, 33.

6. Quoted in James M. Washington, *Conversations with God: Two Centuries of Prayers by African Americans* (New York: HarperCollins, 1994), 51.

7. See Guy Caravan and Candie Caravan, eds., *Sing for Freedom: The Story of the Civil Rights Movement through Its Songs* (Bethlehem, Pa.: Sing Out, 1990).

8. Andrew Young, *An Easy Burden* (New York: HarperCollins, 1996), 183.

9. Martin Luther King, Jr., *Autobiographie* (Paris: Bayard, 2000), 220–21.

10. James Baldwin, *Go Tell It on the Mountain* (New York: Bantam Doubleday Dell, 1985), 204–5.

An Anthology of 210 Spirituals

> *"The reader who wants to have*
> *a precise idea of any Negro Spiritual*
> *must read the original text."*
> —Marguerite Yourcenar

I present the texts of the Negro spirituals either in their contempory transcription or in the original dialect, according to the present practice, which is not uniform.

1. Adam's in the Garden Pinning Leaves

First time God called Adam,
Adam refused to answer,
Adam's in the garden laying low;
Second time God called Adam,
Adam refused to answer,
Adam's in the garden laying low.

Eve, where is Adam,

O, Eve, where is Adam?
Lord, Adam's in the garden pinning
    leaves.

Next time God called Adam,
God hollered louder,
Adam's in the garden pinning leaves.

You, Eve, can't see Adam,
O, Eve, can't see Adam,
Lord, Adam's behind the fig tree
    pinning leaves.

2. Ain't Dat Good News?

Got a crown in de Kingdom, ain't dat
    good news?
I'm a-goin to lay down dis world,

Goin' to shoulder up mah cross,
Goin' to take it home to Jesus, ain't
    dat good news?

Got a harp up in de Kingdom . . .

Got a robe up in de Kingdom . . .

Got a slippers in de Kingdom . . .

Got a Savior in de Kingdom . . .

3. Ain't Going to Tarry Here
Sweep it clean,
Ain't going to tarry here.

I sweep my house with the gospel
    broom,
Ain't going to tarry here.

Sweep it clean,
Ain't going to tarry here.

Going to open my mouth to the Lord,
Ain't going to tarry here.

O-o-o Lordy,
Ain't going to tarry here.

'Cause he's digging down in the grave,
Ain't going to tarry here.

The big bell's tolling in Galilee,
Ain't going to tarry here.

O-o-o Lordy,
Ain't going to tarry here.

4. Ain't Gonna Let Nobody
Turn Me 'Round
Ain't gonna let nobody turn me
    'round,
Turn me 'round,

Ain't gonna let nobody turn me
    'round;
I'm gonna wait till my change comes.
Don't let nobody turn you 'round,
Turn you 'round,
Don't let nobody turn you 'round,
Wait until your change comes.

I say that I'm gonna hold out,
Hold out, hold out;
I say that I'm gonna hold out,
Until my change comes.

I promised the Lord that I would
    hold out,
Hold out;
I promised the Lord that I would
    hold out,
Wait until my change comes.

5. Ain't Got Time to Die
1. Lord, I keep so busy praising my
    Jesus,
Ain't got time to die.
'Cause when I'm healing the sick,
I'm praising my Jesus,
Ain't got time to die.

'Cause it takes all of my time,
To praise my Jesus,
All of my time to praise my Lord.
If I don't praise Him,
The rocks are gonna cry out!
Glory and honor, glory and honor,
Ain't got time to die.

2. Lord, I keep so busy working for
    the Kingdom,
Ain't got time to die.
'Cause when I'm feeding the poor,
I'm working for the Kingdom,
And I ain't got time to die.

3. Lord, I keep so busy serving my
   Master,
Ain't got time to die.
'Cause when I'm giving my all,
I'm serving my Master,
Ain't got time to die.

Now, won't you get out of my way,
Let me praise my Jesus.
Get out of my way,
Let me praise my Lord.
If I don't praise Him,
The rocks gonna cry out!
Glory and honor, glory and honor,
Ain't got time to die!

6. All God's Chillun Got a Song

1. I got a song, you got a song,
All God's chillun got a song;
When I get to heaven, going to sing a
   new song,
Goin' to sing all over God's heaven.

Refrain:
Heaven heaven, everybody talking
   about heaven ain't goin' dere,
Heaven heaven, goin' to shout all over
   God's heaven.

2. I got shoes, you got shoes,
All God's chillun got shoes;
When I get to heaven, goin' to put on
   my shoes,
Goin' to walk all over God's heaven.

3. I got a robe, you got a robe,
All God's chillun got a robe;
When I get to heaven, goin' to put on
   my robe,
Goin' to shout all over God's heaven.

4. I got a harp, you got a harp,
All God's chillun got a harp;

When I get to heaven, goin' to take
   up my harp,
Goin' to play all over God's heaven.

7. Amen
Amen.

See the little baby,
Lying in a manger,
On Christmas morning.

See Him at the temple,
Talking to the elders,
How they marveled at His wisdom.

See Him in the garden,
Praying to His Father,
As Judas betrays Him.

See Him on Calvary,
Dying for our sins,
But He rose on Easter.

8. Balm in Gilead
There is balm in Gilead,
To make the wounded whole;
There is a balm in Gilead,
To heal the sin-sick soul.

1. Sometimes I feel discouraged
And think my work's in vain,
But then the Holy Spirit
Revives my soul again.

2. Don't ever feel discouraged,
For Jesus is your friend,
And if you look for knowledge,
He'll ne'er refuse to lend.

3. If you cannot preach like Peter,
If you cannot pray like Paul,
You can tell the love of Jesus,
And say, "He died for all."

9. Before This Time Another Year

Before this time another year, I may
   be gone,
Out in some lonely graveyard,
O, Lord, how long?

My mother's broke the ice and gone,
O, Lord, how long?

By the grace of God I'll follow on,
O, Lord, how long?

My father's broke the ice and gone . . .

My Savior's broke the ice and gone . . .

10. Blind Man Lying at the Pool

Blind man lying at the pool.

Lying there to be healed,
Blind man lying at the pool.

Crying: O Lord save me,
Blind man lying at the pool.

Save my weary soul,
Blind man lying at the pool.

Pray, remember me,
Blind man lying at the pool.

11. Blow Your Trumpet, Gabriel

1. De talles' tree in Paradise
De Christian call de tree of life;
And I hope dat trump might blow me
   home
To the new Jerusalem.

Refrain:
Blow your trumpet, Gabriel,
Blow louder, louder,
And I hope dat trump might blow me
   home
To the new Jerusalem.

2. Paul and Silas, bound in jail,
Sing God's praise both night and day;
And I hope . . .

12. Bound for Canaan Land

Where're you bound?
Bound for Canaan land.

O, you must not lie,
You must not steal,
You must not take God's name in vain;
I'm bound for Canaan land.

Your horse is white, your garment
   bright,
You look like a man of war;
Raise up your head with courage bold,
For your race is almost run.

How you know?
Jesus told me.

Although you see me going so,
I'm bound for Canaan land;
I have heard trials here below,
I'm bound for Canaan land.

13. But He Ain't Comin' Here t' Die No Mo'

But He ain't comin' here t' die no mo'
Ain't comin' t' die no mo'.

1. Virgin Mary had one Son,
The cruel Jews had him hung.

2. Hallelujah t' de Lamb,
Jesus died for every man.

3. He died for yo', He died for me,
He died t' set po' sinner free.

4. He died for de rich, He died for de po',
He ain't comin' here t' die no mo'.

5. He died for de blind, He died for
de lame,
He bore de pain an' all de blame.

14. Bye and Bye

O bye and bye, bye and bye,
I'm goin' to lay down dis heavy load.

1. I know my robe's goin' to fit me well,
I'm goin' to lay down dis heavy load.
I tried it on at the gates of hell,
I'm goin' to lay down dis heavy load.

2. Hell is deep and dark despair,
I'm goin' to lay down dis heavy load.
Stop, po' sinner, and don't go there,
I'm goin' to lay down dis heavy load.

3. O Christians, can't you rise and tell,
I'm goin' to lay down dis heavy load.
That Jesus hath done all things well,
I'm goin' to lay down dis heavy load.

15. Calvary

Refrain:
Calvary,
Surely He died on Calvary.

1. Ev'ry time I think about Jesus,
Surely He died on Calvary.

2. Don't you hear the hammer
ringing?

3. Don't you hear Him calling His
Father?

3. Don't you hear Him say, "It is
finished"?

5. Jesus furnished my salvation.

6. Sinner, do you love my Jesus?

Another couplet: Make me trouble
thinkin' bout dyin'.

16. Changed Mah Name

Ah tol' Jesus it would be all right, if
He changed mah name.

Jesus tol' me ah would have to live
humble, if He changed mah name.

Jesus tol' me that the world would be
'gainst me, if He changed mah name.

But ah tol' Jesus it would be all right,
if He changed mah name.

17. Children, We All Shall Be Free

Children, we shall be free,
When the Lord shall appear.

1. We want no cowards in our band,
That will their colors fly;
We call for valiant-hearted men,
That are not afraid to die.

2. We see the pilgrim as he lies,
With glory in his soul;
To heav'n he lifts his longing eyes,
And bids this world adieu.

3. Give ease to the sick, give sight to
the blind,
Enable the cripple to walk;
He'll raise the dead from under the
earth,
And give them permission to talk.

18. Chillun, Did You Hear When Jesus Rose?

Chillun, did you hear when Jesus rose?
Did you hear when Jesus rose?

Chillun, did you hear when Jesus rose?
He rose an' ascended on high!
Mary set her table
In spite of all her foes;
King Jesus sat at the center place,
An' cups did overflow.

The father looked at His Son an'
   smiled,
The Son did look at-a Him;
The Father saved my soul from hell
And the Son freed me from sin.

19. City Called Heaven

I am a poor pilgrim of sorrow,
I'm tossed in this wide world alone.
No hope have I for tomorrow,
I've started to make heav'n my home.

Refrain:
Sometimes I am tossed and driven,
   Lord,
Sometimes I don't know where to
   roam,
I've heard of a city called heaven,
I've started to make it my home.

My mother has reached that pure
   glory,
My father's still walkin' in sin.
My brothers and sisters won't own me,
Because I am tryin' to get in.

20. Climbin' up d' Mountain

Climbin' up d' mountain, children.
Didn't come here for to stay,
If ah nevermore see you again,
Gonna meet you at de judgment day.

Hebrew children in de fiery furnace,
   And dey begin to pray,
And de good Lawd smote dat fire out.

Oh, wasn't dat a mighty day! Good
   Lawd, wasn't dat a mighty day!

Daniel went in de lion's den, and he
   begin to pray,
And de angel of de Lawd locked de
   lion's jaw.
Oh, wasn't dat a mighty day! Good
   Lawd, wasn't dat a mighty!

21. Come Go with Me

1. Ole Satan is busy old man,
He roll stones in my way;
Mass' Jesus is my bosom friend,
He roll' em out o' my way.

Refrain:
O come go wid me,
A-walkin' in de heaven I roam.

2. I did not come here myself, my
      Lord,
It was my Lord who brought me here;
And I really do believe I'm a child of
   God,
A-walkin' in de heaven I roam.

22. Come to Jesus

1. Come to Jesus, come to Jesus,
   come to Jesus just now;
Just now come to Jesus, come to Jesus
   just now.

2. He will save you.

3. He is able.

4. He is willing.

5. Come, confess Him.

6. Come, obey Him.

7. He will hear you.

8. He'll forgive you.

9. He will cleanse you.

10. Jesus loves you.

11. Only trust Him.

23. Come to Me
Come to Me, ye who are hard opprest;
Lay your head gently upon my breast;
Come to Me, and I will give you rest;
Weary one, hither come! God is your
  home!

"Come to Me!" Jehovah gently pleads;
"Come to Me, I can supply all needs;
And My way unto green pasture leads;
Free from sin! Enter in! God is your
  home!"

24. Daniel Saw the Stone
1. Daniel saw the stone hewn out of
  the mountain,
Tearing down the kingdom of this
  world.

2. Have you seen that stone,
Tearing down the kingdom of this
  world?

3. Yes, I saw the stone,
Tearing down the kingdom of this
  world.

4. You'd better seek that stone,
Tearing down the kingdom of this
  world.

5. Jesus was the stone,
Tearing down the kingdom of this
  world.

6. Going to preach about that stone,

Tearing down the kingdom of this
  world.

7. O, that holy stone,
Tearing down the kingdom of this
  world.

25. Death Ain't Nothin but a Robber
Death ain't nothin' but a robber, don't
  you see.

Death came to my house, he didn't
  stay long,
I looked in the bed an' my mother
  was gone . . .

I looked in the bed an' my father was
  gone . . .

I looked in the bed an' my sister was
  gone . . .

I looked in the bed an' my brother
  was gone,
Death ain't nothin' but a robber, don't
  you see.

26. Death's Go'n'ter Lay His Col', Icy Hands on Me
Cryin' Oh, Lord, cryin' Oh, my Lord,
  cryin' Oh, Lord.
Death's go'n'ter lay his col', icy hands
  on me.

Oh, sinner, sinner, you better pray.
Death's go'n'ter lay his col', icy hands
  on me.
Or your soul get lost at de judgment
  day.
Death's go'n'ter lay his col', icy hands
  on me.

27. Deep River

Deep river, my home is over Jordan;
Deep river, Lord, I want to cross over
    into campground.
Lord, I want to cross over into
    campground.

1. O don't you want to go to dat
    Gospel feast;
Dat promised land where all is peace?
Lord, I want to cross over into
    campground.

2. I'll walk into heaven and take my seat,
And cast my crown at Jesus' feet.
Lord, I want to cross over into
    campground.

3. O when I get to heav'n, I'll walk all
    about,
There's nobody there for to turn me out.
Lord, I want to cross over into
    campground.

28. De Ol' Ark's a-Moverin'

Oh, de ol' ark's a-moverin', a-moverin',
De ol' ark's a-moverin' an' I'm goin' home.

See dat sistuh dressed so fine?
She ain't got religion on-a her min'.

See dat brudder dressed so gay?
Satan goin' come an' carry him away.

Ol' ark she reel, ol' ark she rock,
Ol' ark she landed on de
    mountaintop.

29. Dere's a Little Wheel a Turnin' in My Heart

Dere's a little wheel a turning' in my heart,
In my heart,
Dere's a little wheel a turnin' in my
    heart.

O, I feel so very happy in my heart,
In my heart,
Dere's a little wheel a turnin' in my
    heart.

O, I don't feel no ways tired in my
    heart,
In my heart,
Dere's a little wheel a turnin' in my
    heart.

O, I feel like shouting in my heart,
In my heart,
Dere's a little wheel a turnin' in my
    heart.

30. Dere's Plenty Good Room

Dere's plenty good room, dere's plenty
    good room,
Plenty good room in my Father's
    kingdom.
Plenty good room, plenty good room,
Just choose your seat and sit down.

O brother, don't stay away, O sister,
    don't stay away,
For my Lord says dere is room enough,
Room enough in Heaven for us all,
My Lord says dere's room enough, so
    don't stay away.

31. Dese Bones Gwine Rise Again

1. De Lawd, He thought He'd make
    a man,
Dese bones gwine rise again,
Made 'im outa mud an' a han'ful
    o' san',
Dese bones gwine rise again.

Refrain:
I knowed it,
Indeed I knowed it, brother,
I knowed it,
Dese bones gwine rise again.

2. Thought He'd make a woman, too,
Didn't know 'xactly what to do.

3. Took a rib from Adam's side,
Made Miss Eve for to be his bride.

4. Put um in a garden fine and fair,
Tole um to eat whatever was dere.

5. But to one tree they mus' not go,
Must leave de apples dere to grow.

6. Sarpint quoiled around a chunk,
At Miss Eve his eye he wunk.

7. First she took a little pull,
Then she filled her apron full.

8. Adam took a little slice,
Smack his lips an' say 'twas nice.

9. De Lord He spoke with a
    'ponstrous voice,
Shook de world to its very jois'.

10. "Stole my apples, I believe."
"No, Marse Lord, I 'spec' it was Eve."

11. "Out of this garden you must git,
Earn yo' livin' by yo' sweat."

12. He put an angel at de do',
Tol' um never come dere no mo'.

13. Of this tale there is no mo',
Eve et the apple and Adam de co'.

32. Didn't My Lord Deliver Daniel?

Didn't my Lord deliver Daniel, d'liver
    Daniel, d'liver Daniel?

Didn't my Lord deliver Daniel, and
    why not every man?

1. He deliver'd Daniel from the lion's den,
Jonah from the belly of the whale,
And the Hebrew children from the
    fiery furnace,
And why not every man?

2. The moon run down in a purple
    stream,
The sun forbear to shine,
And every star disappear,
King Jesus shall be mine.

3. The wind blows east, and the wind
    blows west,
It blows like the judgment day,
And every poor soul that never did pray,
'll be glad to pray that day.

4. I set my foot on the Gospel ship,
And the ship it begin to sail,
It landed me over on Canaan's shore,
And I'll never come back any more.

33. Didn't Old Pharaoh Get Los'?

1. Isaac a ransom,
While he lay upon an altar bound;
Moses an infant cast away,
But Pharaoh's daughter found.

Refrain:
Didn't Pharaoh get los', get los', get
    los'?
Didn't old Pharaoh get los' in de Red
    Sea, true believer, O Red Sea?

2. Joseph by his false brethren sold,
God raised above them all;
To Hanna's child the Lord foretold,
How Eli's house should fall.

3. De Lord said unto Moses:

"Go unto Pharaoh now,
For I have hardened Pharaoh's heart,
To me he will not bow."

4. Den Moses an' Aaron,
To Pharaoh did go:
 "Thus says de God of Israel,
Let my people go."

5. Old Pharaoh said: "Who is de Lord
Dat I should Him obey?"
"His name it is Jehovah,
For he hears his people pray."

6. Hark! hear de children murmur,
Dey cry aloud for bread,
Down came de hidden manna,
De hungry soldiers fed.

7. Den Moses numbered Israel,
Through all de land abroad,
Sayin': "Children, do not
    murmur,
But hear de word of God."

8. Den Moses said to Israel,
As dey stood along de shore:
 "Yo' enemies you see today,
You'll never see no more."

9. Den down came raging Pharaoh,
Dat you may plainly see,
Old Pharaoh an' his host
Got los' in de Red Sea.

10. Den men an' women an'
    children
To Moses dey did flock;
Dey cried aloud for water:
"An' Moses smote de rock."

11. An' de Lord spoke to Moses,
From Sinai's smoking top,
Sayin': "Moses lead de people,
Till I shall bid you stop."

34. Do, Lord, Remember Me

1. Do, Lord, do, Lord, Lord,
    remember me.
Do, Lord, remember me.

2. When I'm in trouble, Lord,
    remember me.

3. When I'm dyin', Lord, remember me.

4. When this world's on fire, Lord,
    remember me.

35. Done Foun' My Los' Sheep

Done foun' my los' sheep, Hallelujah.
I done foun' my los' sheep.

My Lord had a hundred sheep,
One o' dem did go astray,
That jes lef' Him ninety-nine,
Go to de wilderness, seek an' fin',
Ef you fin' him, bring him back,
Cross de shoulders, cross yo' back;
Tell de neighbors all aroun',
Dat los' sheep has to be foun',
Done foun' my los' sheep.

In dat Resurrection Day,
Sinner can't fin' no hidin' place,
Go to de mountain, de mountain
    move,
Run to de hill, de hill run too,
Sinner man trablin' on trembling
    groun',
Po' los' sheep ain't nebber been foun';
Sinner, why don't yo' stop and pray,
Den you'd hear de Shepherd say,
Done foun' my los' sheep.

36. Don't Be Weary, Traveller

Don't be weary, traveller,
Come along home to Jesus.

1. My hand got wet with the
   midnight dew,
Come along home to Jesus,
Angels bear me witness too,
Come along home to Jesus.

2. Where to go I did not know,
Come along home to Jesus,
Ever since He freed my soul,
Come along home to Jesus.

3. I look at de worl' an' de worl' look
   new,
Come along home to Jesus.
I look at my hands an' they look so
   too,
Come along home to Jesus.

37. Don't You View Dat Ship a-Come a-Sailin'?

1. Don't you view dat ship a-come
   a-sailin'? Hallelujah.

2. Dat ship is heavy loaded,
   Hallelujah.

3. She neither reels nor totters,
   Hallelujah.

4. She is loaded wid-a bright angels,
   Hallelujah.

5. Oh, how do you know dey are
   angels? Hallelujah.

6. I know dem by a de'r mournin',
   Hallelujah.

7. Oh, yonder comes my Jesus,
   Hallelujah.

8. Oh, how do you know it is Jesus?
   Hallelujah.

9. I know him by-a his shinin',
   Hallelujah.

38. Down by the Riverside

1. When Christ the Lord was here
   below,
Down by the river,
About the work He came to do,
Down by the river side.

Refrain:
We will end this warfare,
Down by the river,
We will end this warfare,
Down by the river side.

2. Sister Mary wore a golden chain,
Down by the river,
And ev'ry link bear'd my Jesus' name,
Down by the river side.

3. Pilate called for water to wash his
   hands,
Down by the river;
"I find no fault of this good man,"
Down by the riverside.

4. O fishin' Peter led the way,
Down by the river,
But nothing was caught till the break
   of day,
Down by the river side.

5. Sister Mary wept and Martha cried,
Down by the river,
When Christ the Lord was crucified,
Down by the river side.

6. When we meet in the middle of
   the air,
Down by the river,
We hope to meet our friends all there,
Down by the river side.

39. Dry Bones

God called Ezekiel by His word:
"Go down and prophesy!"
"Yes, Lord!"
Ezekiel prophesied by the power of
    God,
Commanded de bones to rise.

Dey gonna walk aroun', dry bones,
Dey gonna walk aroun', wid de dry
    bones,
Dey gonna walk aroun', dry bones,
Why don't you rise an' hear de word
    of de Lord?
"Tell me, how did de bones get
    together wid de long bones?
Prophesy?"

Ah, well, de toe bone connected wid
    de foot bone,
De foot bone connected wid de ankle
    bone,
De ankle bone connected wid de leg
    bone,
De leg bone connected wid de knee
    bone,
De knee bone connected wid de thigh
    bone,
Rise an' hear de word of de Lord!

40. Ev'ry Time I Feel the Spirit

Ev'ry time I feel the Spirit moving in
    my heart,
I will pray.
Oh, ev'ry time I feel the Spirit moving
    in my heart,
I will pray, yes, I will pray.

Up on the mountain my Lord spoke,
Out o' His mouth came fire and
    smoke.
All around me looks so shine,

Ask my Lord if all was mine.

Jordan River is chilly and cold,
Chills the body but not the soul.
Ain't but one train on dis track,
Runs to heaven and right back.

41. Ezek'el Saw de Wheel

Ezek'el saw de wheel
'Way up in de middle o' de air,
De big wheel run by faith,
De little wheel run by de grace o' God,
A wheel in a wheel,
'Way in de middle o' de air.

1. Better min', my sister, how you
       walk on de cross,
   'Way in de middle o' de air,
   Yo' foot might slip an' yo' soul
       be los',
   'Way in de middle o' de air.

2. Let me tell you, brother, what a
       hypocrite will do, . . .
   He'll low-rate you an' he'll low-rate
       me . . .

3. Ol' Satan wears a club-foot shoe, . . .
   If you don' min', he'll slip it on you . . .

42. Fare You Well

O, fare you well, my brother,
Fare you well by the grace of God,
For I'm going home;
I'm going home, my Lord,
I'm going home.

Master Jesus gave me a little broom,
To sweep my heart clean,
Sweep it clean by the grace of God,
And glory in my soul.

43. Father Abraham

Father Abraham sittin' down side ob
    de Holy Lam'.

'Way up on-a de mountain top,
My Lord he spoke an' de chariot stop.

Goodbye mother an' fare you well,
Meet me aroun' dat th'one ob God.

44. Fighting On

Fighting on, Hallelujah! We are
    almost down to de shore.

1. Hallelujah to the Lamb, Jesus died
    for eb'ry man.
We are almost down to de shore.
He died for you, He died for me, He
    died to save de whole world.
We are almost down to de shore.

2. In my room right by my bed, Jesus
    take me when I'm dead.
We are almost down to de shore.
When I get on dat other shore, I'll
    bless my Lord for ever.
We are almost down to de shore.

45. Four and Twenty Elders

Dere are four and twenty elders on
    their knees,
An' we'll rise together,
An' face the risin' sun,
O Lord, have mercy if you please.

Dey are bowin' 'round the altar on
    their knees . . .

See Gideon's army bowin' on their
    knees . . .

See Daniel 'mong the lions on their
    knees . . .

46. Free at Last

Free at last, free at last,
Thank God a'mighty, I'm free at last.

Surely been 'buked, and surely been
    scorned,
Thank God a'mighty, I'm free at last.
But still my soul is a heaven born,
Thank God a'mighty, I'm free at last.

If you don't know that I been
    redeemed,
Thank God a'mighty, I'm free at last.
Just follow me down to Jordan's
    stream,
Thank God a'mighty, I'm free at last.

47. Get on Board, Children

Refrain:
Git on board, children,
For there's room for many a more.

1. The Gospel train is coming,
I hear it jus' at hand,
I hear the car wheels moving,
And rumbling thro' the land.

2. I hear the bell and whistle,
The coming round the curve,
She's playing all her steam an' pow'r,
An' strainin' ev'ry nerve.

3. No signal for another train,
To follow on the line,
O sinner, you're forever lost,
If once you're left behind.

4. This is the Christian banner,
The motto's new and old,
Salvation and repentance,
Are burnished there in gold.

5. She's nearing now the station,
O, sinner, don't be vain,

But come and get your ticket,
And be ready for the train.

6. The fare is cheap an' all can go,
The rich an' poor are there,
No second class aboard the train,
No diff'rence in the fare.

7. There's Moses, Noah, and Abraham,
And all the prophets, too,
Our friends in Christ are all on board,
O, what a heavenly crew.

8. We soon shall reach the station,
O, how we then shall ring,
With all the heavenly army,
We'll make the welcome ring.

9. We'll shout o'er all our sorrows,
And sing forever more,
With Christ and all His army,
On that celestial shore.

48. Give Me Jesus

1. Oh, when I come to die,
Give me Jesus.
You may have all this world,
Give me Jesus.

2. I heard my mother say,
Give me Jesus.

3. Dark midnight was my cry,
Give me Jesus.

4. In the morning when I rise,
Give me Jesus.

5. I heard the mourner say,
Give me Jesus.

49. Glory, Glory, Hallelujah

1. Glory, glory, hallelujah!

Since I laid my burden down.

2. I feel better, so much better,
Since I laid my burden down.

Feel like shouting "Hallelujah!"
Since I laid my burden down.

Burdens down, Lord, burdens down,
     Lord,
Since I laid my burden down.

5. I am climbing Jacob's ladder,
Since I laid my burden down.

6. Ev'ry round goes higher and higher,
Since I laid my burden down.

7. I'm goin' home to be with Jesus,
Since I laid my burden down.

50. Go Down, Moses

Go down, Moses,
'Way down in Egypt land,
Tell ol' Pharaoh,
Let my people go!

1. When Israel was in Egypt's land,
Let my people go.
Oppressed so hard they could not
     stand,
Let my people go.

2. Thus saith the Lord, bold Moses said . . .
If not I'll smite your first-born dead . . .

3. No more shall they in bondage
     toil, . . .
Let them come out with Egypt's spoil . . .

4. When Israel out of Egypt came . . .
And left the proud oppressive land . . .

5. O, 'twas dark and dismal night . . .
When Moses led the Israelites . . .

6. 'Twas good old Moses and Aaron, too . . .
'Twas they that led the armies through . . .

7. The Lord told Moses what to do . . .
To lead the children of Israel through . . .

8. O come along, Moses, you'll not
get lost. . .
Stretch out your rod and come across . . .

9. As Israel stood by the waterside . . .
At the command of God it did divide . . .

10. When they had reached the other
shore . . .
They sang a song of triumph o'er . . .

11. Pharaoh said he would go across . . .
But Pharaoh and his host were lost . . .

12. O, Moses, the cloud shall cleave
the way . . .
A fire by night, a shade by day . . .

13. You'll not get lost in the wilderness . . .
With a lighted candle in your breast . . .

14. Jordan shall stand up, like a wall . . .
And the walls of Jericho shall fall . . .

15. Your foes shall not before you stand . . .
And you'll possess fair Canaan's land . . .

16. 'Twas just about at harvest time . . .
When Joshua led his host divine . . .

17. O let us all from bondage flee . . .
And let us all in Christ be free . . .

18. We need not always weep and moan . . .
And wear the slavery chains forlorn . . .

19. This world's a wilderness of woe. . .
O, let us on to Canaan go . . .

20. What a beautiful morning that
will be . . .
When time breaks up in eternity . . .

21. O brethren, brethren, you'd better
be engaged . . .
For the devil he's out on a big rampage . . .

22. The devil he thought he had me fast . . .
But I thought I'd break his chains at last . . .

23. O take your shoes from off your feet . . .
And walk into the golden street . . .

24. I'll tell you what I like de best. . .
It is the shouting Methodist . . .

25. I do believe without a doubt . . .
That a Christian has the right to shout . . .

51. Go in the Wilderness
I wait upon the Lord,
Weeping Mary . . .
I wait upon the Lord my God,
Who take away the sins of the world.
(Con)flicted sister . . .

If you want to find Jesus,
Half-done Christian . . .
You have to go to the wilderness,
Go in the wilderness,
Come backslider . . .
Leaning on the Lord.
Baptist member . . .

If you want to be a Christian . . .
Seek, Brother Bristol . . .

If you want to get religion . . .
Jesus, a-waiting . . .

(Ex)pect to be converted . . .

52. Go, Tell It on the Mountain
Go, tell it on the mountain,
Over the hills and ev'rywhere;
Go, tell it on the mountain,

That Jesus Christ is born.

1. When I was a sinner,
I prayed both night and day;
I asked the Lord to help me,
And he showed me the way.

2. When I was a seeker,
I sought both night and day;
I asked my Lord to help me,
And he taught me to pray.

3. He made me a watchman,
upon the city wall;
And if I am a Christian,
I am the least of all.

The spiritual is now sung with couplets
focused upon Christmas:

1. While shepherds kept their
watching
O'er silent flocks by night,
Behold throughout the heavens
There shone a holy light.

2. The shepherds feared and trembled
When lo! above the earth,
Rang out the angel chorus
That hailed our Savior's birth.

3. Down in a lowly manger
The humble Christ was born,
And God sent us salvation
That blessed Christmas morn.

53. God Is a God

God is a God! God don't never
change!
God is a God an' He always will be
God!

He made the sun to shine by day,
He made the sun to show the way,

He made the stars to show their light,
He made the moon to shine by night,
say-in'…

The earth His footstool an' heav'n His
throne,
The whole creation all His own,
His love an' power will prevail,
His promises will never fail, say-in'…

54. Going to Set Down and Rest Awhile

Going to set down and rest awhile,
When my good Lord calls me.

Sister Mary went to Heaven,
And she went there to stay,
And she didn't go to come back no
more;
She sang a song that the angels
couldn't sing:
"Hosanna, carry on."

Little children, don't you moan,
When my good Lord calls me.
O, Zion!
When my good Lord calls me.

55. Good Lord, Shall I Ever Be de One?

Good Lord, shall I ever be de one,
To get over in de Promis' Lan'?

1. God placed Adam in de garden,
'Twas about de cool of de day,
Call for ole Adam,
An' he tried to run away.

2. The Lord walked in de garden,
'Twas about de cool of de day,
Call for ole Adam,
An' Adam said: "Hear me Lord."

56. Good News

Good news! The chariot's coming,
And I don't want it to leave me
behind.

There's a long white robe in the
heaven, I know,
And I don't want it to leave me
behind.

Pair of wings . . .

Pair of shoes . . .

Starry crown . . .

Golden harp . . .

57. Great Day

Great day! Great day, the righteous
marching. Great day!
God's going to build up Zion's walls!

1. Chariot rode on the mountain top,
God's going to build up Zion's
walls!
My God spoke, the chariot did stop,
God's going to build up Zion's
walls!

2. This is the day of jubilee,
God's . . .
The Lord has set His people free,
God's . . .

3. We want no cowards in our band,
God's . . .
We call for valiant-hearted men,
God's . . .

4. Going to take my breastplate,
sword, and shield,
God's . . .
And march out boldly in the field,
God's . . .

58. Hammering

Those cruel people! Those cruel
people hammering!
Hammering! Hammering!

They crucified my Lord!

They nailed Him to the tree.

You hear the hammer ringing.

The blood came trickling down.

59. Hard Trials

1. The foxes, they have holes in the
ground,
The birds have nests in the air,
The Christians have a hiding place,
But sinners ain't got nowhere.

Refrain:
Now ain't them hard trials, great
tribulations?
Ain't them hard trials? I'm bound to
leave this land.

2. Old Satan tempted Eve,
And Eve, she tempted Adam,
And that's why the sinner has to pray
so hard,
To get his sins forgiven.

3. Oh, Methodist, Methodist is my
name,
Methodist till I die,
Been baptized on the Methodist side,
And a Methodist will I die.

4. Oh, Baptist, Baptist is my name,
Baptist till I die,
Been baptized on the Baptist side,
And Baptist will I die.

5. While marching on the road,
A-hunting for a home,

You had better stop your differences,
And travel on to God.

60. Have You Got Good Religion?

1. Have you got good religion?
   Cert'nly, Lord;
Cert'nly, Lord, Cert'nly, cert'nly,
   cert'nly, Lord.

2. Have you been redeemed? . . .

3. Have you been to the water? . . .

4. Have you been baptized? . . .

5. Is your name on high? . . .

6. Has your name been changed? . . .

61. He Arose

He 'rose from the dead,
And the Lord shall bear my spirit (*or:*
   His children) home.

1. They crucified my Savior and
   nailed Him to the cross,
And the Lord will bear my spirit
   home.

2. And Joseph begged His body and
   laid it in the tomb,
And the Lord will bear my spirit
   home.

3. The cold grave could not hold Him
   nor death's cold iron band,
And the Lord will bear my spirit
   home.

4. Sister Mary, she came running,
   a-looking for my Lord,
And the Lord will bear my spirit
   home.

5. An angel came from heaven and
   rolled the stone away,
And the Lord will bear my spirit
   home.

6. The angel said He is not here, He's
   gone to Galilee,
And the Lord will bear my spirit
   home.

62. He Is King of Kings

He is King of kings, he is Lord of
   lords,
Jesus Christ, the first and last, no one
   works like him.

He built his throne up in the air,
No one works like him,
And called his saints from everywhere,
No one works like him.

He pitched his tents on Canaan's
   ground,
No one works like him,
And broke the Roman kingdom
   down,
No one works like him.

63. He Nevuh Said a Mumbalin' Word

They crucified my Lord,
An' He nevuh said a mumbalin' word,
Not a word, not a word, not a word.

They nailed Him to the tree . . .

They pierced Him in the side . . .

The blood came streamin' (*or:*
   twinklin') down . . .

He hung (*or:* bow'd) His head and
   died . . .

64. He's Got the Whole World in His Hands

He's got the whole world in His hands,
He's got the big, round world in His hands,
He's got the whole world in His hands.

He's got the wind and the rain…

He's got the little baby…

He's got you and me, sister…
He's got you and me, brother…

65. He's Jus' de Same Today

When Moses an' his soldiers f'om
Egypt's lan' did flee,
His enemies were in behin' him, an'
in front of him de sea.
God raised de waters like a wall, an'
opened up de way,
An' de God dat lived in Moses' time is
jus' de same today.
Is jus' de same today, jus' de same
today,
An' de God dat lived in Moses' time is
jus' de same today.

Daniel faithful to his God, would not
bow down to men,
An' by God's enemy he was hurled
into de lion's den.
God locked de lion's jaw we read, an'
robbed him of his prey,
An' de God dat lived in Daniel's time
is jus' de same today . . .

66. He's the Lily of the Valley

Refrain:
He's the lily of the valley, Oh! my Lord.
1. King Jesus in the chariot rides, Oh!
my Lord;

With four white horses side by side,
Oh! my Lord.

2. What kind of shoes are those you
wear, Oh! my Lord;
That you can ride upon the air, Oh!
My Lord.

3. These shoes I wear are gospel shoes,
Oh! my Lord;
And you can wear them if you
choose, Oh! my Lord.

67. Hear de Angels Singin'

Oh, sing all de way, my Lord,
Hear de angels singin'.

1. We're marchin up to hebben, it's a
happy time; Hear…
An' Jesus is on-a de middle line;
Hear…
Dem-a Christians take up too much
time; Hear…
Dey're idlin' on dat battle line; Hear…

2. Now all things well, an' I don't
dread hell;
I am goin' up to hebben, where my
Jesus dwell;
For de angels are callin' me away;
An' I must go, I cannot stay.

3. Now take your Bible, an' read it
through;
An' ebery word you'll find is true;
For in dat Bible you will see;
Dat Jesus died for you an' me.

4. Say, if my memory serves me right;
We're sure to hab a little shout
tonight;
For I love to shout, I love to sing;
I love to praise my Hebbenly King.

68. His Name So Sweet

Oh Lawd, I jes come from de
    fountain, Lawd,
Jes come from de fountain,
His name so sweet.

1. Po' sinnuh, do you love Jesus?
Yes, yes, I do love mah Jesus.
Sinnuh, do you love Jesus?
His name so sweet.

2. Class leader, do you love Jesus?

3. 'Sidin' elder, do you love Jesus?

69. Hold On!

Keep your hand on-a dat plow!
Hold on!
Keep your hand right on-a dat
    plow!
Hold on!

Noah, Noah, let me come in,
Doors all fastened an de winders
    pinned.
Keep your hand on-a dat plow!
Noah said, You done lost yo' track,
Can't plow straight an' keep
    a-lookin' back.

Sister Mary had a gold chain,
Every link was my Jesus' name.
Keep your hand on-a dat plow!
Keep on plowin'an' don't you tire,
Every row goes high'r an' high'r.

Ef you wanner git to Heben,
I'll tell you how:
Keep your hand right on-a dat
    plow!
Ef dat plow stays in-a your hand,
Land you straight in de Promise'
    Land.

70. Honor, Honor

King Jesus lit the candle by the
    watuh side,
To see the little children when dey
    truly baptize',
Honor, honor unto the dying lamb.

Oh run along, children, an' be
    baptize',
Mighty pretty meetin' by de watuh side,
Honor, honor unto the dying lamb.

I prayed all day, I prayed all night,
My head got sprinkled wid duh mid
    night dew,
Honor, honor unto the dying lamb.

71. How Long?

When the clouds hang heavy and it
    looks like rain,
O Lord, how long?
Well, the sun's drawing water from
    every vein,
O Lord, how long?

About this time another year,
I may be gone,
Within some lonely graveyard.
O Lord, how long?

If I had prayed when I was young,
O Lord, how long?
Well, I would not've had such a hard
    race to run,
O Lord, how long?

72. Hush, Hush, Somebody's Callin' Mah Name

Hush, Hush, somebody's callin' mah
    name,
Oh mah Lawd, what shall I do?

I'm so glad. Trouble don't last always.
Oh mah Lawd, what shall I do?

Sounds like Jesus. Somebody's callin'
mah name...

Soon one mornin', death'll come
creepin' in mah room...

I'm so glad. Ah got mah religion in time...

I'm so glad. I'm on mah journey home...

73. I Ain't Got Weary Yet
I ain't got weary yet,
I've been in the wilderness a mighty
long time,
And I ain't got weary yet.

I've been praying like Silas,
I've been preaching like Paul,
I've been in the wilderness...
I've been walking with the Savior,
I've been walking with the Lord,
I've been in the wilderness...

74. I Am Free
I am free,
I am free, my Lord,
I am free,
I'm washed by the blood of the Lamb.

You may knock me down,
I'll rise again,
I'm washed by the blood of the Lamb;
I fight you with my sword and shield,
I'm washed by the blood of the Lamb.

Remember the day, I remember it
well,
My dungeon shook and my chain
fell off;
Jesus cleaned and made me white,

Said go in peace and sin no more;
Glory to God, let your faith be strong,
Lord, it won't be long before I'll be gone.

75. I Am Seekin' for a City
1. I am seekin' for a city, Hallelujah,
For a city into de heaven, Hallelujah,
Oh, bredren, trabbel wid me,
Hallelujah,
Say will you along wid me? Hallelujah.

Refrain:
Lord, I don't feel noways tired,
Oh, glory, Hallelujah,
Hope to shout glory when dis world
is on fiah,
Oh, glory, Hallelujah!

2. We will trabbel on together,
Hallelujah,
Gwine to war agin de debbel,
Hallelujah,
Gwine to pull down Satan's kingdom,
Hallelujah,
Gwine to build de walls o' Zion,
Hallelujah.

3. Dere is a better day a-comin',
Hallelujah,
When I leave dis world o' sorrer,
Hallelujah,
For to jine de holy number,
Hallelujah,
Den we'll talk de trouble ober,
Hallelujah.

4. Gwine to walk about in Zion,
Hallelujah,
Gwine to talk-a wid de angels,
Hallelujah,
Gwine to tell God 'bout my crosses,
Hallelujah,
Gwine to reign wid Him foreber.

76. I Couldn't Hear Nobody Pray

An' I couldn't hear nobody pray, O Lord,
I couldn't hear nobody pray, O Lord,
O' way down yonder by myself,
An' I couldn't hear nobody pray.

Chilly waters! I couldn't…
In de Jordan!…
Crossin' over!…
Into Canaan! I couldn't…O Lord!

In de valleys! I couldn't…
On my knees!…
Wid my burden!…
An' my Savior!…

Hallelujah!…
Troubles over!…
In de kingdom!…
Wid my Jesus!…

77. I Feel Like My Time Ain't Long

I feel like my time ain't long.

Went to the graveyard the other day,
I feel like . . .
I look'd at the place where my
    mother lay,
I feel like…

Sometimes I'm up, sometimes I'm down,
And sometimes I'm almost on the
    ground.

Better min', my brother, how walk on
    the cross,
Your foot might slip and your soul get lost.

78. I Got a Home in-a Dat Rock

I got a home in-a dat Rock, Don't
    you see?
Between de earth an' sky,

Thought I heard my Saviour cry,
You got a home in-a dat Rock, Don't
    you see?

Poor man Lazarus, poor as I, Don't
    you see?
Poor man Lazarus, poor as I,
When he died he foun' a home on high,
He had a home in-a dat Rock, Don't
    you see?

Rich man, Dives, he lived so well,
    Don't you see?
Rich man, Dives, he lived so well,
When he died he foun' a home in Hell,
He had no home in-a dat Rock, Don't
    you see?

God gave Noah de rainbow sign,
    Don't you see?
God gave Noah de rainbow sign,
No mo' water but fire nex' time,
Better get a home in-a dat Rock,
    Don't you see?

79. I Know de Lord Has Laid His Hands on Me

O I know de Lord, I know de Lord,
I know de Lord has laid his hands on me.
O I know de Lord, I know de Lord,
I know de Lord has laid his hands on me.

Did eber you see de like befo',
I know de Lord…
King Jesus preachin' to de po'?
I know de Lord…

O wasn't dat a happy day,
When Jesus washed my sins away?

My Lord has done just what he said,
He's healed de sick and raised de dead.

80. I Know It Was the Blood

1. I know it was the blood for me.
One day when I was lost,
Jesus died upon the cross.
I know it was the blood for me.

2. It was my Savior's blood for me . . .

3. The blood came streaming down
for me . . .

4. He suffered, bled, and died for me . . .

5. I know He's coming back for me . . .

81. I Saw the Beam in My Sister's Eye

I saw the beam in my sister's eye,
Couldn't see the beam in mine;
You'd better leave your sister's door,
Go keep your own door clean.

And I had a mighty battle like Jacob
and the angel,
Jacob, time of old;
I didn't intend to let him go,
Till Jesus blessed my soul.

And blessed me, and blessed me,
And blessed all my soul;
I didn't intend to let him go,
Till Jesus blessed my soul.

82. I Shall Not Be Moved

I shall not be moved,
Like a tree planted by the water,
I shall not be moved.

When my cross is heavy, I shall not be
moved, like a . . .

The church of God is marching . . .

King Jesus is our Captain . . .

Come and join the army . . .

Fighting sin and Satan . . .

When my burden's heavy . . .

Don't let the world deceive you . . .

If my friends forsake me . . .

83. I Stood on de Ribber ob Jerdon

1. I stood on de ribber ob Jerdon,
To see dat ship come sailin' ober;
Stood on de ribber ob Jerdon,
To see dat ship sail by.

Refrain:
O moaner, don' ya weep, when ya see
dat ship come sailin' ober;
Shout: "Glory Hallelujah!" When ya
see dat ship sail by.

O sister, ya bettuh be ready
To see . . .
Brother, ya bettuh be ready
To see . . .

O preacher . . .

O Deacon . . .

84. I Want Jesus to Walk with Me

I want Jesus to walk with me,
All along my pilgrim journey,
Lord, I want Jesus to walk with me.

1. In my trials, Lord, walk with me,
When my heart is almost breaking,
Lord . . .

2. When I'm in trouble, Lord, walk
with me,

When my head is bowed in sorrow,
  Lord…

More couplets:

1. In my trials, walk with me…
When the shades of life are falling…

2. In my sorrow, walk with me…
When my heart within is aching…

3. In my troubles…
When my life becomes a burden…

85. I Want to Be Ready
I want to be ready
To walk in Jerusalem just like John.

O John, O John, what do you say?
Walk in Jerusalem just like John.
That I'll be there at the coming day,
Walk…

John said the city was just four-square,
And he declared he'd meet me there.

When Peter was preaching at
  Pentecost,
He was endowed with the Holy
  Ghost.

86. I'll Be Singing up There
I'll be singing up there,
Oh! Come on up to bright glory,
I'll be singing up there.

If you miss me singing down here,
Oh, come on up to bright glory,
You'll find me singing up there.
If you miss me praying down here …

If you miss me walking down here…

If you miss me shouting down here …

87. I'm a Poor Wayfaring Stranger
I'm a poor wayfaring stranger,
While journeying through this world
  of woe,
Yet there's no sickness, toil, and danger,
In that bright world to which I go;
I'm going there to see my father,
I'm going there no more to roam,
I'm just going over Jordan,
I'm just going over home.

I know dark clouds will gather 'round me,
I know my way is rough and steep,
Yet bright fields lie just before me,
Where God's redeemed their vigils keep;
I'm going there to see my mother,
She said she'd meet me when I come,
I'm just going over Jordan,
I'm just going over home.

I'll soon be free from every trial,
My body will sleep in the old
  churchyard,
I'll drop the cross of self-denial,
And enter on my great reward;
I'm going there to see my Savior,
To sing His praise in Heaven's dome,
I'm just going over Jordan,
I'm just going over home.

88. I'm a-Rolling
I'm a-rolling, I'm a-rolling, I'm
  a-rolling, through an unfriendly
  world.
O brothers, won't you help me,
O brothers, won't you help me to pray?
O brothers, won't you help me,
Won't you help me in the service of
  the Lord?

O sisters…

O preachers…

89. I'm Gonna Sing

I'm gonna sing (shout, preach, pray)
    when the Spirit says a-Sing,
And obey the Spirit of the Lord.

90. I'm So Glad I Got My Religion in Time

I'm so glad I got my religion in time,
O my Lord, O my Lord, what shall I do?

Make more room, Lord, in my heart
    for thee,
O my Lord, O my Lord, what shall I do?

Run, sinner, run and hunt you an
    hidin' place,
O my Lord, O my Lord, what shall I do?

91. I'm So Glad Trouble Don't Last Always

I'm so glad trouble don't last always,
O my Lord, O my Lord, what shall I do?

1. Christ tol' the blin' man to go to
    the pool and bathe,
O my Lord, O my Lord, what shall I do?

2. Christ tol' Nicodemus, He mu' be
    born again,
O my Lord, O my Lord, what shall I do?

92. I'm Troubled in Mind

I'm troubled in mind,
If Jesus don't help me, I surely will die.

1. O Jesus, my Savior, on thee I'll depend,
When troubles are near me,
You'll be my true friend.

2. When ladened with trouble and
    burdened with grief,

To Jesus in secret I'll go for relief.

3. In dark days of bondage to Jesus I
    prayed,
To help me to bear it and He gave me
    His aid.

93. I've Been 'Buked and I've Been Scorned

I've been 'buked an' I've been scorned,
    children.
I've been 'buked an' I've been scorned,
I've been talked about, sho's you're born.

Dere is trouble all over dis world,
Children, dere is trouble all over dis world.

Ain't gwine to lay my 'ligion down,
Children, ain't gwine to lay my 'ligion
    down.

94. I've Been in de Storm So Long

I've been in the storm so long,
You know I've been in the storm so long,
Oh Lord, give me more time to pray,
I've been in the storm so long.

I am a motherless child,
Singin' I am a motherless child,
Singin' Oh Lord, give me more time
    to pray,
I've been in the storm so long.

This is a needy time
Singin' …

Lord, I need you now …

Lord, I need your prayer…

Stop this wicked race…

Stop all my wicked ways…

Somebody need you now...

My neighbors need you now...

My children need you now...

Just look what a shape I'm in...

Another version:
Oh, let me tell you, Mother, how I
   come 'long,
Oh, gimme little time to pray,
With a hung down head and a
   achin' heart,
Oh, gimme little time to pray.

Now when I get to Heaven I'll take
   my seat,
Oh, gimme little time to pray,
An-a cast my crown at my Jesus' feet,
Oh, gimme little time to pray.

95. I've Been Trying to Live Humble
Humble, humble,
I've been trying to live humble,
   humble;
Ever since my soul's been converted,
I've been trying to live humble,
   humble.

My sister, humble up and humble
   down,
My brother, humble through and
   humble 'round;
Humble, humble.

96. I've Got Peace Like a River
I've got peace like a river in my soul.
I've got river in my soul.

I've got joy like a fountain in my soul.
I've got fountain in my soul.

I've got love like an ocean in my soul.
I've got ocean in my soul.

97. In Bright Mansions Above
In bright mansions above,
Lord, I wan' t' live up yonder,
In bright mansions above.

1. My mother's gone to glory, I wan' t'
   go there too,
Lord, I wan' t' live up yonder,
In bright mansions above.

2. My father's...

3. My sister's...

4. My brother's...

5. My Saviour's...

98. In Dat Great Gittin' Up Mornin'
I'm a-goin' to tell you 'bout de comin'
   of the Savior,
Fare you well, fare you well.

1. Dere's a better day a-comin',
Fare you well, Fare you well;
O preacher, fol' yo' Bible,
Fare . . .
Prayer maker, pray no mo'...
For the las' soul's converted...

Refrain:
In dat great gittin' up mornin',
Fare you well, Fare you well.

2. Dat de time shall be no longer...
For judgment day is comin'...
Den you hear de sinner sayin'...
Down I'm rollin', down I'm rollin' ...

3. De Lord spoke to Gabriel...
Go look behin' de altar...
Take down de silvah trumpet...
Blow yo' trumpet, Gabriel...

4. Lord, how loud shall I blow it...
Blow it right calm an' easy ...
Do not alarm my people...
Tell' em to come to judgment...

5. Gabriel blow yo' trumpet...
Lord, how loud shall I blow it...
Loud as seven peals of thunder...
Wake de livin' nations...

6. Place one foot upon de dry lan'...
Place de other on de sea...
Den you'll see de coffins bustin'...
See de dry bones come a-creepin'...

7. Hell shall be uncapp'd an' burnin',...
Den de dragon shall be loosen'd...
Where you runnin' po' sinner...

8. Den you'll see po' sinners risin'...
Den you'll see de worl' on fiah...
See de moon a bleedin'...
See de stars a fallin'...

9. See de elements a meltin'...
See de forked lightnin'...
Den you'll cry out for cold water...
While de Christians shout in glory...

10. Sayin' Amen to yo' damnation...
No mercy for po' sinner...
Hear de rumblin' of de thunder...
Earth shall reel an' totter...

11. Den you'll see de Christian risin'...
Den you'll see de righteous marchin'...
See dem marchin' home to Heab'n...
Den you'll see my Jesus comin'...

12. Wid all His holy angels...
Take de righteous home to glory...

Dere dey live wid God forever . . .
On de right hand side of my Saviour . . .

99. Is There Anybody Here Who Loves My Jesus?

Is there anybody here who loves my Jesus?
Anybody here who loves my Lord?
I want to know if you love my Jesus;
I want to know if you love my Lord.

This world's a wilderness of woe,
So let us all to glory go.
Religion is a blooming rose,
And none but them who feel it know.

When I was blind and could not see,
King Jesus brought the light to me.

When ev'ry star refuses to shine,
I know King Jesus will be mine.

100. Jacob's Ladder

1. We are climbin' Jacob's ladder,
Soldier(s) of the cross.

2. Ev'ry round goes higher 'n' higher,
Soldier(s) of the cross.

3. Sinner (or: brother), do you love
   my Jesus?
Soldier(s) of the cross.

4. Rise, shine, give God the glory,
Soldier(s) of the cross.

Another couplet:
If you love Him, why not serve Him?

101. Jesus' Blood Done Make Me Whole

Jesus' blood done make me whole,

Since I touched the hem of His
    garment,
Jesus' blood done make me whole.

I don't feel like I used to feel,
Since I touched the hem of His
    garment,
I don't feel like I used to feel.

I don't mourn like I used to mourn...

I don't walk like I used to walk...

I don't talk like I used to talk...

I don't sing like I used to sing...

102. Jesus on the Waterside
Heaven's bell a-ringing,
I know the road,
Jesus is sitting on the waterside.

Do come along,
Do let us go,
Jesus is sitting on the waterside.

103. John Saw
1. John saw, Oh, John saw, John saw
    de holy number,
Settin' on de golden altar.
Worthy is the Lamb,
Worthy, worthy is the Lamb,
Settin' on de golden altar.

2. Mary wept, an' Martha
    cried—Settin'...
To see de'r Saviour crucified—Settin'...
Weepin' Mary, weep no more—Settin'...
Jesus say He gone before—Settin'...

3. Want to go to hebben when I die...
Shout salvation as I fly...
It's a little while longer here below...

Den'a home to glory we shall go...

104. Joshua Fit de Battle of Jericho
Joshua fit de battle of Jericho, Jericho,
    Jericho;
Joshua fit de battle of Jericho,
An' de walls come tumblin' down.

You may talk about yo' king of Gideon,
You may talk about yo' man of Saul;
Dere's none like good ol' Joshua
At de battle of Jericho.

Up to de walls of Jericho
He marched with spear in han';
"Go blow dem ram horns," Joshua cried,
"Cause de battle am in my han'."

Den de lam' ram sheep horns begin to
    blow,
Trumpets begin to soun';
Joshua commanded de chillun to
    shout
An' de walls came tumblin' down.

Dat mornin'
Joshua fit de battle of Jericho, Jericho,
    Jericho;
Joshua fit de battle of Jericho,
An' de walls come tumblin' down.

105. Jubilee
Jubilee, Jubilee, O Lord,
Jubilee, Jubilee, my Lord, Jubilee.

What is the matter, the church won't
    shout?
Somebody in there that ought-a be out!

What is the matter with the mourner?
The devil's in the "amen corner."

What is the matter, the church won't
  move?
Somebody in there that's carryin'
  bad news.

106. Judgment

1. Judgment, Judgment, Judgment
  Day is a-rollin' around,
Judgment, Judgment, Oh, how I long
  to go.
I've a good ole mudder in de heaven,
  my Lord,
Oh, how I long to go dere too;
I've a good ole fadder in de heaven,
  my Lord,
Oh, how I long to go dere too.

2. Dar's a long white robe in de
  heaven for me,
Oh, how I long to go dere too;
Dar's a starry crown in de heaven for me,
Oh, how I long to go.
My name is written in de book ob life,
Oh, how I long to go dere too;
Ef you look in de book you'll fin'em
  dar,
Oh, how I long to go.

3. Brudder Moses gone to de
  kingdom, Lord…
Sister Mary gone to de kingdom,
  Lord…
Dar's no more slave in de kingdom,
  Lord,…
All is glory in de kingdom, Lord…

4. My brudder build a house in
  Paradise…
He built it by dat ribber of life…
Dar's a big camp-meetin' in de
  kingdom, Lord…
Come, let us jine dat-a heavenly crew…

5. King Jesus sittin' in de kingdom,
  Lord…
De angels singin' all around de trone…
De trumpet sound de Jubilo…
I hope dat trump will blow me home …

107. Just a Closer Walk with Thee
Refrain:
Just a closer walk with Thee,
Grant it, Jesus, is my plea,
Daily walking close to Thee,
Let it be, dear Lord, let it be.

1. I am weak but Thou art strong;
Jesus, keep me from all wrong;
I'll be satisfied as long,
As I walk, let me walk close to Thee.

2. Through this world of toil and snares,
If I falter, Lord, who cares?
Who with me my burden shares?
None but Thee, dear Lord, none but Thee.

3. When my feeble life is o'er,
Time for me will be no more;
Guide me gently, safely o'er,
To Thy kingdom shore, to Thy shore.

108. Keep a-Inchin' Along
Keep a-inching along,
Jesus will come by and by.
Keep a-inching along, like a poor
  inchworm,
Jesus will come by and by.

It was by inch that I sought the Lord,
Jesus…
It was inch by inch that He saved my soul,
Jesus…

We'll inch and inch along,
Jesus…

And inch by inch till we get home,
Jesus…

Oh, trials and troubles on the way,
Jesus . . .
But we must watch as well as pray,
Jesus . . .

109. Keep Me from Sinkin' Down

Oh, Lord, oh, my Lord! Oh, my
    good Lord!
Keep me from sinkin' down.

1. I tell you what I mean to do,
Keep me…
I mean to go to heaven too,
Keep me…

2. I look up yonder an' what do I see?
I see de angels beckoning to me.

3. When I was a mourner just like
    you,
I mourned and mourned till I got
    through.

4. I bless the Lord I'm going to die,
I'm going to judgment by and by.

110. King Emanuel

1. Oh, who do you call de King
    Emanuel?
I call my Jesus King Emanuel.

Refrain:
Oh, de King Emanuel is a mighty
    'manuel;
I call my Jesus King Emanuel.

2. Oh, some call Him Jesus, but I call
    Him Lord;
I call my Jesus King Emanuel.

Let's talk about de hebben an' de
    hebben's fine t'ings;
I call my Jesus King Emanuel.

3. Oh, steady, steady, a little while;
I call my Jesus King Emanuel.
I will tell you what my Lord done for me;
I call my Jesus King Emanuel.

4. He pluck-a my feet out de miry clay;
I call my Jesus King Emanuel.
He sot dem-a on de firm Rock o' Age;
I call my Jesus King Emanuel.

111. King Jesus Is a-Listenin'

King Jesus is a-listenin' all day long,
To hear some sinner pray.

1. Some say that John the Baptist was
    nothin' but a Jew,
But the Holy Bible tells us that John
    was a preacher too.

2. That Gospel train is comin',
    a-rumblin' through the lan',
But I hear them wheels a-hum-min',
    get ready to board that train!

3. I know I've been converted, I ain't
    gon' make no alarm,
For my soul is bound for Glory, and
    the devil can't do me no harm.

112. King Jesus Is My Only Friend

King Jesus is my only friend.

When the doctor, the doctor done
    give me over,
Jesus is my only friend.

When the preacher, the preacher done
    give me over,
Jesus is my only friend.

When my house, my house become a
  public hall,
Jesus is my only friend.
When my face, my face become a
  looking glass,
Jesus is my only friend.

113. Kum Ba Yah, My Lord

1. Kum ba yah, my Lord, Kum ba yah!
Oh, Lord, Kum ba yah.

2. Someone's crying, Lord, Kum ba yah!

3. Someone's singing, Lord, Kum ba yah!

4. Someone's praying, Lord, Kum ba yah!

114. Lay This Body Down

I know moon-rise, I know star-rise,
Lay dis body down;
I walk in de moonlight, I walk in de
  starlight,
To lay dis body down.
I'll walk in de graveyard, I'll walk
  through de graveyard,
To lay dis body down;
I'll lie in de grave and stretch out my
  arms,
Lay dis body down.
I go to de judgment in de evenin' of
  de day,
When I lay dis body down;
And my soul and your soul will meet
  in de day,
When I lay dis body down.

115. Let the Church Roll On

Let the church roll on, my Lord,
You can put the Devil out, my Lord,
Let the church roll on, my Lord.

If there's preachers in the church, my
  Lord,
And they're not living right, my Lord;
Just turn preachers out, my Lord,
And let the church roll on.

If there's members in the church, my Lord,
And they're not living right, my Lord;
You can put the members out, my Lord,
And let the church roll on.

If there's liars in the church, my Lord,
And they're not living right, my Lord;
You can put the liars out, my Lord,
And let the church roll on.

If there's sinners in the church, my Lord,
And they're not living right, my Lord;
Just put the sinners out, my Lord,
And let the church roll on.

116. Let Us Break Bread Together

1. Let us break bread together on our
  knees,
When I fall on my knees, with my
  face to the rising sun,
O Lord, have mercy on me.

2. Let us drink wine together…

3. Let us praise God together…

117. Listen to the Lambs

Listen to the lambs, all a-cryin',
All a-cryin'.

He shall feed his flock like a shepherd,
And carry the young lambs in his bosom.

Come on, sister, with you' ups an' downs,
Listen to the lambs, all a-cryin';
Angels waiting for to give you a crown,

Listen to the lambs, all a-cryin'.
Come on, sister, and don't be
  ashamed,
Angels waiting for to write your name;
Mind out, brother, how you walk on
  de cross,
Foot might slip, an' your soul get lost.

118. Lit'le David
Lit'le David, play on yo' harp,
  Hallelu, hallelu,
Lit'le David, play on yo' harp, Hallelu.

Lit'le David was a shepherd boy;
He killed Goliath an' shouted fo' joy.

Joshua was de son of Nun;
He never would quit 'till his work was done.

Done told you once, done told you twice;
There're sinners in hell for shooting dice.

119. Lord, How Come Me Here?
Lord, how come me here?
I wish I never wuz born.

Dere ain't no freedom here.
I wish I never wuz born.

Dey treat me so mean here.
I wish I never wuz born.

Dey sol' my chillun away.
I wish I never wuz born.

120. Lord, I Can't Stay
Here by Myself
Lord, I can't stay here by myself, by
  myself.

My mother has gone and left me here,
My father has gone and left me here,

I'm going to weep like a willow
And mourn like a dove,
O Lord, I cannot stay here by myself.

Yes, I am poor little motherless child,
Yes, I am a poor little child of God
In this world alone,
O Lord, I cannot stay here by myself.

I got my ticket at the low depot,
Low depot.
Yes, I got my ticket at the low depot,
Low depot.
Yes, I got my ticket at the low depot,
O Lord, I cannot stay here by myself.

121. Lord, I Want to Be a Christian
1. Lord, I want to be a Christian in-a
  my heart, in-a my heart;
Lord, I want to be a Christian in-a
  my heart.
In-a my heart, in-a my heart,
Lord, I want to be a Christian in-a
  my heart.

2. Lord, I want to be more holy in-a
  my heart, in-a my heart;
Lord, I want...

3. I don't want to be like Judas in-a
  my heart...

4. I just want to be like Jesus in-a my
  heart...

122. Lord, Until I Reach My Home
Lord, until I reach my home,
I never 'spect to give the journey over,
Until I reach my home, home.
1. Old Satan's mighty busy,
He follows me night an' day,
An' ev'ry time I go to pray,

I find him in my way.
2. Now don't you mind old Satan,
Wid all his temptin' charms,
He wants to steal your soul away,
An' fol' you in his arms.

3. When I was lyin' at hell' dark door,
No one to pity poo' me,
Massa Jesus He come ridin' by,
An' bought my liberty.

123. Mah God Is So High

Mah God is so high, yuh can't get
  over Him;
He's so low, yuh can't get under Him;
He's so wide, yuh can't get aroun' Him;
Yuh mus' come in by an through de Lam'.

One day as I was a-walkin' along de
  Hebenly road,
Mah Savior spoke unto me an' He fill
  mah heart wid His love.
I'll take mah gospel trumpet an' I'll
  begin to blow,
An' if mah Savior help me I'll blow
  wherever I go.

124. Many Thousand Gone

No more auction block for me, No
  more, No more,
No more auction block for me, Many
  thousand gone.

No more peck o' corn for me, No
  more, no more,
Many thousand gone.
No more driver's lash for me...

No more pint o' salt for me...

No more hundred lash for me...

No more mistress' call for me...

125. Mary and Martha

1. Mary and-a Martha's just gone 'long
To ring those charming bells.

Refrain:
Crying free grace and dying love,
Free grace and dying love,
To ring those charming bells.
Oh! way over Jordan, Lord,
Way over Jordan, Lord,
To ring those charming bells.

2. The preacher and the elder's just
  gone 'long...

3. My father and mother's just gone
  'long...

4. The Methodist and Baptist's just
  gone 'long...

126. Mary Had a Baby

Mary had a baby, Yes, Lord!
The people keep a-comin',
And the train done gone.

What did she name him?
She named him King Jesus,
She named him Mighty Counselor.
Where was he born?
Born in a manger,
Yes, Lord!

127. Master Going to Sell Us Tomorrow

Mother, is master going to see us
  tomorrow?
Yes, yes, yes!
O, watch and pray!

Going to sell us down in Georgia?
Yes, yes, yes!
O, watch and pray!

Farewell, mother, I must lebe you.
Yes, yes, yes!
O, watch and pray!

Mother, don't grieve after me.
No, no, no!
O, watch and pray!

Mother, I'll meet you in Heaven.
Yes, my child!
O, watch and pray!

128. My God Is a Rock in a Weary Land

My God is a rock in a weary land,
    weary land,
In a weary land.

My God is a rock in a weary land,
And a shelter in the time of storm!

129. My Good Lord's Done Been Here

Oh, my Good Lord's done been here!
Blessed my soul and gone away,
My Good Lord's done been here,
Blessed my soul and gone.

When I get up in Heaven,
And-a my work is done,
Goin' to sit down by Sister Mary,
And chatter with the darlin' Son.

Hold up the Baptist finger,
Hold up the Baptist hand,
When I get in the Heavens,
Going a-join the Baptist Band.

You may be a white man,

White as the drifting snow,
If your soul ain't been converted,
To Hell you're sure to go.

130. My Lord's a-Writin' All de Time

Come down, come down, my Lord,
    come down,
My Lord's a-writin' all de time;
And take me up to wear the crown,
My Lord...
King Jesus rides in de middle of de air,
My Lord's a-writin' all de time;
He's callin' sinners from everywhere,
My Lord...

Oh, he sees all you do, he hears all
    you say.

131. My Lord, What a Mornin'

My Lord, what a mornin', my Lord,
    what a mornin',
My Lord, what a mornin', when de
    stars begin to fall.

1. You'll hear de trumpet sound, to
    wake de nations underground,
Lookin' to my God's right hand,
    when de stars begin to fall.
2. You'll hear de sinner moan...

3. You'll hear de Christians shout...

132. My Soul's Been Anchored in de Lord

In de Lord, in de Lord,
My soul's been anchored in de Lord.

Befo' I'd stay in hell one day,
My soul's been anchored in de Lord.

I'd sing an' pray myself away,

My soul's been anchored in de Lord.
Goin' shout an' pray an' never stop,
Until I reach de mountaintop.

133. My Way's Cloudy

O brethren, my way, my way's cloudy,
    my way,
Go sen' a dem angels down, O,
    brethren, down.

Dere's fire in de eas' an' fire in de wes',
Sen' dem angels down,
Dere's fire among dem Methodis',
Oh, sen' a dem angels down.

Old Satan is mad and I'm so glad,
Sen' dem angels down,
He missed de soul he thought he had,
Oh, sen' a dem angels down.

134. Nobody Knows de Trouble I've Seen

Nobody knows de trouble I've seen
    (*or:* I see),
Nobody knows but Jesus;
Nobody knows the trouble I've seen,
Glory, halleluiah!

1. Sometimes I'm up, sometimes I'm
    down, oh, yes, Lord;
Sometimes I'm almost to the ground,
    oh, yes, Lord.

2. Although you see me goin' 'long so,
    oh, yes, Lord;
I have my troubles (*or:* trials) here
    below, oh, yes, Lord.

3. One day when I was walking along,
The elements opened, and His love
    came down…

4. I never shall forget that day
When Jesus washed my sins away…

135. No Hidin' Place

Dere's no hidin' place down dere.
Oh, I went to the rock to hide my
    face,
The rock cried out: "No hidin' place."
Dere's no hidin' place down dere.

Oh, de rock cried: "I'm burnin' too,"
Oh, de rock cried out: "I'm burnin'
    too,
I want-a go to hebben as well as you."
Dere's no hidin' place down dere.

Oh, de sinner-man he gambled an'
    fell,
Oh, de sinner-man gambled, he
    gambled an' fell,
He wanted to go to hebben, but he
    had to go to hell.
Dere's no hidin' place down dere.

136. No More Rain Fall for Wet You

1. No more rain fall for wet you,
    Hallelu, hallelu,
No more rain fall for wet you, Hallelujah.

2. No more sun shine for burn you…

3. No more parting in de kingdom…

4. No more backbiting in de kingdom…

5. Every day shall be Sunday…

137. Now Let Me Fly

Way down yonder in de middle o'
    de fiel',
Angel workin' at de chariot wheel,

Not so partic'lar 'bout workin' at de wheel,
But I jes' want-a see how de chariot feel.

Refrain:
Now let me fly
Into Mount Zion, Lord, Lord.

I got a mother in de Promise Lan',
Ain't goin' to stop till I shake her han',
Not so partic'lar 'bout workin' at de
    wheel,
But I jes' want-a get up in de
    Promise Lan'.

Meet dat Hypocrite on de street,
First thing he do is to show his teeth,
Nex' thing he do is to tell a lie,
An' de bes' thing to do is to pass him by.

138. O Daniel

You call yourself a church member,
You hold your head so high,
You praise God with your glitt'ring
    tongue,
But you leave all your heart behind.

Oh my Lord delivered Daniel
O Daniel, O Daniel,
Oh my Lord delivered Daniel,
O why not deliver me too?

139. O Glory, Glory, Hallelujah!

O glory, glory, hallelujah!
O glory, glory to the Lamb;
O glory, glory, hallelujah!
Child of God, that's what I am!

He leadeth me into green pastures,
Child of God, that's what I am!

He leadeth me beside still waters,
Child of God, that's what I am!

140. O, Lord, I'm Hungry

O, Lord, I'm hungry,
I want to be fed.
O, feed me, Jesus, feed me,
Feed me all my days,
O, feed me all the days of my life.

O, Lord, I'm naked,
I want to be clothed.
O, clothe me, Jesus, clothe me,
Clothe me all my days,
O, clothe me all the days of my life.

O, Lord, I'm sinful,
I want to be saved.
O, save me, Jesus, save me,
Save me all my days,
O, save me all the days of my life.

141. Oh! Didn't It Rain

Oh! didn't it rain
Some forty days and nights.

1. They called old Noah a foolish man
Oh! didn't rain.
Cause Noah build de ark upon dry land.
Oh…

2. When it begun to rain,
Women and children begun to scream.

3. It rain all day and it rain all night,
It rain 'til mountain top was out of
    sight.

4. God told Noah by the rainbow sign:
No more water but fire next time.

5. Judgment Day is coming,
Coming in the Prophet's way.
Some folks say they never prayed a
    prayer;
They sho' will pray that day.

142. Oh, Fix Me!

Oh, oh, fix me! Oh, oh, fix me, Jesus!
Oh, oh, fix me, Jesus!
Oh, oh, fix me!

Fix me, Jesus, fix me!
Fix me for my long white robe,
Fix me, Jesus, fix me!

Fix me for my starry crown…

Fix me for my journey home…

143. Oh, Freedom

1. Oh, freedom,
Oh, freedom,
Oh, freedom over me!

Refrain:
An' befo' I'd be a slave,
I'll be buried in my grave,
An' go home to my Lord an' be free.

2. No mo' moanin' over me!
An' befo'…

3. No mo' weepin'…

4. There'll be singin'…

5. There'll be shoutin'…

6. There'll be prayin'…

144. Oh, He Raise-a Poor Lazarus

1. Oh, He raise-a poor Lazuras, raise
him up,
He raise him from de dead, I tol' ye so,
While many were standin' by,
Jesus loosen' de man from under de
groun',
An' tell him: "Go prophesy."

2. He give heal unto de sick, yes, He
did,
He give sight unto de blin', I know
He did,
He done 'able de cripple to walk,
Oh, He raise de dead from under de
groun'
An' give dem permission to talk.

3. Oh, moan along, moan along,
Oh, ye moanin' souls, ye moanin'
souls,
Heaven is my home,
Jesus been here one time, Lord, He's
comin' ag'in,
Git ready and let us go home.

145. Oh, Mary, Don't You Weep, Don't You Mourn

Oh, Mary, don't you weep, don't you
mourn,
Pharaoh's army got drowned.
Oh, Mary, don't you weep.
Sister, what do you want to stay
here for?
Dis old world is no place to live;
Pharoah's army got drowned.
Oh, Mary, don't you weep.

Brother,…

146. Oh, Wasn't Dat a Wide Riber?

Oh, wasn't dat a wide riber, riber ob
Jordan, Lord,
Wide riber, Dere's one more riber
to cross.

1. Oh, you got Jesus, hold him fast,
One more riber to cross.
Oh, better love was nebber told,
One more riber to cross.

'Tis stronger dan an iron band,
One more riber to cross.
'Tis sweeter dan dat honey comb,
One more riber to cross.

2. Oh, de good ole chariot passing by,
One more...
She jarred de earth an' shook de sky,
One more...
I pray, Good Lord, shall I be one?
One more...
To get up in de chariot, trabbel on,
One more...

3. We're told de fore-wheel run by
love,...
We're told dat de hind-wheel run by
faith...
I hope I shall get dere timeby...
To jine de number in de sky...

4. Oh, one more riber we hab to
cross...
'Tis Jordan's riber we hab to cross...
Oh, Jordan's riber am chilly an' cold...
But I got de glory in-a my soul...

147. Oh! What a Beautiful City

Oh! what a beautiful city
Twelve gates-a to the city-a, Hallelu!

1. Three gates in-a de east, three gates
in-a de west;
Three gates in-a de north, and three
gates in-a de south;
Making it twelve gates-a to de city-a,
Hallelu!

2. My Lord built-a dat city, said it was
just-a fo' square;
Wanted all-a you sinners to meet Him
in-a de air;

'Cause He built twelve gates-a to de
city-a, Hallelu!
3. Who are all-a those children all
dressed up in white?
They must be the children of the
Israelites;
'Cause He built twelve gates-a to the
city, Hallelu!

4. Who are all-a those children all
dressed up in red?
They must be the children that
Moses led;
The Lord built twelve gates-a to the
city, Hallelu!

5. When I get to Heaven I'm gonna
sing and shout;
Ain't nobody up there gonna take
me out;
'Cause He built twelve gates-a to the
city, Hallelu!

148. Ole-Time Religion

Gimme dat ole-time religion,
It's good enough for me.

1. It was good for my ole father,
It's good enough for me.

2. It was good for my ole mother...

3. It was good for Paul and Silas...

4. Makes me love ev'rybody...

5. It is good when I'm in trouble...

6. It will do when I am dying...

7. It will take us all to heaven...

Another couplet: It brought me out of
bondage...

149. On Mah Journey

On mah journey now, Mount Zion,
Well I wouldn't take nothin', Mount
  Zion,
For mah journey now, Mount Zion.

One day, one day, I was walking along,
Well, the elements opened an' de love
  come down, Mount Zion.

I went to de valley an' I didn't go to stay,
Well, my soul got happy an' I stayed
  all day, Mount Zion.
Just talk about me just as much as
  you please,
Well, I'll talk about you when I bend
  my knees, Mount Zion.

150. Open the Window, Noah!

Open the window, Noah!
Open the window,
Let the dove come in.

The little dove flew in the window
  and mourned,
Open the window,
Let the dove come in.

The little dove brought back the
  olive leaf,
Open the window,
Let the dove come in.

Open the window, Noah!

151. Over My Head

Over my head I hear music in the air,
There must be a God somewhere.

1. Over my head I hear singing in the
   air…

2. Over my head I see color in the air…

3. Over my head I see glory in the air . . .

4. Over my head I see Jesus in the air . . .

152. Peter, Go Ring-a Them Bells

Oh, Peter, go ring-a them bells,
I heard from heaven today.
(1) I thank God, and I thank you, too,
I heard from heaven today…
(2-3) It's good news, and I thank
    you too,
I heard from heaven today.
(4-5) He's gone where Elijah has gone,
I heard from heaven today.

1. I wonder where my mother is gone,
I heard from heaven today.

2. I wonder where sister Mary's
   gone…

3. I wonder where sister Martha's
   gone…

4. I wonder where brother Moses is
   gone…

5. I wonder where brother Daniel's
   gone…

153. Prayer Is the Key of Heaven

Refrain:
Prayer is the key of Heaven,
Faith unlocks the door;
I know that.

I think it was about twelve o'clock,
When Jesus led me to the rock;
I remember the day, I know the time,
Jesus freed this soul of mine;
My head got wet with the midnight
    dew,
The morning star was witness too.

154. 'Rastlin' Jacob

'Rastlin' Jacob, let me go,
I will not let you go.

1. Day is breakin', Jacob let me go,
I will not let you go.

2. If you'll bless my soul, I'll let you go,
I will not let you go.

3. When I'm sinkin' down, pity on me,
I will not let you go.

155. Religion So Sweet

1. O walk Jordan long road,
And religion so sweet.

2. O religion is good for anything,
And religion so sweet.

3. Religion make you happy (*or:*
humble)…

4. Religion gib me patience…

5. O member, get religion…

6. I long time been a-huntin'…

7. I seekin' for my fortune…

8. O I gwine to meet my Savior…

9. Gwine to tell him 'bout my trials…

10. Dey call me boastin' member…

11. Dey call me turnback Christian…

12. Dey call me 'struction maker…

13. But I don't care what dey call me…

14. Lord, trials 'longs to a Christian…

15. O tell me 'bout religion…

16. I weep for Mary and Martha…

17. I seek my Lord and I find him…

156. Ride On, King Jesus

Ride on, King Jesus,
No man can a-hinder me.

1. I was but young when I begun, No
man…
But now my race is almost done, No
man…

2. King Jesus rides on a milk-white
horse, No man…
The river of Jordan He did cross, No
man…

3. If you want to find your way to
God, No man…
The gospel highway must be trod, No
man…

4. When I get to Heaven gonna wear
a robe,…
Gonna see King Jesus sittin' on the
throne,…

5. Gonna walk all over those streets of
gold,…
Goin' to a land where I'll never grow
old…

Another version:
Walk in, kind Savior, No man can
hinder me!
Walk in, sweet Jesus, No man can
hinder me!

1. See what wonder Jesus done,
O no man can hinder me!

2. Jesus make de dumb to speak…

3. Jesus make de cripple walk…

4. Jesus give de blind his sight…

5. Jesus do most anything…

6. Rise, poor Lazarus, from de tomb…

7. Satan ride an iron-gray horse…

8. King Jesus ride a milk-white horse…

157. Rise an' Shine

Oh, rise an' shine, an' give God de
 glory,
Rise an' shine, an' give God de glory,
For de year of Juberlee.
Jesus carry de young lambs in his
 bosom, bosom,
Carry de young lambs in his bosom,
For de year of Juberlee.

Oh, come on, mourners, get you
 ready, ready,
Come on, mourners, get you ready,
 ready
For de year of Juberlee;
You may keep your lamps trimmed
 an' burning, burning,
Keep your lamps trimmed an'
 burning, burning,
For de year of Juberlee.

Oh, come on, children, don't be
 weary, weary,
Come on, children, don't be weary, weary,
For de year of Juberlee.
Oh, don't you hear dem bells
 a-ringin', ringin',
Don't you hear dem bells a-ringin', ringin',
For de year of Juberlee?

158. Rise Up, Shepherd, and Follow

1. There's a star in the East on
 Christmas morn,

Rise up, shepherd, and follow,
It will lead to the place where the
 Christ was born,
Rise up, shepherd, and follow.

Refrain:
Follow, follow,
Rise up, shepherd, and follow,
Follow the Star of Bethlehem,
Rise up, shepherd, and follow.

2. If you take good heed to the
 angel's words,
Rise up, shepherd, and follow,
You'll forget your flocks, you'll forget
 your herds,
Rise up, shepherd, and follow.

3. Leave your sheep, leave your lambs,
Rise up, shepherd, and follow,
Leave your ewes, leave your rams,
Rise up, shepherd, and follow.

159. Rock o' My Soul

Rock o' my soul in de bosom of
 Abraham,
Lord, rock o' my soul.
He toted the young lambs in his
 bosom,
And leave the old sheep alone.

160. Roll, Jordan, Roll

Roll, Jordan, roll, roll, Jordan, roll,
I want to go to heaven when I die,
To hear Jordan roll.

Oh, brothers, you ought t' have been
 there, Yes, my Lord,
A sitting in the Kingdom, to hear
 Jordan roll.

Oh, preachers, you ought…

Oh, sinners,...

Oh, mourners,...

Oh, seekers,...

Oh, mothers,...

Oh, sisters,...

161. Rolling in Jesus' Arms
I'm a-rolling in Jesus' arms,
On the other side of Jordan,
I'm a-rolling in Jesus' arms.

One day when I was walking,
Along that lonesome road,
My Savior spoke unto me,
And filled my heart with love.

He chose me for a watchman,
To blow the trumpet of God,
To join the weary traveler,
Along that heavenly road.

Why do you tarry, sinner,
Why do you wait so long?
Your Savior is a-waiting for you,
Why don't you come along?

You need not look for riches,
Nor either dress so fine,
The robe that Jesus gives you,
Outshines the glittering sun.

162. Run, Mary, Run
Run, Mary, run,
Oh, run, Mary, run,
I know the other world is not like this.

1. Fire in the east, and fire in the west,
I know...
Bound to burn the wilderness,
I know...

Jordan's river is a river to cross,
I know...
Stretch your rod and come across,
I know...

2. Swing low, chariot, into the east,
Let God's children have some peace;
Swing low, chariot, into the west,
Let God's children have some rest;

3. Swing low, chariot, into the north,
Give me the gold without the dross;
Sing low, chariot, into the south,
Let God's children sing and shout;

4. If this day was Judgment Day,
Every sinner would want to pray;
That trouble it comes like a gloomy cloud,
Gather thick, and thunders loud.

163. Run to Jesus
Refrain:
Run to Jesus, shun the danger,
I don't expect to stay much longer here.

1. He will be our dearest friend,
And will help us to the end.
I don't expect to stay much longer here.

2. O, I thought I heard them say,
There were lions in the way.
I don't expect to stay much longer here.

3. Many mansions there will be,
One for you and one for me.
I don't expect to stay much longer here.

164. Satan's Camp a-Fire
Fier, my Savior, Fier,
Satan's camp a-fire;
Fier, believer, fier,
Satan's camp a-fire.

165. Scandalize' My Name

Well, I met my sister de other day,
Give her my right han',
Just as soon as ever my back was
    turned,
She took'n' scandalize' my name.
Do you call dat a sister?
No! No! you call dat a sister?
No! No! scandalize' my name.

2. ...my brother...

3. ...my preacher...You call dat a
    'ligion?...

166. Shine on Me

1. I heard the voice of Jesus say:
"Come unto me and rest (and rest);
Lay down, thou weary one, lay down
Thy head upon my breast."

Refrain:
Shine on me.
Let the light from the lighthouse
(Lord,) Shine on me.
Let the light from the lighthouse
Shine on me.

2. With pitying eyes the Prince of Peace
Beheld our helpless grief (our grief);
He saw, and O amazing love!
He came to our relief!

167. Shout for Joy

O Lord, shout for joy!
Mary had a Baby, shout for joy!
Born in a stable, shout for joy!
They laid Him in a manger, shout
    for joy!
They named Him King Jesus, shout
    for joy!
He was the Prince of Peace,

A mighty Counselor,
The King of Kings,
That Christmas, in the morning.

Shepherd came to see Him, shout
    for joy!
Wise men bought Him presents,
    shout for joy!
King Herod tried to find Him, shout
    for joy!
They went away to Egypt, shout
    for joy!
Mary rode a donkey, shout for joy!
Joseph walked beside her, shout
    for joy!
Angels watching over, shout for joy!

O Lord, shout for joy!
He was the Prince of Peace,
A mighty Counselor,
The King of Kings,
O Lord, shout for joy!!!

168. Singin' wid a Sword in Ma Han'

Singin' wid a sword in ma han',
    Lord, singin' wid a sword in ma
    han'.

Purtiest singin' ever I heard,
'Way ovah on de hill,
De angels sing an' I sing too,
Singin' wid a sword...

Purtiest shoutin' ever I saw,
'Way ovah on de hill,
De angels shout an' I shout too,
Shoutin' wid a sword...

Purtiest preachin' ever I heard...

Purtiest prayin' ever I heard...

Purtiest mournin' ever I heard...

169. Sing Till the Power of the Lord Comes Down

I'm gonna sing till the power of the
    Lord comes down,
Lift up your head, don't be afraid,
I'm gonna sing till the power of the
    Lord comes down.

170. Sinner, Please Don't Let This Harvest Pass

Sinner, please don't let this harvest
    pass, harvest pass;
Sinner, please don't let this harvest pass,
And die and lose your soul at last,
    soul at last.

I know that my Redeemer lives, yes,
    He lives;
I know that my Redeemer lives,
Sinner, please don't let this harvest
    pass, harvest pass.

Sinner, O see the cruel tree, cruel tree;
Sinner, O see the cruel tree,
Where Christ died for you and me,
    you and me.

My God is a mighty man of war, man
    of war;
My God is a mighty man of war,
Sinner, please don't let . . .

My Jesus, He's a rock in a weary land,
He's a shelter in de time of storm.

171. Sister Mary Had-a but One Child

Sister Mary had-a but one child,
Born in Bethlehem.
And-a every time-a that baby cried,
She'd-a rocked him in a weary land.

Oh, three wise men to Jerusalem came,
They traveled very far.
They said: "Where is he born King of
    the Jews,
For we have a-seen his star."
King Herod's heart was troubled,
He marveled but his face was grim.
He said: "Tell me where the Child
    may be found,
I'll go and worship him."

An angel appeared to Joseph,
And gave him-a this-a command:
"Arise ye, take-a your wife and child,
Go flee into Egypt land."

For yonder comes old Herod,
A wicked man and bold.
He's slayin' all the children,
From six to eight days old.

172. Sit Down, Servant, Sit Down

Sit down, servant, sit down!
Sit down an' rest a little while.
1. (I) Know you mighty tired, so sit down!

2. Know you shoutin' happy, so sit down!

173. Slavery Chain

Slavery chain done broke at last,
    broke at last,
Slavery chain done broke at last,
Going to praise God till I die.

Way down in-a dat valley,
Praying on my knees,
Told God about my troubles,
And to help me ef-a He please.

I did tell him how I suffer,
In de dungeon and de chain,

And de days I went with head bowed
   down,
And my broken flesh and pain.

I did know my Jesus heard me,
'Cause de Spirit spoke to me,
And said: "Rise, my child, your chillun,
And you shall be free."

I done 'p'int one mighty captain,
For to marshall all my hosts,
And to bring my bleeding ones to me,
And not one shall be lost.

Now no more weary trav'lin',
'Cause my Jesus set-a me free,
An' dere's no more auction block for me,
Since He give me liberty.

174. Somebody's Knockin' at Your Door

Somebody's knockin' at your door,
O sinner, why don't you answer?
Somebody's knockin' at your door.

1. Knocks like Jesus, somebody's…
O sinner, why don't you answer?
Somebody's knockin' at your door.

2. Can't you hear Him?…

3. Answer Jesus…

4. Jesus calls you…

5. Can't you trust Him?…

175. Some o' Dese Days

1. I'm go'n'ter set down at de welcome
   table, yes,
I'm go'n'ter set down at de welcome
   table, some o' dese days, Hallelujah!
I'm go'n'ter set down at de welcome
   table.

2. I'm go'n'ter feast on milk an'
   honey, yes,
I'm go'n'ter feast on milk an' honey,
   some o' dese days, Hallelujah!
I'm go'n'ter…

3. I'm go'n'ter drink from de golden
   fountain, yes,
I'm go'n'ter drink de golden fountain,
   some o' dese days, Hallelujah!
I'm go'n'ter…

4. I'm go'n'ter sing and never get
   tired, yes…

5. I'm go'n'ter tell God all of my
   troubles, yes…

6. I'm go'n'ter tell God how you treat
   me…

7. God's go'n'ter set this world on fire…

8. God's go'n'ter stop that
   long-tongue liar…

176. Sometimes I Feel Like a Motherless Chile

Sometimes I feel like a motherless chile,
A long ways (*or:* far away) from
   home, a long ways from home,
True believer, a long ways from home.

Sometimes I feel like I'm almos' gone,
'Way up in the heavenly land, 'way up
   in the heavenly land,
True believer, 'way up in the heavenly
   land.

Another text: Then I get down on my
   knees an' pray,
Get down on my knees an' pray.

Then I get down on my knees an' pray,
Get down on my knees an' pray.

Another text: Sometimes I feel like a
feather in the air,
And I spread my wings and I fly.

177. Soon-a Will Be Done

Soon-a will be done with the troubles
of the world,
Troubles of the world, the troubles of
the world,
Soon-a will be done with the troubles
of the world,
Goin' home to live with God.

No more weepin' and a-wailing,
I'm goin' to live with God.

I want t' meet my mother,
I'm goin' to live with God.

I want t' meet my Jesus,
I'm goin' to live with God.

178. Standin' in the Need of Prayer

It's me, it's me, O Lord,
Standing in the need of pray'r.

1. Not my brother, not my sister, but
it's me, O Lord,
Standing in the need of pray'r.

2. Not my father, not my mother…

3. Not the preacher, not the deacon…

4. Not the stranger, not my neighbor…

179. Steal Away to Jesus

Steal away, steal away,

Steal away to Jesus!
Steal away, steal away home.
I ain't got long to stay here!
1. My Lord calls me,
He calls me by the thunder;
De trumpet sounds within-a my soul:
I ain't got long to stay here.

2. Dark clouds arisin' (*another version:*
Green trees a-bending),
Poor sinners stand a-tremblin';
De trumpet sounds within-a my soul:
I ain't got long to stay here.

3. Tombstones are bursting,
Poor sinners stand a tremblin';
De trumpet…

4. My Lord calls me,
He calls me by the lightning;
De trumpet…

180. Study War No More

1. Going to lay down my sword
and shield,
Down by the riverside;
Going to study was no more,
I ain't going to study war no more.

2. Going to lay down my burden
Down by the riverside…

3. Going to try on my starry crown…

4. Going to meet my dear old father…

5. Going to meet my dear old mother…

6. Going to meet my loving Jesus…

181. Sweet Jesus

1. Sweet Jesus, sweet Jesus,
He's the Lily of the Valley,

He's the Bright and Morning Star.
Sweet Jesus, sweet Jesus,
He's the Fairest of ten thousand to
my soul.

2. How I love Him, how I love Him...

3. I'll serve Him, I'll serve Him...

4. He's worthy, He's worthy,
He's the Lily of the Valley,
He's the Bright and Morning Star.
He's worthy, He's worthy,
He's the governor of the nations, bless
His name.

182. Swing Low, Sweet Chariot
Swing low, sweet chariot, comin' for
to carry me home.

1. I looked over Jordan, an' what did I
see, comin' for to carry me home?
A band of angels comin' after me,
comin' for to carry me home.

2. If you get dere before I do, comin'
for to carry me home,
Tell all my friends I'm comin' too,
comin' for to carry me home.

3. I'm sometimes up, I'm sometimes
down, comin' for to carry me home,
But still my soul feels heavenly bound,
comin' for to carry me home.

183. Take Me to the Water
1. Take me to the water to be baptized.

2. None but the righteous shall see God.

3. I love Jesus, yes I do.

4. He's my Savior, yes He is.

184. That Lonesome Valley
O, you got to walk-a that lonesome
valley,
You got to go there by yourself;
No one here to go there with you,
You got to go there by yourself.

When you walk-a that lonesome valley,
You got to walk it by yourself;
No one here may walk it with you,
You got to walk it by yourself.
When you reach the River Jordan,
You got to cross it by yourself;
No one here may cross it with you,
You got to cross it by yourself.

When you face that judgment
morning,
You got to face it by yourself;
No one here to face it for you,
You got to face it by yourself.

Loud and strong your Master calling,
You got to answer by yourself;
No one here to answer for you,
You got to answer by yourself.

You got to stand your trial in
judgment,
You got to stand it . . .

Jordan's stream is strong and chilly,
You got to wade it . . .

When my dear Lord was hanging
bleeding,
He had to hang there by Hisself;
No one there could hang there for Him,
He had to hand there by Hisself.

You got to join that Christian army,
You got to join it . . .

You got to live a life of service,
You got to live it . . .

185. The Angels Done Bowed Down

O, the angels done bowed down,
O, yes, my Lord.
While Jesus was hanging upon the
  cross,
The angels kept quiet till God went off,
And the angels hung their harps on
  the willow trees,
To give satisfaction till God was
  pleased.

His soul went up on the pillar of
  cloud,
O, God He moved and the angels did
  bow,
Jehovah's sword was at His side,
On the empty air He began to ride.

Go down angels to the flood,
Blow out the sun, turn the moon into
  blood!
Come back angels, bolt the door,
The time that's been will be no
  more!

186. The Blind Man Stood on the Road and Cried

The blind man stood on the road
  and cried,
Oh, the blind man stood on the road
  and cried,
Crying, oh my Lord, save-a me.
The blind man stood on de road
  and cried.

Cryin': "Help me, O Lawd, if you
  please."
Cryin': "O Lawd, show me de way."
The blind man stood on de road
  and cried.

When I was a sinner I stood on de
  way an' cried,
Cryin': "O Lawd, show me de way."
The blind man stood on de road
  and cried.

187. The Downward Road Is Crowded

Refrain:
O, the downward road is crowded,
Crowded, crowded,
O, the downward road is crowded,
With unbelieving souls.

Come, all ye wayward travelers,
And let us all join and sing,
The everlasting praises,
Of Jesus Christ our King.

Old Satan's mighty busy,
He follows me night and day,
And everywhere I'm appointed,
There's something in my way.

When I was a sinner,
I loved my distance well,
But when I came to find myself,
I was hanging over Hell.

188. The Old Sheep Know the Road

Refrain:
O, the old sheep know the road,
The old sheep know the road,
The young lambs must find the way.

O, sooner in the morning when I rise,
With crosses and trials on every side;
My brother, ain't you got your
  accounts all sealed?
You'd better go get them before you
  leave this field.

O, shout, my sister, for you are free,
For Christ has brought you liberty;
I really do believe without one doubt,
That the Christian has a mighty right
    to shout.
My brother, better mind how to walk
    on the cross,
For your foot might slip and your
    soul get lost;
Better mind that sun and see how she
    runs,
And mind, don't let her catch you
    with your work undone.

189. Then My Little Soul's Going to Shine

I'm going to join the great association,
Then my little soul's going to shine,
    shine,
Then my little soul's going to shine
    along.

I'm going to climb up Jacob's ladder,
I'm going to climb up higher and
    higher,
I'm going to sit down at the welcome
    table,
I'm going to feast off milk and honey,
I'm going to tell God how-a you
    starved me,
I'm going to join the big baptizing.

Then my little soul's going to shine,
    shine,
Then my little soul's going to shine
    along.

190. There's a Meeting Here Tonight

Get you ready, there's a meeting here
    tonight,
Come along, there's...

I know you by your daily walk, there's...

1. Camp-meeting down in the
    wilderness, there's...
I know it's among the Methodes',
    there's...

2. My father says it is the bes',...
To live an' die a Methodes',...

3. There's fire in the eas',...
I know it's among the Methodes',...

191. They Led My Lord Away

They led my Lord away, away,
They led my Lord away,
O tell me where to find Him, find Him.

1. The Jews and Romans in-a one
    band,
Tell me where to find Him,
They crucified the Son of Man,
Tell me...

2. They led Him up to Pilate's bar,
Tell me...
But the Jews could not condemn
    Him there,
Tell me...

3. Old Pilate said: "I wash my hands,"
Tell me...
"I find no fault in this just man,"
Tell me...

192. This Little Light of Mine

1. This little light of mine, I'm going
    to let it shine,
Let it shine.

2. Ev'ry where I go, I'm gonna to let
    it shine.

3. Jesus (or: God) gave it to me...

Other couplets:
All in my heart,…

All in my house,…

All through the night,…

193. 'Tis the Old Ship of Zion
'Tis the old ship of Zion,
Git on board.

1. It has landed many a thousand,
Git on board.

2. Ain't no danger in de water…

3. It was good for my dear mother…

4. It was good for my dear father…

5. It will take you home to Glory…

194. Trampin'
I'm trampin', trampin', tryin' to make
 Heaven ma home,
Hallelujah, I'm a-trampin', trampin',
 tryin'…

I've never been to Heaven, but I've
 been tol',
Try'n' to make Heaven ma home;
Dat de streets up dere are paved
 wid gol'.
Try'n'…

If you git dere befo' I do,
Try'n'…
Tell all ma friends I'm comin' too,
Try'n'…

195. Trouble Done Bore Me Down
O Lord, O Lord,
What shall I do?

Trouble done bore me down.
O Lord, O Lord,
What shall I do?
O, trouble done bore me down.

He's gone on high to prepare a place,
Trouble done bore me down;
For to prepare a place for me and you,
Trouble…

O Lord, O Lord, have mercy on
 me,
Trouble…
O Lord, O Lord, have mercy on
 me,
Trouble…

I've seen some strangers quite
 unknown,
I'm a child of misery,
I'm sometimes up and sometimes down,
I'm sometimes level with the ground,
O Lord, O Lord, what shall I do?

I bent my knees and smote the
 ground,
I asked God almighty for to run me
 'round,
O Lord, O Lord, what shall I do?

196. Wade in de Water
Wade in de water, children,
God's a-going to trouble the water.

1. See that host all dressed in white,
God's…
The leader looks like the Israelite
 [John the Baptist],
God's…

2. See that host all dressed in red…
Looks like the band that Moses led…

3. Look over yonder, what do I see?…

The Holy Ghost a-coming on me...

4. If you don't believe I've been
   redeemed...
Just follow me down to Jordan's
   stream...

197. Walk Togedder, Children

Oh, walk togedder, children, don't
   you get weary,
Walk togedder, children, don't you get
   weary,
Oh, walk togedder, children, don't
   you get weary,
Dere's a great camp-meetin' in de
   Promised Land.
Gwine to mourn, and nebber tire,
Mourn and nebber tire, mourn an'
   nebber tire,
Dere's a great camp-meetin' in de
   Promised Land.

Oh, get you ready, children, don't you
   get weary,
Get you ready, children, don't you
   get weary,
Dere's a great camp-meeting...
For Jesus is a comin', don't get weary,
Jesus is a comin', don't get weary,
Dere's a great...
Gwine to hab a happy meetin', don't...
Hab a happy meetin', don't...
Dere's a great...

Refrain:
Gwine to pray an' nebber tire,
Dere's a great camp-meetin' in de
   Promised Land.

Gwine to hab it in hebben, don't...
Dere's...
Gwine to shout in hebben, don't...
Shout in hebben...

Dere's...
Oh, will you go wid me? don't...
Will you go wid me?...
Dere's...

Refrain:
Gwine to shout an' nebber tire,
Shout an' nebber tire...
Dere's...

Dere's a better day a-comin', don't...
Better day a-comin',...
Dere's...
Oh, slap your hands, children, don't...
Dere's...
Oh, pat your foot, children, don't...
Pat your foot, children...
Dere's...

Refrain:
Gwine to live with God forever,
Live wid God forever...
Dere's...

Oh, feel de Spirit a-movin', don't...
Feel de Spirit a-movin'...
Dere's...
Oh, now I'm getting' happy...
Dere's...
I feel so happy...
Feel so happy...
Dere's...

Refrain:
Oh, fly an' nebber tire,
Fly an' nebber tire...
Dere's...

198. We Are Building on a Rock

We are building on a Rock,
On high, on high,
We are building on a Rock,
On high, thank God.

2. It's a mighty true Rock,
On high, on high,
It's a mighty true Rock,
On high, thank God.

3. It's a mighty solid Rock...

4. Christ Jesus is the Rock . . .

5. The very gates of hell...

6. Will not 'gainst it prevail...

7. Help me build on the Rock...

199. We'll Stand the Storm
Oh! stand the storm, it won't be long,
We'll anchor by and by,
Stand the storm, it won't be long,
We'll anchor by and by.

1. My ship is on the ocean,
We'll anchor by and by.

2. She's making for the Kingdom,
We'll...

3. I've a mother in the Kingdom,
We'll...

200. We've Come a Long Way, Lord
We've come a long way, Lord, a
    mighty long way,
We've borne our burdens in the heat
    of the day,
But we know the Lord has made
    the way,
We've come a long way, Lord, a
    mighty long way.

1. I've been in the valley and I prayed
    night and day,
And I know the Lord has made the way.

2. I've had trials each and ev'ry day,
But I know the Lord has made the way.

201. Were You There?
Were you there when they crucified
    my Lord?
Oh! Sometimes it causes me to
    tremble, tremble, tremble.
Were you there...

Were you there when they nailed
    Him to the tree?

Were you there when they pierced
    Him in the side?

Were you there when the sun refused
    to shine?

Were you there when the laid Him in
    the tomb?

*The following verses do not seem to be
in the original text:*

Were you there when he rose up from
    the dead?

Were you there when they rolled the
    stone away?

202. What Yo' Gwine to Do When Yo' Lamp Burn Down?
O, po' sinner, O, now is yo' time, O
    po' sinner, O,
What yo' gwine to do when yo' lamp
    burn down?

Fin' de Eas', fin' de Wes',
What yo' gwine to do when yo' lamp
    burn down?
Fire gwine to burn down de
    wilderness,

What you' gwine to do when yo' lamp
    burn down?
Head got wet wid de midnight dew,
What yo' gwine to do when yo' lamp
    burn down?
Morn'n' star was a witness too,
What yo' gwine to do when yo' lamp
    burn down?
Dey whipp'd Him up and dey
    whipped Him down,
What yo' gine to do when yo' lamp
    burn down?
Dey whipp'd dat man all over town,
What yo' gwine to do when yo' lamp
    burn down?
Dey nail'd His han' an dey nail'd
    His feet,
What yo' gwine to do when yo' lamp
    burn down?
De hammer was heard on Jerusalem's
    street,
What yo' gwine to do when yo' lamp
    burn down?

203. Where Shall I Be When de Firs' Trumpet Soun'?

Where shall I be when de firs'
    trumpet soun',
Where shall I be when it soun' so loud,
When it soun' so loud till it wake up
    de dead,
Where shall I be when it soun', O,
    Brethren?

Gwine to try on ma robe when de
    firs' trumpet soun',
Gwine to try on ma robe when it
    soun' so loud,
When it soun' so loud till it wake up
    de dead,
Where shall I be when it soun', O
    Brethren?

204. Who'll Be a Witness for My Lord?

My soul is a witness for my Lord.
You read in de Bible an' you
    understan',
Methuselah was de oldes' man;
He lived nine hundred an' sixty nine,
He died an' went to heaven in a
    due time.
O, Methuselah was a witness for my Lord.

You read in de Bible an' you
    understan',
Samson was de strongest man;
Samson went out at-a one time,
An' he killed about a thousan' of de
    Philistine.
Delilah fooled Samson, dis-a we know,
For de Holy Bible tells us so;
She shaved off his head jus' as clean as
    yo' han',
An' his strength became de same as
    any natch'al man.
O, Samson was a witness for my Lord.

Now Daniel was a Hebrew child,
He went to pray to his God a while;
De king at once for Daniel did sen',
An' he put him right down in de
    lion's den;
God sent His angels de lions for to keep,
An' Daniel laid down an' went to
    sleep.
O, Daniel was a witness for my Lord.

O, who'll be a witness for my Lord?
My soul is a witness for my Lord.

205. Wish I Was in Heaven Sitting Down

Wish I was in heaven sitting down,
O, Mary, O, Martha,

Wish I was in heaven sitting down.

Wouldn't get tired no more, tired no
    more,
Wouldn't have nothing to do, nothing
    to do.

Try on my long white robe, long
    white robe,
Sit at my Jesus' feet, my Jesus' feet.

206. Woke up Dis Mornin'

1. Oh, I woke up dis mornin' wid
    mah min', an it was stayed,
Stayed on Jesus.
Woke up dis mornin' wid mah min',
    an' it was stayed,
Stayed on Jesus,
Hallelujah.

2. Can't hate your neighbor in your
    min', if you keep it stayed,
Stayed on Jesus…

3. Makes you love everybody with your
    min', when you keep it stayed…

4. De devil can't catch you in your
    min', if you keep it stayed…

5. Jesus is de captain in your min',
    when you keep it stayed…

207. Wonder Where Is Good Ole Daniel

1. Wonder where is good ole Daniel,
Way over in de Promise' Lan'.

2. He was cas' in de den ob lions,
Way over in de Promise' Lan'.

3. By an' by we'll go an' meet him…

4. Wonder where's dem Hebrew
    children…

5. Dey come thro' de fiery furnace…

6. By an' by go an' meet dem…

7. Wonder where is doubtin'
    Thomas…

8. Wonder where is sinkin' Peter…

208. You Goin' to Reap Just What You Sow

You goin' to reap just what you sow,
Upon the mountain, down in the valley,
You goin' to reap just what you sow.
Let the gambler gamble on,
O let the gambler gamble on.

Let the liar lie right on,
O let the liar lie right on.

Let the preacher preach right on,
O let the preacher preach right on.

209. You Got a Right

You got a right, I got a right,
We all got a right to de tree of life,
Yes, tree of life.

De very time I thought I was los',
De dungeon shuck an' de chain fell off.
You may hinder me here,
But you cannot dere,
'Cause God in de heav'n
Gwinter answer prayer.

O, brother, O, sister,
You got a right, I got a right,
We all got a right to the tree of life,
Yes, tree of life.

210. You Hear the Lambs a-Cryin'

You hear the lambs a-cryin', hear the
   lambs a-cryin',
O Shepherd, feed my sheep.
You feed my sheep.

My Savior spoke these words so sweet;
O Shepherd, feed my sheep.
"Peter, if you love me, feed my sheep";
O Shepherd, feed my sheep.

Lord, I love Thee, Thou dost know;
O Shepherd, feed my sheep.
O give me grace to love Thee more;
O Shepherd, feed my sheep.

Wasn't that an awful shame?
O Shepherd, feed my sheep.
He hung three hours in mortal pain;
O Shepherd, feed my sheep.

A List of All the Spirituals Quoted

The Thirty-Three Best CDs of Spirituals

A Capella Spirituals: The Series, CD EK 57113 and 7019444600, Word, Incorporated, 1993 and 1995.

Marian Anderson, *He's Got the Whole World in His Hands,* CD 09026-61960-2, BMG Music, 1994

Marian Anderson, *Negro-Spirituals 1924–1949,* FA 184, Frémeaux & Associés, 2000.

Louis Armstrong, *Louis and the Good Book,* MCD 01300, MCAD 1300, 1980-92.

Kathleen Battle and Jessye Norman, *Spirituals in Concert,* CD 429 790-2, Deutsche Grammophon, 1991.

Harry Belafonte, *My Lord What a Mornin',* 74321 26049 2, RCA Victor, 1995.

Black Christmas: Sprituals in the African American Tradition, CD 1011, ESS.A.Y. Recordings, 1990.

Barbara Conrad, *Spirituals,* CD 8.553036-F, Naxos, 1995.

The Fairfield Four, *I Couldn't Hear Nobody Pray,* CD 9 46698 2, Warner Bros, 1997.

Golden Gate Quartet, *Our Story,* Columbia 493248 2, 1999.

Gospels and Spirituals, The Gold Collection, R2CD 40-26, 1997.

Great American Spirituals, Kathleen Battle, Barbara Hendricks,

Florence Quivar, CD 513725Z, Musical Heritage Society, 1994.

Barbara Hendricks, *Negro Spirituals*, CDC 7 47026 2, EMI, 1983.

Barbara Hendricks, *Give Me Jesus: Spirituals*, CD 5 56683 2, EMI, 1998.

The Moses Hogan Chorale, *The Best of the Moses Hogan Chorale*, 2 CE, MGH-2581, 1998.

The Moses Hogan Chorale, *I Can Tell the World*, Our Choral Heritage Series, vol. 1, Disc Makers, 1997.

The Moses Hogan Singers, *A Home in That Rock*, 3000MGH, 1999.

Mahalia Jackson, *Gospel, Spirituals, and Hymns*, CD 468663 2, Columbia, 1991.

Mahalia Jackson, *Best Loved Spirituals*, CD A 13582, Sony Music, 1993.

John Littleton, *Spirituals*, 2 vols., CD 12 2303 and 12 2333, Studio SM, 1994.

Montreal Jubilation Gospel Choir, *Jubilation IV*, CD 46-2, Justin Time Records, 1992.

The Mormon Tabernacle Choir, *An American Heritage of Spirituals*, BWE 0097, 1996.

Negro Spirituals, CD 5 72790 2, EMI, 1998.

Negro Spirituals. La Tradition du concert, 1909–1948, Frémeaux & Associés, FA 168, 1999.

Les plus beaux Negro Spirituals, CD 456 530-2, Philips, 1997.

Les plus Beaux Negro Spirituals/Gospel Songs, CD A 6180, Auvidis, 1991.

My Lord, What a Mornin': Spirituals in Arrangements by Hall Johnson, Roland Hayes, and H. T. Burleigh, CD MHS 512250K, Musical Heritage Society, 1988.

Jessye Norman, *Spirituals*, CD 416 462-2, Philips, 1979.

Jessye Norman, *Amazing Grace*, CD 432 546-2, Philips, 1991.

Florence Quivar with the Harlem Boys Choir, *Ride On, King Jesus*, CD 7 49885 2, EMI Records, 1990.

Derek Lee Ragin, *Negro Spirituals*, CD 100196, Aria, 1996.

Bernice Johnson Reagon, *African American Spirituals: The Concert Tradition*, Wade in the Water Series, vol. 1, CD SF 40072, Smithsonian/Folkways Recordings and National Public Radio, 1994.

Take Me to the Water, CD 329, GIA Publications, 1994.

The CD Included with This Book

Moses Hogan (1957–2003)

Moses Hogan, who was born in New Orleans in 1957, was a pianist, orchestra leader, and composer. He studied music at the Oberlin Conservatory (Ohio) before attending the Juilliard School of Music in New York and Louisiana State University at Baton Rouge.

A multitalented musician, he won the 28th Kosciuszko Foundation National Contest. His adaptations of the spirituals have been sung by Barbara Hendricks on the CD *Give Me Jesus* (EMI, 1998) and by Derek Lee Ragin on the CD *Negro Spirituals* (Aria, 1996).

Moses Hogan died on February 11, 2003.

The Moses Hogan Chorale

In 1980 Moses Hogan began to explore choral music with the creation of the *New World Ensemble,* which in 1993 became the Moses Hogan Chorale. This chorale, specializing in singing spirituals, has been invited just about everywhere in the United States and in the world.

The Moses Hogan Singers

This group replaced the chorale in 1998. Four of the songs on the CD are interpreted by this ensemble: "Go Down, Moses," "He's Got the Whole World," "I Got a Home in-a Dat Rock," and "Ride On, King Jesus."

The Making of the CD

For ease in finding the songs, we have recorded the spirituals in alphabetical order and have indicated in parentheses the reference number to

the anthology in appendix 1. I have
been careful to choose songs that
correspond to the various aspects of
my analysis, though of course I would
have needed even more to present all
the themes. These spirituals are
presented in one form only: the
choral form.

Ain't Dat Good News? (2)
Amen (7)
Balm in Gilead (8)
Didn't My Lord Deliver Daniel ?
    (32)
Ev'ry Time I Feel the Spirit (40)
Go Down, Moses (50)
He Nevuh Said a Mumbalin' Word
    (63)
*He's Got the Whole World in His
    Hands* (64)
I Got a Home in-a Dat Rock (78)
In Bright Mansions Above (97)
Joshua Fit de Battle of Jericho (104)
Nobody Knows de Trouble I've Seen
    (134)
Ride on, King Jesus (156)
Soon-a Will Be Done (177)
Steal Away to Jesus (179)
Study War No More (180)
Swing Low, Sweet Chariot (182)
Wade in de Water (196)